AF847710

Violent Conflicts, Crisis,
State of Emergency, Peacebuilding

Recht, Sicherheit und Verwaltung in internationaler Perspektive

Law, Security and Public Administration in an International Perspective

Herausgegeben von

Prof. Dr. Oesten Baller

Band 6 / Volume 6

Oesten Baller (ed.)

Violent Conflicts, Crisis, State of Emergency, Peacebuilding

Constitutional Problems, Amendments and Interpretation

Berliner
Wissenschafts-Verlag

Bibliografische Information der Deutschen Nationalbibliothek:
Die Deutsche Nationalbibliothek verzeichnet diese Publikation in der Deutschen Nationalbibliografie; detaillierte bibliografische Daten sind im Internet über http://dnb.d-nb.de abrufbar.

Dieses Werk einschließlich aller seiner Teile ist urheberrechtlich geschützt. Jede Verwertung außerhalb der engen Grenzen des Urheberrechtes ist unzulässig und strafbar.

© 2019 BWV | BERLINER WISSENSCHAFTS-VERLAG GmbH,
Markgrafenstraße 12–14, 10969 Berlin,
E-Mail: bwv@bwv-verlag.de, Internet: http://www.bwv-verlag.de

Druck: Memminger MedienCentrum, Memmingen
Gedruckt auf holzfreiem, chlor- und säurefreiem, alterungsbeständigem Papier.
Printed in Germany.

ISBN Print 978-3-8305-3964-3
ISBN E-Book 978-3-8305-4126-4

Foreword

Constitutional law can appear differently in political crises, states of emergency or national and international conflicts. Negative implications are likely to occur, where constitutional law is abused in states of emergency situations or exploited by the political elite to enforce its own positions and to escalate crises and conflicts. However, constitutional law can also be a valid yardstick for maintaining a sense of proportion in crises and exceptional situations, as well as for respecting the constitutionality of the political system. Most importantly, constitutional law provides a recognised framework for finding solutions to conflicts, crises or states of emergency situations – and for making peace.

This volume is based on lectures given by constitutional lawyers from Africa, Asia, Europe and South America at the 10th World Congress of Constitutional Law (IACL-AIDC), held from 18–22 June 2018 at SungKyunKwan University in Seoul, Korea, on Violent Conflicts, Peace-Building, and Constitutional Law. The English and French contributions originate from three Congress workshops: No. 3 (State of Emergency), No. 14 (Constitutional Amendments), and No. 19 (Violent Conflicts, Peacebuilding and Constitutional Law).

The first thematic block describes violent conflicts. *Abiodun Odusote* explores the perennial and violent clashes between herdsmen, farmers and indigenous ethnic communities across West Africa, which result from scarce rural resources and heterogeneous, partly traditional, forms of living and economic activities. From this point of view, he looks at both the constitutional embedding of these forms of living, and the attempted solutions on domestic and supranational levels. Based on an, as objective as possible, factual assessment of the Russian-Ukrainian conflict, *Oesten Baller* examines the constitutional development and the constitutional interpretation as well as the main political decisions with constitutional law relevance, both in Ukraine and Russia. Even though the main responsibility for the conflict clearly lies with Putin's Russia, the analysis shows that deficiencies in the rule of law are characteristic in both countries.

Crises of constitutional relevance and such of a constitutional nature are in the focus of the second, the largest, at the same time, thematic block. *Sacha Sydoryk* asks whether, and if so, to what extent, a constitution may be amended at all in times of severe crises. To this end, he examines the constitutions of many member states of the European Union and concludes with the presentation of model solutions. Two contributions deal with the constitutional problems associated with national measures to combat terrorism. *Audrey de Montis* and *Priscilla Jensel-Monge* ask about the institutional and functional balance between the executive and legislative branches in the French anti-terrorist struggle, and as a result, favour a strong controlling function of parliament, even in times of terrorism. *Xavier Miny* and *Quentin Pironnet* analyse the Belgian legal anti-terror system, and conclude that, even in a state of emergency, the rule of law does not allow the end to justify the means.

Rubens Beçak and *Jairo Lima* deal with judicial review of constitutional amendments in the light of the political constitutionalism critiques. Since the power to amend a constitution has greater democratic potentials than ordinary legislation, constitutional amendments require a judicial scrutiny compatible with this nature. Supermajority rules in Constitutional Courts are the way they develop their argument. In his article on the evaluation of Taiwan's Act of Ill-gotten Political Party Assets in Taiwan, dated 2016, *David KC Huang* asks whether a Bill of Attainder should be regarded as transitional justice or transitional injustice. Obviously, the author tends towards the latter – with a comparative law view to Germany's two historical attempts to cope with its past – when he states that revenge can never create justice.

Oyelowo Oyewo covers a wide geographical span when he looks at the challenges of constitutional reforms in democratising states in Sub-Saharan Africa, and asks about Nigeria's chances of playing an active role in this process. In any case, he concludes, there will be no stable democracy without far-reaching constitutional changes. *Paul Zibi's* contribution deals with the chances to overcome the crisis in Cameroon, which has been known as Anglophone Crisis since 2016. As a result, he proposes a constitutional reform that takes account of the country's specifics and strengthens the use of the English language accordingly, making Cameroon a bilingual decentralised state. This is the only way to avoid separatism and unwanted federalisation. *Anne-Laure Youhnovski Sagon* examines the jurisprudence of the European Court of Human Rights on the right to life in connection with deadly governmental violence in times of crisis. In concluding, she states that, even in extreme crises, the Court fails to perform the necessary comprehensive proportionality analysis.

Three articles in the third thematic block deal with constitutional exception regimes, martial law and state of emergency. *Olivier Le Bot* asks whether, in France, there is a right to judicial review during a state of emergency, and whether this right can be restricted or denied. He notes that it was a decision by the French Constitutional Council that, in the interests of the executive, severely infringes upon the right to judicial review in a state of emergency. *Maciej Pisz* examines extra lege legislative powers for the executive during martial law in contemporary Polish constitutional law. In conclusion, the author considers these exceptions to Parliament's primacy in legislation to be permissible at least within the framework of Polish constitutional law, in particular with regard to the principle of separation of powers. *Eva Schulev-Steindl* deals with the question of resilience of law in times of crisis in Austria, with a comparative view to other European countries. In the end, she proposes elements of a regulatory model to optimise Austrian law, and emphasises the importance of a system of checks and balances even in exceptional situations and crises. Last, but not least, *Manon Bonnet's* contribution focusses on the peacebuilding function of constitutions, emphasizing the dualism of peace and democracy. This would require a new understanding of the old concept of democratic peace. It should not be forgotten, however, that constitutions in post-conflict settings play just a limited role among other factors.

The diversity of aspects presented in these contributions, and the interesting perspectives chosen by the authors characterise this volume, as well as the often comparative approach. The global communication and the excellent cooperation within this book project have been very gratifying for the editor and give hope for a follow-up volume after the next World Congress of Constitutional Law in Johannesburg/South Africa in December 2022.

Berlin, September 2019 Oesten Baller

Content

Perennial Conflicts between Farmers, Herdsmen and Communities in West Africa: Perspectives on Clashes of Rights to Livelihoods

Abiodun Odusote

Abstract

Perennial and violent clashes between herdsmen, farmers and indigenous ethnic communities across West Africa are widespread. Various arguments have been advanced to find the root causes of and factors that exacerbate these conflicts. There have been accusations and counter accusations among the warring factions. The change on ecosystems that limit the amount of land for grazing purposes characterized by retreating natural resources and population bloat have and are occasioning continued migration of herdsmen and their cattle from the North to the South hemisphere in search of greener pastures for their herds. Balancing the rights of the herdsmen and farmers to livelihoods amidst competing and diverse claims to land, road access, water, grass and other limited resources makes the conflicts more difficult to manage by government authorities and relevant stakeholders. The herdsmen are desirous of grazing land and cattle passages whilst the farmers seek to protect their farmlands, plantations and farm products from the scavenging cattle. It is not unusual for cows to stray into children's parks, schools, offices, residential homes, care homes, hospitals, airport runways and farmlands; thereby destroying farm produce, farmlands and generally occasioning great nuisance. There are also ethno-religious undertones exacerbating the conflicts. This often results in very violent clashes and confrontation leading to severe loss of lives and properties on both sides. This research employs doctrinal perspective to make enquiries on the root causes of the violent conflicts, interrogates how to address the competing rights and claims on land, forests, water and agricultural resources to avoid conflicts and review governmental mechanism of fostering inclusivity and harmonious cohabitation between the herdsmen and farmers. In conclusion, credible legal and institutional frameworks that promote peaceful co-existence of the farmers, communities and herdsmen are recommended.

I. Introduction

1. Problem Statement

On the 1st of January, 2018 Nigerians were greeted with the tragic killings of about 73 people by herdsmen in a violent and despicable attack on Logo and Guma in Benue State, Nigeria. Some commentators attributed the violent attack to the enactment of Grazing Prohibition Law by the Benue State Government[1]. This argument can-

1 *Umar Tanko Al-Makura,* the Nasarawa State Governor has disclosed that the implementation of the anti-grazing law in Benue State is responsible for herdsmen attacks. Available at <https://www.eagleee.com/detail?newsId=602490>, accessed on 20 March, 2018; *Mansur Dan-Ali,* Minster of

not hold water in view of the fact that there has been many reckless killings of farmers and inhabitants of host communities across the country before the enactment of the Grazing Prohibition Law in Benue State. Subsequent to the New Year killings in Logo and Guma, there have been numerous other killings in other states of the federation by herdsmen. Many of the other states of the federation that have and are still experiencing herdsmen killings have no anti-grazing laws. However, in his reaction to the killings masterminded by the herdsmen in Logo and Guma, the Emir of Kano, and seemingly justifying the killings as retaliation, *Alhaji Sanusi*[2] claimed that over 800 Fulani herdsmen and people were killed on the Mambilla Plateau in Taraba State in one weekend[3].The Taraba State Government acknowledged there was a conflict between the farmers and the herdsmen on the Mambilla Plateau but contend that both parties suffered causalities and the figure of deaths from both sides put together is nowhere close to 800. A Judicial Commission of Enquiry was set up to investigate the conflicts and make appropriate recommendations. The Judicial Commission had since submitted its report but the state is yet to take any action or make the content of the report known to the public. The death recorded on the New Year's Day is not in isolation. Study has shown that recently "deaths from Fulani extremists resulted in more than 3000 deaths across four countries, with 92 % fatalities taking place in Nigeria."[4] Based on the above, this study investigates the factors responsible and exacerbating these conflicts. This paper is divided into four parts. Part one is the introductory. Part two interrogates the clashes of rights to livelihoods by reason of the competing and divergent interests of the parties, using the constitution and other statutory remedies as panacea to the seemingly irretraceable conflicts. Part three offers insights to the nature and experiences of other West African countries in managing and sometimes resolving these conflicts. Part four concludes by way of summing up the expositions in the paper and proposing credible solutions that have the potential of ushering in lasting and enduring peace between the herdsmen, farmers and the indigenous communities across West African states.

Defence of the Federal Republic of Nigeria also blamed anti-open grazing law for killings by herdsmen. Available at <https://www.premiumtimesng.com/news/headlines/256685-nigerian-govt-blames-anti-open-grazing-law-killings-herdsmen.html>, accessed on 20 March, 2018.

2 *Alhaji Sanusi* is also a patron of the Miyeti-Allah, an umbrella body of the herdsmen trade/pressure union.

3 This claim has been disputed by the Taraba State Government and the Christian Association of Nigeria chapter in Taraba State. Cf. Nigerian Punch Newspaper, Sanusi's claim that 800 Fulani were killed, a lie – Taraba govt, CAN, available at <http://punchng.com/sanusis-claim-that-800-fulani-were-killed-a-lie-taraba-govt-can/>, accessed on 18 April, 2018.

4 Global Terrorism Index (GTI) 2017.

2. Historical Background

In the early 19th Century the Northern Nigeria was conquered by the Fulani jihadist. Invariably the Fulani appropriated all lands in the conquered territories in accordance with Maliki Law of Islam.[5] The Maliki Law stipulates that lands which come into the possession of the faithful through conquest become public property and no individual has title to it[6]. In consonance with this principle some parcels of land were placed under the Emir to hold in trust for the people. Under this land system land was not owned by the family, the village but in trust by the Emir for public good. Thereafter, the Grazing reserve was introduced in Nigeria by the Fulani that invaded, conquered and ruled Northern Nigeria prior to British colonial rule[7]. The Fulani rulers demarcated and carved out grazing routes.[8] At this time, it was purely a customary arrangement, there was no statutory backing. Hence, herdsmen lived in perpetual fear of being ejected from the grazing reserves by their overlords. However, formal grazing reserves in Nigeria did not start until the 1950 s.[9] The Fulani Amenities Proposal aimed at supporting the Fulani herdsmen was later incorporated into the Grazing Reserve Law of the Northern Nigeria to assuage their fears. With the support of World Bank and the United States Agency for International Development, the Survey Department surveys the Grazing Reserve. It is on record[10] that as at 1980, Nigeria had 2.3 million hectares for grazing reserves, just about 11 % of the planned size[11]. *Iro* further stated in his findings:

> 'The government acquired less than five percent of the ten million hectares proposed as grazing land. Of the forty-five planned dams, twenty-four have been completed.

5 *I. O. Smith*, Practical Approach to Law of Real Property in Nigeria, Ecowatch Publications 2013, 28.

6 *F. H. Ruxton*, Maliki Law, being a Summary from French Translations of the Mukhtaṣar of Sîdî Khalîl, Political Department, Nigeria, London: Luzac & Co.1916, available at <https://www.cambridge.org/core/journals/journal-of-the-royal-asiatic-society/article/maliki-law-being-a-summary-from-french-translations-of-the-mukhtasar-of-sidi-khalil-by-f-h-ruxton-political-department-nigeria-london-luzac-co1916/BBE35DA01BCBF9CE93F193731AAB174D>.

7 *S. Bako, and S. Ingawa,* Animal traction in Nigeria: A Review. Paper presented to the Third Regional Workshop on animal Traction for Agricultural Development in West Africa. Selv, Senegal, July 7–12, 1988.

8 *Ismail Iro*, Grazing Reserve Development: A Panacea to the Intractable Strife Between Farmers and Herders, available at <http://www.gamji.com/fulani8.htm>.

9 Ibid.

10 Ibid.

11 *C. Omaliko, O. Mammah, O.* and *Agbakoba, A.*, Some Aspects of Rangeland Improvement in a Derived Savannah Ecosystem, Journal of Range Management 37 (September 1984), 415–419.

> Five boreholes have been sunk. Of the expected 722 roads, 150 have been built, showing a huge deficit. At the close of 1992, the government has identified over 300 areas with twenty-eight million hectares for grazing reserve development. About forty-five of these areas, covering some 600,000 hectares, have been gazetted. Eight of these reserves, totaling 225,000 hectares, are fully established. Already, 350 of the projected 950 pastoral families and 11,600 of the planned 46,000 cattle are using these reserves (National Livestock Project Division record 1992).[12] Apart from acquiring the land, the government regulates how the Fulani should use the grazing reserves.'

However, the grazing reserves and grazing routes were later abandoned while other grazing reserves could not be acquired and gazetted because those earlier acquired lack required facilities (water, boreholes, Veterinary hospitals etc) and where facilities were provided, they were not maintained. Thus, the laudable project was abandoned by successive governments.

3. Root Causes of Farmers and Herdsmen Conflicts

Nigerian population has since grown exponentially from about 45 million in 1950 to about 194 million today[13]. Inevitably, there is more pressure on land, water and other natural resources used by farmers and herdsmen. There has been constant encroachment on grazing reserves and grazing routes. Findings have revealed that one of the implications of the pressure on the available resources is the blockage of transhumance routes and loss of grazing land to agricultural, housing and industrial expansion[14]. It has also been well established that as a result of climate change resulting from global warming and desertification herdsmen now migrate towards the south to find greener pasture for their cattle and stock. For example, research finding has shown that Lake Chad that is reputed to be the primary wetland in the semi-arid Sahel corridor has decreased substantially.[15] The water and other aquatic resources of

12 The full report in four volumes, Nigerian Livestock Resources (ISBN 1 898 028 00 1) published in 1992 is available from the sales and distribution agents: Environmental Research Group Oxford Ltd, Oxford.

13 Worldmeters, Nigeria Population Live, available at <http://www.worldometers.info/world-population/nigeria-population/>., accessed on 18 April, 2018.

14 *Shettima and Tar*, Farmer-Pastoralist Conflict in West Africa: Exploring the Causes and Consequences, Information, Society and Justice (2008) Vol 1.2 163–184; *Olaniyan, Francis and Okeke-Uzodike*, The Cattle are 'Ghaninans' but the Herders are Strangers: Farmer-Herder Conflicts, Expulsion Policy, and Pastoralist Question in Agogo, Ghana' African Studies Quarterly (2015) Vol. 15, Issue 2.

15 GIWA Report, Lake Basin: Giwa Regional Assessment (2004) 43 Nairobi: UNEP, the Global International Waters Assessment. Lake Chad Basin, GIWA Regional assessment 43, available at

Lake Chad support about 11 million people including pastoralists, farmers, fishermen and others from four countries; Chad, Cameroon, Niger and Nigeria.[16] The recession of the Lake due to environmental factors has led to a decline in resources on which the pastoralists, farmers, fishermen and others from these four countries depend for livelihoods. This has occasioned intense competition and rivalries, particularly between the herdsmen and farmers resulting in perennial conflicts.[17]

As shown above, prior to the enactment of the Grazing Reserve Act of 1965, the herdsmen had exercised customary grazing rights over large tracts of land. The customary rights have been exercised over a long period of time. In contemporary times, the grazing routes and reserves are fast depleting. Herdsmen are now demanding a reactivation and preservation of grazing routes and reserves. The herdsmen are of the opinion that the reactivation of the grazing routes and reserves will reduce instances of seasonal migration and the incidental burdens, promote co-operation and bonding amongst herdsmen inter se and among the rural dwellers. Incidents of cattle rustling will also be eliminated. Unfortunately, these expectations have not been met by both the state and federal governments. Hence, farmers and rural dwellers compete with the herdsmen for the same limited land and resources.

Findings have shown that the scarcity of pastoral land is the primary reason why there are nomadic pastoralist in every nook and crannies of West Africa in search of the proverbial; greener pasture. Hence, pastoralist take their stock to hitherto unimaginable places for pasturing, including airport runways, parks, schools, motorway, railway, farmlands and golf courses. The flock litters the ground with accompany stench, feces and chaos. Attendant consequences include, delayed flights, near accidents, annoyance, confrontations, threat to food security and fighting. A combination of factors often escalate the annoyance into conflicts, this includes low literacy level, religious bias, historical tensions, strained relationships and economic depression. Most often these exacerbate into cattle rustling, human killings and genocide. In Nigeria, several thousands of lives have been lost in 2018. Other identified problems militating against peaceful co-existence between farmers, herdsmen and host communities

<http://wedocs.unep.org/bitstream/handle/20.500.11822/8398/-Lake%20Chad%20Basin-GIWA%20Regional%20Assessment%2043-20043745.pdf?sequence=3&isAllowed=y>.

16 *Caterina Batello, Marzio Marzot, Adamou Harouna Touré* , The Future is an Ancient Lake: Traditional Knowledge, biodiversity and genetic resources for food and agriculture in Lake Basin Ecosystem, FAO Interdepartmental Working Group on Biological Diversity, Rome 2004, available at <http://www.fao.org/3/y5118e/y5118e00.htm>.

17 *Shettima* and *Tar*, Farmer-Pastoralist Conflict in West Africa: Exploring the Causes and Consequences, Information, Society and Justice (2008) Vol 1.2 163–184.

include: land conflict between the farmers and herdsmen, Illegal occupation of land by farmers and herdsmen, tribalism, hatred, rumor-mongering, oppression, religious differences[18] and political differences/lack of justice.

II. Clashes of Rights to Livelihoods: The Constitution to the Rescue

The clashes of rights to livelihoods between the herdsmen and farmers and the host communities include the rights of movement, property rights, right to food, right to water, right relating to work, right to sanitation and to take part in cultural life.[19] Some of these rights will be discussed below.

1. Right of Movement

Section 15 (2) of the Constitution of the Federal Republic of Nigeria, CFRN 1999, as amended, encourages government to promote national integration irrespective of place of origin, sex, religion, status, ethnic or linguistic association or ties and Section 17 (3) (a) CFRN requires the State to direct its policies to secure adequate means of livelihood in a non-discriminatory manner. This section enjoins government to secure the livelihoods of the farmers, herdsmen and the residents of the host communities. Section 41 CFRN guarantees the right to freedom of movement. The section provides that "every citizen of Nigeria is entitled to move freely throughout Nigeria and to reside in any part thereof, and no citizen of Nigeria shall be expelled from Nigeria or refused entry thereby or exit therefrom." Every Nigerian is entitled to work, and live anywhere within the country. Every Nigerian is entitled to move freely within the country and come into the country without any form of hindrances.[20] Hence, nomadic herdsmen have the constitutional right to move about doing their lawful trade and not to be harassed by anyone. In the course of engaging in their livelihoods, it is

18 *Adamu* and *Ben*, Nigeria: Benue State under the shadow of 'herdsmen terrorism' (2014 – 2016), with update: 1 January – 31 August 2017, 2017, available at <https://www.worldwatchmonitor.org/wp-content/uploads/2017/11/Nigeria-Benue-State-2017-WWR.pdf>, accessed on 4th April, 2018.

19 See the African Charter on Human and Peoples' Rights, available at <http://www.achpr.org/instruments/achpr/>.

20 See also Article 12 of the ICCPR, and Article 12 of the African Charter; Shugaba v Minister for Internal Affairs (1981) 1 NCLR 25; Director of State Security Service & Anor v Olisa Agbakoba (2003) 10 WRN 93.

well documented that the herdsmen have caused unspeakable and wanton destruction to lives, crops, farms and other properties across several states in Nigeria. There have also been several allegations against the herdsmen of rape and kidnapping for ransom. The right to movement is however a restrictable right. Section 45 of the Constitution provides that the right to movement may be restricted in the interest of defence, public safety, public order, public morality or public health or for the purposes of protecting the rights and freedom of other person. Perhaps it is in consonance with section 45 CFRN that four states[21] have prohibited open grazing within their territorial space and encourage the establishment of ranches. This legal approach has been criticized by *Saleh Alhassan,* Miyetti-Allah Cattle Breeders Association's secretary. He lamented that "anti-grazing laws are nothing but populist agenda designed by visionless and desperate politicians to destroy the means of livelihood of the herdsmen." He further opined that "these laws are oppressive and negative and are fundamentally against our culture as Fulani pastoralists."[22] A cursory perusal of Section45 CFRN and a review of the antecedents and perennial conflicts between the herdsmen and farmers will put the seeming conflict between the right of movement of the herdsmen and the right of the state governments to protect lives and properties in perspective, Section17 (3) (a) CFRN. The primary obligation of a responsible government is to protect the lives and property of its people. The anti-open graze law does not preclude anyone from doing livestock business in the state. The laws actually encourage the establishment of ranches for livestock business. Open grazing is however precluded because of the perennial conflicts between the herdsmen and farmers because of crop destruction by straying cattle.

In Burkina Faso, Guinea, and Mali, legislations affirm the right of herdsmen to move their animals within and across national borders.[23] In Ghana the conflict between herdsmen and famers is pronounced in Northern Ghana. The violence con-

21 Ekiti state: Prohibition of Cattle and Other Ruminants Grazing in Ekiti, 2016; Taraba state: Anti-Open Grazing Prohibition and Ranches Establishment Bill 2017; Edo State Bill: A Bill for A Law to Establish the Edo State Control of Nomadic Cattle Rearing/Grazing Law and for Other Purposes; and Benue State Law: A Law to Prohibit Open Rearing and Grazing of Livestock and Provide for the Establishment of Ranches and Livestock Administration, Regulation and Control and for Other Matters Connected Therewith, 2017.

22 The Nigerian Punch Newspapers Editorial, Implementing states' anti-open grazing laws, available at <http://punchng.com/implementing-states-anti-open-grazing-laws/>, accessed on 13 December, 2017.

23 IIED 2006, Innovation en matière de sécurisation des droits fonciers en Afrique : leçons tirées de l'expérience; Document de synthèse; 12p made pursuant to the ECOWAS Transhumance Protocol, 1998 under Decision A/DEC.5/10/98.

flicts between the herdsmen and farmers have become more frequent in recent times due to the adverse climate conditions and stiffer competition for limited resources. The herdsmen and herds continue to move southward due to adverse inclement climate conditions. Frequent clashes between these groups have led to the expulsion of the herdsmen from Agogo, Ghana and they are equally declared persona non grata. They are banned from entering the country in future.[24] Research findings however reveal that despite the court order, there are still remaining Fulani herdsmen in Agogo, Ghana[25]. The court order has invoked some constitutional challenges. Some of the herdsmen were born in Ghana and had acquired Ghanaian citizenship. They have Ghanaian voters' cards and identity cards[26]. They have never lived outside Ghana, in the eyes of the law, they are Ghanaian citizens but in the perception of majority of the Ghanaian people, the Fulani herdsmen are strangers and immigrants from the neighboring countries. In a study by *Bukari* and *Schareika* on 'stereotypes, prejudices and exclusion of Fulani pastoralists in Ghana', *Kwesi Aning*, sums up the maltreatment and prejudices against the Fulani herdsmen as follows:

> 'What poses a threat to our collective security is the so-called "indigenous" Ghanaians perspective of the Fulanis, most of whom are actually Ghanaian citizens. Ghana's handling of the Fulani grazers is a complete violation of the ECOWAS Protocol on TransHumans, which Ghana has signed up to. The protocol regulates the movement of nomadic herdsmen within West Africa. It spells out rules and regulations of where they should pass with the cattle, is a failure of the state, plus a deliberate manipulative process by communities in where there should be boreholes for their water and where there should be veterinary outposts to treat them… We (the Ghanaians authorities) are not following the protocol. This which Fulanis either pass through or are located, to intimidate, to steal, to abuse and to attack them…'[27]

This study further reveals systemic discriminatory practices against the Fulanis as some other ethnic groups have been conferred Ghanaian citizenship by virtue of their ethnicity , citing example of the Akan, Mole-Dagomba, Ga-Dangme and Ewe, the Fulanis are not recognized by the Ghanaian state. The Fulanis despite having set-

24 *Olaniyan, Francis and Okeke-Uzodike*, 'The Cattle are 'Ghaninans' but the Herders are Strangers: Farmer-Herder Conflicts, Expulsion Policy, and Pastoralist Question in Agogo, Ghana', African Studies Quarterly (2015) Vol. 15, Issue 2.

25 Ibid., at 55.

26 Ibid., at 56.

27 *Bukari and Schareika,* Stereotypes, prejudices and exclusion of Fulani pastoralists in Ghana, Research, Policy and Practice, 2015, p.7, available at <https://pastoralismjournal.springeropen.com/articles/10.1186/s13570-015-0043-8>, accessed on 14 February, 2018.

tled in Ghana far before her independence are not recognized as part of the Ghanaian ethnicities.[28]

The policy of expulsion has been practiced in Ghana, Liberia and Libya[29] and to some extent in parts of Nigeria though without judicial intervention in the latter. This is regardless of Article 2 2(d) of the Economic State of West African States (ECOWAS) treaty that encourages member states to abolish all obstacles to free movement of persons, services and capital. Article 27(1) of the ECOWAS treaty assures Community citizenship on the citizens of member states. It also enjoins member states to remove every obstacle to freedom of movement and residence within the West African states. Further Article 27 (2) permits citizens of member states to work and undertake commercial and industrial activities within West Africa territories without the need to hold visitor's visa or residence permits[30].

The ECOWAS treaty on Transhumance Protocol of 1998 gives grazing rights to herdsmen by permitting herders to move across West African borders in search of pasture for their herds. It allows the free movement of persons and property within and across West African states. However, herdsmen still face many challenges in transhumance practice, including non domestication of the ECOWAS treaty in host countries, local land tenure system, historical fractured relationship between the herdsmen and farmers, inadequacy of local laws to address the challenges, inadequate enforcement mechanism, and lack of awareness of the treaty by locals in the host communities. Research has also shown that "the regulations signed by ECOWAS states in 1998 are not applied; at the same time, each coastal country adopts for herself its own texts, often in total contradiction with the laws sub-regional, letting agents and decentralized structures, especially municipalities, dictate their own laws on farmers and transhumant herds"[31] For example, in 2010 a High Court in Kumasi Ghana gave approval to the expulsion of the Fulani herdsmen and their cattle from the Agogo Afram plains by the Ashanti Regional Security Council (REGSEC).[32] This is obviously in violation of Article 11 (1) of the Protocol relating to the free movement of persons, residence

28 Ibid., at 8.

29 *Steve Tonah,* The Politics of Exclusion: The Expulsion of Fulbe Pastoralists from Ghana in 1999/2000. Working Paper for Max Planck Institute for Social Anthropology, 2002.

30 See also Art 2 of Protocol A/P.1/5/79 Relating to free movement of persons, residence and establishment, it states that Community citizens shall have the right to enter, reside and establish in the territory of Member States. By Article 13, the Protocol shall definitively enter into force upon ratification by seven signatory states in accordance to the constitutional procedures applicable to each state.

31 FAO, at 80.

32 Ghana news Agency, 2012; *Olaniyan, Francis and Okeke-Uzodike* (note 23), at 54.

and establishment requiring that a decision to expel any citizen of the Community must be communicated to the government of his state and the Executive Secretary of ECOWAS. It also violates Article 11 (2) that requires that the expenses incurred in the expulsion of a citizen must be borne by the member state which expels him.

In sum, the political and environmental changes and the perennial conflicts between the farmers and the herdsmen have generally affected the nomadic communities across West Africa. The nomadic man sees himself struggling for livelihood in an ever increasingly hostile environment. He must struggle to fend for himself and the survival of his herd. Hence, he is always living on the edge and ready to defend himself with the last drop of blood in his vein.

2. Property Rights, Livelihood Rights and the Grazing Reserve Act, 1965

In the context of this discourse property rights and livelihood rights include in one part, the rights of the herdsmen, farmers and the indigenous communities to communal land, water, cattle grazing, crop farming, fishing and right o other natural resources. This bundle of rights cannot be privately owned. It embraces the rights of both the herdsmen and the famers to access the river, to access public land, and to use same as they please but within the confines of the law. The resources have been described as open access resources[33] and when limited open access resources is perceived as being over used by one group to the detriment of other users, there is bound to be conflict. The herdsmen have been accused by the farmers of grazing their cattle both day and night thereby resulting in over grazing, occasioning land degradation. Land degradation invariably affects crop production and fish farming. The herdsmen have also accused farmers of planting on grazing routes and killing of their cattle. Hence, there is need for regulations on these bundles of rights by the state government and regional authorities.

In other part, property rights include individual rights to acquire and own properties such as land and the right to exclusive use of same. The Federal Government of Nigeria had proposed cattle colonies as panacea for lasting peace and harmonious co-existence between the farmers and the herdsmen.[34] Aside from the fact that the word colony is offensive to many indigenous communities because it brings back memories of Fulani conquest and dominion and the British rule, the extant legal in-

33 *Fielmua et al*, Managing Pastoralism and Water Rights in the Upper West Region of Ghana: A Blame Game Among Actors, Journal of Sustainable Development 2014, Vol. 7 (1), at 75.

34 Less controversial descriptive words should be 'grazing reserves'.

struments do not permit for seizure of land from state governments, communities or individual owners to be given, donated or appease Fulani herdsmen as cattle colony. Section 1 of the Land Use Act 1978,[35] entrust all land comprised in the territory of each State in the Federation in the Governor of each State and such land can only be held in trust and administered for the use and common benefit of all Nigerians in accordance with the provisions of the Act. Most state governors have already declined the request for tracts of land for the proposed cattle colony[36]. The Federal Government does not have and cannot acquire forcefully any land for the purpose of cattle colony. Section 43 of the Constitution of the Federal Republic of Nigeria provides for the right of every Nigerian to acquire and own immovable property anywhere in Nigeria. Section 44 of the Constitution prohibits compulsory acquisition of property and deals with the procedure of acquiring vested interest in an immovable property by the Government. It provides that no movable property or any interest in an immovable property shall be taken possession of compulsorily and no right over or interest in such property shall be acquired compulsorily in any part of Nigeria except in the manner prescribed by law. In acquiring a vested property for public good, the owner must be promptly compensated and must have access to challenge the acquisition in open court, *Guinness Nigeria Ltd v Engr Alex Udeani*[37]; *Okenwa v Military Governor Imo State*[38] Section 44 (2) of the Nigerian Constitution highlights issues or circumstances that may affect one's right to property or the compensation to be paid.[39] Section 44 is to be read along with the provisions of sections 28 and 29 of the Land Use

35 Available at <http://www.nigeria-law.org/Land%20Use%20Act.htm>.

36 All the 17 states of Southern Nigeria have rejected cattle colony while 16 Northern States have agreed to donate 5000 hectres each. See Daily Post Newspapers of 23 January, 2018, available at <http://dailypost.ng/2018/01/23/cattle-colonies-list-16-states-volunteered-land/>, accessed on 24 April, 2018.

37 2000, 18 WRN 27.

38 1997, 6 NWLR (PT.507) 136.

39 Kano v Government of Adamawa State (2015) All FWLR (Pt. 775) 308 at 337. The court held in this case that if any of the incidents set out below occur, it may adversely affect the right of an individual to hold land or the compensation to be paid to the individual in the event of compulsory acquisition by government: (a) imposition or enforcement of tax, or duties; (b) penalties or forfeitures for the breach of any law; (c) covenants running with lands; (d) administration of persons adjudged or declared bankrupt, insolvent, unsound, deceased, or a company being wound up; (e) execution of judgments or orders of court; (f) properties in dangerous condition, including abandoned properties; (g) enemy property; (h) property under trusts and trustees; (i) where limitation of action applies; (j) properties vested in body corporate; (k) temporary taking of property for examination, investigation or enquiry; (l) carrying out of work on land for the purpose of soil conservation or; (m) acquisition for public good.

Act. These sections permit the Governor to revoke a right of occupancy for overriding public purpose.[40] This position has been confirmed by the Supreme Court decision in *Osho* v *Foreign Finance Corporation*[41]. For the revocation to be valid it must be for public good, the ground of revocation must be expressly stated in the notice of revocation and the notice of revocation must be properly served on the holder.[42] Acquisition of land or compulsory acquisition of land for cattle business of some individuals cannot be said to be for public good.

3. The Grazing Reserve Act of 1965: then and now

Farming has historically remained a popular and perhaps the main vocation in Northern Nigeria. As discussed above, farmers were encroaching on the customary grazing routes. Hence, noticeable misunderstanding began to evolve between the farmers and the herdsmen. To arrest the conflict the Grazing Reserve Act of 1965[43] was enacted by the Northern Regional Government. It was argued that grazing reserve will boost livestock production, ease herding challenges and reduce seasonal migrations of herdsmen. It was a deliberate policy measure to address some of the constraints confronting pastoralists in Nigeria at that time. The grazing Act mapped out grazing routes and reserves for the exclusive use of the herdsmen. This Act created and gazetted 313 grazing reserves particularly in North Central. Only few grazing routes was formally gazetted leaving the original objectives largely unfulfilled[44] Huge land compensation approved by the Land Use Act and other associated expenses prevented

40 Under Section 51 of the Land Use Act public purposes include: (a) for exclusive Government use or for general public use;(b) for use by anybody corporate directly established by law or by anybody corporate registered under the Companies Act 1968 as respects which the Government owns shares, stocks or debentures; (c) for or in connection with sanitary improvements of any king; (d) for obtaining control over land contiguous to any part or over land the value of which will be enhanced by the construction of any railway, road or other public work or convenience about to be undertaken or provided by the Government; (f) for obtaining control over land required for or in connection with mining purposes; g) for obtaining control over land required for or in connection with planned urban or rural development or settlement;(h) for obtaining control over land required for or in connection with economic, industrial or agricultural development.

41 1991, 4 NWLR (Part 184) 157.

42 Goldmark Nigeria Limited and Others v Ibafon Company Limited and Others, 2012, LPELR-SC.421/2001.

43 The Act was absorbed into state laws when the Northern Region ceased to exist as an entity. See Grazing Reserves Law, Ca59 Laws of Yobe State, 1994; Grazing Reserves Law, No. 4, Laws of Northern Nigeria, 1965 of Plateau State.

44 A. *Waters-Bayer* and *E. Taylor-Powell,* Population and Land Use in the Sub humid Zone of Nigeria. In Livestock Systems Research in Nigeria's Sub humid Zone: Proceedings of a second

state governments from creating additional routes.[45] The North-Central region had excellent pasture areas because of its low population density at the time when the Act was passed in 1964. The excellent pasture is no longer available because the population density in the North-Central is now as high as any part of the North. Following the collapse of Nigeria's First Republic, the grazing routes set out in the 1964 Act slowly went into disuse and diverse encroachment set in.

Recently there was an attempt to reintroduce the Grazing Reserve Act through the National Assembly. The Grazing Reserve Bill[46] proposed the constitution of National Grazing Reserves and Stock Routes on lands at the disposal of the Federal Government; any land in respect of which it appears to the Commission that Grazing on such land should be practiced and any land acquired by the commission through purchase, assignment gift or otherwise howsoever; any land in respect of which it appears to the Commission that primary secondary or tertiary routes be established. The assumptions underlying theses proposals are flawed. They contradict and are against the intent and purposes of the Land Use Act, LUA. The LUA does not confer any right on any agency of government including the Federal Government to take over anyone's land. In addition, the Federal Government does not have enough land for the purposes of establishing grazing routes neither does it have enough resources to purchase tracts of land for the intended purses of grazing reserves and routes. It is to be noted that land is not within the legislative competence of the National Assembly. It is a residual matter within the exclusive legislative competence of the state Assemblies. Meanwhile, four states within the Nigerian federation had already enacted laws prohibiting open grazing but establishing ranches within their respective states. The anti-open grazing law makes provision for livestock owners to apply for land for the ranches and follow a laid down procedure to get the land. From this quagmire, it is apparent that a uniform national legislation on grazing reserves and stock routes might not offer effective solution to the perennial conflicts between the herdsmen and farmers.

I. L. C. A./N. A. P. R. I. symposium held in Kaduna, Nigeria, October 29-November 4, 1984, edited by R. von Kaufmann, S. Chater, and R. Blench, 37–58, Addis Ababa: I. L. C. A., 1986b.

45 Ibid.

46 The Bill (available at <http://nass.gov.ng/document/download/879> was sponsored by Senator *Zainab Kure*, representing Niger Central in the Seventh Senate was presented for consideration but was rejected by the last Senate. The Bill was however revived in the present political dispensation and equally rejected. The Bill was titled: National Grazing Reserve (Establishment) Bill 2016, sponsored by *Hon. Sadiq Ibrahim*. Read more at <https://www.vanguardngr.com/2016/04/nigerians-say-no-national-grazing-reserves-bill/>, accessed on 12 January, 2018.

Despite the many potential benefits of the Grazing Reserve Bill, it was rejected.[47] In the opinion of the National Assembly, grazing matter or livestock does not fall within the legislative competence of the National Assembly.[48] It is doubtful if the stance of the National Assembly can stand judicial scrutiny. Development of agriculture[49] is clearly an item within the legislative competence of the National Assembly. A Grazing Reserve Bill falls within the purview of agriculture. Section 17 Part II of the Second Schedule of the CFRN empowers the National Assembly to make laws for the federation or any part thereof for the regulation of business, including development of agriculture. There were many other criticism of the Grazing Bill while some were constructive others were based on socio-cultural and religious sentiments. For example, the Kachia Grazing Reserve has been used to illustrate some reservations of a Grazing Reserve Act. Critics observed that the indigenous people whose lands were appropriated for the Kachia reserve are yet to be compensated till date, while the Kachichera Fulani herdsmen have since settled and gained rights to the land. The Kachichera Fulani herdsmen are now making a demand for Ladduga chiefdom,[50] in Africa chiefdom is associated with land ownership and control. Hence, the resistance to the idea of cattle colony or grazing reserve by other indigenous communities and some state governors.

Following from this experience and the perceived domineering nature of the herdsmen most state governments under pressure from indigenous communities are unwilling to allow their ancestral land and means of livelihood to be appropriated for grazing reserves. It is generally agreed that grazing reserve has contemplated and uncontemplated consequences. Grazing reserves will potentially breed more conflicts in the future as the herdsmen will grow in number and make a demand for more tracts of land. Again, what is the justification of taking parcels of land belonging to an indigenous community and is given to the Fulani herdsmen? In addition, there is no scientific proof that previous Grazing reserves in Nigeria have reduced clashes between herdsmen, farmers and communities in the past rather the conflicts have been exac-

47 Despite the fact that this Bill has been rejected, it is imperative that its provisions be discussed in this paper because it offers a potential to ameliorate the farmer and herdsmen conflict f refined. It might also be re-introduced because the primary reason for its rejection by the National Assembly is not tenable.

48 Cf. <www.thisdaylive.com/index.php/2016/11/10/senate-rejects-grazing-reserve-bill-says-its-unconstitutional/>, accessed 22 February, 2018.

49 Agriculture has widely been defined as including farming, raising livestock and rearing fishes.

50 *Z.A.Gundu*, The matter of grazing reserves, The Nation Newspapers; available at <http://thenationonlineng.net/matter-grazing-reserves/>, accessed on the 15th of April, 2018.

erbated in those areas. This opinion is supported by a study of factors underlying the conflicts between herdsmen and farmers in the Benue Valelley of Kogi State. Findings reveal that conflicts over "land matter accounted for the highest percentage (42.9) of conflicts, followed by political (32.08 %) and chieftaincy matters (28.3 %) respectively. A high percentage of conflicts arising from land disputes have to do with land matters and conflict between Fulani herdsmen and farmers over grazing land"[51] The conflicts that occurred in the villages where grazing is permitted led to violent destructions of crops, farms, and pollution of water, ponds, fish and fishery resources.[52] The wanton destruction from the conflict adversely affected the livelihoods of the indigenes and the herdsmen. Thousands of lives have been lost on both sides, properties destroyed, farms burnt and cattle poisoned or killed. This informs the public furore, hysteria, phobia, contempt, and opprobrium that greeted the introduction of the grazing reserve Bill at the National Assembly. In most communities, the Fulanis are considered strangers because they do not belong to the host communities by their way of life and are deemed to be different and confrontational.

In sum, a national Grazing Reserve legislation or cattle colony is not a guarantee for fostering peace. Research findings have shown that the perennial conflicts between the farmers, the Fulani herdsmen and the host communities have far reaching consequences. Peaceful coexistence and harmonious living have been impeached and acrimony, hatred and distrust now exist between the herdsmen, farmers and the host communities across West Africa and Nigeria in particular. It is not likely to have peace without a process of reconciliation and atonement.

III. Herdsmen and Famers Conflicts across West African States and beyond the Conflicts

There are over 12 million pastoralists in the West Africa sub-region and over 70 million people depend on livestock for their livelihoods.[53] There is an estimated 256.9 million head of livestock in West Africa. Nigeria has "41.8 % of the total number in

51 *Tenuche and Ifatimehin,* Resource Conflict among Farmers and Fulani Herdsmen: Implications for Resource Sustainability, African Journal of Political Science and International Relations 2009, Vol. 3(9), 360–364.

52 Ibid., at 363.

53 *S. Nura,* Agricultural development in the age of sustainability: Livestock production, in: Benneh, G., et al (eds), Sustaining the Future: Economic, Social, and Environmental Change in Sub-Saharan Africa Tokyo, United Nations University Press, 1996.

the sub-region followed by Niger, Mali and Burkina Faso which have 14.2 %, 12.7 % and 11.9 % respectively.[54]" The West African pastoralists are popularly known and referred to as the Fulani herdsmen. These pastoralists are predominantly nomadic. They operate between their base in the semi-arid north during the rainy season and migrate to the wet south during the dry season. They move across West African countries in the process, in search of water and pasture for their herds. In the process they graze on farmlands belonging to crop farmers. The farmers often also benefit from the dairy products produced by the herdsmen. They share land, water, fodder and other resources. Problems and conflicts are inevitable. There are always problems over resource use and control. This has been a recurring problem over the years. Some herdsmen are also accused of intentionally damaging cash crops[55] and setting farmlands on fire particularly in Northwest and Northeast of Nigeria tracks. This is induced by reason of blockage of the corridors or tracks by construction of schools, cemetery, crop farmlands etc. Research findings have identified blockages of agreed corridor of passage in Zinder province (Niger), an entire Matameye neighbourhood developed in the international transhumance corridor, in Nigeria identified and agreed corridor is full of large agricultural estates[56]. In contemporary times, there is a tendency to prevent the herdsmen from advancing to hinterlands and indigenous communities in search of grazing water and pasture land, this usually provoke violent conflicts between herdsmen and farmers.

Some other constraints being faced by the herdsmen in the process of transhumance have been identified in a study by FAO and they include "pronounced climate change and environmental degradation, land policy without taking into account of pastoral mobility; limited consideration of policies, institutions and legal and regulatory texts regarding pastoralism; population growth and urbanization that requires a very high increase in the supply of animal products"[57]. In addition, there is lack of access to education, water and vet veterinary services. The pastoralists are poor and cannot afford to buy medicine for their herds or prevent diseases. "Their movements

54 FAOstat, 2009, available at <https://www.documentcloud.org/documents/3884375-ECOWAS-CrossBorder-Transhumance-WA-Final-Report-1.html>, accessed on 01 January, 2018.

55 FACU, Farmer-Pastoralist Conflict in the core states of the National Fadama Development Project, 1999.

56 Food and Agricultural Organization of the United Nations, The cross-border transhumance in West Africa. Proposal for Action Plan, 2012, 30; available at < http://ecpf.ecowas.int/wp-content/uploads/2016/01/CrossBorder-Transhumance-WA-Final-Report-1.pdf>, accessed on 13th February, 2018.

57 Op. cit., at 10.

combined with the diversity of trypanotolerant breeds, are a way to avoid animal diseases and vectors such as tsetse flies.[58]" They remain vulnerable to epidemics, prejudices and xenophobia attacks.

However, beyond the contest for land and other resources, contemporary West African communities have witnessed a mix of herdsmen militancy, religious conflict and terrorism unleash on farmers and the host communities. Now the herdsmen are fully armed with the ability to call for very devastatingly effective enforcement within a twinkle of an eye[59]. It has been alleged that the Fulani herdsmen use modern weaponry and mercenaries across West African states[60]. The conflicts in respect of quest for grazing land and resources have now evolved into a complex and almost irretraceable conflict of religion, ethnicity, identity, and terrorism. Foreign Fulani herdsmen and mercenaries from Chad, Mali, Libya, Niger and Ghana have been identified during vicious attacks on Nigerian communities.[61]

1. Finding Solutions: Lessons from Selected West African Countries on Inclusivity

Published findings have shown steps adopted in some West African countries to curtail the persistent conflicts between the herdsmen and farmers.[62] Niger inaugurated projects like the Livestock Sector Support Program (PASEL), and engage reputable NGOs like CARE International with globally acclaimed integrity and other financial partners to delineate and mark traditional and historical corridors of passage[63]. All stakeholders were consulted and diverse interests taking into consideration. All provinces were involved in the peace process and a committee is set up to take charge of the corridors. It must be acknowledged that little challenges remain; herdsmen rest area is sometimes located quite far from the grazing area due to refusal of farmers to give up their lands for the construction of rest areas. The study concludes that though

58 Ibid., at 20.

59 The 2015 Global Terrorism Index identified the Fulani herdsmen as the fourth deadliest terrorist group in the world.

60 *A. Ahmed-Gamgum,* Herdsmen and Farmers Conflict in Nigeria: Another Dimension of Insecurity, Journal of Public Administration and Social Welfare Research, 2018, Vol. 3 No. 1.

61 Ibid.

62 Ibid., 36–38.

63 *N. Diakité,* Transhumances transfrontalières en Afriques de l'Ouest, Communication Rencontre de Bamako (Mali), Praia Sahel Consult, 2003.

there are penalties for the violation of the peace plan, no legal or administrative sanction has been implemented.

To draw up a peace plan and end the persistent conflicts in Benin, the farmers and the herdsmen have to negotiate by having constructive dialogue. The antidote to the conflict includes the setting up of pastoral tracks and access to water and grazing land along the tracks.[64] In the South-Eastern province of Borgu herdsmen-farmers committee which developed into an association was set up to manage the land and relationship between the stakeholders. This model has been adopted by Mali and Senegal successfully.[65] In addition, livestock and farming infrastructural facilities and development plans including corridors, guaranteed access to water and rest slots were provided. This has greatly improved relationship between the parties and helped in crop protection and improved nomadic pastoral experiences.[66]

A dual-approach model that offers preventive and healing perspectives was implemented in Ivory Coast. The preventive approach includes establishment of close crop farmlands in risk areas including the supply of free barbed wire, grazing routes with needed facilities, creation of animal restraining areas with mandatory night padlocks to enforce the restrain, herdsmen and farmers are made to carry identity cards. The healing approach includes peaceful settlement of damage to crops, encouragement and promotion of mixed crop and livestock farming.

A national management committee of transhumance with administrative authorities was set up in Togo. This committee is made up of representatives of the herdsmen, farmers and the traditional rulers. The committee is charged with the responsibility of controlling the movement of nomadic herdsmen and their stock, assist them to locate the grazing areas, to ensure the herdsmen respect the regulations in force in the country, to settle all disputes between the farmers, the herdsmen and third parties and to apply sanctions provided by law against any offender against the laws Togolese.

Conflict prevention and resolution mechanism exist in every region in Senegal. They hold frequent reconciliatory meetings between the parties and apply regulatory measures. These meetings enjoy the collaboration of the administrative authorities and traditional authorities. All the stakeholders are committed to the peace pro-

64 B. *Rosier*, Des couloirs pastoraux pour la paix, in : Information agricole 2009, no. 839, Monde, 37–38.

65 *L. J. De Hann*, Changements dans les modes de vie au Nord Bénin et leurs effets sur l'environnement, Le Courrier 1992, no. 133, Mai-Juin, 89 – 90.

66 *A. Marty*, Etude sur le pastoralisme, droits, tenure et changements climatiques, IRAM – Montpellier –Paris 2011, IUCN – Right Ressources.

cess and take proactive and preventive measures, including the development of new cross-border valleys.

2. Moving Forward

To mitigate or eliminate the perennial conflicts between herdsmen and farmers it is imperative for both parties to shift their positions. The herdsmen, farmers and militias in host communities must be disarmed. There are far too many arms in Nigeria and across West Africa. Ranches, grazing reserves and stock routes redevelopment must be given priority particularly in the Northern states of Nigeria where the Fulani herdsmen live and reside in significant large numbers. Nationwide the herdsmen should be encouraged to embrace modern breeding methods and jettison old tradition of nomadic cattle rearing which is now considered obsolete. Open grazing surely must be curtailed and restricted particularly in states that have limited land mass and insignificant number of resident herdsmen. With ranches adequate food and medical facilities will be provided for the cattle. Cattle will be more productive and healthier. There will be far less conflict and confrontation with farmers. Ranches are owned by individuals while grazing reserve is jointly owned by the community of herdsmen.

A mutually beneficial stakeholders' driven and inclusive framework should be developed and implemented as done in Togo, Benin and Senegal discussed above. The process must be consultative, deliberate and painstaking. A holistic legislative framework and harmonization is required to address the challenges associated with nomadic cattle rearing. The fragmented laws as presently constituted are not adequately effective to tackle the menace of the herdsmen[67]. That ranching is an enduring solution is not in doubt. However, there is need for strategic and long time planning and implementation.

Regional instruments governing pastoralism should be respected, protected and domesticated where possible. Federal grazing reserves, grazing routes should be mapped out identified and protected in the Northern Nigerian states. Identified international corridors must be protected and maintained with functional facilities such as boreholes, veterinary hospitals, grazing routes, etc. The Federal Government must create multi-level incentives to modernize and optimize livestock just as its doing for plant cultivation. It is recognized that agriculture is on the concurrent list, the Federal Government however should provide a platform that sets the standards on the implementation of the desired transition from nomadic animal husbandry to modern ranching. Approaches that are not deeply thought and exclusionary are bound

67 There are now diverse state laws that have been enacted to regulate the practice of livestock.

to fail. Recently, the National Economic Council (NEC) is reported to have banned open grazing.[68] NEC is an economic advisory body, no more. Apart from the fact that NEC does not have the power to ban open grazing,[69] this approach will only inflame the already volatile situation. Ban or restriction on open grazing should be phased out gradually and with discussion and understanding of the herdsmen.

The ECOWAS must create a platform to address the emerging transnational dimension of the herdsmen militancy across West Africa. The herdsmen have been wreaking havoc across Africa and particularly in West Africa. The national approach to land issues must be harmonized at ECOWAS regional level.

IV. Conclusion

In an empirical study conducted by *Olaniyan et al*[70] discussed earlier above, findings reveal that the farmers and the herdsmen blame each other for the rampant and vicious attacks; accusing each other of perpetuating crimes such as destruction of properties, destruction of crops, killing of cattle, rape and genocide. It has however been shown above that all parties; the herdsmen, farmers and the indigenous people of the host communities are all victims. They are victims of abysmal failure of some West African governments to plan ahead and take effective steps at the national and regional levels to forestall the potential violence that is now spreading across the West African states between the herdsmen, farmers and the indigenous people of the host communities. More worryingly is the neglect of the Nigerian Government to take adequate step to reconcile the parties. Killings and maiming among the parties have become a daily occurrence in some part of Northern and North central Nigeria, Benue, Kaduna, Taraba and Plateau states are most affected. The Nigerian Army and other securities personnel have been drafted to those states to curtail the very violent and vicious attacks but the conflict is not abating. Some communities and notable indi-

68 Guardian Newspapers, NEC bans open grazing as herdsmen attacks persists, <https://guardian.ng/news/nec-bans-open-grazing-as-herdsmen-attacks-persist>; New Telegraph, NEC bans open grazing nationwide, <https://newtelegraphonline.com/2018/04/nec-bans-open-grazing-nationwide/>, accessed on 24 April, 2018.

69 Part I Third Schedule S. 19 states that NEC "shall have power to advise the President concerning the economic affairs of the Federation, and in particular on measures necessary for the co-ordination of the economic planning efforts or economic programmes of the various Governments of the Federation".

70 Cf. *Olaniyan, Francis and Okeke-Uzodike*, note 24.

viduals are not convinced the security personnel are neutral[71]. The Nigerian Army has been accused of giving tactical support to the Fulani herdsmen. The Nigerian Army has vehemently denied the accusation. The Army and other security personnel can only restore immediate peace; they cannot restore stability, mutual co-existence and enduring peace. The nature of the conflicts require more than security intervention.

From the expositions above, approaches to peace and reconciliation among the herdsmen, farmers and the indigenous host communities must be strategic and all embracing. Reconciliation here "means that the victims and perpetrators, or members of hostile groups, do not see the past as defining the future as simply a continuation of the past. It means that they come to see the humanity of one another, accept each other, and see the possibility of a constructive relationship.[72] The narratives promoting exclusiveness, divisiveness and diverse form of xenophobia will certainly not bring enduring peace. The narratives must feed inclusiveness, diversity and multi-culturalism. There must be a channel of communicating grievances and receiving remedies as adapted by the selected West African states discussed above. This channel must be effective in communicating information to all stakeholders. Reconciliation and Atonement committee consisting of credible representatives[73] of the herdsmen, farmers, indigenous communities and government must be statutorily established. They must be charged with the responsibility of maintaining peace, adjudicating minor infractions, mediating and provision of vital information.

71 Former Chief of Army Staff, Lieutenant General *Yakubu Danjuma* (rtd) accused the army of collusion with the Fulani herdsmen: "The armed forces are not neutral. They collude; they collude; they collude with the armed bandits that kill people and kill Nigerians. They facilitate their movement. They cover them". *Danjuma* was a former defence Minister of the Federal Republic of Nigeria; cf *The Nation Newspapers*, March 25, 2018, Danjuma: Military colluding in herdsmen killings, available at < https://thenationonlineng.net/danjuma-blasts-military-allegedly-aiding-killer-herdsmen/>, accessed on April 23, 2018.

72 *Ervin Staub*, Reconciliation after Genocide, mass killing, or intractable conflict: Understanding the Roots of Violence, Psychological Recovery, and Steps toward a General Theory, Political Psychology 27.6 2006, at 868.

73 Previously a similar mediation council existed in Northern Nigeria but it later became bias and corrupt. The arbitral proceedings were flawed and susceptible to distortions. Summation of its activities is aptly captured by FAO of the United Nations: 'most disputes between farmers and herders require arbitration of traditional leaders. They have developed a type of judicial procedures with witnesses, the site inspection and an independent assessment of costs. However, some of them, pronounce arbitrary sentences, and are often accused of taking bribes. In some areas, for example, pastoralists are favoured in all cases because they are richer than farmers and can afford more. Elsewhere, sentences are always pronounced in favour of farmers', Food and Agricultural Organization of the United Nations, 2012, 69. See note 56 above.

The reality is that the herdsmen cannot be wished away neither can they be expelled without far reaching consequences, including but not limited to war, genocide, instability, entrenched poverty and perhaps religious and tribal antagonism. Policy of expulsion of the Fulani herdsmen as shown above in Ghana and some parts of Nigeria has not really proven effective. Likewise, the herdsmen cannot continue to recklessly destroy or allow their cattle to destroy crops, farmlands and indigenous communities' livelihoods and expect muted response or peace. Government must make deliberate effort to address and tackle disobedience, contempt for local rules, regulations and custom by the herdsmen and farmers. Any breach of regulations and laws must be appropriately sanctioned. Lessons can be drawn from the other West African countries discussed above. The Government of Taraba state should immediately publish the reports of its Judicial Commission of enquiry on the Mambilla Plateau killings and Benue State should equally publish the report of the Logo and Guma killings. All perpetuators of these horrific killings should be brought to face justice. This is the right signal to send to would-be trouble makers.

It is also a giving that there will always be pressure on land and other natural resources as population continues to bloat. Crop farming and livestock business will outlive all parties. Hence, the only viable intervention for national and regional governments within West Africa is to put in deliberate measures that will promote peace, reconciliation and atonement with a motto of live and let live. Application of any other measure will only exacerbate the problems and promote more violent conflicts. A top-down approach is also not the solution but an all stockholders reconciliatory approach.

Constitutional Development and Constitutional Interpretation in Ukraine and Russia in the Light of the Russian-Ukrainian Conflict

Oesten Baller

Abstract

Five years ago the Maidan Revolution (or, as the Ukrainian mainstream calls it: The Revolution of Dignity) marked the cornerstone for the outbreak of the Russian-Ukrainian conflict. Based on the facts, beginning with the prehistory and ending in August 2015, the political decisions of Russia, Ukraine and Crimea are evaluated here, as well as the primary decisions of the constitutional courts of Ukraine and Russia. The framework of this analysis is not limited to the respective national constitutions and legislations of Ukraine and Russia. As the conflict is an international one, the impact of international law is crucial, too. A precise evaluation of the main events shows, that the main players are Russia and Ukraine, because Crimea was and is not a subject of international law. The essential conclusion is that in both countries it is not Law, which determines political decision-making and jurisdiction, but vice versa, the political mainstream which determines the law-making and the jurisdiction of the Constitutional courts. Despite the many victims of the bloody conflict, both states are not only uncompromising, but stay with post-Soviet traditions.

Introduction

The Russian-Ukrainian conflict, which has led to the *de facto* separation of the Crimea and its incorporation into the Russian Federation, is often considered from an international law perspective. The scenarios and events of the conflict and the two actors Crimea and the Russian Federation were and are often in the centre of interest, whereas Ukraine is treated rather as an object of implicit reference. Of course, the Ukrainian crisis as such is also dealt with in numerous studies. This study tries a different approach. Based on a detailed chronological account of events, the ones most important in constitutional terms are correlated either to Russia or to Ukraine, depending on which country the events are directly and exclusively attributable to. Accordingly, Crimea is not seen as an independent subject of international law, whilst the actions under review are considered from within the framework of the Ukrainian Constitution and the Constitution of the Autonomous Republic of Crimea. Of course, the assessment should not be anticipated by this view, as only from the assessment the results are deduced. In the presentation of the legal basis of the attributable events, international law does not play the first fiddle from the outset. The focus is rather on the constitutional basis and, depending on the field of action, on simple laws. International law comes on the scene, when the constitutions and laws refer to international law. Special attention is paid on how events and decisions are reflected in the jurisdiction of the constitutional courts in Ukraine and Russia.

I. The Facts

The evaluation of constitutional problems in the Russian Federation and Ukraine should be preceded by a presentation of the underlying facts. Accordingly, it must be determined in advance, which sources are suitable and which periods should be covered. The answer to the first question depends on which sources can be found to have a high degree of objectivity and fairness. With regard to the two aforementioned standards, the prehistory and the main story of the Russian-Ukrainian conflict have led to a deplorable decline in the constitutional and international law science standards in Russia. A clear evidence for this thesis is, on the one hand, the controversy about the case law of the Russian Constitutional Court on the incorporation of Crimea into the Russian Federation that was carried out in Russian newspapers between the professor of constitutional law, *Elena Luk'ianova,*[1] and the Chairman of the Constitutional Court of the Russian Federation, *Valerij Zor'kin*[2], and, on the other hand, the open letter of the Executive Board of the Russian Association of International Law to the Executive Council of the International Law Association from June 2014.[3]

Among other things, *Elena Luk'ianova* states in her contribution that the Russian Constitutional Court has made eight serious legal mistakes in its decision to incorporate the Crimea. *Valerii Zor'kin* responds with derogatory and sometimes insulting words, completely abandoning the self-restraint constitutional court judges prac-

1 *Elena Luk'ianova,* O prave nalevo. K voprosu o verkhovenstve prava v kontekste rossiiskoi vneshnei politiki, ili Pochemu, soglasno zakonu Rossiiskoi Federatsii, Krym vse-taki ne sovsem nash (The rule of law inside out. The precedence of law in the context of Russian foreign politicy, or why, according to the Law of the Russian Federation, Crimea is not quite ours), Novaia Gazeta (New Gazette), 19 March 2015, available at <https://www.novayagazeta.ru/articles/2015/03/19/63473-o-prave-nalevo>.

2 *Valerii Zor'kin,* Pravo – i tol'ko pravo. O vopiiushchikh pravonarusheniiakh, katorye uporno ne zamechaiut (Law and only law. About egregious offenses that persistently remain unnoticed), Rossiiskaia gazeta (Russian Gazette) No. 6631, 24 March 2015, available at <https://rg.ru/2015/03/23/zorkin-site.html>.

3 The Russian and English version are available at <http://www.ilarb.ru/html/news/2014/5062014.pdf>.

tice in developed democracies – although he declared that he, as a citizen of Russia, is writing not a political but a philosophical and even an existential article:

> 'I would never answer the article of any lawyer, even more professional and deeply immersed in the specifics of constitutional law. In this case, we are not talking about the article of Ms. *Luk'ianova,* who constantly strives to sit on two chairs – pseudo-communist and pseudo-liberal – and constantly changing her position in accordance with the conjuncture.'[4]

The open letter of the Russian Association of International Law lists, under six headlines, facts and assessments that correspond to a good part and often literally with the political state doctrine of the Russian Federation, as well as with the speeches and statements of President *Putin,* and are thus part of the propaganda machinery[5], which was launched preceding the onset of the Russian-Ukrainian conflict. Therefore, numerous works of Russian international and constitutional lawyers, with few exclusions,[6] fail to provide a basis for the description of underlying facts, as well as some western international and constitutional lawyers, whose articles fully or in some details overlap with the official propaganda machinery.[7] Another reason not to trust the Russian sources too much is that all the respective long-term historic-chronological accounts keep silent about the deportation of the Crimean Tatars and the genocide against them at the end of the Second World War.[8] As a result, I have chosen a

4 See for this controversy *Caroline von Gall,* Ist die Krim wirklich russisch? Russische Juristen diskutieren über die Rechtmäßigkeit der Aufnahme der Krim (Is Crimea Russian, indeed? Russian jurists debate legality of Crimea's accession), russland analysen (Analyses of Russia) No. 295, 8.5.2015, 2–7.

5 See *Oleksandr Merezhko,* Crimea's Annexation in the Light of International Law. A Critique of Russia's Legal Argumentation, Kyiv-Mohyla Law and Politics Journal 2 (2016), 36–89, at 55.

6 Above all, the works of *Elena Luk'ianova* and *Maria Sissaeva;* cf. *Elena Luk'ianova,* On the Rule of Law in the Context of Russian Foreign Policy, Russian Law Journal (hereinafter RLJ), Vol. III (2015) Issue 2, at 10; *Maria Sissaeva,* A Nationalized Approach to International Law: the Case of Russia, available at <https://voelkerrechtsblog.org/a-nationalized-approach-to-international-law-the-case-of-russia/>; A Quarter of a Century on from the Soviet Era. Reflexions on Russian Doctrinal Responses to the Annexation of Crimea, RLF Vol. V (2017) Issue 3, at 86.

7 Cf. *John J.A. Burke and Svetlana Panina-Burke,* Eastern and Southern Ukraine's Right to Secede and Join the Russian Federation, RLJ Vol. III (2015) Issue 1, at 33; *John J.A. Burke,* Economic Sanctions Against the Russian Federation are illegal under Public International Law, RLJ Vol. III (2015), Issue 3, at 126.

8 Cf. *Brian Glyn Williams,* The Crimean Tatars. From Soviet Genocide to Putin's Conquest, Hurst Publishers, 2015.

selected mixture of global researchers on the Russian-Ukrainian conflict.[9] Contributions were written in part as an immediate response to the escalation of the Russian-Ukrainian conflict, sometimes with a certain interval allowing for critical reflection.

As regards the time frame, the events which can be attributed to the escalation of the Russian-Ukrainian conflict or have to be seen as a direct causal link with the breaking out of the conflict should be outlined. The changeable history of the Crimean peninsula in the last 75 years is not retold here; where historical references are part of constitutional or international law analysis, this will be done at the respective place in this contribution. The starting point was November 28, 2013. At the Eastern Partnership Summit, which took place in Vilnius, November 28–29, 2013, the President of Ukraine, *Viktor Yanukovych,* informed on the decision by the Ukrainian Government to suspend preparations for signing the Association Agreement (AA) and the Deep and Comprehensive Free Trade Area (DCFTA) between the EU and Ukraine.[10] Large parts of Ukraine were shocked by this decision: unlike in the neighbouring countries Moldova and Georgia, the further Europeanisation of Ukraine was now put on ice. It was not his fickleness that prompted *Viktor Yanukovych* to make that decision. On the one hand, long-term negotiations, both within the European Union and between the EU and the Eastern Partnership countries, took place on the

9 The main sources are *David R. Marples and Frederick V. Mills* (eds.), Ukraine's Euromaidan. Analyses of a Civil Revolution, Stuttgart 2015; *Viktor Stepanenko and Yaroslav Pylynskyi* (Eds.), Ukraine after the Euromaidan, Bern 2015; *Otto Luchterhandt,* Der Anschluss der Krim an Russland aus völkerrechtlicher Sicht (Crimea's accession to Russia in the light of international law), Archiv des Völkerrechts, Vol. 52, 137–174, at 137–141, 155–161 f.; *Christian Marxsen,* The Crimea Crisis. An International Law Perspective, ZaöRV 74 (2014), 367 – 391, at 368 – 370; *Maria Issaeva* (note 6), at 89–94; *G. Matteo Bacaro-Incisa,* Crimea's Secession from Ukraine and Accession to the Russian Federation as an Instance of North(-West) v. South(-East) Divide in the Understanding of International Law, Santa Clara Journal of International Law, Vol. 14, Issue 2, 4-1-2017, 125–156, at 133–135; *Konstiantyn Fedorenko,* The Two Movements: Liberals and Nationalists During Euromaidan, Ideology and Politics, No. 1(5), 2015, 4–35; *Robin Geiß,* Russia's Annexation of Crimea: The Mills of International Law Grind Slowly but They Do Grind, International Law Studies, U. S. Naval War College, Vol. 91. 2015, 424–449, at 429–431; *Michel Kofman, Katya Migacheva, Brian Nichiporuk et al.,* Lessons from Russia's Operation in Crimea and Eastern Ukraine, I-110; at 6–12; with limitation also *John Burke and Svetlana Panina-Burke,* The Reunification of Crimea and the City of Sevastopol with the Russian Federation, RLJ, Vol. V (2017), Issue 3, 29–68, at 39–47.

10 Cf. Joint Declaration of the Eastern Partnership Summit, Vilnius, 28–29 November 2013, Eastern Partnership: the way ahead; available at <http://static.eu2013.lt/uploads/documents/Programos_12/131129%20Vilnius%20Summit%20Declaration.pdf>. Decision of the Ukrainian Government not to sign the AA dates from November 21, see *Alexander Kratochvil and Carmen Scheide,* EuroMaidan. Chronology of Events, in: Carmen Scheide, Ulrich Schmid (Eds.), The EuroMaidan in Ukraine. November 2013 till February 2014, Euxeinos. Governance and Culture in the Black Sea Region, 13/2014, at 52.

terms and conditions of rapprochement of these countries with the EU.[11] The closer the deadline for signing the AA and the DCFTA came, the stronger became the economic pressure of the Russian president on the neighbouring country Ukraine.[12] The breakout of the rally of demonstrations in Kiev, which were later well known as Euro-Maidan[13] was right after the decision of the Ukrainian Government in the night from November 22 to 23, 2013. The day after, ten thousands demonstrated peacefully for the Europeanisation of Ukraine.

The *Yanukovych* regime did not wait long for a violent and unconstitutional reaction to the peaceful and non-violent exercise of the fundamental rights to freedom of assembly and opinion guaranteed by the Ukrainian Constitution.[14] First, the Kiev City State Administration requested the competent District Administrative Court to impose a large-scale and extensive ban on peaceful gathering throughout the city centre of Kiev, which was decided on the same day of November 30.[15] Secondly, heavily armed special police forces, Berkut, were sent to the Maidan during the night, striking with incredible brutality at peaceful students who had slept in tents. This happened under the pretext of setting up a Christmas tree on the Maidan and has therefore been referred to as 'Bloody Christmas Tree'. This is clear evidence that the escalation of violence on Kiev's streets was not caused by the protestors, but by the Ukrainian state in the seat of the President, the Mayor of Kiev, the state administration, the administrative courts and the police.[16]

The following weeks showed manifold events. The overture to anti-Soviet and slowly growing, partly anti-Russian protest came with the so-called 'Leninfalls'[17] – in many cities of Ukraine and at the place of the Bessarabs'kij Rynok in Kiev Lenin

11 Cf. Joint Staff Working Document. Implementation of the European Neighbourhood Policy in Ukraine. Progress in 2014 and recommendations for actions, Brussels, 25. March 2015, available at <https://eur-lex.europa.eu/legal-content/EN/TXT/?uri=CELEX%3A52015SC0074>.

12 *Luchterhandt* (note 9), at 139.

13 The specific chronology of the events at the Maidan and in Kiev city follows *Alexander Kratochvil* and *Carmen Scheide*, EuroMaidan (note 10) and *Andriy Portnov and Tetiana Portnova*, The Ukrainian 'Eurorevolution': Dynamics and Meaning, in: Viktor Stepanenko and Yaroslav Pylsynski (Eds.), Ukraine after the Euromaidan. Challenges and Hopes, Bern 2015, 59–72.

14 Konstytutsiia Ukrainy (The constitution of Ukraine) with subsequent amendments, signed 28 June 1996, Vidomosti Verkhovnoi Rady Ukrainy (Bulletin of the Verkhovna Rada, VVR), 1996, No. 30, item 141 (hereinafter ConstUA).

15 Postanova (Decision) No. 826/19020/13-a, signed 30 November 2013, available at <http://archive.is/KYsht#selection-185.0–185.94>.

16 *Andriy Portnov and Tetiana Portnova* (note 13), at 60.

17 Cf. *Konstiantyn Fedorenko* (note 9), at 7.

monuments were smashed. In keeping with the Soviet tradition of guided demonstrations, on December 14, 2013, the government organised an anti-Maidan demonstration close to the Maidan, whose aggressive and violence-prone participants were bussed and trained into Kiev by the Party of Regions and the Government. This period is marked by many not always peaceful demonstrations in many Ukrainian cities on the one hand, by arbitrary arrests and state repression on the other. On December 17, President *Yanukovych* travelled to Moscow for a friendly visit with President *Putin.* The latter promised a loan of 15 billion US dollars and a significant reduction of gas prices for Ukraine.[18] Gradually, also leaders of the three largest opposition parties of Ukraine at that time joined in the events. These were *Vitalii Klichko, Oleg Tyagnybok* and *Arseniy Yatsenyuk.* From a political point of view, the party 'UDAR' headed by *Klichko,* and the party 'Bat'kivshyna, headed by *Yatsenyuk,* belong to the liberal party family, while the 'Svoboda' party under T*yagnybo*k must be classed with the right-winged party family. The three party leaders founded on December 22 the National Maidan Association (NOM).[19]

Even before Orthodox Christmas and Orthodox New Year, the Kiev district administrative court renewed its large-scale ban on peaceful gatherings on 6 January 2014 until March 8. The ban addressed the leaders of the abovementioned political parties and other social organisations, and included a ban to conduct events, to use loudspeakers, vehicles, posters, install tents, stages, canopies, starting from January 8, 2014 to March 8, 2014 and extending over central Kiev with the addresses, mentioned in the decision.[20] On January 16, 2014, the Verkhovna Rada not only decided on the state budget for 2014, according to the agreement between *Putin* and *Yanukovych.*[21] More seriously, Verkhovna Rada passed nine real illiberal package-laws that not only tightened sanctions in criminal and administrative regulatory law, above all in the area of exercising constitutional rights, such as freedom of opinion and of assembly, but also limited the rights of parliamentarians and accused persons and vested police and secret services with more rights, and, last but not least, *à la russe,* served

18 See *A. Eremenko et al.*, Zapomni, kak vse nachinalos' (Remember how it all began), Kiev: Zerkalo nedeli (Mirror of the week), 2013, available at <http://gazeta.zn.ua/internal/zapomni-kak-vse-nachinalos-_.html>.

19 *Andriy Portnov and Tetiana Portnova* (note 13), at 64.

20 The official court registry of Ukraine can accessed only from computers in Ukraine. The court decision is Postanova No. 826/145/14, signed 6 January 2014; cf. <https://kiev.unian.net/872609-sud-zapretil-massovyie-aktsii-v-tsentre-kieva-do-8-marta.html> (Court bans mass rallies in center of Kiev).

21 Zakon Ukrainy 'Pro Derzhavniy biutzhet Ukrainy na 2014 rik' (Law of Ukraine 'On the 2014 state budget of Ukraine'), No. 719-VII, signed 16 January 2014, VVR 2014, No. 9, item 93.

to brand social organisations that receive funding from abroad, as foreign agents.[22] All in all, these packages of *ad hoc* legislation are not only severely violating the provisions of the Ukrainian Constitution, but also provided the main conditions for the break-out of uncontrollable violence with severe consequences in the following weeks.

As a result, Right Sector, a right-wing nationalistic organisation called to arms and founded a militant self-defence. From this point on, at the latest, one must assume that the Maidan movement had a militant branch, which did not shy away from violence, including the use of firearms.[23] On January 22, called the 'Black Day' of Ukraine[24], there were snipers in the city, shooting at innocent people. Many peaceful people in Ukraine became victims of this violence. In detail, it is still unclear who shot where and when in the city. An immediate criminalistic and forensic investigation, led by international teams, could have brought light into the darkness.[25] The political will for this has been missing from January 2014 up to today in Ukraine.

February 21, 2014 brought two related events. On the one hand, President *Yanukovych*, Russian special envoy *Vladimir Lukin*, and three foreign ministers from Germany, France and Poland, as well as the three opposition leaders mentioned above signed an Agreement on the Settlement of Crisis in Ukraine.[26]. The agreement foresaw an immediate end to violence, early detection and investigation of the events, surrender of all illegal weapons, a comprehensive constitutional reform, early presidential elections in Ukraine, and a return to the 2004 Constitution of Ukraine.[27] *DmytroYarosh*, the leader of the militant Right-Sector, disagreed and demanded the immediate resignation of President *Yanukovych*. During the night, the latter left secretly Kiev, heading for eastern Ukraine (Kharkiv).[28]

On February 22, referring to Art. 108 No. 1 of the Ukrainian Constitution (Resignation of the President), the Verkhovna Rada decided that President *Yanukovych*

22 Cf. *Konstiantyn Fedorenko,* at 9.

23 Cf. *Konstiantyn Fedorenko* (note 9), at 14 ff., *Christian Marxsen,* Crimea Crisis (note 9), at 369.

24 *Andriy Portnov and Tetiana Portnova* (note 13), at 66.

25 The report on Maidan Investigations, 31 March 2015, of the Council of Europe lists some details, but cannot resolve the decisive question, available at <https://www.coe.int/en/web/kyiv/report-on-maidan-investigations>.

26 See full text at <https://www.theguardian.com/world/2014/feb/21/agreement-on-the-settlement-of-crisis-in-ukraine-full-text>.

27 Zakon Ukrainy 'Pro vidnovlennia dii okremykh polozhen' Konstytutsii Ukrainy' (Law of Ukraine 'On Restoring Specific Provisions of the Constitution of Ukraine'), No. 742-VII, signed 21 February 2014, VVR 2014, No. 11, item 143.

28 Cf. *Alexander Kratochvil and Carmen Scheide,* EuroMaidan (note 10), at 54.

had withdrawn from office.[29] Presidential elections were scheduled for 25 May 2014. The execution of an impeachment procedure under Art. 111 of the Constitution would, of course, have been more precise than the analogy in question.[30] The same day began the Russian invasion of the Crimean peninsula. Initially, special units were transferred;[31] other land operations that may have supported the evacuation of *Yanukovych,* as well as a snap inspection with 150.000 soldiers, followed shortly thereafter. On February 24, the City Council of Sevastopol elected a Russian citizen as mayor; Three days later, Russian special forces disguised as local self-defense militia occupied the Crimean parliament and hoisted the Russian flag. The Crimean Parliament then decided to hold a referendum on May 25, parallel to the presidential elections in Kiev.[32] The same day, *Arseniy Yatsenyuk* from the party Bat'kivshyna was elected Prime Minister of Ukraine.

On February 28, the day on which the Sevastopol City Soviet voted in favor of a referendum, Crimean Prime Minister *Aksenov* announced that the referendum had been brought forward to March 30. Five days later, a joint decision by the Supreme Soviet of the Crimea and the City Soviet preponed the referendum date to March 16. Only on March 1, 2014, nearly a week after the first invasion of the Crimea by Russian troops, the Russian Duma authorized President *Putin* to send troops to Ukraine. Then it happened in quick succession. On March 6, the Supreme Soviet of the Crimea decided to join the Russian Federation as a new federation subject.[33] The Declaration of Independence of the Crimea took place on March 11.[34] Three days later, the Ukrainian Constitutional Court ruled the planned referendum in the Crimea to be contra-

29 Postanova Verkhovnoi Rady Ukrainy 'Pro samousunennia Prezydenta Ukrainy vid vykonannia konstytutsiinykh povnovazhen' ta pryznachennia pozachergovykh vyboriv Prezydenta Ukrainy' (On Self-Removal of the President of Ukraine from his Constitutional Authority and Early Elections of the President of Ukraine), No. 757-VII, signed 22 February 2014, VVR 2014, No. 11, item 158.

30 Cf. also *Luchterhandt* (note 9), at 140, note 14.

31 Cf. for the military aspects of the invasion of Crimea *Michael Kofmann, Katya Migacheva,* et al, Lessons from Russia's Operation in Crimea and Eastern Ukraine, Luchterhandt (note 9), at 161 ff.

32 A good overview on the events in Crimea can be found in the Russian version of Wikipedia, at <https://ru.wikipedia.org/wiki/%D0%A0%D0%B5%D1%84%D0%B5%D1%80%D0%B5%D0%BD%D0%B4%D1%83%D0%BC_%D0%BE_%D1%81%D1%82%D0%B0%D1%82%D1%83%D1%81%D0%B5_%D0%9A%D1%80%D1%8B%D0%BC%D0%B0_(2014)>.

33 Postanovlenie VR ARK 'O provedenii obsczekrymskogo referenduma' (Decision of the Verkhovna Rada of the Autonomous Republic of Crimea 'On the execution of an All-Crimean Referendum') No. 1702–6/14, signed 6 March 2014 , available at <http://crimea.gov.ru/act/11689>.

34 Parlament Kryma, Deklaratsii o nezavisimosti Avtonomnoi Respubliki Krym i g. Sevastopolia (Parliament of Crimea, Declaration of Independence of the Autonomous Republic of

dictory to the Ukrainian Constitution,[35] and on on March 20, with the same result on the Declaration of Independence.[36] A move to preserve Ukraine's sovereignty, independence, unity and territorial integrity in the Security Council of the UN has been blocked by Russia's veto on March 15, against 13 positive votes.[37]

On March 16, the referendum took place under strong Russian military presence. The dispute over the results is shown below.[38] A day later, *Putin* issued an Ukaz in which he recognized the Crimea, and with it, the city of Sevastopol as a sovereign and independent state.[39] President *Putin,* the Republic of Crimea and the City of Sevastopol signed the 'Contract between the Russian Federation and the Republic of Crimea on the incorporation into the Russian Federation of the Republic of

Crimea and the city of Sevastopol, signed 11.3.2014, available at<http://www.crimea.gov.ru/news/11_03_2014_1>.

35 Rishennia Konstytutsiinogo sudu Ukrainy u spravi za konstytutsiinymy podanniamy vykonuiuchogo obov'iazky Prezydenta Ukrainy, Golovy Verkhovnoi Rady Ukrainy ta Upovnovazhenogo Verkhovnoi Rady Ukrainy z prav liudyny schodo vidpovidnosti Konstytutsii Ukrainy (konstytutsiinosti) Postanovu Verkhovnoi Rady Avtonomnoi Respubliky Krym 'Pro provedennia zagal'nokryms'kogo referdendumu' (sprava pro provedennia mistsevogo referendum v Avtonomniy Respublitsi Krym) (Ruling of the Constitutional Court of Ukraine in the case of the constitutional petitions of the Acting President of Ukraine, the Chairman of the Verkhovna Rada of Ukraine and the Commissioner of the Verkhovna Rada of Ukraine on Human Rights on the compliance of the Constitution of Ukraine (constitutionality) with the Resolution of the Verkhovna Rada of the Autonomous Republic of Crimea 'On the All-Crimean Referendum' (case on holding a local referendum in the Autonomous Republic of Crimea), Spravo No. 2-rp/20 14, 14 March 2014, available at <http://zakon3.rada.gov.ua/laws/show/v002p710–14>.

36 Rishennia Konstytutsiinogo sudu Ukrainy u spravi za konstytutsiinym podanniam vykonuiuchogo obov'iazky Prezydenta Ukrainy Golovy Verkhovnoi Rady Ukrainy schodo vidpovidnosti Konstytutsii Ukrainy (konstytutsiinosti) Postanovu Verkhovnoi Rady Avtonomnoi Respubliky Krym 'Pro Deklaratsiiu pro nezaleshnist' Avtonomnoi Respubliky Krym i mista Sevastopolia'(Ruling of the Constitutional Court of Ukraine in the case of the constitutional petition of the Acting President of Ukraine, the Chairman of The Verkhovna Rada of Ukraine on the compliance of the Constitution of Ukraine (constitutionality) of the Resolution of the Verkhovna Rada of the Autonomous Republic of Crimea 'On the Declaration on the Independence of the Autonomous Republic of Crimea and the City of Sevastopol'), Sprava NQ 1–15/2014, NQ 3-rp/2014, 20 March 2014, available at <http://zakon5.rada.gov.ua/laws/show/v003p710–14>.

37 Cf. <https://news.un.org/en/story/2014/03/464002-un-security-council-action-crimea-referendum-blocked>.

38 See under III.3.

39 Ukaz Prezidenta Rossiiskoi Federatsii 'O priznanii Respubliki Krym' (Ukaz of the President of the Russian Federation 'On the recognition of the Republic of Crimea'), No. 147, signed 17 March 2014, SZ RF 2014, No. 12, item 1259.

Crimea and the formation of new subjects of the Russian Federation' the next day.[40] On March 20 and 21, the two chambers of the Russian Parliament ratified the contract.[41] With 100/11/24 votes the UN General Assembly affirmed the referendum's invalidity by Resolution 68/262.[42]

A new violent page of the Russian-Ukrainian conflict was opened in April 2014, when pro-Russian rebels began occupying government buildings in the Donbass region of Ukraine, including the industrial centres of Donetsk and Luhansk. A hybrid war started with many victims on both sides, as well as many violations of Human Rights, on both sides, too.[43] Perhaps it was Russia's President *Putin,* who gave the start-

40 Dogovor mezhdu Rossiiskoi Federatsiei i Respublikoi Krym o priniatii v Rossiiskuiu Federatsiiu Respubliki Krym i obrazovanii v sostave Rossiiskoi Federatsii novykh sub'ektov (Treaty between the Russian Federation and the Republic of Crimea on the admission to the Russian Federation of the Republic of Crimea and the formation in the Russian Federation of new subjects within the Russian Federation), signed in Moscow 18 March 2014), available at <http://kremlin.ru/events/president/news/20605>.

41 Postanovlenie Gosudarstvenoi Dumy Federal'nogo Sobraniia Rossiiskoi Federatsii 'O проекте Federal'nogo konstitytsionnogo zakona No 475944–6 'O priniatie v Rossiiskuiu Federatsii Respubliki Krym i obrazovanii v sostave Rossiiskoi Federatsii novykh sub'ekov Respubliki Krym i goroda federal'nogo znacheniia Sevastopol' (Decision of the State Duma of the Federal Assembly of the Russian Federation 'On the draft federal constitutional Law 'On the admission to the Russian Federation of the Republic of Crimea and the creation within the Russian Federation of new subjects – Republic of Crimea and the city of federal significance Sevastopol''), dated 20 March 2014, SZ RF 2014, No. 12, item 1258; Postanovlenie Soveta Federatsii Federal'nogo Sobrania Rossiiskoi Federatsii 'O Federal'nom konstitytsionnom zakone 'O priniatie v Rossiiskuiu Federatsii Respubliki Krym i obrazovanii v sostave Rossiiskoi Federatsii novykh sub'ekov Respubliki Krym i goroda federal'nogo znacheniia Sevastopol'' (Decision of the Federal Council of the Federal Assembly 'On the federal constitutional Law 'On the adoption to the Russian Federation of the Republic of Crimea and the creation within the Russian Federation of new subjects – Republic of Crimea and a city of federal significance city of Sevastopol'') No. 69-SF, dated 21 March 2014, SZ RF 2014, No. 12, item 1204.

42 Cf. <http://www.un.org/en/ga/search/view_doc.asp?symbol=A/RES/68/262>.

43 Cf. Amnesty International, available at <https://www.amnesty.org/en/countries/europe-and-central-asia/ukraine/>, above all, the reports 'Summary Killing during the Conflict in Eastern Ukraine', available at <https://www.amnestyusa.org/wp-content/uploads/2017/04/eur500422014en_final.pdf>, and 'Breaking Bones. Torture and Summary Killing in Eastern Ukraine', 2015, available at <https://www.amnestyusa.org/reports/breaking-bodies-torture-and-summary-killings-in-eastern-ukraine/>; OECD Special Monitoring Mission to Ukraine (SMM), available at <https://www.osce.org/press-releases?filters=+im_taxonomy_vid_1:(896)>; UN Human Rights Monitoring Mission in Ukraine, available at <http://www.un.org.ua/en/publications-and-reports/un-in-ukraine-publications/3592-un-reports-on-human-rights-situation-in-ukraine>; from an Ukrainian perspective see <http://uacrisis.org/> with many, sometimes daily reports.

ing shot, when he used for the first time the term 'Novorossiia'.[44] In the meanwhile, Crimea adopted a new Constitution on April 11.[45] One month later, local referendums were held in Donetsk and Luhansk, widely criticized by Ukraine, the EU and the US.[46] To pacify the bloody conflict in eastern Ukraine, a tripartite contact group was set up, which was composed of Swiss Ambassador *Heidi Tagliani* for the OSCE, the second President of Ukraine, *L. D. Kuchma,* the Ambassador of Russia in Ukraine, *M.Yu. Surabov, A. V. Sacharchenko* for Donetsk and *I. V. Plotnisky* for Luhansk. The so-called Minsk-1 Agreement of 1 September 2014 contains 12 measures to calm the crisis, including ceasefire, improving the humanitarian situation, releasing all hostages, and decentralisation.[47] This agreement did not have much success, just as little as the Minsk-2 agreement of 12 February 2015, even if this sounds much clearer than its predecessor does.[48] After all, implementing the Minsk-1 Agreement, Ukraine had on 16 September, 2014 already passed a special law 'On the Special Procedure of Local Self-Government in Some Districts of Donetsk and Lugansk Oblasts'.[49]

However, it is quickly told, how difficult it is to find a way towards the constitutional reform necessary for decentralization: At the beginning of March 2015, the President set up a constitutional commission with some international participation,[50] which was to work in various areas, including decentralization.[51] The concrete composition was decided on March 31, including the appointment of the then spokesman for Verkhovna Rada, *Volodymyr Grojsman,* as chairman of the commission. An intensive cooperation with the Venice Commission was planned and implemented.

44 Cf. *Adrian A. Basora and Aleksandr Fisher,* Putin's 'greater Novorossiya' – the Dismemberment of Ukraine? May 2, 2014, available at <https://www.fpri.org/article/2014/05/putins-greater-novorossiya-the-dismemberment-of-ukraine/>.

45 Konstitutsiia Respubliki Krym (Constitution of the Republic of Crimea), adopted 11 April 2014, available at <http://constitution.garant.ru/region/cons_krim/>.

46 *Sofia Cavandoli,* The unresolved dilemma of self-determination: Crimea, Donetsk and Luhansk, The International Journal of Human Rights, 2016, Vol. 20, No. 7, 875–892, at 883.

47 Cf. <https://www.osce.org/ru/home/123258?download=true>.

48 Cf. <https://www.ft.com/content/21b8f98e-b2a5-11e4-b234–00144feab7de>.

49 Zakon Ukrainy 'Pro osoblyvnyi poriadok mistsevogo samovriaduvannia v okremykh raionakh Donet s'koi ta Lugans'koi oblastei' (Law of Ukraine 'On a special procedure of local self-government in some districts of the Donetsk and Luhansk oblasts') with subsequent amendments, No. 1680-VII, signed 16 September 2014, VVR 2014, No. 45, item 2043.

50 Cf. <http://constitution.gov.ua/en>.

51 Polozhennia pro Konstytutsiiny Komisiiu (Statute on the constitutional commission), adopted by Ukaz of the President No. 119/2015, signed 3 March, Oficijnyi visnyk Prezydenta Ukraïny (Official bulletin of the President of Ukraine, OVP) 16 March 2015, No. 7, page 22, item 464.

Additional time was allotted, because the self-proclaimed republics in Donetsk and Luhansk in May requested to participate in the constitution-making process. On 8 June, they submitted a revised version of their amendments, which was partly in line with the Minsk-2 Agreement. On the other hand, they called for a semi-autonomous status with a mixture of treaty and constitutional federalism.[52] However, the Constitutional Commission, did not pay much attention to this draft which gave rise to significant political unrest. Subsequently, at the 103rd plenary session on 19 and 20 June, the Chairman of the Constitutional Commission *Volodymyr Grojsman* asked the Venice Commission for a short-term opinion on the draft law on constitutional amendments.[53] Since the final draft version was worked out during the development work, a description of the draft version is not given here.[54] The overwhelmingly positive opinion of the Venice Commission concludes that the draft work is based on a concept of decentralization that is largely consistent with the European Charter of Local Self-Government[55], and that the proposed changes are carefully prepared and worth supporting. Only two small changes are proposed.[56]

A revised bill was forwarded to the Ukrainian Constitutional Court in July. The court ruled on 30 July 2015 that the draft complied with the Constitution.[57] In the

52 Dopolneniia i izmeneniia DNR i LNR v Konstitutitsiiu Ukrainy (Addenda end changes to the Constitution of Ukraine, proposed by the Donetsk and Luhansk People's Republics), dated 8. June 2015, available at <https://politikus.ru/articles/51812-dopolneniya-i–izmeneniya-dnr-i–lnr-v-konstituciyu-ukrainy.html>.

53 Venice Commission, Opinion No. 803/2015, CDL-PI (2015) 008, 26 October 2015, Preliminary Opinion on the proposed Constitutional Amendments, regarding the Territorial Structure and Local Administration of Ukraine, available at <http://www.venice.coe.int/webforms/documents/?pdf=CDL-PI(2015)008-e>.

54 The Venice Commission has published a non-official comparison table between the current constitution and the draft bill, cf. <http://www.venice.coe.int/webforms/documents/default.aspx?pdffile=CDL-REF(2015)021-e>.

55 Dated 15 October 1985, cf. <https://rm.coe.int/CoERMPublicCommonSearchServices/DisplayDCTMContent?documentId=090000168007a088>.

56 Venice Commission, Opinion No. 803/2015, CDL-PI (2015) 008, 26 October 2015, Preliminary Opinion on the proposed Constitutional Amendments, regarding the Territorial Structure and Local Administration of Ukraine <http://www.venice.coe.int/webforms/documents/?pdf=-CDL-PI(2015)008-e>.

57 Vysnovok Konstitutsiinogo Sudy Ukrainy u spravi za svernenniam Verchovnoj Rady pro nadannia vysnovku schodo vidovidnosti zakonoproektu zmin do Konstitutsii Ukrainy schodo detsentralisatsii vlady vymogam statei 157 i 158 Konstitutsii Ukrainy (Ruling of the Constitutional Court of Ukraine in the case on the appeal of the Verkhovna Rada of Ukraine on the conclusion on compliance with the draft law on amendments to the Constitution of Ukraine regarding the decentralization of power to the requirements of Articles 157 and 158 of the Constitution of Ukraine),

first reading on 31 August 2015, the bill was debated controversially among all parties, including the governing coalition, and was passed with a majority of members of the governing coalition and other parties.[58] Following this, there were right-wing demonstrations and bloody riots in front of the Parliament. During the protests, about 30 armed demonstrators attacked the security forces. The situation escalated when a grenade was thrown out of this group, resulting in many casualties and the deaths of three policemen.[59] Consequently, the second reading, for which a qualitative two-thirds majority is required for adoption, has been postponed and has not yet taken place.

II. Ukraine

1. The Course of the Events

The events directly and exclusively attributable to Ukraine, and therefore legally assessed under this heading, are:

- Maidan legislation under President *Yanukovych* and bans imposed by the Administrative Court
- Declaration of Independence of Crimea and decision of the Ukrainian Constitutional Court
- Referendum in Crimea and decision of the Ukrainian Constitutional Court
- Defining the status of the crisis in eastern Ukraine
- Decision of the Ukrainian Constitutional Court and draft constitutional amendments on decentralisation

Sprava No. 1–18/2015, 30 July 2015, available at <http://www.ccu.gov.ua/sites/default/files/ndf/2-v/2015.pdf>.

58 The exact result of the vote as well as statements of leading politicians can be found here: without author, Dezentralisierung: Politischer Konflikt und gewaltsame Proteste (Decentralisation: Political conflict and violent protests), Ukraine-Analysen No. 155, 16.9.2015, page 8–14.

59 Ukraine-Analysen, a. a.O; see also the daily report of the OSCE Mission in Ukraine, available at <http://www.osce.org/ukraine-smm/179251>.

2. The Legal Requirements

2.1. Constitution of Ukraine

Ukraine is a sovereign and independent, democratic, social, law-based state (Art. 1 ConstUA). The current constitution defines Ukraine[60] as unitarian state (Art. 2 ConstUA), whose territorial structure follows the principles of unity and indivisibility, and the combination of centralization and decentralization in the exercise of state power (Art. 132 ConstUA). All people are free and equal in their dignity and rights, and human rights and freedoms are inalienable and inviolable (Art. 21 ConstUA). Art. 28 emphasizes the respect of human dignity and forbids any torture, cruel, inhuman or degrading treatment or punishment that violates the human dignity. Everyone is guaranteed the right to freedom of thought and speech, and to free expression of his or her views and beliefs, as well as citizens have the right to assemble peacefully without arms and to hold meetings, rallies, processions and demonstrations, upon notifying in advance the bodies of executive power or bodies of local self-government (Art. 34, 39 ConstUA). Restrictions on the exercise of the right to assembly may be established by a court in accordance with the law and only in the interests of national security and public order, with the purpose of preventing disturbances or crimes, protecting the health of the population, or protecting the rights and freedoms of other persons (Art. 39 (2) ConstUA). Formally, the Constitution of Ukraine is not as international law friendly as the Constitution of the Russian Federation. According to Art. 9 ConstUA only international treaties agreed to be binding by the Verkhovna Rada of Ukraine are part of the national legislation of Ukraine.

Art. 5 ConstUA states that the constitutional order may only be changed by the sovereign (the people of the state). Constitutional amendments are made by a law of the Verkhovna Rada, which requires a qualified quorum of one third of the deputies and a qualified quorum of two-thirds for the legislative initiative (Art. 85 (1), 154, 155 ConstUA). Amendments to Chapters I (General Principles), III (Elections, Referendum) and XIII (Amendments to the Constitution) require a two-thirds majority for legislative initiative and legislative resolution, followed by a general referendum (Art. 156 ConstUA). Constitutional changes are banned if fundamental and human rights are abolished or restricted, or if the changes aim at liquidating independence or violating the territorial indivisibility of Ukraine. If martial law is imposed or there is a state of emergency, the constitution must not be changed (Art. 157 ConstUA). Fi-

60 Cf. note 14. An English version is available at <http://www.partylaw.leidenuniv.nl/party-law/4c8b8dea-7838-45f1-8e92-1b537287acdc.pdf>.

nally, according to Art. 159 ConstUA, Verkhovna Rada can not deal with a bill amending the constitution unless it has a vote by the Constitutional Court that the provisions of Art. 157 and 158 ConstUA do not preclude the constitutional amendment. An All-Ukrainian referendum is designated by the Verkhovna Rada of Ukraine or by the President of Ukraine, in accordance with their authority established by this Constitution. An All-Ukrainian referendum is called on popular initiative on the request of no less than three million citizens of Ukraine who have the right to vote, on the condition that the signatures in favour of designating the referendum have been collected in no less than two-thirds of the oblasts, with no less than 100 000 signatures in each oblast. Issues of altering the territory of Ukraine are resolved exclusively by an All-Ukrainian referendum (Art. 72 and 73 ConstUA). A law of Ukraine (Art. 92 (13) ConstUA) effects the factual altering of the territory of Ukraine.

The President of Ukraine has to confess in his oath (Art. 104 ConstUA):

> 'I, (name and surname), elected by the will of the people as the President of Ukraine, assuming this high office, do solemnly swear allegiance to Ukraine. I pledge with all my undertakings to protect the sovereignty and independence of Ukraine, to provide for the good of the Motherland and the welfare of the Ukrainian people, to protect the rights and freedoms of citizens, to abide by the Constitution of Ukraine and the laws of Ukraine, to exercise my duties in the interests of all compatriots, and to enhance the prestige of Ukraine in the world.'

According to Art. 106 ConstUA the President of Ukraine adopts a decision in accordance with the law on general or partial mobilisation and introduction of martial law in Ukraine or in its particular areas, in the event of a threat of aggression, danger to the state independence of Ukraine (20) or, in the event of necessity, on the introduction of state of emergency in Ukraine or in its particular areas (21). The powers of the President of Ukraine terminate prior to the expiration of term in cases of: 1) resignation; 2) inability to exercise his or her powers for reasons of health; 3) removal from office by the procedure of impeachment; or 4) death (Art. 108 ConstUA).) If the President of Ukraine commits state treason or other crime, he can be removed from office by the procedures of impeachment (Art. 111 ConstUA).

In the Constitution of Ukraine, minority rights are at least protected by a basic standard, and the constitution contains a whole chapter (X) on the protection of the autonomy of the Crimean peninsula. Even if Ukrainian is the exclusive state languages of Ukraine, the Constitution guarantees the free development, use and protection of Russian and other languages of national minorities of Ukraine (Art. 10 ConstUA). According to Art. 134 ConstUA, the Autonomous Republic of Crimea is an inseparable constituent part of Ukraine and decides on the issues ascribed to its competence within the limits of authority determined by the Constitution of Ukraine. Legal acts of the Verkhovna Rada of the Autonomous Republic of Crimea and decisions of the Council of Ministers of the Autonomous Republic of Crimea shall not contradict the Constitution and the laws of Ukraine and are adopted in accordance with the Constitution of Ukraine, the laws of Ukraine, acts of the President of Ukraine and the Cabinet of Ministers of Ukraine, and for their execution (Art. 135 ConstUA). The Constitution of Ukraine assigns to the Autonomous Republic of Crime a good package of legislative and executive competences, including the organisation and conduction of local referendums (Art. 136–138 ConstUA).

2.2. Maidan Laws

The nine so-called Maidan laws[61] enacted on January 16, 2014, are omnibus amending acts with major changes to some laws, particularly made to restrict freedom of assembly and related activities, and to criminalize participation therein, which in democratic states are protected areas of freedom of assembly,. Sanctions for many violations, irrespective of the severity of the infringement, were drastically tight-

61 The laws in this note are given with English titles, in order to roughly inform on the content. Law of Ukraine 'On Amendments to the Law of Ukraine 'On the Judiciary and the Status of Judges' and 'Procedural Laws on Additional Measures to Protect the Security of Citizens' No. 721-VII , signed 16 January, 2014, VVR 2014, No. 22, item 801; Law of Ukraine 'On Amendments to Certain Legislative Acts of Ukraine regarding Liability for committing Administrative Offenses during the Conduct of Football Matches' No. 722-VII, signed 16 January, 2014, VVR 2014, No. 22, item 802; Law of Ukraine 'On Amendments to Certain Legislative Acts of Ukraine Regarding Liability for Administrative Offenses in the Field of Road Traffic Safety, Recorded in the Automatic Mode' No. 723-VII, signed 16 January, 2014, VVR 2014, No. 22, item 811; Law of Ukraine 'On Amendments to the Rules of Procedure of the Verkhovna Rada of Ukraine' No. 724-VII, signed 16 January, 2014, VVR 2014, No. 22, item 804; Law of Ukraine 'On Amendments to the Criminal Procedural Code of Ukraine for Correspondence Criminal Proceedings' No. 725-VII, signed 16 January 2014, VVR 2014, No. 22, item 805; Law of Ukraine 'On Amendments to the Law of Ukraine 'On Free Legal Aid' the postponement of the entry into force of the provisions of clause 6 of Section VI 'Final and Transitional Provisions" No. 726-VII, signed 16 January, 2014, VVR 2014, No. 22, item 806; Law of Ukraine 'On Amendments to Article 197 of the Tax Code of Ukraine for Exemption from Taxation of Value Added Tax on Transshipment of Natural Gas to the Customs Territory of Ukraine' No. 727-VII, signed 16 January, 2014, VVR, 2014, No. 22, item 807; Law of Ukraine 'On Amendments to Article 297 of the Criminal Code of Ukraine regarding liability for the desecration or destruction of monuments built in memory of those who fought against Nazism during the Second World War – Soviet soldiers liberators, members of the partisan movement, underground, victims of Nazi persecution, as well as international soldiers and peacekeepers' No. 728-VII, signed 16 January, 2014, VVR', 2014, No. 22, item 808; Law of Ukraine 'On Amendments to the Criminal Code of Ukraine on Responsibility for Denying or Excusing Fascist Crimes' No. 729-VII, signed 16 January, 2014, VVR 2014, No. 22, item 809.

ened. All these laws had a short but violent life, as they were repealed on January 28, 2014, by a law signed by President *Yanukovych.*[62] To give you some examples: The law No. 721-VII introduced a new Art. 185–1 (Violation of the order of organizing and holding meetings, rallies, street processions and demonstrations) in the Code of Administrative Offences[63], with foreseen fines from 20 – 100 minimum monthly wages (further: MMW). The masked participation in a demonstration or accompanying a masked person in a demonstration could now be punished with a penalty from 150 to 250 MMW. The unauthorized setting up a tent could now be punished with a penalty from 250 to 300 MMW or with an arrest up to 15 days[64]. In the Criminal Code[65] the fines for Crime against the bases of national security of Ukraine were tightened or new crimes were introduced into the Criminal Code. Imprisonment for violations of Art. 109 (Actions aimed at the forcible change or overthrow of the constitutional order or the seizure of state power) was now possible for terms from 5 to 10 years. A new offense was added to the Criminal Code, Art. 110–1 (Extremist activity):

> 1. Manufacture, storage for the purpose of distribution or distribution, as well as the sale or distribution of extremist materials, including through the media, the Internet, social Internet networks, the use or demonstration of extremist materials before a mass meeting of people, including at meetings, rallies, during street processions, demonstrations, public utterances or appeals of an extremist nature, as well as funding for these activities or otherwise facilitating their organization or implementation, including by providing information services, money, real estate, educational, printing or material and technical facilities, telephone, facsimile or other types of communication, in the absence of signs of a more serious crime, entail the imposition of a fine of two hundred to eight hundred non-taxable minimum incomes of citizens with the confiscation of extremist materials.

The fine was fixed from 200 – 800 MMW. Law No. 724 created the possibility of imposing arrest on parliamentary deputies, judges of the Constitutional Court and judges in ordinary jurisdiction. Law No. 726 amended the entry into force of the

62 Zakon Ukrainy 'Pro vyznannia takymy, scho vtratyly chynist, deiakykh zakoniv Ukrainy' (Law of Ukraine 'On the recognition of some laws of Ukraine as repealed'), No. 732-VII, signed 28 January, 2014, VVR 2014, No. 22, item 811.

63 Kodeks Ukrainy pro administratyvni pravoporushennia (Code of Ukraine on administrative offences), art. 1 - 212-20, with subsequent amendments, No. 8073-X, signed 7 December, 1984, Vidomosti Verkhovnoi Rady Ukrainskoi RSF (Bulletin of the Verkhovna Rada of the Ukrainian Soviet Socialist Republic) 1984, No. 51, item 1122.

64 With the risk of being beaten or tortured there.

65 Kryminal'nyi kodeks Ukrainy (Criminal Code of Ukraine), with subsequent amendments, No. 2341, signed 5 April 2001, VVR 2001, No. 25–26, item 131.

Law 'On Free Legal Aid'[66] with retroactive effect from 1 January 2014 to 1 January 2015. Last but not least, another new offence was added to the Criminal Code, i. e. Art. 436–1 (Public denial or justification of the crimes of fascism, propaganda of neo-Nazi ideology, the production and (or) distribution of materials that justify the crimes of the fascists and their supporters).[67]

2.3. Emergency Laws

For understanding the legal design of Ukrainian military operation in Donbass, it is useful to briefly overview the security options, which are also anchored in the Constitution of Ukraine. First, there is the 2015 Law 'On the legal regime of martial law'.[68] This Law determines the content of the martial law regime, the procedure for its introduction and abolition, the legal basis for the activities of state authorities, military commanders, military administrations, local governments, enterprises, institutions and organizations in a state of martial law, the protection of human and civil rights and freedoms, and of the rights and legitimate interests of legal entities. The definition in Art. 1 of this law corresponds to the equivalent definition in the predecessor Act[69]:

Martial law is a special legal regime introduced in Ukraine or in its particular regions in the event of armed aggression or threat of attack, the danger to state independence of Ukraine, its territorial integrity and provides for the provision of appropriate state authorities, military command, military administrations and local self-government powers necessary to prevent a threat, repulse armed aggression and ensure national security, eliminate threats dangerous the state independence of Ukraine, its territorial integrity, as well as a temporary restriction of the constitutional rights and

66 Zakon Ukrainy 'Pro bezoplatnu pravovu dopomogu' (Law of Ukraine 'On free legal aid'), with subsequent amendments, No. 3460-VI, signed 2 June 2011, VVR 2011, No. 51, item 577.

67 The public denial or justification of the crimes of fascism against humanity committed during the Second World War, in particular the crimes committed by Waffen-SS, its subordinate structures, those who fought against the anti-Hitler coalition and collaborated with fascist occupiers, as well as propaganda of neo-Nazi ideology, manufacture and (or) distribution of materials that justify the crimes of the fascists and their supporters shall be punishable by a fine of five hundred to one thousand minimal monthly wages, or restraint of liberty for a term up to two years, or imprisonment for the same term.

68 Zakon Ukrainy 'Pro pravovii rezhym voiennogo stanu' (Law of Ukraine 'On the legal regime of martial law'), with subsequent amendments, No. 389-VIII, signed 12 Mai 2015, VVR 2015 No. 28, item 250.

69 Zakon Ukrainy 'Pro pravovy rezhym voiennogo stanu' (Law of Ukraine 'On the legal regime of martial law') No. 1647-II, signed 6 April 2000, VVR 2000, No. 28, item 224.

freedoms of a person and citizen, the rights and legitimate interests of legal entities with the indication of the validity of these restrictions.

The second option is the law 'On combatting terrorism'.[70] In Art. 1 this law defines terrorism and terroristic action: 'Terrorism' is a socially dangerous activity that consists in the conscious, purposeful use of violence by taking hostages, arson, murder, torture, intimidation of the population and authorities, or committing other attacks on the lives or health of innocent people or threats of committing criminal acts with the aim of achievement of criminal goals; 'terrorist activities' are activities that cover planning, organization, preparation and implementation of terrorist acts, incitement to commit terrorist acts, violence against individuals or organizations, destruction of material objects for terrorist purposes, organization of illegal armed groups, criminal groups (criminal organizations), organized criminal groups for the commission of terrorist acts, as well as participation in such acts.

2.4. Constitution of Crimea

As far as Crimea did not adopt a new constitution until April 11, 2014,[71] all Crimea-related activities up to incorporating Crimea into the Russian Federation are also to be judged on the basis of the Crimean Constitution at that time, i. e., the Constitution of the Autonomous Republic of Crimea (ConstCrimea).[72] In accordance with the Ukrainian Constitution, the Constitution of Crimea stated in Art. 1, that the Autonomous Republic of Crimea shall be an integral part of Ukraine and it shall solve, within the powers conferred upon it by the Constitution of Ukraine, any and all matters coming within its terms of reference. According to Art. 2 ConstCrimea, the legal foundation of the status and powers of the Autonomous Republic of Crimea, the Supreme Rada of the Autonomous Republic of Crimea and the Council of Ministers of the Autonomous Republic of Crimea shall be the Constitution of Ukraine, Ukrainian laws and the Constitution of the Autonomous Republic of Crimea. If the provisions of legislation of the Supreme Rada of the Autonomous Republic of Crimea and the acts of the Council of Ministers of the Autonomous Republic of Crimea contradict

70 Zakon Ukrainy 'Pro borot'bu z teroryzmom (Law of Ukraine 'On fighting terrorism'), with subsequent amendments, No. 638-IV, signed 20 March 2003, VVR 2003, No. 25, item 180.

71 Cf. note 45.

72 Zakon Ukrainy 'Pro zatverdzhennia Konstytutsii Avtonomnoi Respubliky Krym' (Law of Ukraine 'On Approval of the Constitution of Autonomous Republic of Crimea'), with subsequent amendments, No. 350-XIV, signed 23 December 1998, VVR 1999, No. 5–6, item 43.

the Constitution of Ukraine and/or Ukrainian laws, the provisions of the Constitution of Ukraine and Ukrainian laws shall prevail.

As concerns the holding of referendums, Art. 18 ConstCrimea states that the powers of the Autonomous Republic of Crimea include calling and holding of republican (local) referendums upon matters coming under the terms of reference of the Autonomous Republic of Crimea; equally, the powers of the Supreme Rada of the Autonomous Republic of Crimea are limited to all matters, coming under the Constitution of Ukraine, the Constitution of the Autonomous Republic of Crimea and Ukrainian laws, within the terms of reference of the Autonomous Republic of Crimea, except those as shall be required to be solved by a republican (local) referendum or the Council of Ministers of the Autonomous Republic of Crimea and other executive bodies of the Autonomous Republic of Crimea (Art. 26).

2.5. International Law

With regard to the international law framework, two levels must be distinguished in advance: on the one hand, universal international law, on the other hand, regional international law and bilateral international treaties. The two antagonists in the *jus cogens* of universal law are, on the one hand, the principle of territorial integrity or political independence of the states, on the other hand the principle of equal rights and self-determination of peoples.[73] The rights of territorial integrity and political independence are closely linked to the prohibition of violence addressed to all other states. The right of peoples to self-determination and their right to secession have long been discussed intensively in international law, originally in the context of decolonization in the 20th century.[74] The so-called Friendly Relations Declaration[75] highlights the prohibition of violence, the principles of sovereign equality and non-intervention and the principle of equal rights and self-determination of peoples. With the aim to bring

73 Art. 2 (4) and 1 (2) UNCh.

74 For a small selection, see *Margret Moore* (ed.), National Self-Determination and Secession, New York, 1998; *Bruno Coppieters and Richard Sawka* (eds.), Contextualizing Secession. Normative Studies in Comparative Perspective, New York, 2003; *Stephan Macedo and Allen Buchanan*, Secession and Self-Determination, New York and London, 2003; *Andrew K. Coleman*, Resolving Claims to Self-Determination. Is there a role for the International Court of Justice, New York and London, 2013; *Christian Walter, Antje von Ungern-Sternberg and Kavus Abushov* (eds.), Self-Determination in International Law, New York, 2014; *Juan Francisco Escudero Espinosa*, Self-Determination and Humanitarian Secession in International Law of a Globalized World. Kosovo v. Crimea, Springer International Publishing, 2017.

75 Declaration on Principles of International Law Friendly Relations and Co-Operation amongst States in Accordance with the Chapter of the United Nations, adopted 24 October 1970.

a speedy end to colonialism the Friendly Relations Declaration, provides a regulation, which cannot be transferred to the Crimea and the Russian-Ukrainian conflict because of not having a reference to overcome colonialism:[76]

> 'The establishment of a sovereign and independent State, the free association or integration with an independent State or the emergence into any other political status freely determined by a people constitute modes of implementing the right of self-determination by that people.'

Another important brick for consideration and evaluation of international law is the Kosovo-decision of the International Court of Justice, issued in 2010.[77] In this advisory opinion, the court has stated that Kosovo's unilateral declaration of independence is consistent with international law. The question of whether Kosovo and Crimea are comparable is being discussed vigorously. Like a prayer wheel, the Russian propaganda machine and, for the most part, the Russian scientific publications emphasize that the cases are identical.[78] Almost unanimously, western publications emphasize the opposite.[79] Since this can be decided only through evaluating the facts, the own assessment is coming soon. In the discussion of international law, however, the opinion emerges that the concept of a 'remedial secession' can be used to balance self-determination with state sovereignty and territorial identity.[80] In any case, the concept of a remedial secession is so far a concept, but not *jus cogens.*

76 *Simone F. van den Driest*, Crimea's Separation from Ukraine: An Analysis of the Right to Self-Determination and (Remedial) Secession in International Law, NILR (2015) 62, 329–363, at 336.

77 Accordance with International Law of the Unilateral Declaration of Independence in Respect of Kosovo, Advisory Opinion, I. C. J. Reports 2010, 403.

78 Cf. *V. A. Tomsinov*, 'Krymskoe Pravo' ili iuridicheskie osnovania dlia vossoedineniia Kryma s Rossii ('Crimean Law' or legal grounds for the reunification of the Crimea with Russia), Vestnik Moskovskogo Universiteta, Ser. 11, Pravo (Journal of the Moscow State University, Series 11, Law) 2014 No. 5; 3–32; *A. M. Ibragimov*, Vossoedinenie Kryma i Sevastopolia s Rossiiskoi Federatsiei v prizme mezhdunarodnogo prava i mirovoi politiki, Iuridicheskii Vestnik DGU 2014, No. 4, 75–77.

79 Cf. *Otto Luchterhandt* (note 9), at 152; *Marko Milanovic*, Crimea, Kosovo, Hobgoblins and Hypocrisy, available at <https://www.ejiltalk.org/crimea-kosovo-hobgoblins-and-hypocrisy/>; *Christian Marxsen,* The Crimea Crisis from an International Law, Kyiv-Mohyla Law and Politics Journal 2 (2016), 13–36, at 27; *Matteo Bacaro-Incisa* (note 9), at 131.

80 Cf. only *Tanita Pechalova*, Remedial secession as right of self-determination: The cases of Kosovo and Abkhazia, Tilburg, the Netherlands 2017; *Ieva Vezgergaitė*, Remedial Secession as an Exercise of the Right to Self-Determination of Peoples, Budapest 2011; *R. Huseynov, T. Linnus,* Remedial secession: A right to external self-determination as a remedy to serious injustices. The Politicon 2017, available at <http://thepoliticon.net/essays/428-remedial-secession-a-right-to-external-self-determination-as-a-remedy-to-serious-injustices.html>; *Simone F. van den Driest,* Remedial

A right to remedial secession could possibly be customary law if there were a clear and widespread state practice and an *opinio juris*. Whether the cases of Bangladesh and Kosovo are sufficient for such a practice seems to be worthy of discussion. If one wishes to apply this concept, then, of course the crystallizing preconditions must be in place.

> 'The first is substantive in nature and requires that the people at issue suffers from a persistent refusal of internal self-determination by the central authorities of the State. The presence of gross human rights violations are either viewed as an expression of this denial, or as an additional requirement. The second prerequisite is procedural in nature and requires that any viable peaceful options to resolve the situation internally are absent. That is to say that remedial secession operates as an ultimum remedium'.[81]

Otherwise, the principle of self-determination has to be implemented by internal, and not by external (= unilateral secession) self-determination.

If we now look at the regional and bilateral international law in force at the time of the outbreak of the Russian-Ukrainian conflict, the picture is clear: in all the agreements, Russia pledged to renounce violence and to respect the sovereignty and territorial integrity of Ukraine.[82] In the 1994 Budapest – Memorandum[83] the United States of America, the Russian Federation, and the United Kingdom of Great Britain and Northern Ireland reaffirmed their obligation to refrain from the threat or use of force against the territorial integrity or political independence of Ukraine, as well as their commitment to refrain from economic coercion designed to subordinate to their own interest the exercise by Ukraine of the rights inherent in its sovereignty (Art. 2–4). The Memorandum of the Commonwealth of Independent States[84], which concluded the Heads of the States of the successor states of the Soviet Union on 10

Secession- A Right to External Self-Determination as a Remedy to Serious Injustices? Cambridge, 2013.

81 *Simone F. van den Driest*, (note 76), at 347.

82 Earlier agreements that reach into the Soviet Union and the Commenwealth of Independent States are left out here. The entire bilateral Russian-Ukrainian international law history is told in *Oleksandr Merezhko*, Crimea's Annexation in the Light of International Law. A Critique of Russia's Legal Argumentation, Kyiv-Mohyla Law and Politics Journal 2 (2016), 36–89, at 40–48.

83 Memorandum on Security Assurances in connection with Ukraine's accession to the Treaty on the Non-Proliferation of Nuclear Weapons, adopted on 5 December 1994.

84 Memorandum Soveta glav gosudarstv Sodruzhestva Nezavisimykh Gosudarstv of 10 February 1995 'Memorandum of poderzhanii mira i stabil'nostiv v Sodruzhestve Nezavisimykh Gosudarstv' (Memorandum of the Council of the Heads of State of the Community of Independent States 'On Supporting Peace and Stability in the CIS'), available at <http://pravo.levonevsky.org/bazaby/org513/basic/text0177.htm>.

February 1995, rules that the Commonwealth states will mutually refrain from military, political, economic and other forms of pressure (Art. 1), intend to suppress in accordance with their national law the creation and operation on their territories of organizations, groups or individuals directed against independence, territorial integrity and inviolability of borders (Art. 2) and will, in accordance with national law and international norms, take measures to suppress any manifestations of seperatism, nationalism, chauvinism and fascism (Art. 7).

In the 1997 Treaty of Friendship, Cooperation, and Partnership between Ukraine and the Russian Federation[85] the two states obliged themselves in Art. 3 to build the relations with each other on the basis of the principles of mutual respect, sovereign equality, territorial integrity, inviolability of borders, peaceful settlement of disputes, non-use of force or threat of force, including economic and different ways of pressure. The 1997 Black Sea Fleet Agreement between the Ukraine and the Russian Federation and the associated troop statute provide the details of the division of the Black Sea Fleet and the conditions of stationing the Russian Black Sea Fleet with the associated military personnel in the port of Sevastopol. The last Russian-Ukrainian treaty was terminated after the complete separation of the Crimea and its incorporation into the Russian Federation.[86]

3. My assessment

3.1. Maidan Legislation under President Yanukovych and the Bans, imposed by the Administrative Court

The Maidan laws, already described above as illiberal, may have had only one purpose, to make it as difficult as possible for Ukrainian citizens (and foreign supporting activists) who protested initially and later mainly peacefully in the center of Kiev and especially on the Maidan, not only to exercise their guaranteed in Articles 34 and 39 of the Ukrainian Constitution rights to freedom of expression and assembly, but also to exercise their basic rights without permanent fear of being arrested, beaten or even tortured, or being fined with penalties, which could cause them great financial difficulties. Of course, not all demonstrators were peaceful, and right wing and

85 Federal'nyi Zakon 'O ratifikatsii Dogovora o drushbe, sotrudnichestve i partnerstve mezhdu Rossiiskoi Federatsiei i Ukrainoi (Federal Law 'On ratifying the treaty on Friendship, Cooperation and Partnership between the Russian Federation and Ukraine), No. 42-FZ, signed 2 March 1999, SZ RF1999, No. 10 , item 1159 (the text of the agreement in SZ RF 1999, No. 20, item 2413).

86 Has expired from 2 April 2014, by Federal Law No. 38-FZ, signed 2 April 2014, SZ RF 2014, No. 14, item 1530.

extremely violent people started taking on an increasingly determining role in in the further development of the protest.[87]

Art. 39 (2) ConstUA permits restrictions on the freedom of assembly in the interest of national security and public order, with the purpose of preventing violations of the public order or crimes, protecting the health of the population, or protecting the rights and freedoms of other persons. Constitutionally, it is doubtful whether restrictions on the freedom of assembly are allowed even if disturbances of public order or other administrative offenses are present. On the one hand, the legislator has only used its options here. On the other hand, such restrictions are only permissible under strict observance of the principle of proportionality, which was probably a foreign word for the Verkhovna Rada (and the President) at that time. All the new regulations are far away from the principle of proportionality, because they often do not differentiate according to the weight of the violation of the order, or whether there is an administrative offence or a crime. Generally, many regulations are comparable with the widespread erosion of the freedom of assembly in Russia by the Law of June 8, 2012.[88] The new facts of a crime 'Extremist activity', which was added to the Criminal Code, is more likely to be misused under the given circumstances, because a slight infringement of the rules can easily lead to criminal investigation.

Cumulative anti-constitutional effects arise when two ad hoc decisions of the Administrative Court come together. An all-encompassing and comprehensive prohibition of assemblies throughout Kiev's center on the one hand effects, that everyone who participates in a rally, is confronted with the prosecution for administrative or criminal offence. On the other hand, it is to be understood as an invitation to the special units of the police forces and intelligence to act with all severity against peaceful demonstrators. This is topped by the fact that free-of-charge legal aid – an important instrument to defend oneself against unlawful acts by the police and the secret service – has been suspended. As far as the Administrative Court bans aim at the leaders of the three main opposition parties, further provisions of the constitution are violated by judgments of the Administrative Court: Art. 36 granted Ukrainian citizens the right to freedom of association in political parties and public organisations, according to Art. 80 ConstUA People's Deputies of Ukraine are guaranteed parliamentary immunity and shall not be held criminally liable, detained or arrested without the consent of the Verkhovna Rada of Ukraine. Branding social organisations that

87 Cf. *Konstiantyn Fedorenko* (note 9), overall and at 14.

88 Cf. *Oesten Baller*, Artikel 31 (Versammlungsfreiheit) [Freedom of Assembly], in: Bernd Wieser (ed.), Handbuch der russischen Verfassung (Manual of the Russian Constitution), Wien 2014, Art. 31, point 2.

receive funding from abroad, as agents is a clear violation of the right of association, granted by Art. 39 ConstUA.

Cartes blanches for police and secret service to execute barely constitutional government decisions were issued generously. The possibility of arresting deputies, prosecutors, judges and constitutional judges can only be understood as muzzling any critical voices that do not join the political mainstream. Moreover, it would not occur to any (constitutional) judge to adorn a justifying decision with a dissenting vote, which does not merely repeat political decisions.

3.2. Declaration of Independence of Crimea and Decision of the Ukrainian Constitutional Court

The constitutional and international law assessment of the Declaration of Independence of Crimea, effected on 11 March 2014, notwithstanding the numerous pertinent academic evaluations, is quickly summarized. On the one hand, the Declaration of Independence of 11 March 2014 violates both the Constitution of Ukraine and the Constitution of Crimea itself. The territorial structure of Ukraine's unitarian state, including the peninsula of Crimea, follows the principle of unity and indivisibility. The, at that date, legally valid Constitution of Crimea defines Crimea itself in Art. 1 as an integral part of Ukraine. The constitutional norms in the Ukrainian Constitution and the Crimean Constitution are explicit and clear. Whether one can find any differences in international law must first be clarified. The principle of territorial integrity or political independence of the states is the central building block of the UN Charter. The prohibition of violence in Article 1 (4) of the Charter expressly refers to the inviolability of this central principle of international law. International law does not know an external realization of the principle of self-determination of peoples by unilateral secession, at least in the post-colonial period.

If, in the case of conflicts between territorial integrity and self-determination, the so-called remedial secession is attributed at least to customary law, this does not absolve of the duty to examine the prerequisite of a unilateral secession. The main precondition requires that a people suffers from persistent denial of internal self-determination by the central state.[89] In the history of the Ukrainian Crimea, the relationship between Kiev and Crimea was not always without conflict and controversy. Of course, these were always carried out without violence. At the time of the Declaration of Independence, an entire chapter in the Ukrainian Constitution was and still is dedicated to the Autonomous Republic of Crimea. A denial of an internal self-determina-

89 Cf. only *Simone F. van den Driest* (note 80), at 260.

tion and certainly not a permanent denial can hardly be substantiated. The presence of large human rights violations, whether considered as an additional or alternative condition of a remedial secession, can neither be substantiated by facts. This is why the Kosovo decision of the International Court of Justice[90] cannot be used to justify the Declaration of Independence.[91] The Declaration of Independence refers to the Kosovo decision itself.

As far as can be seen, there is no real argumentation with this clear international law legal situation in the Russian scientific discussion. The main argumentation, why the Declaration of Independence is in accordance with international law is instead based on an alleged unconstitutional coup d'état in Ukraine or future nazification of Ukraine.[92] The vast majority of the global international law community, like myself, considers the Declaration of Independence contrary to international law.

The Constitutional Court of Ukraine decided on March 20 on the Declaration of Independence.[93] In its decision, the Constitutional argued only formally by citing the provisions of the Ukrainian Constitution, which were outlined in this contribution. The first sentence of the decision emphasizes that Ukraine recognizes and enjoys the rule of law principle. Therefore, it could have discussed and assessed any aspect of international law, a transfer of the Kosovo decision of the International Court of Justice to the case of Crimea, and an application of the controversial principle of remedial secession in the judgment. This would not necessarily have led to a different outcome of the decision. The court does not say a word about it, but argues elsewhere that Crimea is not a state and the people of Crimea are not a people.

3.3. Referendum in Crimea and Decision of the Ukrainian Constitutional Court

With regard to the referendum in Crimea, two aspects have to be assessed. First, it is about the decision itself to hold a referendum, including the alternative questions

90 Cf. <http://www.icj-cij.org/files/case-related/141/141-20100722-ADV-01-00-EN.pdf>.

91 Cf. for many others *G. Matteo Vaccaro-Incisa* (note 9), at 131 f.; *Marko Milanovic*, (note 77).

92 Cf. for many others *Georgii M. Vel'iaminov*, Vossoedinenie Kryma s Rossiei: Pravovoi rakurs (Reunification of Krym and Russia: a legal point of view), Gosudarstvo i Pravo, 2014, No. 9, 12–18. *Anatoly Kapustin* weighs, at least partly, the pros and cons, but argues mainly with a focus on a coup d'etat in Kiev and the idea that Crimea historically belongs to Russia, see *Anatoly Kapustin*, Crimea's Self-Determination in the Light of Contemporary International Law, ZaöRV 75 (2015), 101–118.

93 Cf. note 36.

put to vote. Second, it is about the actual conduct and the circumstances of the referendum and the determination of the results.

The first question about the legality of the referendum can be answered quickly. The first alternative of the referendum – Do you support the reunification of the Crimea with Russia as a subject of the Russian Federation?[94] – violates both the constitutional principles of Ukraine and the Crimea, as well as the international law principle of territorial integrity.[95] As stated before, the Constitution of Ukraine emphasizes the territorial integrity of Ukraine and the Crimean Constitution defines Crimea as integral part of Ukraine. The territorial structure of Ukraine and the legal regime of the state border shall be determined exclusively by law of Ukraine (Art. 92 (13), (18) ConstUA. Although the Crimean Constitution provides for the holding of local referenda, this is limited by the precedence of the Constitution of Ukraine and the Constitution of Ukraine. Constitutional amendments that violate the principle that the territory of Ukraine is indivisible, and this is the question 1 of the referendum, are banned by constitution. Any changes of the territory of Ukraine can only be made through an all-Ukrainian referendum. The second alternative – Do you support the restoration of the Constitution of the Republic of Crimea as of 1992 and the status of Crimea as a part of Ukraine? – is considered individually as compliant with both Constitutions, because increasing the degree of autonomy as a form of internal self-determination within Ukrainian can be a topic of a consultative local referendum in Crimea. However, considering the two voting questions together as an alternative, there are doubts about the second question. The two questions are not a real alternative in the sense of yes or no. In addition, an important aspect is missing. On the one hand, asking for integration into the Russian Federation and, on the other hand, a return to the 1992 Constitution, is not a clear alternative. Correct and in accordance with international referendum standards[96] would be a yes / no to the

94 For a general assessment cf. the Opinion of the European Commission on Democracy through Law (Venice Commission), Whether the decision taken by the Supreme Council of the Autonomous Republic of Crimea in Ukraine to organise a referendum on becoming a constituent territory of the Russian Federation or restoring Crimea's 1992 Constitution is compatible with constitutional Principles, adopted by the Venice Commission at its 98th Plenary Session (Venice, 21–22 March 2014), available at <http://www.venice.coe.int/webforms/documents/default.aspx?pdffile=CDL-AD(2014)002-e>.

95 Cf. *Christian Marxsen*, Territorial Integrity in International Law – Its Concept and Implications for Crimea, ZaöRV 75 (2015), 7–26.

96 Cf. *Anne Peters*, Das Völkerrecht der Gebietsreferenden. Das Beispiel der Ukraine 1991–2014 (International law on territorial referenda 1991–2014) , Osteuropa 2014, Vol. 5/6, 101–133; European Commission on Democracy through Law (Venice Commission), Code of Good Practice om Referendums, for Democratic Elections, adopted by the Council for Democratic Elections at its

integration into the Russian Federation or a second question about the maintenance of the current legal situation.

The conduct and the circumstances of the referendum show many violations of international standards. First, it is the presence of Russian military forces in Crimea described above and considered illegal, and their behavior on the day of the referendum.[97] In addition, the multiple shortening of the period up to the referendum has tended to make it difficult or even impossible to publicly discuss the voting questions, and to include into the necessary political discourse all ethnic groups, especially the Crimean Tartars. The official result of the referendum is not presented here, as it is now proven that there was a case of electoral fraud. This is also the result of a statement by a member of the Russian Human Rights Council under the President of the Russian Federation.[98] According to his statement, the overwhelming majority of residents of Sevastopol voted in a referendum for joining Russia (turnout 50–80 %), in Crimea, according to different data for joining Russia, 50–60 % of voters voted yes at a total turnout of 30–50 %.

On March 14, the Ukrainian Constitutional Court ruled to recognize as non-conforming with the Constitution the resolution of the Verkhovna Rada of the Autonomous Republic of Crimea No. 1702–6 / 14 'On holding of the all-Crimean referendum' dated March 6, 2014. In his decision, the Constitutional Court referred to the known norms s of the Ukrainian Constitution. In a short paragraph, the court, referring to UN Charter, also states that the decision is unlawful also under international law.[99]

3.4. *Defining the Status of the Crisis in Eastern Ukraine*

The decision of the Ukrainian President *Petr Poroshenko* to lead the military fight against the separatist rebels in the Donbass as an Anti-Terrorist Operation (ATO)

19th meeting (Venice, 16 December 2006) and the Venice Commission at its 70th plenary session (Venice, 16–17 March 2007), available at <http://www.venice.coe.int/webforms/documents/default.aspx?pdffile=cdl-ad(2007)008-e>.

97 See before all Office of the United Nations, High Commissioner for Human Rights, Report on the human rights situation in Ukraine, 15 April 2014, point 82 ff.

98 Sovet pri Prezidente Rossiiskoi Federatsii po raszvitiiu grazdanskogo obshchestva i pravam cheloveka (Council under the President of the Russian Federation on civil society development and human rights), the statement is available at <http://president-sovet.ru/members/blogs/bobrov_e_a/problemy-zhiteley-kryma-/>. Cf. also *Otto Luchterhandt* (note 9), at 158 f.

99 Cf. note 35; an English translation is available at <http://mfa.gov.ua/en/news-feeds/foreign-offices-news/19573-rishennya-konstituci>.

must be seen as a political pretext. From this point of view, the decision reminds of the two Chechen wars, which were conducted by Russia under this label. Thus, all fighters on the part of the Donetsk People's Republic DNR[100] and the Luhansk People's Republic LNR[101] can be described as terrorists and all hostilities as terrorist activities. Additionally, the legal terms in the law 'On combatting Terrorism' actually refer to smaller groups and not to larger groups with a partly state and military structure. This hasty classification also obscures the view that many severe human rights violations and war crimes are committed not only by the fighters of the DNR / LNR, but also by the Ukrainian army and in particular by the volunteer battalions, fighting for the central government.[102] The Azov and Aidar Battalions are at the 'forefront' and, not least, the voluntary battalions of the Right Sector. Even though these associations have increasingly been formally classified in the security structure of Ukraine, they cannot be overlooked as belonging to the extremely right-wing spectrum, and their symbols clearly refer to the army of Nazi Germany.[103]

The bloody conflict in the Donbass is, to some extent, reminiscent of a civil war, partly because of Russia's military involvement in an international armed conflict. As fighting goes on and leaves many dead and wounded, it is not a frozen, but a live conflict, which is often labelled as a hybrid war.[104] According to the Ukrainian Constitution (Art. 83 and 85) and the Law 'On the legal regime of martial law', the legally clear solution would have been the proclamation of martial law. In particular, the legal definition of martial law, which implies danger to state independence and territorial integrity, fits very well with the conflict situation in Donbass. And, last but not least, under the regime of martial law, the Ukrainian constitution allows to restrict fundamental

100 In Russian: Donetskaia narodnaia respublika.

101 In Russian: Luganskaia narodnaia respublika.

102 See note 43, and Amnesty International Briefing, Ukraine: Abuses and war crimes by the Aidar Volunteer Battalion in the north Luhansk region, dated 8 September 2014, available at <https://www.amnesty.org/download/Documents/8000/eur500402014en.pdf>.

103 Cf. <https://www.globalsecurity.org/military/world/ukraine/volunteers.htm>.

104 *Hans-Georg Erhardt* speaks of an unconventional and hybrid war, Unkonventioneller und hybrider Krieg in der Ukraine: zum Formenwandel des Krieges als Herausforderung für Politik und Wissenschaft (Unconventional and hybrid warin Ukraine: The metamorphosis of war as a challenge to politics and science), Zeitschrift für Außen- und Sicherheitspolitik, published 21. April 2016, S. 1–16; cf. *Wolfgang Hingst*, Brandstiftung in Europa!! Der 'Bruderkrieg' in der Ukraine. Essays und Notizen April 2014 bis Februar 2015. Mit einen kurzen historischen Abriss, 2015 (Arson in Europe!! The 'war of brothers' in Ukraine. Essays and notes from April 2014 until February 2015, with a short historical overview, 2015); *Reinhard Lauterbach*, Bürgerkrieg in der Ukraine. Geschichte, Hintergründe, Beteiligte (Civil war in Ukraine. History, backgound, participants), 2nd ed. 2014.

rights in individual cases (Article 64 (2) ConstUA). This, too, would be constitutional progress and would at least remedy some factual fundamental rights violations.

3.5. Decision of the Ukrainian Constitutional Court and Draft Constitutional Amendments on Decentralisation

In the process of implementing the provisions of the Minks-2 agreement and thus contributing to the pacification of the Donbass conflict, the Verkhovna Rada drafted a bill to change the Ukrainian Constitution, with a view to decentralize state power. The draft law proposes amendments to Articles 85, 92, 106, 118, 119, 121, 132, 133, 140, 141, 142, 143, 144, 150, the title of Section IX, and Section XV 'Transitional Provisions' of the Constitution of Ukraine. In a statutory constitutional proceeding, the Ukrainian Constitutional Court ruled on 30 July 2015[105] that the draft law complied with the Constitution, in particular with the provisions of Art. 157 and 158 of the ConstUA. In examining this crucial question, the Court contented itself with just a short paragraph:

> 'The Constitutional Court of Ukraine proceeds from the fact that at the time of giving them this opinion in Ukraine or in its individual regions, no military or state of emergency has been imposed on the procedure established by the Constitution of Ukraine. The Constitutional Court of Ukraine, taking into account its Conclusion of June 16, 2015 No. 1-v / 2015 and the position of the President of Ukraine, states that the decision to introduce a regime of martial law or a state of emergency in Ukraine or in its separate areas according to the procedure established by the Constitution of Ukraine is not adopted. In view of the above, the Constitutional Court of Ukraine considers that the Draft Law meets the requirements of part two of Article 157 of the Constitution of Ukraine.'

A legal examination of the exciting question, what consequences the bloody conflict in Donbass could have on the procedure, did not take place. Quite formally and without any visible constitutional awareness of the problem, the majority of the court found

105 Vysnovok Konstytutsiynogo sudu Ukrainy u spravi za zvernniam Verkhovnoi Rady Ukrainy pro nadanniia vysnovky schodo detsentralizatsii vladi vymogam statei 157 i 158 Konstitutsii Ukrainy (Ruling of the Constitutional Court of Ukraine in the case on the appeal of the Verkhovna Rada of Ukraine on the conclusion on compliance with the draft law on amendments to the Constitution of Ukraine regarding the decentralization of power to the requirements of Articles 157 and 158 of the Constitution of Ukraine), 30 July 2015 № 2-c/2015, sprava № 1–18/2015. available at <https://zakon.rada.gov.ua/laws/main?find=2&dat=20150730&user=a&text=&textl=1&bool=and&org=79&typ=0&datl=0&yer=2015&mon=07&day=30&numl=2&num=&minjustl=2&minjust=>.

that at the time of the application neither martial law had been imposed nor an exception had been decided, as provided for by the constitution (Article 106 (1) (20) or (21) ConstUA) process. In my opinion, there is much to suggest that the formally correct imposition of martial law equates to a de facto war. The purpose of the provision of Art. 157 ConstUA is that the sovereign cannot participate to the required extent in the democratic constitutional decision-making process. It makes no difference whether martial law is imposed or whether war is being waged under the guise of an anti-terrorist operation in important parts of Ukraine. The dissenting votes of two judges *M. I. Mel'nik* and, above all, *S. V. Shevchuk* clearly criticize the purely formal view of the Court. The latter clearly argues against a formal view that contradicts the idea and spirit of the constitution.[106] In summary, it can be seen that the Constitutional Court obviously had no deep awareness of solving constitutional problems, and the Ukrainian President has initiated no further attempt, probably for reasons of maintaining his power, to make a significant contribution to the pacification of the country.

III. The Russian Federation

1. The Course of Events

The events directly and exclusively attributable to Russia, and therefore legally assessed under this heading, are:

- Military intervention in Crimea and partly in Donbass, and temporary occupation of Crimea and the military support in carrying out the referendum in the Crimea
- Recognition of Crimea as an independent state, conclusion of an international agreement with Crimea and the city of Sevastopol and legal accession of Crimea and the city of Sevastopol, and corresponding constitutional amendments.

106 In a personal conversation in September 2018 with the judge of the Constitutional Court *Viktor Gordorovenko,* who himself was not involved in the decision, it became clear that in a difficult political situation the court had to take a more than a difficult decision.

2. Legal Requirements

The framework for legal assessment is a combination of Russian (constitutional) law and international law.[107] The Russian Constitution, which entered into force on 25 December 1993[108], places a high value on the validity of international law and is therefore considered friendly with international law.[109] For some provisions of the Russian Constitution that are relevant to this essay, the Russian Law contains implementing statutes, some of which are provided as simple federal laws, some as federal constitutional laws. These statutes are included in the context of the presentation of the provisions of the constitution.

The Russian Constitution (hereinafter: ConstRF) addresses international law in several places. According to Art. 15 (4) ConstRF the universally accepted principles and norms of international law and the international treaties of the Russian Federation are part of its legal system. According to the wording of the provision, an international treaty has precedence over the legislation. The basic and human rights are in accordance with Art. 17 (1) ConstRF recognized and guaranteed in accordance with universally accepted principles and norms of international law, and in accordance with the Constitution. The interpretation of these constitutional norms is not easy for two reasons. First, the Russian Constitution does not use the usual international law triad, such as international treaties, customary law, and general legal principles.[110] On the other hand, the actually clear legal precedence of international law in the Russian Constitution is relativized in part in Russian constitutional law commentaries, arguing that the federal constitutional laws very relevant in the context of this essay are supposed to over international treaties.[111] This would build up a new hierarchy: Constitution (supreme legal force, Art. 15 (1) ConstRF), federal constitutional legislation, international treaties and international law principles norms and treaties,

107 For international Law please cf. part II.2.5., too.

108 Konstitutsiia Rossiiskoi Federatsii with subsequent amendments, signed12 December 1993, Rossiiskaia gazeta 25. December (hereinafter ConstRF).

109 Cf. *Angelika Nußberger and Yury Safoklov*, Art. 15 (Vorrang der Verfassung, Kundmachungspflicht, Völkerrecht (Precedence of law, obligation to announce, international law)), in: Handbuch der russischen Verfassung (note 88), point 20.

110 Op. cit., point 22.

111 Cf. *V.F. Andrianov*, in: L.V. Lazarev (ed.), Kommentarii k Konstitutsii Rossiiskoi Federacii, Moscow 2010 (Commentary on the Constitution of the Russian Federation), at 103; *B.S. Ebzeev*, in: V.D. Zor'kin (ed.), Kommentarii k Konstitutsii Rossiiskoi Federacii (Commentaryon the Constitution of the Russian Federation), Moscow 2013, at 163.

simple federal legislation. This legal view blurs the original intention of the Russian Constitution and is hardly compatible with the clear wording of the constitution.

With regard to international treaties, Art. 86 lit. b) ConstRF authorizes the President to negotiate international treaties and to sign them. Details of the conclusion and ratification of international treaties of the Russian Federation are contained in the Law 'On International Treaties of the Russian Federation'.[112] The preamble to this law is undoubtedly a call for peaceful coexistence of peoples.

> 'International treaties form the legal basis of interstate relations, promote the maintenance of universal peace and security, the development of international cooperation in accordance with the purposes and principles of the Charter of the United Nations. International treaties play an important role in protecting human rights and freedoms, in ensuring the legitimate interests of states.'

Article 5 of the law repeats the constitutional provisions on the precedence of international treaties. Articles 14 to 16 govern the ratification of international treaties by a single federal law. A constitutional court review of an international treaty that has not yet entered into force provides for Art. 125 (2) lit. d) ConstRF. Eligible to apply are, among others, the President or the Houses of Parliament. The wording that it is about the verification of the constitutionality of the international treaty, points toward an interpretation in the sense of 'Who has doubts, can make an application'. The precise design of entitlement in the Law 'On the Constitutional Court'[113] confirms this view, although the law provides admissibility regulations in two places. Both Art. 36 and Art. 89 No. 1 ConstCourtAct consider any possible doubt as to the constitutionality of the treaty. The intention of an application to court should not be to seek positive confirmation of the own view, but to confirm the compliance of the treaty with the Constitution.[114]

Since Russia is at least formally a federation, the constitution contains a chapter on the federal structure of the country. Art. 65 (1) ConstRF lists all subjects of the federation. If a new territory is incorporated as a subject into the Russian Federation,

112 Federal'nyi Zakon 'O mezhdunarodnych dogovorakh Rossiiskoi Federatsii' (Federal law 'On International Treaties of the Russian Federation') with subsequent amendments, No. 101-FZ, signed 15 July 1995, SZ RF 1995, No. 29 , item 2757.

113 Federal'yi Konstitutsinonnyi Zakon 'O konstitutsionnom sude Rossiiskoi Federatsii' with subsequent amendments (Federal constitutional law 'On the constitutional court of the Russian Federation), No. 1 FKZ, signed 21 July 1994, SZ RF 1994, No13, item1447 (hereinafter Law of the Constitutional Court of the Russian Federation = ConCourtAct).

114 Cf. similarly *Elena Luk'ianova*, O prave nalevo (The rule of law inside out), 24 March 2015, available at <https://echo.msk.ru/blog/novaya_gazeta/1517374-echo/>.

then the prerequisites of both constitutional amendment and incorporation of a new subject of the federation must be fulfilled. Art. 65 (2) ConstRF states that the conditions for the incorporation of a new subject must be regulated by a federal constitutional law. This law is the Federal Constitutional Law 'On the Procedure for the Incorporation into the Russian Federation and the Formation of a new subject of the Russian Federation'.[115] Art. 4 IncorporationAct reads like an outline of the Russian-Ukrainian conflict:

> '1. As a new entity in the Russian Federation may accede a foreign state or a part of it. 2. The incorporation of a foreign state or its part into the Russian Federation as a new subject is carried out by mutual agreement of the Russian Federation and this foreign state in accordance with an international (interstate) treaty on the accession of the foreign state or a part of it (hereinafter referred to as the international agreement) to the Russian Federation as a new entity concluded by the Russian Federation with this foreign state.'

If Crimea – *de facto* – is an independent state, then the regulation works. If Crimea – *de jure* – is a part of Ukraine, then an international treaty with Ukraine has to be concluded. Art. 9 IncorporationAct regulates two options: the ratification of an international treaty on the accession of a new subject to the Russian Federation is carried out by a simple law according to Art. 105–107 ConstRF; the factual incorporation of a new subject is effected by a federal constitutional law according to Art. 108 ConstRF. The latter article, however, only opens up a further reference, because federal constitutional laws are adopted on issues, covered by the Constitution of the Russian Federation. This is ruled by a quorum: A federal constitutional law is adopted if it is approved by a majority of at least three quarters of the total votes of members of the Federation Council and at least two-thirds of the of the total number of deputies of the State Duma. The reference leads to Art. 137 (1) ConstRF: According to this regulation, amendments to Article 65 of the Constitution of the Russian Federation are effected on the basis of a federal constitutional law on the accession to the Russian Federation of a new subject of the Russian Federation.

In summary, there is a system of rules with pitfalls and a different ratification procedure for international treaties and accession laws on new subjects of the Federation.

115 Federal'yi Konstitutsinonnyi Zakon 'O poriadke priniatiia v Rossiiskuiu Federatsiiu i obrazovaniia v ee sostave novogo sub'ekta Rossiiskoi Federatsii' (Federal constitutional law on the constitution: On the Procedure for the Adoption to the Russian Federation and the Formation of a new subject of the Russian Federation) with subsequent amendments, No. 6 FKZ, signed 17 December 2001, SZ RF 2001, No. 52, item 4916 (hereinafter IncorporationAct).

3. My Assessment

3.1. Military Intervention in Crimea and partly in Donbass, and Temporary Occupation of Crimea and the Military Support in Carrying out the Referendum in Crimea

The Russian military intervention in Crimea and in parts of eastern Ukraine, as well as the military occupation of Crimea during a large number of reported events, significantly violate the Constitution of the Russian Federation, international law and international treaties concluded by Russia. The international treaties referred to in Art. 15 (4) ConstRF are as plain as they can be. In addition, the Principle of the Prohibition of the Use of Force in Art. 2 (4) UN Charter obliges the Russian Federation to refrain from any acts of violence against other states, violating their territorial integrity and independence. This principle is violated in the event of any use of armed force by one state against another state, irrespective of the scope and aims of the use of force.[116] Comprehensive intervention bans and prohibitions of violence can be found in all bilateral treaties between Russia and Ukraine, as well as in the multilateral treaties in which both countries are involved: the 1994 Budapest – Memorandum, the Memorandum of the Commonwealth of Independent States, and the 1997 Treaty of Friendship, Cooperation, and Partnership between Ukraine and the Russian Federation. Russia has violated all these treaties through its military intervention and occupation.[117]

Russia and President *Putin* have put forward three political, but not legal justifications for breaking the principle of the prohibition on violence:

- Protection of nationals abroad and of the Russian-speaking population in Crimea and Donbass;
- Enforcement of self-determination, and
- Intervention upon invitation

President *Putin* used the argument to protect Russian citizens, Russian nationals and Russian-speaking people abroad, before all in Crimea and Donbas twice: first in his letter on the use of the Russian Armed Forces in Ukraine, referring to the pending

116 Cf. *Erika Leonaitė and Dainius Žalimas,* The Annexation of Crimea and Attempts to Justify it in the Context of International Law, Lithuanian Annual Strategic Review 2015–2016, Vol. 14, 11–63, at 14.

117 For a good description of the actions taken by Russia, see op. cit., at 15 ff.; for the treaties, see above, part II.2.5.

situation of the current political crisis in that country, to the Federation Council.[118] He argued as follows:

> 'In connection with the extraordinary situation in Ukraine, the threat to the lives of citizens of the Russian Federation, our compatriots, the personnel of the military contingent of the Armed Forces of the Russian Federation deployed in the territory of Ukraine (Autonomous Republic of Crimea) in accordance with an international treaty, and pursuant to Article 102–1(d) of the Constitution of the Russian Federation, I hereby submit to the Federation Council of the Federal Assembly of the Russian Federation a letter on the use of the Armed Forces of the Russian Federation in the territory of Ukraine pending normalisation of the public and political situation in that country'.

He repeated this argumentation in his so-called Kremlin Crimean speech[119] to the deputies of the Russian Parliament, the representatives of the Republic of Crimea and of Sevastopol, including Russian citizens and citizens of Crimea and Sevastopol. Under international law, the rescue of nationals who are in danger on the territory of another state can under specific circumstances partly be regarded as legitimate self-defence under Article 51 UN Charter or, alternatively, as an customary exemption from the prohibition of the use of force in Art. 2(4) UN Charter.[120] Such exemption can be justified, on the one hand, by occurrence of an armed attack against the Russian territory or, on the other hand, by clear evidence that Russian military personnel or Russian citizens in Crimea would be exposed to significant dangers to life and limb, as well as by danger to other fundamental rights, or in the event that Ukraine is unwilling to protect these rights.[121] Neither *Putin* nor the Russian Federation have presented believable proofs for this.

An official letter, dated 18 March 2014, from the Permanent Representative of the Russian Federation to the United Nations addressed to the Secretary-General, dated 19 March 2014, included the second argumentation – to enforce self-determination in another state or in a part of a foreign state.[122] *Putin* stated: 'First, we had to help cre-

118 Dated 1 March 2014; cf. <http://tass.com/russia/721586>.

119 Obrashchenie Prezidenta Rossiiskoi Federatsii (Speech of the president of the Russian Federation), dated 18 March 2014, available at <http://kremlin.ru/events/president/news/20603>.

120 Cf. *Christian Marxsen*, The Crimea Crisis from an International Law Perspective, Kyiv-Mohyla Law and Politics Journal 2 (2016), 13–36, at 17 f.

121 Cf. *Daniel Wisehart*, The Crisis in Ukraine and the Prohibition of the Use of Force: A Legal Basis for Russia's Intervention? Published on March 4, 2014, available at <https://www.ejiltalk.org/the-crisis-in-ukraine-and-the-prohibition-of-the-use-of-force-a-legal-basis-for-russias-intervention/>.

122 Cf. <https://undocs.org/pdf?symbol=en/A/68/803>.

ate conditions so that the residents of Crimea for the first time in history were able to peacefully express their free will regarding their own future.'[123] This is a nice argument, but could not justify a military intervention.[124]

The last argument – Intervention upon Invitation – is deeply discussed in international law, based on global experience, above all, from post-Soviet time.[125] Many questions are still under discussion, but the main opinion is that the highest available governmental authority is required for the invitation in order to identify attempts of abuse and to avoid a split of the authorities in a country. The most relevant precondition is that the invitation for intervention must be attributable to a/the state.[126] Two events must be taken into consideration. First, in a speech of *Mr. Churkin*, Permanent Representative of the Russian Federation to the United Nation, held on 1 March, 2014, he mentioned, 'that *Mr. Aksyenov*, Prime Minister of Crimea, went to the President of Russia with a request to restore peace in Crimea. That appeal was agreed with *Mr. Yanukovych*, whose removal from office, we believe, was illegal.'[127] The second event is an annex to a letter dated 3 March 2014 from the Permanent Representative of the Russian Federation to the United Nations addressed to the Secretary-General, with a statement of the (former) President of Ukraine:

> 'As the legally elected President of Ukraine, I hereby make the following statement. The events on the Maidan and the illegal seizure of power in Kyiv have brought Ukraine to the brink of civil war. Chaos and anarchy reign in the country, and people's lives, safety and human rights are under threat, particularly in the southeast and in Crimea. With the influence of Western countries, open acts of terror and violence are being perpetrated and people are being persecuted on political and linguistic grounds.' signed *V. F. Yanukovych.*[128]

Both events cannot be interpreted as an official invitation to intervention. The Prime Minister of Crimea is not the highest official of a state, because the Autonomous Re-

123 At 5.

124 *Christian Marxsen*, (note 120), at 20.

125 Cf. *Georg Nolte*, Intervention by Invitation, from: Oxford Public International Law, Oxford University Press, 2015, available at <http://opil.ouplaw.com/view/10.1093/law:epil/9780199231690/law-9780199231690-e1702?prd=EPIL>.

126 *Christian Marxsen*, op. cit., at 21; *Georg Nolte*, op. cit., point 12 and 23.

127 Cf. United Nations, Security Council, 7421th meeting, 1 March 2014, S/PV. 7124, at. 5, available at <https://www.securitycouncilreport.org/atf/cf/%7B65BFCF9B-6D27-4E9C-8CD3-CF6E4FF96FF9%7D/s_pv_7124.pdf>.

128 Cf. United Nations, Security Council, S/2014/146, dated 3 March 2014, available at <http://dag.un.org/bitstream/handle/11176/32341/S_2014_146-EN.pdf?sequence=3&isAllowed=y>.

public of Crimea is de jure still an integrated part of Ukraine, and a letter of the former President *Yanukovych* is no more attributable to the State of Ukraine. The question, whether the decision of 22 February 2014 of the Verkhovna Rada of Ukraine, that President *Yanukovych* had withdrawn from office fully complies with the Ukrainian Constitution, is here irrelevant, because virtually *Mr. Yanukovych* flew from his office and saw himself more belonging to Russia then to Ukraine, as we can see from the letter, presented by the representative from the Russian Federation and not from Ukraine.[129]

To conclude with, an exemption from the principle of Prohibition of the Use of Force for the Russian military intervention, the occupation of Crimea and all the related activities does not exist.

3.2. Recognition of Crimea as an Independent State, Conclusion of an International Agreement with Crimea and the City of Sevastopol, Legal Incorporation of Crimea and the City of Sevastopol, and Corresponding Constitutional Aamendments

All of these decisions are interlinked and can be assessed, along with an analysis of the decision of the Russian Constitutional Court of March 21, 2014 on the incorporation agreement between Russia and the Republic of Crimea,[130] because their examination must, by law, be included in that decision. As a guide to this analysis, the critical essay by *Elena Luk'ianova*[131] is ideally suited, because she formally deconstructs the decision of the Constitutional Court with eight arguments. The central arguments, which take into account all of the topics above, are processed here:

129 See also *Daniel Wisehart*, op. cit., at 4; *Christian Marxsen*, (note 120), at 33 f.

130 Postanovlenie Konstitutsionnogo Suda Rossiiskoi Federatsii 'Po delu o proverke konstitutsionnosti ne vstupivshego v silu mezhdunarodnogo dogovora mezhdu Rossiiskoi Federatsiei i Respublikoi Krym o priniatii v Rossiiskuiu Federatsiiu Respubliki Krym i obrazovanii v sostave Rosiiskoi Federatsii novykh sub'ektov' (Ruling of the Constitutional Court of RF on the case of the verification of the constitutionality of an international agreement that has not entered into force between the Russian Federation and the Republic of Crimea on the admission to the Russian Federation of the Republic of Crimea and the formation of new subjects within the Russian Federation), No. 6-P, 19 March 2014, available at <http://doc.ksrf.ru/decision/KSRFDecision155662.pdf>.

131 See note 114.

- 'The Constitutional Court failed to comply with the mandatory review procedure;
- The Constitutional Court itself refrained from assessing the content of the regulations of the Treaty referring to the compliance with the constitutional framework of Russia;
- The Court did not proof the compliance of the Treaty with Art. 15 (2) and (4) ConstRF;
- The Court excluded from the verification of the Treaty the analysis of the documents which such a treaty must refer to;
- The Constitutional Court has withdrawn from evaluating the Treaty with regard to the procedure of its signing
- The Court excluded from the subject of the verification of the Treaty the complience with the Law 'On the Procedure for the Incorporation into the Russian Federation and the Formation in a new subbject of the Russian Federation'
- The Constitutional Court ruled against its own legal opinion.'

With the exception of the last point, all these shortcomings relate to the extent of the constitutional judicial review. Although the court itself states in its decision that, according to Art. 90 in conjunction with Art. 86 ConstCourtAct, the examination of international treaties that have not yet come into force must include a comprehensive review of the formal and material content of the treaty as well as of its compliance with the constitutional framework, such comprehensive review on the merits is missing in the decision. The constitutional framework conditions are primarily the international law references of the constitution and the related laws. Be that as it may, from Article 15 (4) ConstRF follows that the *jus cogens* of international law, above all the principles of the UN Charter, but also the treaties concluded by Russia with Ukraine are relevant. In the preamble of the Law 'On International Treaties of the Russian Federation' the relevance of the principles of international law and the UN Charta are also highlighted and therefore form the legal basis of international treaties of the Russian Federation. New international treaties may not contradict existing international treaties of the Russian Federation. The principle of Prohibition of the Use of Force, the respect for territorial integrity and independence, as well as the aforementioned international treaties of Russia have been violated by the Russian military intervention in Crimea, the Declaration of Independence and the referendum of Crimea made possible by it, so that these are unlawful. From this also follows that Crimea is not a subject of international law that can conclude an international treaty, and not at all the mayor of Sevastopol, who also signed the contract. Thus, the incorporation agreement, which expressly refers to the declaration and the referendum, becomes illegal.

It is a good tradition in constitutional courts, that they have a permanent memory of the jurisdiction of the own court in the past. Otherwise, the court rules against its own decisions. Art. 6 ConstCourtAct states, that all decisions of the Constitutional Court of the Russian Federation are binding also the judicial bodies of state power, i. e. the Constitutional Court itself. Of course, a court can dissent to a former jurisdiction, above all, when the legal framework has changed. However, this should be made clear in the amended decision. In the past there are two main decisions of the Russian Constitutional Court on territorial integrity and self-determination. The first is the so-called Tatarstan decision of 13 March 1993, which was made still under the old constitution of the Russian Soviet Federal Socialist Republic (RSFSR).[132] The second decision is the Cechnia-Decision of 31 July 1995.[133] Interesting for the court's mem-

132 Postanovlenie Konstitutsionnogo Suda Rossiiskoi Federatsii po delu o proverke konstitutsionnosti Deklaratsii o gosudarstvennom suverenitete Respubliki Tatarstan ot 30 avgusta 1990 goda, Zakona Respubliki Tatarstan ot 18 aprelia 1991 goda 'Ob iszmeneniiakh i dopolneniiakh Konstitutsii (Osnovnogo Zakona) Respubliki Tatarstan', Zakona Respubliki Tatarstan ot 29 noiabria 1991 goda 'O referendume Respubliki Tartastan', Postanovleniia Verkhovnogo Soveta Respubliki Tatarstan ot 21 fevralia 1992 goda 'O provedeniia referenduma Respubliki Tatarstan po voprosu o gasudarstvennom statuse Respubliki Tatarstan (Ruling of the Constitutional Court of the RSFSR on the case of checking the constitutionality of the Declaration on State Sovereignty of the Republic of Tatarstan of August 30, 1990, Law of the Republic of Tatarstan of April 18, 1991 'On Amendments and Additions of the Constitution (Basic Law) of the Republic of Tatarstan' , Law of the Republic of Tatarstan of November 29, 1991 'On the referendum of the Republic of Tatarstan', Resolution of the Supreme Soviet of the Republic of Tatarstan of February 21, 1992 'On holding a referendum in the Republic of Tatarstan on the issue of the state status of the Republic of Tatarstan'),13 March 1992, available at <http://doc.ksrf.ru/decision/KSRFDecision40636.pdf>.

133 Postanovlenie Konstitutsionnogo Suda Rossiiskoi Federatsii po dely o proverke konstitutsionnosti Ukaza Prezidenta Rossiiskoi Federatsii ot 30 noiabria 1994 goda No. 2137 'O meropriiatiiakh po vosstavleniu konstitutsionnoi zakonnosti i pravoporiadka na territorii Chechenskoi Respubliki', Ukaza Prezidenta Rossiiskoi Federatsii ot 9 dekabria 1994 goda No. 2166 'O merakh po presecheniiu deiatel'nosti nezakonnykh vooruzhennykh formirovannii na territorii Chechenskoi Respubliki i v zone ositiiu – ingushkogo konflikta', postanovleniia Praitel'stva Rossiiskoi Federatsii ot 9 dekabria 1994 goda No. 1360 'O obespechenii gosudarstvennoi bezopastnosti i territorial'noi tselostnosti Rossiiskoi Federatsii, zakonnosti, prav i svobod grazhdan, razoruzhenniia nezakonnykh vooruzhennykh formirovanii na territorii Chechenskoi Respubliki i prilegaiushchikh k nei regionov Severnogo Kavkaza', Ukaza Prezidenta Rossiiskoi Federatsii ot 2 noiabria 1993 goda No.1833 'Ob Osnovnykh polozheniiakh voennoi doktriny Rossiiskoi Federatsii' (Ruling of the Constitutional Court of the Russian Federation in the case of verifying the constitutionality of

ory is that three judges were involved in all decisions including the Crimea case. This includes the former and again current President of the Russian Constitutional Court, *Valery Zor'kin*. Another judge was involved in the decisions on Crimea and Chechnya.

Let me cite some main findings of both decisions. The Tatarstan-Decision ruled on the Declaration of Independence of the Republic of Tatarstan, at that time a subject of the RSFSR und today a subject of the Russian Federation. With many references to international law and the UN-Charta, the Constitutional Court argued: 'self-determination is one of the basic principles of international law … Thus, while not denying the right of the people to self-determination through legitimate will, one must proceed from the premise that international law restricts it to compliance with the requirements of the principle of territorial integrity and the principle of respect for human rights.' In the Chechnia-Decision the Constitutional Court ruled on an Ukaz of the President of the Russian Federation 'On measures to restore constitutional legality and law and order in the territory of the Chechen Republic', again with many references to international law.

> 'The Constitution of the Russian Federation …does not provide for the possibility of unilateral decision on the issue of changing the status of the subject of the Russian Federation and its withdrawal from the Russian Federation. According to Article 66 (part 5) of the Constitution of the Russian Federation, the status of a subject of the Russian Federation can be changed by mutual agreement of the Russian Federation and the subject of the Russian Federation in accordance with the federal constitutional law… State integrity is one of the foundations of the constitutional system of the Russian Federation. … The constitutional goal of preserving the integrity of the Russian state is consistent with universally recognized international norms on the right of the people to self-determination. From the Declaration of Principles of International Law adopted on 24 October 1970 concerning friendly relations and cooperation among States in accordance with the Charter of the United Nations, it follows that the exercise of the right to self-determination 'should not be interpreted as authorizing or en-

the Decree of the President of the Russian Federation of November 30, 1994 No. 2137 'On measures to restore constitutional legality and law and order in the territory of the Chechen Republic', Decree of the President of the Russian Federation of December 9, 1994 No. 2166 'On measures to suppress activities of illegal armed groups on the territory of the Chechen Republic and in the zone of the Ossetian-Ingush conflict', regulation of the Government of the Russian Federation of 9 December 1994 No. 1360 'On ensuring state security and territorial integrity of the Russian Federation, the rule of law, the rights and freedoms of citizens, disarmament of illegal armed groups in the Chechen Republic and adjacent regions of the North Caucasus', Decree of the President of the Russian Federation dated November 2, 1993 No. 1833 'On Basic Provisions of the military doctrine of the Russian Federation'), No. 10-P, 31 July 1995, available at <http://doc.ksrf.ru/decision/KSRFDecision30248.pdf>.

> couraging any action that would lead to the dismemberment or complete violation of the territorial integrity or political unity of sovereign and independent states acting in accordance with the principle of equality and self-determination of the peoples'.

What a bang it would have been, had the Russian Constitutional Court rummaged in their own decisions, and had simply transferred the principles and arguments found there – and then logically had ruled, that the 'Contract between the Russian Federation and the Republic of Crimea on the incorporation into the Russian Federation of the Republic of Crimea and the formation of new subjects of the Russian Federation' and all related events and decisions were unconstitutional and contradictory to international law? Probably this would be possible only in another, and then democratic and law-based Russia. The reality is different. In a hasty procedure, in less than 5 days, from March 16 to 21, *Putin* recognized the Declaration of Independence of Crimea, signed the contract on the incorporation of Crimea into the Russian Federation, the Constitutional Court ruled on the legality of the contract, and both chambers of the Russian Parliament voted nearly unanimously to ratify the contract.[134] There was no time for reflection, discussion, or legal scrutiny worthy of the name. In compliant obedience, Parliament and Constitutional Court followed the will of the Russian President.

Conclusion

The assessment of the Russian-Ukrainian conflict has shown that all the decisions of Crimea to secede from Ukraine and all the decisions of Russia to incorporate Crimea into the Russian Federation are incompatible with both their own law and international law. Now five years have passed since these decisions, and the de jure status and the de facto status of Crimea are vague, even if Russia's legal assessment of it remains unchanged, because so far the international community has shown no tendency to recognize the factual status. When considering the respective decisions and constitutional jurisdiction in Russia and Ukraine, there is a lack of rule of law, which is still common to both countries. The courts do not judge according to law and constitution, but only in a formal way and only in accordance with the respective political mainstream.

134 Cf. <https://apostrophe.ua/article/society/2018-06-07/putin-snova-ugrojaet-ukraine-est-region-opasnee-donbassa/18778>.

The two countries face each other irreconcilably, not only with regard to the assessment of the events, but also with regard to the solution of the ongoing bloody conflict in Eastern Ukraine. A will to compromise for peace cannot be seen. There is no need to quarrel over who is responsible for breaking up this conflict, as Russian President *Putin's* recent statement shows, which threatens consequences for Ukraine's statehood, if the Ukrainian army attacks the separatist territories in Donbass during the World Cup. The hope is on the side of the Ukrainian civil society, which is increasingly pressing for a solution to the conflict in the Donbass, and perhaps in the future forces its own government to compromise.

Les Limites Directes aux Révisions Constitutionnelles en Période de Crise: Modélisation au Sein de l'Union Européenne*

Sacha Sydoryk

Abstract

The idea of constitutional amendments is for a specific legal order to provide for the modification of its own highest positive norm. Among the member States of the European Union, constitutional provisions show that it is possible to distinguish between limits to constitutional amendments in time of institutional crisis, or in time of security crisis. Those limits are either general one, forbidding from amending the whole constitution, or specific one, forbidding the amendment of only some constitutional provisions. The question of the control of these limits to constitutional amendments is altogether an entirely other one, since the existence of substantial limits does not imply the control of the respect of the limits. With the data provided by the constitutions, it is possible to create a schematic representation of the limits to constitutional amendments during crisis. Such a representation is not some ideal to fulfil, but rather an image of what is found in the various positive constitutions of members of the European Union. It follows, then, that such a representation would become ineffective should the constitutional provisions be amended.

Résumé

Le principe même des révisions constitutionnelles est pour un système juridique donné de prévoir la modification de sa propre norme suprême positive. Au sein des États de l'Union européenne, les dispositions constitutionnelles montrent qu'il est possible de distinguer des limites à la révision en cas de crise institutionnelle ou de crise sécuritaire, ces limites étant soit générales pour l'ensemble de la constitution, soit spécifiques à certaines dispositions. La question du contrôle du respect de ces limites est tout autre, puisque l'existence de limites matérielles n'implique pas l'existence d'un contrôle du respect de ces limites. On peut ainsi, grâce à ces données, proposer un modèle schématique des limites aux révisions constitutionnelles en temps de crise, modèle qui n'est pas un idéal à atteindre, mais plus simplement une représentation des différents exemples fournis par les droits positifs constitutionnels des États membres de l'Union européenne, représentation qui devient donc inopérante en cas de changement des droits positifs.

* Nous tenons à remercier *Camille Bordere, Matthieu Gaye-Palettes* et *Marie-Céline Pallas* pour leur relecture poussée et discussion la animée que celle-ci a permis. Toutes les opinions et erreurs demeurent évidemment du fait de l'auteur.

I. Introduction: Cadre Général de la Réflexion

Étudier les limites aux révisions constitutionnelles en temps de crise impose de préciser d'abord quelques définitions, afin d'éviter et de dissiper tout malentendu terminologique. Nommément, il s'agit de préciser ce qui sera entendu par 'constitution', par 'révision', par 'limites' et par 'temps de crise'. Il faudra pour cela préciser également ce que nous entendrons lorsque nous parlerons de 'droit', mais aussi de 'modèle'.

1. Définitions Générales

Par 'droit', nous désignerons un ensemble de normes, récursif et dynamique, globalement efficace et sanctionné. La norme sera considérée comme la signification, déontiquement modalisée (c'est-à-dire qui oblige, permet ou interdit), d'un énoncé ou d'un fait considéré par le droit lui-même comme appartenant à l'ordre juridique.[1] C'est ici que s'illustre le caractère récursif: le droit prévoit sa propre création, et une norme n'est juridique que parce qu'une autre norme le prévoit. Pour éviter une régression à l'infini, il est nécessaire de considérer la norme la plus haute de l'ordre considéré comme étant valide, cette supposition étant qualifiée de 'norme fondamentale supposée, ou 'grundnorm'.[2] Cette supposition n'est ni une réintroduction de la morale dans le système, ni une incohérence interne à la théorie kelsénienne. Il s'agit simplement de résoudre la question de la validité de la seule norme du système qui d'une part ne tire sa validité d'aucune norme juridique identifiable, et d'autre part fonde la validité de toutes les autres normes du système, directement ou indirectement.[3] C'est,

1 Nous empruntons cette définition du droit à *Otto Pfersmann*, Pour une typologie modale des classes de validité normative, 27 Cahiers de philosophie politique et juridique de l'Université de Caen, 1995, 69.

2 *Hans Kelsen*, Théorie pure du droit (traduit de l'allemand par Charles Eisenmann), Paris, Bruxelles 2e éd 1999, 194.

3 La question de la supposition de la validité d'une norme pour permettre l'étude d'un système pose une question particulière, celle du nombre de normes supposées valides. C'est, pour le dire autrement, le problème posé par les rapports entre l'ordre juridique international et les différents ordres (ou sous-ordres) juridiques internes. Plusieurs façons de procéder sont possibles, selon les éléments observés et l'étude effectuée. Intellectuellement, il nous semble que la position la plus correcte consiste à adopter une position 'moniste internationaliste', c'est-à-dire à supposer l'ordre juridique international valide. C'est cet ordre juridique international qui lui-même habilite de façon très vague l'adoption des ordres juridiques nationaux, qui sont donc, dans cette vision, des sous-ordres d'un seul et unique ordre juridique. Cette vision, cependant, n'a pas l'avantage de la simplicité pour s'intéresser aux normes qui seront définies par la suite comme constitutionnelles. Dans la mesure où nous ne serons pas confrontés aux rapports entre droit international et droit interne, nous simplifierons le raisonnement en considérant directement les normes constitutionnelles valides, sans nous interroger sur leur lien avec le droit international. Pour une position dé-

en cela, un postulat de travail essentiel au juriste.[4] Cette norme dont on suppose la validité est la constitution au sens formel du terme.

Il est ainsi possible de définir la constitution d'un point de vue formel ou matériel, et de donner même plusieurs sens à chacun de ces termes. La constitution sera ici considérée d'un point de vue formel. Ce qui détermine la forme constitutionnelle, quel que soit par ailleurs le nom donné à cette forme au sein de son ordre juridique, c'est la procédure par laquelle elle est édictée. La constitution formelle est alors l'ensemble des énoncés normatifs produits par une procédure spécifique, distincte de la procédure classique de production des normes générales et abstraites, procédure qui est en outre renforcée par rapport à cette procédure ordinaire. La constitution formelle ne peut pas être révisée de la même manière que les lois ordinaires, mais par une procédure plus contraignante d'un point de vue politique. Cette constitution formelle contient aussi, bien souvent, des éléments relatifs aux droits fondamentaux. Elle contient généralement, au moins en partie et pas en exclusivité, les énoncés normatifs de la constitution matérielle. Ce n'est toutefois pas une nécessité. En droit français, le droit constitutionnel formel correspond à l'ensemble normatif appelé ' Constitution de la Ve République ', dont la procédure de modification est prévue par l'article 89 de ladite Constitution. La constitution au sens formel n'est donc, *in fine*, qu'une question de spécificité de production de la norme constitutionnelle par rapport aux autres normes du système juridique.[5]

Dans une telle vision, qualifiable de 'normativiste', certains phénomènes sont exclus du champ d'étude spécifiquement juridique. Il en va ainsi de la coutume, sauf à ce que le système juridique lui-même n'en fasse mention comme étant un élément inscrit dans l'ordre juridique,[6] mais également des motifs des décisions juridictionnelles, sauf là encore à ce que le droit positif lui-même habilite les juridictions à édicter des normes générales et abstraites, s'appliquant au-delà du litige qu'elles ont à trancher.

Cela ne signifiera pas pour autant que la jurisprudence sera exclue de l'étude. Elle sera utilisée pour indiquer ce que sont, factuellement, les interprétations retenues

fendant l'existence d'une unité de l'ordre juridique, et donc une présentation unitaire du droit, *Xavier Magnon*, Repenser la frontière droit externe-droit interne au profit d'une approche unitaire du droit, in: Baptiste Bonnet (éd.), Traité des rapports entre ordres juridiques, Paris 2016, 653–666.

4 Sur ce choix et sa justification, *Thomas Hochmann*, Retour en Rhodésie: Kelsen, la norme fondamentale et l'efficacité, 105 Revue française de droit constitutionnel 2016, 37–56.

5 *Otto Pfersmann*, La Constitution comme norme, in: Louis Favoreu (éd.), Droit constitutionnel, Paris 2017, 19e éd, 61–149, à 84.

6 Le Code civil français fait ainsi encore quelques références à la coutume comme mode de création du droit, notamment aux articles 593 et 2511.

dans les systèmes juridiques considérés. En effet, dans une tentative de modélisation et face à des énoncés dont le cadre des significations[7] est important, certains éléments spécifiques ne sont pas déterminés par l'ordre juridique, mais sont laissés à la discrétion des organes d'application du droit, les juridictions pouvant imposer leur dernier mot le cas échéant. C'est spécifiquement le cas, dans cette étude, du contrôle des limites aux révisions par les différentes cours constitutionnelles. En l'absence de dispositions spécifiques d'une part, et en fonction des énoncés normatifs constitutionnels d'autre part, certains systèmes peuvent s'interpréter comme autorisant ou n'autorisant pas le contrôle du respect des limites dans le cadre des révisions constitutionnelles.

2. Principe des Limites aux Révisions Constitutionnelles: Limites Générales et Limites Spécifiques

La constitution formelle n'est pas nécessairement modifiable. Par définition, elle a été édictée par un corps de règle prévoyant une procédure spécifique,[8] mais il est possible qu'il se soit agi d'un corps de règles *ad hoc*, spécifique à l'élaboration ponctuelle d'une constitution. Ainsi en France, la Constitution de 1958 tire sa validité formelle d'une loi constitutionnelle spécifique, la loi constitutionnelle du 3 juin 1958 portant dérogation transitoire aux dispositions de l'article 90 de la Constitution (de 1946). Cette loi habilitait spécifiquement le gouvernement investi le 1er juin 1958 à édicter une nouvelle constitution, en suivant certaines conditions de fond et de forme. Les constitutions ne peuvent donc pas toutes être modifiées, soit qu'elles ne prévoient aucune procédure de modification en leur sein,[9] soit qu'elles interdisent expressément toute modification.

7 Sans adhérer aux théories réalistes de *Ricardo Guastini*, nous considérons à sa suite qu' 'à chaque disposition légale ne correspond pas une norme seulement, mais une multiplicité de normes disjointes, séparées: autant de normes que de possibles interprétations différentes': *Ricardo Guastini*, Interprétation et description des normes, in: Paul Amselek (éd.), Interprétation et droit, Aix-en-Provence, Bruxelles 1995, 96.

8 Sauf s'il s'agit de la 'première constitution historique'. Mais dans la majorité des cas, la constitution en vigueur dans un État a été élaborée selon un certain corps de règles, substantielles ou procédurales, et ce même si la constitution considérée est historiquement la première. La notion de 'première constitution historique' renvoie au premier corps de règles constitutionnel par définition et dont il faut supposer la validité. V. *Otto Pfersmann*, La Constitution comme norme, in: Louis Favoreu (éd.), Droit constitutionnel, Paris 2017, 19e éd, 61–149, à 111, et *Xavier Magnon*, Théorie(s) du droit, Paris 2007, 73 et 74.

9 En France, par exemple, les constitutions napoléoniennes, les deux chartes de 1814 et de 1830 ainsi que la Constitution du Second Empire ne comportaient aucune procédure de révision constitutionnelle. Cela ne signifie évidemment pas qu'il était impossible de modifier ces constitutions,

Mais les constitutions, dans la majorité des cas, prévoient des procédures de modification, plus ou moins rigides. Une révision constitutionnelle est alors toute disposition formellement constitutionnelle, édictée en suivant la procédure spécifiquement prévue par la constitution formelle elle-même. La révision tire sa validité de la constitution, ce qui fait de la constitution la seule norme qui peut prévoir la procédure de sa propre modification.[10] Par définition, toute procédure de révision est intrinsèquement une limite à la révision.[11] En effet, même si les dispositions constitutionnelles n'imposent pour réviser la constitution qu'une procédure presque identique à la procédure législative ordinaire, cette simple différence est, en elle-même, une première limite. L'aspect procédural montre d'ailleurs bien son caractère de limite en cas d'impossibilité matérielle de suivre la procédure de révision. Si par exemple c'est le Parlement qui doit se prononcer sur la révision, mais que celui-ci ne peut pas se réunir, soit pour des raisons juridiques (par exemple si la session parlementaire est achevée et qu'il n'est pas possible de convoquer une session extraordinaire) soit pour des raisons matérielles (par exemple si le lieu de réunion du parlement est inaccessible), alors la révision ne peut être entreprise. De même, si le gouvernement doit nécessairement intervenir dans la procédure mais qu'en raison d'une crise politique il n'y a pas de gouvernement en fonction, réviser la constitution est impossible. De telles limites, indirectes, ne seront cependant pas étudiées ici.

Si cet aspect procédural est une première forme de limite, les constitutions prévoient également certaines limites matérielles, touchant au contenu des dispositions constitutionnelles pouvant être révisées. Il arrive ainsi que certaines dispositions ne puissent être modifiées que selon certaines procédures, différentes de la procédure ' normale ' de révision constitutionnelle. Un exemple réside dans l'article 66 de la Constitution de Malte, qui prévoit trois procédures de révision distinctes — bien que proches — en fonction des domaines révisés. Il arrive également que certaines dispositions ne puissent être modifiées du tout, soit de façon générale soit dans certaines circonstances.

mais que toute modification doit être interprétée comme une révolution juridique (v. *infra*, notes 19 et 20).

10 Il est possible que des actes réglementaires prévoient eux-mêmes leur procédure de modification, mais ce n'est pas une nécessité. À l'inverse, la constitution au sens formel, si elle est modifiable, doit nécessairement, par définition, prévoir elle-même la procédure de sa propre modification.

11 Pour une réflexion spécifique aux limites aux révisions constitutionnelles, *Jean-Philippe Derosier*, Enquête sur la limite constitutionnelle: du concept à la notion, 76 Revue française de droit constitutionnel 2008, 785–795.

Les limites générales aux révisions constitutionnelles sont communément appelées des 'clauses d'éternité', terme issu de la doctrine allemande pour les désigner.[12] Elles visent, la plupart du temps, des éléments considérés comme essentiels à l'identité de l'État ou de la constitution. Ainsi en France la Constitution dispose que 'la forme républicaine du Gouvernement ne peut faire l'objet d'une révision',[13] alors que la Constitution allemande[14] dispose que 'toute modification de la présente Loi fondamentale qui toucherait à l'organisation de la Fédération en Länder, au principe du concours des Länder à la législation ou aux principes énoncés aux articles 1 et 20, est interdite',[15] les articles 1 à 19 constituant une première partie intitulée 'les droits fondamentaux' et l'article 20 étant intitulé 'Fondements de l'ordre étatique, droit de résistance'.

Outre ces limites générales, interdisant la modification de dispositions spécifiques en toute circonstance, d'autres dispositions constitutionnelles peuvent encadrer la révision uniquement pendant certains évènements spécifiques. La Constitution grecque dispose par exemple qu' 'aucune révision de la Constitution n'est permise avant que cinq ans se soient écoulés à partir de la fin de la révision précédente'.[16] De façon plus courante, cependant, les révisions constitutionnelles sont encadrées ou interdites en temps de 'crises'.

Les limites aux révisions constitutionnelles ne seront cependant pas ici étudiées en général,[17] mais spécifiquement pendant les périodes de 'crise'. La notion de 'crise' est nécessairement au moins partiellement subjective. Sur le plan strictement juridique, les limites aux révisions constitutionnelles sont de deux formes différentes. La première limite, intrinsèque au concept de révision, est la limite formelle de la procédure

12 Ibid., 792.

13 Art. 89, al. 5 de la Constitution française de 1958.

14 On utilise ici le terme de 'constitution' et pas celui de 'loi fondamentale' afin de faciliter l'expression. Le terme 'loi fondamentale' est l'expression interne au droit allemand pour désigner sa constitution, entendu comme un concept général. Il s'agit d'un concept métajuridique qui désigne des objets présentant des caractéristiques communes malgré leur dénomination dans leur ordre juridique propre. De même en ce qui concerne les noms des différents parlements, nous utiliserons le vocable conceptuel de 'parlement' (sans véritablement le définir, il faut le concéder) plutôt que le nom de chaque assemblée étatique.

15 Art. 79, al. 3 de la Constitution allemande de 1949.

16 Art. 110, al. 6 de la Constitution grecque de 1975.

17 Notre étude s'inscrit nécessairement — mais modestement — dans le contexte de l'étude des limites aux révisions constitutionnelles. Elle vise cependant à développer spécifiquement celles relatives aux périodes de crise. Pour une étude globale et récente des limites aux révisions constitutionnelles, *Yaniv Roznai*, Unconstitutional constitutional amendments. The limits of Amendment Powers, Oxford 2017.

à suivre pour réviser la constitution. Schématiquement elle est de la forme: 'Pour édicter une norme constitutionnelle, il est nécessaire de suivre la procédure P', plusieurs procédures pouvant exister pour différentes normes constitutionnelles. Les limites matérielles sont quant à elles de la forme 'Pendant l'évènement X, la constitution (ou certaines de ses normes) ne peut faire l'objet d'une modification'. Notons d'ailleurs qu'il pourrait exister, dans l'absolu, une combinaison de ces deux formes, qui impliquerait en cas de survenue d'un évènement particulier de suivre une procédure spécifique pour réviser tout ou partie de la constitution, cependant les énoncés de droit positifs ne révèlent pas l'existence de cette forme au sein des constitutions étudiées. Tous les évènements pris en compte pour limiter la révision ne peuvent pas être considérés comme des 'crises', comme l'illustre le cas grec mentionné précédemment, qui exige simplement un délai entre deux révisions. Il est alors nécessaire de construire une définition de ce qui sera considéré comme des 'crises au sens de cette étude.

La définition des périodes de 'crise' ici proposée sera 'stipulative'.[18] Il ne s'agit pas de chercher le ou les sens de l'emploi d'un mot par une communauté linguistique, mais de poser une définition sans tenir compte des multiples usages du terme, en tâchant toutefois, afin que la définition conserve sa pertinence, de ne pas s'éloigner des usages courants du terme. Une crise sera entendue ici comme 'tout évènement, prévu ou non par la constitution, qui bouleverse le fonctionnement régulier des institutions publiques sur tout ou partie du territoire de l'*État de façon durable*'.

La crise ici entendue est un évènement, c'est donc un fait, qui peut avoir des traductions ou des conséquences juridiques. Ce fait peut être prévu ou non par la constitution de l'État ou plus largement son ordre juridique. Évidemment, si une crise spécifique est une limite directe à la révision constitutionnelle, alors elle est prévue par la constitution, mais de façon générale une constitution donnée peut ne pas prévoir précisément ce qui doit se passer en cas de crise. La crise affecte le fonctionnement régulier des institutions. Elle peut d'abord le faire de façon juridique en prenant la forme d'une exception, par exemple si un énoncé prévoit que dans le cas spécifique d'une crise particulière, un régime exceptionnel dérogatoire au droit commun s'applique ou peut s'appliquer. C'est par exemple le cas de l'état de guerre ou de l'état de siège, s'ils existent dans le droit positif. Elle peut ensuite le faire factuellement et matériellement, en empêchant les services de l'État de fonctionner correctement, par exemple en cas de catastrophe naturelle. Par 'institutions publiques', il faut entendre de façon large l'État et ses services. Il peut ainsi s'agir du bon fonctionnement des

18 La classification des définitions lexicales, stipulatives et explicatives, et plus généralement nos développements sur les définitions, sont directement tirés d'*Umberto Scarpeli*, Qu'est-ce que le positivisme juridique?, Paris 1996, 5.

institutions principales de la conduite des affaires de l'État comme le parlement ou le gouvernement, mais également du contrôle effectif de ces institutions du territoire ou d'une portion du territoire. La crise doit au demeurant affecter le fonctionnement des institutions sur la durée, et pas simplement de façon ponctuelle. Cette durée peut être plus ou moins longue, mais il ne s'agit pas d'un simple évènement de la vie politique. Une dissolution du parlement par le pouvoir exécutif, ou une motion de censure réussie, sont sur le plan politique souvent appelées des 'crises'. Elles se résolvent cependant en quelques jours. Dans le cas où la nomination d'un nouveau gouvernement n'est pas immédiate, que cela fasse suite à des élections législatives ou à une motion de censure, on pourra parler de crise selon la définition que nous avons retenue.

Les limites aux révisions constitutionnelles, qu'elles soient générales ou spéciales, ne sont cependant pas infranchissables. Si l'on considère le système juridique lui-même et sa continuité, les limites peuvent en effet être elles-mêmes supprimées dans certains cas de figure. L'article 89 de la Constitution française de 1958 interdit la révision de la 'forme républicaine du Gouvernement'. Sur le plan strictement juridique, il serait possible de supprimer par une première révision cette disposition, afin d'ensuite modifier la forme républicaine du gouvernement.[19]

Mais si l'on sort du système constitutionnel considéré, les limites semblent encore moins opérantes. Elles ne sont qu'une façon, pour une constitution donnée, de couper toute parenté intellectuelle et institutionnelle avec une constitution future qui ne respecterait pas certains principes, forçant ainsi une révolution juridique.[20] Ainsi une 'révision' d'une constitution C1 qui ne respecterait pas les limites posées, qu'elles soient purement procédurales ou substantielles, ne serait pas une révision de C1. Ces

19 Cette opinion n'est cependant pas partagée. Pour *Georges Liet-Veaux* il s'agit d'une 'fraude à la constitution' en ce que cette façon de procéder va à l'encontre de l'esprit de la constitution (*Georges Liet-Veaux*, 'La fraude à la constitution. Essai d'une analyse juridique des révolutions communautaires récentes, Revue du droit public et de la science politique en France et à l'étranger 1943, 116–150). De même *Jean-Philippe Derosier* considère que la limite à la révision constitutionnelle est 'absolue et éternelle' afin d'éviter une régression à l'infini de dispositions limitant la révision des limites (*Jean-Philippe Derosier*, Enquête sur la limite constitutionnelle: du concept à la notion, 76 Revue française de droit constitutionnel 2008, 785–795, 795). Il nous semble, quant à nous, qu'il faut distinguer entre les limites autoréférentielles qui ne peuvent être révisées et les limites non autoréférentielles qui peuvent l'être. Si l'article 89 de la Constitution française, en plus d'interdire la révision de la 'forme républicaine du Gouvernement', interdisait également toute modification de son propre contenu, alors la limite serait éternelle. Pour une position plus modérée qui semble accepter au moins en principe la possibilité d'amender des limites non autoréférentielles, *Yaniv Roznai*, Unconstitutional constitutional amendments. The limits of Amendment Powers, Oxford 2017, 139.

20 *Jean-Philippe Derosier*, Qu'est-ce qu'une révolution juridique? Le point de vue de la théorie générale du droit, 102 Revue française de droit constitutionnel 2015, 391–404.

nouvelles dispositions ne tireraient pas leur validité de C1. Mais si factuellement ces nouvelles dispositions trouvent à s'appliquer sans remise en cause, alors la constitution aura été modifiée d'une façon contraire au droit positif. C1 aura disparu, au profit d'une nouvelle constitution C2. Cette modification n'emporte pas de véritable conséquence sur le reste du droit positif, si ce n'est la substitution non prévue par le système d'une constitution par une autre. En revanche sur le plan politique cette modification illustre le non-respect par les détenteurs du pouvoir politique du droit positif, sans qu'un jugement de valeur ne soit intrinsèquement porté sur cette violation.[21]

Il s'agira alors d'étudier au sein des États de l'Union européenne les différentes limites explicites aux révisions constitutionnelles pendant ces périodes de crise, et de tenter d'en donner un modèle. Par 'limites explicites' sont évoquées les limites aux révisions qui sont expressément et explicitement mentionnées dans les énoncés normatifs des constitutions des États membres, à l'exclusion des limites qui découlent des exigences procédurales. Ainsi, pour illustrer le propos, tous les États considérés font intervenir d'une façon ou d'une autre leur parlement dans la procédure de révision. Une crise qui empêcherait la réunion du parlement empêcherait alors, *de facto*, toute révision constitutionnelle. À coup sûr tout évènement empêchant durablement la réunion du parlement est une crise selon la définition que nous en avons retenue. Cependant, à moins que l'évènement ne constitue par ailleurs une crise expressément prévue par la constitution, nous ne l'inclurons pas dans l'étude.

Les États considérés sont ceux de l'Union européenne disposant d'une constitution formelle. Parmi les vingt-huit États membres, seul le Royaume-Uni ne dispose pas d'une telle constitution, il sera donc exclu de l'étude. Pourquoi se concentrer sur les États de l'Union ? La réponse n'a rien de strictement scientifique. Le but de la présente étude est de tenter de proposer une modélisation des types de limites en temps de crise, mais pour ce faire il est nécessaire d'observer différents droits positifs. Les États membres de l'Union européenne permettent de délimiter sans trop d'arbitraire un tel échantillon. Il aurait également été possible de s'intéresser aux États membres du Conseil de l'Europe, leur nombre nous en a cependant dissuadé.

Cette remarque implique de préciser dès maintenant un élément de méthode. Le fait d'étudier les constitutions de vingt-sept États pose le problème de l'accès linguistique aux sources. Lorsque les institutions des États proposaient sur internet des versions françaises de leur constitution, nous avons utilisé ces versions. Dans les autres

21 Ainsi l'ordonnance du 9 août 1944 relative au rétablissement de la légalité républicaine sur le territoire continental constitue une révolution au sens juridique du terme, et ce malgré ce qu'elle affirme elle-même. La qualifier de révolution juridique n'est pas synonyme de jugement de valeur, positif ou négatif.

cas, les traductions utilisées ont été celles fournies par la Digithèque de matériaux juridiques et politiques (digithèque MJP) sur son site internet,[22] à l'exception de la Constitution de Malte que nous avons consultée dans la version anglaise. Ainsi les articles cités le seront dans les versions traduites soit par les institutions des États, soit par la digithèque MJP.

Cette utilisation d'énoncés normatifs constitutionnels traduits implique un présupposé particulier. Nous sommes en effet contraints de considérer les traductions comme permettant de retrouver au moins partiellement le cadre des significations porté par les énoncés originaux. Nous considérerons ainsi que malgré la traduction le sens 'global' de l'énoncé, c'est-à-dire les normes, n'est pas dénaturé. La contrepartie de ce présupposé est qu'il impose une certaine humilité dans l'étude, ainsi qu'une certaine généralité, puisque l'on ne peut connaître exactement les normes des systèmes étudiés, mais simplement une représentation de ces normes par la traduction de leur support.[23]

3. Principe de la Modélisation des Limites aux Révisions Constitutionnelles en Période de Crise Proposée

La modélisation proposée ici ne vise pas à proposer un modèle *idéal* qui serait prescriptif, indiquant ce que serait une bonne ou une meilleure façon de poser des limites aux révisions en temps de crise. Il s'agit d'une classification, qui vise à restituer le résultat d'une analyse comparative. Cette classification n'est pas essentialiste. Les classes utilisées n'existent pas en elles-mêmes, ce sont simplement des éléments saillants qui ressortent de l'analyse des constitutions des vingt-sept États. Sa portée scientifique est en outre limitée.[24] Elle ne permet pas de suggérer d'explication, ou de déduire logiquement un caractère moins apparent qui serait par ailleurs nécessairement partagé par les individus d'une même classe. De plus la classification proposée ne sera pas purement logique, certaines constitutions apparaissant dans plusieurs classes.

22 Digithèque de matériaux juridiques et politiques, disponible sur <http://mjp.univ-perp.fr/mjp.htm>.

23 La norme n'est certes pas traduite, c'est l'énoncé porteur de norme qui est traduit. Cependant, le lien entre le support de la norme et la norme implique que toute traduction du support risque de modifier même légèrement la norme qui est la signification de l'énoncé.

24 Sur la portée scientifique des classifications, *Michel Troper*, Les classifications en droit constitutionnel, Revue du droit public et de la science politique en France et à l'étranger 1989, 945–956, à 950.

Le but de la classification proposée, que l'on pourrait qualifier de typologie, 'vise à produire un effet de connaissance'.[25] Il s'agit de présenter synthétiquement les dispositions constitutionnelles des différents États de l'Union européenne relatives aux limites à la révision en période de crise, permettant 'd'obtenir rapidement quelques informations sur l'existence de quelques règles juridiques simples'[26] au sein de telle ou telle constitution concrète. Il s'agit d'une ébauche, qu'il serait pertinent de compléter tant en amont en l'affinant sur le plan logique et théorique qu'en aval en la confrontant à d'autres données relatives à des constitutions actuelles ou passées.

En observant les constitutions écrites des vingt-sept États membres de l'Union européenne, on peut d'abord noter que peu d'entre elles — moins de la moitié — prévoient des limites matérielles aux révisions constitutionnelles, des clauses d'éternité. Encore moins prévoient des limites aux révisions constitutionnelles en période de crise, ou un contrôle des limites posées (II). Une fois ces dispositions présentées, on tentera de modéliser les différents types de limites aux révisions en période de crise. On peut en effet distinguer les crises institutionnelles et les crises sécuritaires, ainsi que, dans ces deux catégories, des limites substantielles générales ou des limites substantielles spécifiques (III). Seront également présentés, dans deux annexes, un tableau récapitulatif de la classification proposée, ainsi qu'une carte géographique illustrant les différentes limites.

II. Les Limites aux Révisions Constitutionnelles en Période de Crise: des Limites Restreintes

De façon générale, au sein de l'Union européenne, une minorité d'États utilise le mécanisme des clauses d'éternité au sein de leur constitution, et une partie encore plus faible des États prévoit le mécanisme des limites à la révision en période de crise (1). Il est à noter en outre que les États mettant en place ces limites ne disposent pas nécessairement de procédures visant à garantir leur respect (2), et qu'il n'existe pas de corrélation entre l'existence de régimes constitutionnels de crise déterminés et de limites à la révision pendant ces périodes spécifiques (3).

25 Pour *Jean-Marie Denquin*, la 'typologie est censée produire un effet de connaissance': *Jean-Marie Denquin*, Éléments pour une théorie constitutionnelle, 8 Annales de la faculté de droit de Strasbourg 2006, 123.

26 *Arnaud Le Pillouer*, La notion de 'régime d'assemblée' et les origines de la classification des régimes politiques, 58 Revue française de droit constitutionnel 2004, 305–333, à 318–319.

1. Le Faible Nombre d'États ayant Recours aux Limites: Présentation Générale des Dispositions Constitutionnelles

Parmi les États membres de l'Union européenne, neuf ont recours, dans leur constitution, à des dispositions limitant d'une façon ou d'une autre les révisions constitutionnelles en période de crise. Il s'agit de la Belgique, l'Espagne, l'Estonie, la France, la Lituanie, le Luxembourg, le Portugal et la Roumanie. L'Allemagne présente aussi, semble-t-il, de telles dispositions, mais uniquement dans le cas d'une révision totale de sa Constitution.

L'inventaire à la Prévert commence donc par la Constitution belge, dont l'article 196 dispose qu' 'aucune révision de la Constitution ne peut être engagée ni poursuivie en temps de guerre ou lorsque les Chambres se trouvent empêchées de se réunir librement sur le territoire fédéral', et l'article 197 que 'pendant une régence, aucun changement ne peut être apporté à la Constitution en ce qui concerne les pouvoirs constitutionnels du Roi et les articles 85 à 88, 91 à 95, 106 et 197 de la Constitution'. Deux limites sont donc posées, l'une générale soit en temps de guerre soit si les chambres du parlement ne peuvent se réunir librement,[27] l'autre spéciale, et qui concerne les pouvoirs du monarque pendant les périodes de régence.[28] L'état de guerre est prévu par la Constitution. Déclaré par le Roi,[29] la Constitution prévoit l'existence de tribunaux militaires pendant sa durée.[30]

La Constitution espagnole dispose à son article 169 qu' 'on ne peut engager la révision de la Constitution en temps de guerre ou lorsque l'un des états prévus à l'article 116 est en vigueur', ces états étant 'les états d'alerte, d'urgence et de siège'. Si la Constitution belge mentionnait l'engagement et la poursuite de la révision comme étant empêchés ici c'est seulement l'engagement qui est interdit. Cela semble signifier, d'après la lettre du texte, qu'une révision qui serait engagée avant ces périodes pourrait être poursuivie.

27 L'adverbe 'librement ' a ici toute son importance. En effet, l'article 195 de la Constitution belge prévoit par principe le rôle du Parlement dans la révision de la Constitution. Si le Parlement est dans l'incapacité de se réunir, la révision est donc impossible puisque la procédure ne peut être mise en œuvre. Il est cependant possible que le Parlement soit contraint de se réunir, et c'est là que l'exigence de sa liberté de réunion est importante pour la validité de la révision constitutionnelle.

28 Nous considérons la régence comme une période de crise, puisque c'est une période durant laquelle le chef de l'État n'est pas le chef de l'État normal, mais un remplaçant dont l'office ne doit durer qu'un minimum de temps.

29 Art. 167, § 1er, al. 2 de la Constitution belge.

30 Art. 157, al. 1 de la Constitution belge.

La Constitution estonienne dispose au second alinéa de son article 161 que 'l'initiative de la révision ne peut être exercée, ni la Constitution modifiée pendant l'état d'urgence ou l'état de guerre'. Les états d'urgence et de guerre sont mentionnés par la Constitution. Le contenu de l'état d'urgence est défini par la loi, et durant ces deux états certains droits et libertés peuvent être restreints.[31] Ici aussi sont visées tant l'initiative de la révision que la révision elle-même, ce qui bloque toute discussion relative à la révision, sauf à considérer que l'on pourrait discuter d'une révision introduite avant la crise sans jamais l'adopter.

La France prévoit deux limites distinctes aux révisions en période de crise dans sa Constitution, une troisième ayant été précisée par la jurisprudence du Conseil constitutionnel. L'article 89 de la Constitution, consacré entièrement à la procédure de révision constitutionnelle, dispose dans son quatrième alinéa qu' 'aucune procédure de révision ne peut être engagée ou poursuivie lorsqu'il est porté atteinte à l'intégrité du territoire', et le onzième alinéa de son article 7 qu' 'il ne peut être fait application [...] de l'article 89 de la Constitution durant la vacance de la Présidence de la République'. Dans une décision,[32] le Conseil constitutionnel a précisé qu'il considère que pendant les période d'utilisation des 'pleins pouvoirs' de l'article 16 de la Constitution, la révision est également impossible. Cet article peut être mis en œuvre, entre autre, lorsque l'intégrité du territoire est menacée, mais cette justification n'est pas suffisante à justifier une interdiction de la révision pendant l'utilisation de l'article 16 puisque l'article 89 interdit déjà toute révision en cas d'atteinte au territoire. L'article mentionne que les décisions prises dans le cadre de cet article doivent l'être pour assurer aux ' pouvoirs publics constitutionnels' 'les moyens d'accomplir leur mission'. On pourrait alors interpréter cette mention des pouvoirs publics constitutionnels comme interdisant de modifier ces pouvoirs et leurs missions, et donc la Constitution. Cependant, même dans un tel cas, ce seraient uniquement les dispositions relatives aux pouvoirs publics qui ne devraient pas pouvoir être modifiées. Cette précision jurisprudentielle, qui n'a pas de valeur normative puisqu'elle se trouve dans la motivation de la décision, semble donc devoir être écartée, sauf à ce que le Conseil démontre dans sa motivation en quoi l'interprétation de l'article 16 implique une limitation de la possibilité de révision constitutionnelle.

Cette 'limite' prétorienne des révisions totales lors de l'utilisation de l'article 16 ne doit pas être confondue avec une interdiction d'une révision par les pouvoirs de

31 Art. 131 de la Constitution estonienne.

32 Décision n° 92–312 DC du 2 septembre 1992 – Maastricht II -, Considérant 19.

l'article 16.[33] En effet, la Constitution ne précise pas l'étendue de la compétence du Président de la République dans le cadre de l'article 16, parlant seulement de 'mesures'. S'il peut décréter des mesures normalement législatives ou réglementaires, la Constitution ne dit rien sur d'éventuelles modifications de la Constitution. L'indétermination de l'article 16 semble permettre *a priori* d'accepter les deux interprétations. Cependant, quand bien même l'article 16 devrait être interprété comme interdisant au Président de la République de réviser la Constitution par l'utilisation des compétences qu'il tire de cet article, une telle interprétation ne peut s'étendre à une révision suivant la procédure normale de l'article 89 de la Constitution.

Notons qu'ici, l'interdiction des révisions concerne tous les aspects de la procédure, de son introduction en passant par sa discussion et son adoption. Sur le plan constitutionnel, la France connaît l'état de siège[34] et l'état spécifique des pleins pouvoirs de l'article 16 de la Constitution, que l'on pourrait qualifier de dictature dans le sens qu'avait ce terme sous la Rome antique.[35] Il existe un état d'urgence dont la nature est purement législative, celui-ci n'étant pas même mentionné dans la Constitution. Il n'existe pas à proprement parler d'état de guerre, même si la Constitution prévoit les modalités de déclaration de guerre.[36] L'interdiction de l'article 89 mentionne une atteinte à l'intégrité du territoire, notion qui ne recoupe pas un état de siège, de guerre ou d'urgence. En effet un État peut être en guerre sans que pour autant ses frontières ne soient menacées. L'état de siège peut être préventif, bloquant les opposants hors des frontières, et alors l'intégrité du territoire est protégée, bien qu'elle soit menacée. De même l'état d'urgence, du moins dans le droit français,[37] peut recouvrir des cas de catastrophes naturelles même si une telle éventualité ne s'est jamais présentée, ou des cas de violences urbaines qui ne menacent pas l'intégrité du territoire.[38]

La Lituanie dispose également de limites aux révisions constitutionnelles en périodes de crise. Ainsi selon l'alinéa second de son article 147 dispose que 'pendant la durée de l'état d'urgence ou de la loi martiale, la Constitution ne peut être révi-

33 V. not. *Jean Lamarque*, La théorie de la nécessité et l'article 16 de la Constitution de 1958, Revue du droit public et de la science politique en France et à l'étranger 1961, 558–628, à 617, et *Michèle Voisset*, L'article 16 de la Constitution du 4 octobre 1958, Paris 1969, 68.

34 Art. 36 de la Constitution française.

35 'Sous la République, magistrat unique et souverain, nommé extraordinairement en certaines circonstances critiques, et pour une durée qui ne pouvait excéder six mois': 'Dictateur', Dictionnaire de l'Académie française, 9e éd., 1992. disponible sur <http://atilf.atilf.fr/academie9.htm>.

36 Art. 35, al. 1er de la Constitution française.

37 Loi n° 55–385 du 3 avril 1955 relative à l'*état d'*urgence.

38 Ainsi il a été décrété du 8 novembre 2005 au 4 janvier 2006 pour assurer l'ordre dans certains quartiers français en situation d'émeute.

sée'. L'état d'urgence est réglementé par la loi,[39] et lorsque ces deux états sont déclarés, certains droits peuvent être restreints.[40] C'est ici la révision de la Constitution qui est visée, donc le résultat de la révision, et non son processus. On pourrait ainsi considérer qu'une procédure de révision peut être introduite et discutée tant qu'elle n'est pas définitivement adoptée.

Le Luxembourg prévoit dans sa Constitution une limite similaire à celle de la Belgique en ce qui concerne les périodes de régence. Ainsi son article 15 dispose que 'pendant une régence, aucun changement ne peut être apporté à la Constitution en ce qui concerne les prérogatives constitutionnelles du Grand-Duc, son statut ainsi que l'ordre de succession'. Là aussi ce sont des limites spécifiques qui sont posées, mais à la différence de la Belgique ces dispositions ne sont pas autoréférentielles et n'interdisent donc pas leur propre modification en période de régence.

Le Portugal prévoit également des limites aux révisions constitutionnelles pendant les périodes de crise. Ainsi l'alinéa second de l'article 289 de sa Constitution dispose qu' 'aucun acte de révision constitutionnelle ne peut être accompli pendant l'état de siège ou l'état d'urgence', ces deux états étant prévus par la Constitution et délégués au législateur dans leur contenu.[41] Puisque l'interdiction porte sur des 'actes de révision constitutionnelle', il semble possible de considérer qu'interdiction est faite de procéder à n'importe quels éléments de procédure relatif à la révision de la Constitution.

En ce qui concerne la Roumanie, enfin, le troisième alinéa de l'article 152 de sa Constitution dispose que 'la Constitution ne peut être révisée pendant la durée de l'état de siège ou de l'état d'urgence, ni en temps de guerre'. L'état d'urgence et l'état de siège sont réglementés par une loi organique.[42]

Doit également être évoqué ici le cas de l'Allemagne. Son article 146 prévoit en effet la caducité de la Constitution au moment de l'adoption d'une nouvelle constitution. Cette caducité est cependant conditionnée, puisque la nouvelle constitution doit être 'adoptée par le peuple allemand en pleine liberté de décision'. La notion de 'pleine liberté de décision' semble pouvoir s'interpréter comme une limite à la révision totale de la Constitution, un peuple allemand qui ne serait pas en pleine liberté de décision ne pouvant alors pas, juridiquement, adopter de nouvelle constitution.[43]

39 Art. 144, al. 3 de la Constitution lituanienne.

40 Art. 145 de la Constitution lituanienne.

41 Art. 164, e) de la Constitution portugaise.

42 Art. 72, al.3, e) de la Constitution roumaine.

43 Pour une analyse plus détaillée, *Otto Pfersmann*, La révision constitutionnelle en Autriche et en Allemagne fédérale: théorie, pratique, limites, in: Association française des constitutionnalistes (éd.), La révision de la Constitution, Paris, Aix-en-Provence, 1993, 6–65, à 62 et 63.

Cette limite est particulière en ce qu'elle ne concerne que le cas de la révision totale de la Constitution. Bien que s'appliquant à une procédure très spécifique, elle constitue une limite de portée générale.

Cette énumération, rébarbative mais nécessaire, permet d'illustrer une certaine parenté entre les limites aux révisions outre le cas de l'Allemagne. Elle illustre qu'un faible nombre d'États a fait le choix d'instaurer de telles limites dans l'Union européenne, seulement un tiers d'entre eux. De plus, parmi ce faible nombre, seule l'Allemagne contrôle *de facto* les révisions constitutionnelles.

2. L'Absence de Contrôle Systématique du Respect des Limites

Nous l'avons dit plus haut, le principe même de révision de la constitution introduit une idée de hiérarchie formelle de validité entre des dispositions constitutionnelles. Les normes de révisions sont valides, elles ont une existence juridique, uniquement parce qu'elles ont été édictées en suivant la procédure de révision. L'idée de limite aux révisions constitutionnelles, en général ou en période de crise, introduit nécessairement l'idée de l'existence de plusieurs 'étages'constitutionnels non plus sur le strict plan de la validité, mais au moins partiellement sur celui de la conformité[44] des normes. Ainsi une norme de révision constitutionnelle qui irait à l'encontre des limites aux révisions, générales ou spéciales, serait une norme constitutionnelle inconstitutionnelle.[45] Puisqu'une hiérarchie entre les normes d'une même constitution existe, il n'est pas impensable alors qu'un contrôle soit effectué par une cour consti-

44 La validité d'une norme est son existence juridique dans le système. Validité et existence sont synonymes. La conformité d'une norme au système renvoie à l'idée d'une norme qui aurait été édictée en suivant les procédures prescrites par l'ordre juridique, qui serait donc valide et existerait, mais qui, dans son contenu, contiendrait des éléments contraires à l'ordre juridique. Cette norme existe, elle s'applique, mais du fait de sa non-conformité elle peut possiblement être retirée de l'ordre juridique par des juridictions en suivant certaines procédures spécifiques. C'est typiquement le cas d'une loi déclarée inconstitutionnelle par une cour constitutionnelle lors d'un contrôle *a posteriori*. Entre son édiction et son annulation, la loi existait, elle produisait des effets juridiques; elle était valide. Son absence de conformité a cependant entraîné son annulation. L'introduction d'un contrôle de conformité des normes introduit une deuxième forme de hiérarchie entre les normes (qui souvent recoupe plus ou moins dans les grandes catégories la hiérarchie de la validité). Sur le plan de la validité, deux normes sont dans un rapport hiérarchique lorsque l'une prévoit la création de l'autre. Sur le plan de la conformité, deux normes sont dans un rapport hiérarchique lorsque l'une doit respecter le contenu matériel prescrit par l'autre. Sur les notions de validité, de conformité et de calcul des défauts, *Otto Pfersmann*, La Constitution comme norme, in: Louis Favoreu (éd.), Droit constitutionnel, Paris 2017, 19e éd, 61–149, à 74.

45 Il faut admettre qu'il est discutable de dire que ces 'normes' sont valides. On peut en effet considérer que les limites aux révisions, comme les interdictions de réviser la constitution pendant certaines périodes, sont des éléments procéduraux qui rendent ces révisions non valides, et donc juri-

tutionnelle entre celles-ci.[46] Ce contrôle peut avoir lieu avant l'entrée en vigueur des normes,[47] ou bien après.

Pour qu'un tel contrôle existe, cependant, il faut que les énoncés normatifs le prévoient, ou du moins qu'ils soient suffisamment vagues et indéterminés pour ne pas l'interdire. Dans ce dernier cas, il faut en outre que la juridiction constitutionnelle se saisisse du pouvoir politique requis pour effectuer ce contrôle.

Parmi les neuf États qui utilisent le mécanisme des limites constitutionnelles en période de crise, aucun n'interdit directement le contrôle de la constitutionnalité de ses lois de révisions, que ce soit sur le simple aspect matériel de la procédure ou sur l'aspect du fond des dispositions modifiées. Aucun ne l'autorise directement non plus. Les énoncés normatifs restent indéterminés quant à ce contrôle.

Une seule des juridictions a décidé d'effectuer un contrôle, *a priori*, des lois de révisions constitutionnelles. Il s'agit du Tribunal constitutionnel fédéral allemand.[48] Les énoncés constitutionnels permettaient ce contrôle malgré l'absence de compétence explicite.[49] En effet, l'article 79 relatif à la révision constitutionnelle mentionne ces révisions comme des 'lois'. Le Tribunal constitutionnel peut donc, sans méconnaître la constitution, appliquer les dispositions générales relatives au contrôle de constitutionnalité des lois *a priori*.

Le contrôle portait ici sur les limites des clauses d'éternité, mais il n'est pas impensable que le Tribunal contrôle également la clause de l'article 146 exige la 'pleine liberté' de la décision du peuple allemand pour poser une nouvelle constitution.

À l'inverse, en France le Conseil constitutionnel s'est explicitement prononcé contre un tel contrôle, alors que les énoncés constitutionnels ne le lui interdisaient

diquement inexistantes. Il nous semble cependant, pour les besoins de la réflexion, plus pertinent de les considérer ici comme valides, mais non conformes.

46 *Claude Klein*, Le contrôle des lois constitutionnelles – Introduction à une problématique moderne, 27 Cahiers du Conseil constitutionnel (2010), 9–12.

47 Dans ce cas-là il ne s'agit techniquement pas d'un contrôle de conformité entre deux normes, mais entre une norme et un texte qui va entrer dans le système juridique et donc dont le sens sera porteur de norme. Ainsi, et malgré les notes précédentes, si le contrôle avait lieu *a priori*, il ne serait même pas question de validité puisque la norme n'existerait pas encore dans l'ordonnancement juridique. Pour faciliter le propos, nous préférons toutefois parler de validité et de conformité même avant l'entrée en vigueur des dispositions, afin d'éviter une terminologie trop indigeste.

48 BVerfGE 1, 14 (Southwestern State).

49 V. not. *Yaniv Roznai*, Unconstitutional constitutional amendments. The limits of Amendment Powers, Oxford 2017, 203.

pas explicitement.[50] Ce choix était esquissé dès 1962,[51] et a été confirmé en 2003.[52] Cette position n'est pas étonnante sur le plan politique, bien qu'elle ait été critiquée par la doctrine.[53] Le Conseil constitutionnel est en France une institution récente, qui a dû politiquement s'imposer au sein d'un système dont les acteurs principaux considéraient la loi comme la quintessence de l'expression du Droit. La loi, 'expression de la volonté générale',[54] était considérée comme parfaite, et il était impensable qu'elle puisse être contrôlée dans son contenu. La Constitution de 1958 constitue alors une révolution, et le Conseil constitutionnel s'est toujours, dans sa jurisprudence, montré très déférent vis-à-vis du Parlement mais aussi du peuple.[55] Sur le plan juridique,

50 *Vincent Auriol*, siégeant alors au Conseil constitutionnel, a tiré argument de l'absence de délai de promulgation des lois de révision, qui aux termes de l'article 89 sont 'définitive[s]' après leur adoption par référendum ou par le Congrès. Cet argument ne semble cependant pas dirimant, puisqu'il concerne la validité de la révision et non pas la possibilité de contrôler sa conformité aux dispositions encadrant la révision. 'Séance du 6 novembre 1962. Décision n° 62–20 DC, Loi référendaire relative à l'élection du Président de la République au suffrage universel direct. Incompétence pour connaître d'une loi référendaire', in: Ferdinand Mélin-Soucramanien, Bertrand Mathieu, Jean-Pierre Machelon, Dominique Rousseau, Xavier Philippe (éd.), Les grandes délibérations du Conseil constitutionnel. 1958–1986, Paris 2e éd. 2014, 113–124, à 119.

51 Décision n° 62–20 DC du 6 novembre 1962, 'Loi relative à l'*élection du Président de la République au suffrage universel direct*'. Ici la question qui se posait au Conseil était particulière dans la mesure où la procédure de l'article 89 de la Constitution relatif à la révision n'était pas suivie, puisqu'avait été utilisé l'article 11 relatif au référendum des lois (la Constitution ne précisant pas 'ordinaires' ou 'constitutionnelles'). La question qui se posait été donc double, tant sur l'aspect procédural du contrôle d'une loi de révision de la Constitution que sur l'aspect plus politique du contrôle d'une loi adoptée par référendum et donc par le peuple. Si c'est cette dernière considération que le Conseil utilise pour rejeter sa compétence, ses délibérations révèlent que l'aspect du contrôle des lois de révision était présent à l'esprit de ses membres, ceux-ci le rejetant explicitement. V. 'Séance du 6 novembre 1962. Décision n° 62–20 DC, Loi référendaire relative à l'élection du Président de la République au suffrage universel direct. Incompétence pour connaître d'une loi référendaire', in: Ferdinand Mélin-Soucramanien, Bertrand Mathieu, Jean-Pierre Machelon, Dominique Rousseau, Xavier Philippe (éd.), op. cit., 113–124.

52 Décision n° 2003–469 DC du 26 mars 2003, 'Révision constitutionnelle relative à l'organisation décentralisée de la République'.

53 *Olivier Beaud*, Pour/contre un tel contrôle en France: Un plaidoyer modéré en faveur d'un tel contrôle, 27 Cahiers du Conseil constitutionnel 2010, 43–45, *Guy Carcassonne*, Pour/contre un tel contrôle en France: Un plaidoyer résolu en faveur d'un tel contrôle sagement circonscrit, 27 Cahiers du Conseil constitutionnel 2010, 46–47.

54 Art. 6 de la Déclaration des Droits de l'Homme et du Citoyen de 1789, inspirée des théories de *Jean-Jacques Rousseau contenues* dans 'Du contrat social ou Principes du droit politique'.

55 Ce n'est pas *stricto sensu* le Conseil qui s'est montré déférent, mais ses membres. L'anthropomorphisme traduit ici une facilité de langage.

cependant, ce déclinatoire de compétence aboutit à laisser *de facto* lettre morte les limites encadrant la révision constitutionnelle.[56]

La Belgique semble de même avoir fait le choix explicite de l'absence de contrôle des révisions constitutionnelles et donc des limites à celles-ci. C'est du moins ce qu'exprime la Commission de Venise du Conseil de l'Europe dans plusieurs rapports, sans cependant citer ni dispositions constitutionnelles, ni décisions, ni travaux doctrinaux.[57] Nous n'avons, de même, pas pu corroborer l'affirmation ni par des décisions ni par des travaux de recherche.[58]

En ce qui concerne les autres États, c'est-à-dire l'Espagne, l'Estonie, la Lituanie, le Luxembourg, la Roumanie et le Portugal, l'incertitude semble régner. *Prima facie* les dispositions constitutionnelles n'interdisent ni explicitement ni implicitement de tels contrôles.[59] Les juridictions constitutionnelles de ces États ne semblent pas s'être saisies des contrôles de constitutionnalité des lois de révisions constitutionnelles, bien qu'il semble que leur système constitutionnel respectif ne semble pas interdire un tel contrôle. Les juridictions *pourraient* donc contrôler le respect des limites par les révisons, mais *choisissent* de ne pas le faire, ou n'ont jamais été confronté à de telles questions, cette dernière hypothèse semblant la plus probable.

La situation est donc, *in fine*, que sur neuf États de l'Union européenne prévoyant des limites aux révisions constitutionnelles en période de crise, aucun ne prévoit explicitement de mécanisme de contrôle. Seule la juridiction constitutionnelle allemande a utilisé sa compétence implicitement permise de contrôler les révisions constitutionnelles, et il faut noter que son mécanisme de limite des révisions en périodes de crise est très spécifique par rapport à ceux des huit autres États, l'Allemagne ne limitant que la révision totale de sa Constitution.

56 Il ne s'agit pas de dire qu'une norme, pour être juridique, doit être sanctionnée. La Constitution a une valeur obligatoire pour tous, et spécifiquement les organes chargés de l'appliquer doivent la respecter. Les limites, cependant, servent précisément à encadrer la compétence de révision dans le cas où ces organes seraient tentés de réviser la Constitution dans une certaine direction. L'existence d'un contrôle permet alors de rajouter une étape, et même possiblement de dissuader d'une révision qui irait ouvertement à l'encontre des limites posées par le texte constitutionnel.

57 Commission de Venise, Avis relatif à la révision de la Constitution de la Belgique, Avis n° 679/2012, CDL-AD (2012) 010, paragraphes 48 et 49, et Commission de Venise, Rapport sur l'amendement constitutionnel, Étude n° 469/2008, CDL-AD (2010) 001, 53 pages.

58 Cependant, il faut admettre ici que certaines références doctrinales en langue anglaise ne nous ont pas été accessibles.

59 Il faut ici reconnaître qu'à part en ce qui concerne le Luxembourg, les constitutions n'ont pas été consultées dans leur langue d'origine.

Cependant, même sans contrôle juridictionnel ces dispositions n'en sont pas moins juridiques. Il peut, au mieux, être souligné le paradoxe politique qui est de ne pas organiser de procédure de contrôle de limites posées spécifiquement pour les périodes de crises, c'est-à-dire pendant une période où politiquement la situation est la plus propice à voir s'installer un régime contraire aux valeurs portées par les constitutions, mais ce paradoxe ne limite en rien la portée juridique des limites. Les organes de révision de la constitution y sont juridiquement tenus, même dans le cas où factuellement ils s'en détachent.

Outre cette obligation juridique, il existe une utilité politique à l'existence de limites aux révisions constitutionnelles en période de crise. *Yaniv Roznai* parle d'un 'Chilling effect',[60] d'un 'effet paralysant'. Pour lui, de telles clauses permettent par leur existence d'ouvrir un débat public et politique dans le cas où il serait tenté de les amender elles-mêmes[61] par une révision à 'double détente'.[62]

3. L'Absence de Corrélation entre la Prise en Compte des Crises dans la Constitution et la Limitation des Révisions Constitutionnelles durant ces Périodes

Il n'est pas possible d'observer une corrélation, et encore moins donc une 'causalité' politique, entre la présence d'un état constitutionnel de crise et l'existence de limites au pouvoir de révision constitutionnelle pendant ces périodes de crise.

Sur les neuf États limitant les révisions constitutionnelles pendant certaines crises, les neuf présentent dans leur Constitution des états spéciaux de crise. La particularité du Luxembourg est qu'il ne présente que l'existence de période de régence comme crise, là où les autres constitutions prévoient, sous une forme ou une autre, l'existence d'état de guerre, de siège ou d'urgence. Toutefois, les dix-huit autres États prévoient tous, sous une forme ou une autre, les mêmes états d'exception, qu'il s'agisse de l'état de guerre, d'urgence, de circonstances exceptionnelles ou de vacance du chef de l'État.

La présence ou l'absence de clauses limitatives des révisions constitutionnelles en période de crise n'a donc rien d'automatique, sur le plan politique, avec l'existence de périodes spécifiques et exceptionnelles en cas de crise dans la constitution. Afin d'expliquer la présence de limites aux révisions constitutionnelles en période de

60 *Yaniv Roznai*, Unconstitutional constitutional amendments. The limits of Amendment Powers, Oxford 2017, 141.

61 *Idem.*

62 La suppression des limites avant de modifier dans un second temps les dispositions dont la révision était précédemment interdite.

crise dans une constitution, l'histoire semble plus à même de fournir des réponses. Ainsi, pour le cas français, la présence de la clause de l'article 89 de la Constitution interdisant toute révision ' lorsqu'il est porté atteinte à l'intégrité du territoire', ainsi d'ailleurs que celle de l'alinéa suivant interdisant tout modification de la 'forme républicaine du Gouvernement', est un stigmate de la Seconde Guerre mondiale et du régime de Vichy. En effet, la IIIe République avait été révisée, après l'occupation allemande et l'armistice, afin de donner tous les pouvoirs, dont celui de faire des lois constitutionnelles, au Maréchal Pétain.[63] La volonté était alors née, après la guerre, d'interdire toute révision forcée de la constitution qui abolirait la démocratie. Les articles 94 et 95 de la Constitution de 1946 reprenaient alors ces deux limites, qui sont restées dans la Constitution de 1958. La limitation faite à la révision pendant les périodes de vacance du Président obéit à une autre logique. Le Président de la République est au sein de la Ve république la 'clé de voûte'[64] des institutions. En l'absence d'un Président désigné selon la procédure normale, que cet empêchement soit temporaire ou définitif, il apparaissait aux rédacteurs impensable politiquement de réviser la Constitution.

En Allemagne, tant la limite de l'article 79 alinéa 3 de la Constitution que celle de l'article 146 semblent inspirées par les mêmes évènements. Outre l'histoire interne, il semble aussi possible que le principe de limiter les révisions constitutionnelles pendant certaines périodes ait été emprunté entre plusieurs États. Cette thèse a été développée pour les clauses d'éternité,[65] et il n'est pas impossible de penser que si des emprunts ont eu lieu en ce qui concerne le principe général de l'encadrement des révisions constitutionnelles, des emprunts similaires ont pu avoir lieu en ce qui concerne les limites circonstancielles.

Les limites aux révisions constitutionnelles en période de crise dans les États de l'Union européenne ainsi présentées, explicitées et contextualisées, il semble possible de les systématiser, du moins de tenter de les ordonner afin d'en présenter une modélisation qui permette une vision d'ensemble de la situation.

63 Loi constitutionnelle du 10 juillet 1940.

64 *Michel Debré,* Discours devant le Conseil d'État, 27 août 1958.

65 *Yaniv Roznai,* Unconstitutional Constitutional Amendments – The Migration and Success of a Constitutional Idea, 61 American Journal of Comparative Law (2013), 657–720.

III. Classification des Limites aux Révisions Constitutionnelles en Période de Crise: des Crises Institutionnelles ou Sécuritaires et des Limites Matérielles Générales ou Spécifiques

Tenter de proposer une modélisation des données précédemment évoquées nécessite d'essayer de créer des catégories plus générales dans lesquelles 'ranger' chaque exemple national. Il n'y a rien à déduire juridiquement de chacune de ces catégories, et elles ne sont que le reflet de certains droits positifs donnés à un instant donné. Il semble ainsi que, globalement, les limites aux révisions constitutionnelles en période de crise soient les seules limites spécifiques aux révisions constitutionnelles (1). On peut d'ailleurs, au sein des crises prises en compte par le droit positif, distinguer entre des crises 'institutionnelles' et des crises 'sécuritaires', les deux pouvant être prises en compte dans une constitution (2). Il s'avère que pendant les crises sécuritaires, les limites aux révisions sont en grande majorité générales, alors que pendant les crises sécuritaires elles sont aussi bien générales que spécifiques (3). Enfin, il est notable que, globalement, les limites aux révisions constitutionnelles en période de crise sont toutes des limites matérielles et non des limites procédurales (4).

1. Les Limites aux Révisions Constitutionnelles en Période de Crise comme Seules Limites Spécifiques aux Révisions Constitutionnelles

Une typologie des limites aux révisions constitutionnelles doit tout d'abord distinguer entre les limites formelles et les limites matérielles. Les premières recouvrent toutes les limites procédurales, c'est-à-dire les procédures de révision de la constitution, procédures qui peuvent être multiples selon les circonstances ou les énoncés constitutionnels révisés. Ces limites sont intrinsèques au concept de constitution formelle. Si aucune procédure de révision existe, la constitution ne peut être changée, ce qui constitue une limite infranchissable juridiquement, et si une procédure de révision existe, elle constitue alors une limite qui encadre la compétence pour réviser la constitution.[66]

66 *Richard Albert* propose ainsi un gradient de cinq formes différentes de dispositions en fonction de leur procédure d'adoption et de modification: la loi, la loi renforcée, la constitution, la constitution renforcée, et les clauses d'éternité. *Richard Albert*, Constitutional Handcuffs, 42 Arizona State Law Journal 2010, 663–715, à 670.

Les secondes limites sont les limites matérielles. Ces clauses visent à limiter la révision de la Constitution non plus dans la procédure à suivre, mais dans le fond des dispositions, précisant lesquelles peuvent faire l'objet d'une révision et, le cas échéant, les conditions dans lesquelles une telle révision est possible.

Parmi les limites matérielles aux révisions constitutionnelles, on peut distinguer les limites générales des limites spécifiques à certaines situations. Les limites générales sont celles posées par les clauses d'éternité, qui interdisent de modifier certaines dispositions spécifiques de la constitution. Les limites spécifiques interdisent quant à elles la révision de la constitution, en tout ou en partie, pendant certaines circonstances, et peuvent être résumées sous la forme 'pendant que les circonstances X se produisent, le révisions de la Constitution ou de certaines de ses disposition est impossible', comme précisé en introduction.

C'est parmi ces limites matérielles spécifiques que l'on peut distinguer les limites posées pour les périodes de crise. Il s'avère d'ailleurs que parmi les limites matérielles spécifiques, les limites en période de crises sont les seules qui ressortent, globalement, des limites posées par les constitutions des États membres de l'Union. La Grèce prévoit une interdiction totale de réviser sa Constitution dans les cinq années suivant une révision.[67] C'est cependant la seule occurrence d'une limite matérielle spécifique qui ne soit pas posée pour une circonstance de crise.[68] Dans les vingt-six autres États de l'Union, les limites matérielles sont toutes prévues pour des périodes de crise.

Aucune raison strictement juridique ne peut expliquer ce choix, qui est politique. On peut cependant avancer la raison que le choix est fait par les constituants de ne pas entraver outre mesure les compétences du pouvoir de révision de la constitution. Des limites matérielles trop rigides peuvent en effet empêcher de proposer des changements politiquement souhaités, changements qui n'iraient en outre pas contre la philosophie du régime.

2. Les Deux Types de Crises Prises en Compte: des Crises Institutionnelles et des Crises Sécuritaires

Parmi les limites matérielles spécifiques aux révisions constitutionnelles, il est donc possible de distinguer un groupe qui semble partager certains éléments, il s'agit des

67 Article 110 § 6 de la Constitution grecque.

68 L'article 284 de la Constitution portugaise peut sembler poser une limite similaire dans son premier alinéa. Son second, cependant, précise qu'il est possible de passer outre cette restriction à la majorité des quatre cinquièmes, ce qui *de facto* aboutit à seulement poser une procédure de révision renforcée dans les cinq ans qui suivent une révision.

limites posées pendant les circonstances de crise. L'observation du droit positif permet de distinguer deux grandes catégories de crise.

On trouve d'abord les crises que l'on peut qualifier d'institutionnelles. Il s'agit des périodes durant lesquelles les institutions ne fonctionnent pas normalement parce qu'elles n'arrivent pas à se mettre d'accord, ou alors parce que le titulaire d'une fonction s'est trouvé empêché de l'exercer avant que son remplaçant ne soit en capacité de le faire. Parmi les neuf États de l'Union européenne prévoyant des limites aux révisions en période de crise, trois États prévoient une interdiction de révision dans le cas où le chef de l'État légitime du point de vue du droit positif est en incapacité d'exercer sa fonction. On trouve ainsi la Belgique, la France et le Luxembourg. La France interdit toute révision constitutionnelle lorsque le Président de la République élu[69] est définitivement empêché et que de nouvelles élections doivent être organisées. La Belgique et le Luxembourg prévoient un mécanisme qui s'inscrit dans la même idée. En cas de régence, soit de décès du Roi avant que son successeur ne soit en âge de gouverner, les révisions constitutionnelles touchant au statut constitutionnel du Roi sont interdites.

On peut également distinguer une autre forme de crises, qualifiables de 'sécuritaires'. Ces crises sont caractérisées par des périodes durant lesquelles l'ordre public est gravement et durablement menacé. Du point de vue des droits fondamentaux, ce sont des périodes pendant lesquelles l'État ne peut assurer la sûreté des résidents. Les limites, cependant, ne portent en général pas sur les circonstances elles-mêmes mais sur les régimes d'exception applicables durant ces périodes. Ainsi il faut lier deux énoncés de la forme 'Pendant les évènements X, le régime d'exception R est applicable' et 'Si le régime R est appliqué, alors la Constitution ne peut être révisée'. L'interdiction de réviser la constitution est alors liée, dans ce cas, non pas tant aux évènements eux-mêmes qu'à la mise en place du régime d'exception permettant de remédier à ces évènements. La Belgique,[70] l'Espagne, l'Estonie, la Lituanie, le Portugal et la Roumanie présentent des dispositions de ce type.

La France présente également une limite aux révisions constitutionnelles en période de crise sécuritaire, sans pour autant que la crise soit liée à un état constitution-

69 Par opposition au Président intérimaire accédant automatiquement à la fonction.

70 L'article 196 de la Constitution belge mentionne les 'temps de guerre', sans en faire à part entière un régime spécifique dans le même sens que peut l'être un régime d'état d'urgence. L'article 167, § 1er, al. 2 dispose que 'Le roi [...] constate l'état de guerre', mais l'expression semble davantage désigner un état de fait qu'un régime juridique spécifique. La seule autre mention de l'état de guerre est à l'article 157, al. 1er de la Constitution qui mentionne l'existence de juridictions militaires durant cet 'état'.

nel spécifique. Les dispositions de l'article 89 alinéa 4 de la Constitution interdisent en effet la révision 'lorsqu'il est porté atteinte à l'intégrité du territoire', ce qui inclut nécessairement l'état de siège,[71] mais pas nécessairement les périodes de guerre, les périodes d'état d'urgence ou les périodes d'utilisation des 'pleins pouvoirs' de l'article 16 de la Constitution. La crise sécuritaire est ici directement liée au territoire, sans par ailleurs qu'il soit nécessaire qu'un état d'exception soit en place.

La Belgique présente, au-delà de son interdiction des révisions en périodes de guerre, une disposition interdisant la révision de la Constitution 'lorsque les Chambres se trouvent empêchées de se réunir librement sur le territoire fédéral'.[72] La situation exigée ici est plus importante que l'idée française 'd'atteinte à l'intégrité du territoire', cependant il semble que la philosophie générale derrière l'interdiction soit la même. Si les chambres sont empêchées de se réunir librement sur le territoire, c'est qu'il existe une menace pressante pesant sur ledit territoire, constituant ainsi une crise sécuritaire et justifiant aux yeux des constituants l'interdiction de révision.

La limite allemande de l'article 146 de la Constitution s'inscrit également dans cette idée de crise sécuritaire générale, mais elle en est peut-être la plus éloignée. En effet, l'article prévoit une procédure spécifique d'adoption d'une nouvelle constitution. Celle-ci doit être adoptée par le peuple, donc par référendum, mais par un peuple 'en pleine liberté de décision'. Nul doute que si le peuple n'a pas sa pleine liberté de décider de sa Constitution, c'est que l'État traverse une situation de crise sécuritaire particulière, que la violence vienne de l'intérieur ou de l'extérieur de celui-ci.

3. Les Limites en Cas de Crises Sécuritaires Majoritairement Générales, les Limites en Cas de Crises Institutionnelles Mitigées

Si l'on peut diviser les situations de crise en crises institutionnelles et en crises sécuritaires, il est également possible d'observer un niveau de subdivision supplémentaire dans les mesures limitatives de révisions durant ces deux types de crises. On peut en effet distinguer des limites totales aux révisions constitutionnelles et des limites partielles. Les limites totales interdisent toutes les révisions de la constitution, alors que les limites partielles n'interdisent que la révision de certaines dispositions.

Parmi les limites en temps de crises institutionnelles, qui sont déjà moins nombreuses que les limites sécuritaires, aucune tendance ne se dégage entre limites totales et partielles. En effet sur les trois États instituant ces limites, la France interdit toute

71 Art. 36 de la Constitution française.

72 Art. 196 de la Constitution belge.

révision en cas de vacance ou d'empêchement du Président de la République, alors que la Belgique et le Luxembourg n'interdissent que les révisions partielles des compétences et attributs du monarque en période de régence. À ce propos, il est d'ailleurs notable que le Luxembourg a vu une évolution de son encadrement. Initialement, en effet, l'article 115 de la Constitution du Luxembourg posait une interdiction totale de révision pendant les périodes de régence. Après une révision de la Constitution du 12 janvier 1998, cette interdiction est devenue partielle.

Parmi les limites en temps de crise sécuritaire, cependant, une tendance claire se dégage. Tous les États utilisant ces limites en font des limites totales. Pendant les crises sécuritaires, qu'il s'agisse d'évènements spécifiques ou de la durée d'application de régimes d'exception liés à ces états de crise, aucune révision de la constitution n'est autorisée.

L'Allemagne se retrouve cependant encore dans une position spécifique, de par la rédaction de sa clause limitant les révisions en temps de crise. En effet, l'article 146 de la Constitution interdit en période de crise la révision *totale* de la Constitution. Sa révision partielle, elle, reste permise. La possibilité de révision totale peut d'ailleurs se lire comme une exception à la limite de l'article 79 alinéa 3 qui interdit la modification des articles 1 et 20. Il nous semble cependant plus cohérent de classer ces dispositions parmi les limites totales.

En tout état de cause, même en considérant qu'ils ne posent qu'une limite partielle à la révision en période de crise sécuritaire, la tendance n'est pas infléchie. Les sept autres États instaurant des limites aux révisions en période de crise sécuritaire en font des limites totales. Ici non plus aucune raison *juridique* n'impose ce choix. On pourrait très bien imaginer de permettre les révisions pendant ces périodes mais en agrandissant le champ des clauses d'éternité. Le choix des constituants semble cependant être d'exiger une stabilité constitutionnelle totale pendant les crises sécuritaires. Ainsi, selon l'issue de la crise, soit l'État en question la surmonte et sa constitution, démocratique et libérale en l'espèce, est préservée, soit l'État ne la surmonte pas et de toute façon la constitution sera modifiée par la force des choses. Pour prendre un exemple historique, si la Constitution française de la IIIe République avait interdit toute révision lorsqu'il est porté atteinte à l'intégrité du territoire, le régime de Vichy aurait quand même existé. Il n'aurait pas pu s'inscrire dans la continuité formelle de la IIIe République, peut-être sur le plan politique la légitimité du régime aurait-elle dû être plus fortement justifiée, mais il n'empêche que factuellement, toute considération faite du contexte géopolitique dans lequel la France se trouvait, une nouvelle constitution aurait été adoptée, avec les mêmes acteurs. La façade politique aurait seulement été plus difficile à maintenir.

4. Des Limites en Période de Crise Uniquement Matérielles

Les limites aux révisions constitutionnelles ici observées l'étaient uniquement sous l'angle des limites matérielles, c'est-à-dire des limites encadrant le fond des révisions. Dans l'absolu, les périodes de crise pourraient être également mobilisées pour les limites formelles, comme des conditions spécifiques exigeant des procédures particulières. De tels énoncés constitutionnels seraient de la forme 'Pour réviser la Constitution, il faut suivre la procédure P, sauf dans les circonstances particulières X dans lesquelles il faut suivre la procédure P_2', avec X comme une situation de crise et avec P_2 comme procédure différente de la procédure P. Cette procédure peut d'ailleurs être plus ou moins contraignante, peu importe en soi tant qu'elle est différente, même si l'on imagine plus facilement, rationnellement, une procédure complexifiée en période de crise.

Cependant, dans les constitutions des États membres de l'Union européenne, les périodes de crises ne sont prises en compte que pour limiter matériellement les révisions constitutionnelles. À aucun moment les crises ne sont envisagées pour complexifier la procédure de révision. Cela peut s'expliquer parce que les crises sont perçues comme des périodes d'exception dans la vie institutionnelle des constitutions, qui ne doivent pas se pérenniser.

Conclusion

Les limites aux révisions constitutionnelles en période de crise couvrent deux types de crises, les crises politiques internes et les crises liées à la sécurité générale de l'État. C'est déjà là un élément notable, tant il aurait été imaginable de proposer d'autres limitations aux révisions constitutionnelles, même en dehors des périodes de crises.

Il appert des observations précédentes une certaine 'unité dans la diversité', pour reprendre la devise de l'Union européenne. Il n'est en effet pas possible de trouver de corrélation, et encore moins de causalité à compter que cela soit même possible, entre l'existence de limites spécifiques aux révisions constitutionnelles comme la forme du gouvernement ou le type de contrôle de constitutionnalité. De même, sur le plan historique, l'existence de ces limites ne semble pas possible à établir avec certitude de façon généralisée, chaque État ayant choisi de les introduire pour des raisons qui lui sont propres. On retrouve cependant une unité dans ces mesures, d'abord dans l'analyse de leur structure générale qui est relativement proche dans chaque État les implémentant. On retrouve ensuite une proximité géographique entre les trois seuls

États prévoyant des limites en période de crise politique, puisqu'il s'agit de la France, la Belgique et le Luxembourg.

Sur le plan de l'efficacité des limites enfin, on peut formuler plusieurs remarques. Sur le plan strictement juridique, aucune n'apparaît redondante par rapport à la procédure de révision prévue. Sur le plan strictement politique, en revanche, les limites semblent vaines au-delà d'un certain point. En effet, s'il peut exister un effet dissuasif certain rien ne peut empêcher, matériellement, la violation de l'interdiction des limites aux révisions constitutionnelles lors justement des périodes de crise, la création d'une nouvelle constitution et ainsi une révolution juridique. De ce point de vu, le droit est indéniablement soumis au fait politique de puissance.

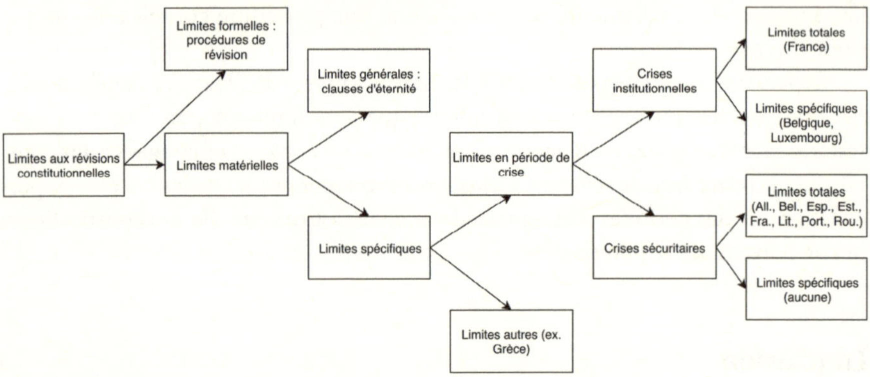

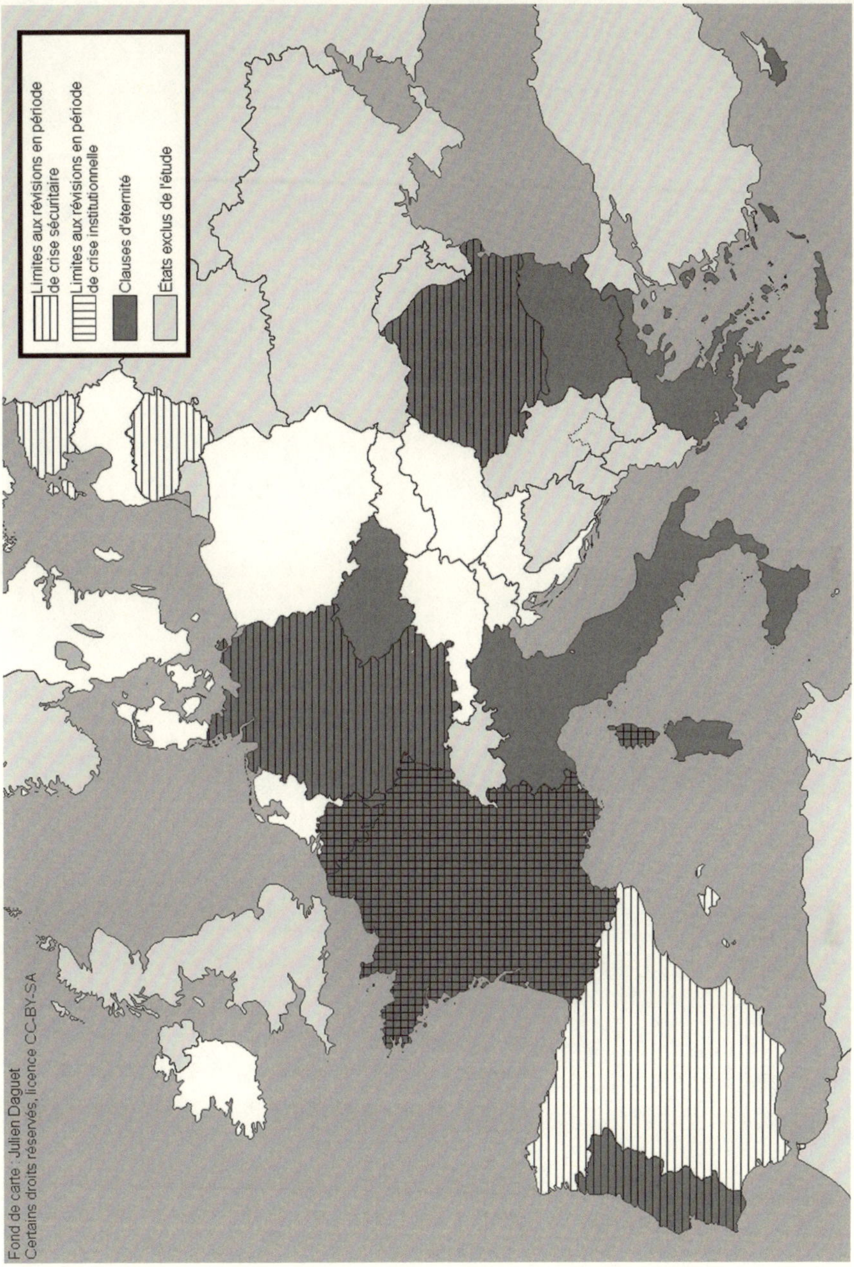
Limites aux révisions en période de crise sécuritaire
Limites aux révisions en période de crise institutionnelle
Clauses d'éternité
États exclus de l'étude
Fond de carte : Julien Daguet
Certains droits réservés, licence CC-BY-SA

Le Parlement Français et la Lutte contre le Terrorisme: une Atténuation du Déséquilibre Institutionnel de la Ve République

Audrey de Montis and Priscilla Jensel-Monge

Abstract

In the particular context of terrorism, the question of institutional and functional balances between the legislative and executive bodies is particularly acute in France. The French Parliament has reinvested its representation function, through its constitutional functions of voting the law and controlling the Government. On such a sensitive subject which confronts security and freedom, Parliament has therefore chosen to strengthen its place within the institutions and, more precisely, to assert its role as guarantor of freedoms, both in the context of its legislative mission and in controller. This analysis therefore aims to contribute to the reflection on the separation of powers in a particular context that is the fight against terrorism.

I. Préface

„Monsieur le Président du Congrès, Monsieur le Président du Sénat, Mesdames, Messieurs les Parlementaires, vous qui représentez la Nation tout entière, vous la représentez dans toutes ses sensibilités, dans toute sa diversité mais aussi dans son unité. Vous êtes les représentants d'un peuple libre qui est invincible quand il est uni et rassemblé. C'est notre bien le plus précieux et nous devons éviter surenchères et dérives, c'est aussi notre devoir de républicain. C'est en renonçant au combat que la République devait mener qu'elle a pu s'éloigner d'elle-même dans certaines circonstances; nous devons veiller qu'il n'en soit pas aujourd'hui le cadre. La République, nous voulons l'investir de toute la force nécessaire qu'appelle ce contexte nouveau de guerre, pour lui permettre d'éradiquer dans le respect de nos valeurs le terrorisme et sans rien perdre de ce que garantit l'État de droit" (*François Hollande*, Versailles, 16 novembre 2015).

En s'exprimant devant les parlementaires réunis en Congrès le 16 novembre 2015,[1] le Président de la République *François Hollande* envoie un geste symbolique fort aux représentants de la Nation. Au-delà de l'unité nationale imposée par les circonstances,

1 Au moment de la révision constitutionnelle du 23 juillet 2008, *François Hollande* avait exprimé son hostilité à l'égard de cette nouvelle faculté offerte au Président de la République par l'article 18 de la Constitution. C'est donc dans un contexte particulier que l'article 18 a révélé une autre utilité : celle de provoquer l'union nationale de toutes les sensibilités politiques autour du chef de l'État, gardien de la Constitution (art. 5 C.).

le chef de l'État en appelle à 'l'unité institutionnelle' pour lutter contre le terrorisme. Pour cela, il n'hésite pas à éveiller le sentiment d'appartenance à la représentation nationale des parlementaires.[2] Dans un contexte aux enjeux sécuritaires inédits, ce discours souligne l'importance de la présence du Parlement, aux côtés du Gouvernement et du Président de la République, pour apporter une réponse adaptée au terrorisme. Dans 'ce contexte nouveau de guerre', les pouvoirs exécutif et législatif doivent ainsi aller de concert. Mais, face à la menace, le chef de l'État rappelle aussi les risques de dérive et le cadre de la réponse qui doit être apportée, celui de l'État de droit. Dit autrement, il rappelle la nécessité de ne pas sacrifier les libertés sur le terrain de la sécurité, sauf pour la République à 's'éloigner d'elle-même'.

Le système politique de la Ve République a conduit l'institution parlementaire à subir un double encadrement juridique et politique la réduisant à n'être, *a priori*, qu'une chambre d'enregistrement. D'aucuns s'interrogent, depuis près de cinquante ans, sur son utilité.[3] Cependant, la lutte contre le terrorisme a été l'occasion pour le Parlement de se réapproprier ses fonctions essentielles de législateur et de contrôleur. Pleinement investi dans son rôle de représentant de la Nation, le Parlement a veillé de façon consécutive à s'ériger véritablement en un 'Parlement législateur' et en un 'Parlement contrôleur'. La poursuite de cet objectif de lutte contre le terrorisme permet alors de mesurer clairement l'évolution de la théorie de la séparation des pouvoirs d'une conception classique à une conception aujourd'hui plus moderne. La doctrine, théorisée notamment par Montesquieu, permettait au départ d'identifier au sein d'un État, les trois grandes 'puissances': 'la puissance législative, la puissance exécutrice des choses qui dépendent du droit des gens, et la puissance exécutrice de celles qui dépendent du droit civil'.[4] Ne pouvant être réunies dans les mêmes mains, elles étaient réparties entre plusieurs autorités qui interagissaient ensemble pour modérer le pouvoir. Or, en raison de l'apparition des partis politiques et des élections au suffrage universel, l'organe exécutif, dans les régimes parlementaires, est aujourd'hui généralement soutenu par une majorité parlementaire. Ensemble, ils créent un bloc majoritaire soudé et homogène qui absorbe la fonction législative. Dès lors, cette configuration laisse progressivement place à une nouvelle articulation, que la lutte contre le terrorisme en France a révélé : la distinction fonctionnelle entre, d'un côté, la fa-

2 Dans les deux premières phrases de l'extrait choisi, l'idée de représentation est mobilisée à trois reprises.

3 À titre d'exemple, *André Chandernagor*, Un Parlement, pour quoi faire ?, Paris, Gallimard, coll. Idées, 1967; *Pierre Birnbaum/Francis Hamon/Michel Troper*, Réinventer le Parlement, Paris, Flammarion, coll. La rose au poing, 1978.

4 *Montesquieu*, De l'esprit des lois (I), Livre XI – Chapitre VI 'De la Constitution d'Angleterre'.

culté de 'statuer' ou de 'gouverner' et de l'autre, la faculté de 'contrôler' ou 'd'empêcher'. Dans cet ordre d'idées, le fait que le Parlement renforce son positionnement au sein des institutions permet de tempérer la prééminence exécutive, qui a été désirée par les auteurs de la Constitution du 4 octobre 1958 mais qui avait conduit à un déséquilibre institutionnel majeur. Dans un contexte qui met donc les institutions et la démocratie sous pression, le Parlement a fait le choix de sortir de l'ombre.

Face à ce phénomène évolutif et insaisissable qu'est devenu le terrorisme,[5] les solutions apportées par les institutions politiques pouvaient logiquement être variées. Dans un contexte national dominé par l'émotion, une réponse constitutionnelle a immédiatement été envisagée et annoncée le 16 novembre 2015, au Congrès, par le Président de la République. Mais cette volonté de l'exécutif s'est confrontée à la résistance des parlementaires qui ont refusé d'entrer dans l'ère de la constitutionnalisation émotionnelle. En revanche, ils ont décidé d'investir pleinement le terrain législatif et celui du contrôle afin de réaffirmer leur rôle de représentant de la Nation.

En premier lieu, le Parlement a d'abord choisi de se saisir pleinement de sa fonction législative. Dans le cadre des discussions relatives à la détermination et à la prorogation de l'état d'urgence, ou plus récemment de celles relatives à la loi renforçant la sécurité intérieure, il a participé activement à la définition des instruments juridiques de la lutte contre le terrorisme. Il s'est positionné comme un garde-fou essentiel pour assurer le respect des droits et libertés et l'État de droit.

Mais c'est surtout sur le second volet, celui du contrôle, qu'il s'est démarqué et qu'il s'est positionné comme un organe incontournable dans la mise en œuvre des mesures de lutte contre le terrorisme. Au cours des débats législatifs, grâce à des initiatives déterminées de certains parlementaires, un contrôle parlementaire fort a été défini, reposant sur des outils nouveaux, en dehors des mécanismes traditionnels de contrôle déjà prévus par la Constitution et les règlements des assemblées notamment. Ainsi, le retour du 'Parlement législateur' a réveillé le 'Parlement contrôleur'. Le domaine de la lutte contre le terrorisme a donc permis à l'institution d'investir pleinement sa fonction de contrôle, à laquelle elle est désormais principalement destinée.

5 Le 'terrorisme' peine à être défini clairement par le droit. *Olivier Le Bot* rappelle dans son article que 'ni la notion de *terrorisme* ni celle d'*actes de terrorisme* ne sont définies par les nouvelles dispositions du CSI' (code de sécurité intérieure). *Olivier Le Bot*, Un état d'urgence permanent ? (loi n° 2017–1510 du 30 octobre 2017 renforçant la sécurité intérieure et la lutte contre le terrorisme), RFDA 2017, n° 6, 1115. En droit international, le terrorisme semble s'identifier grâce à trois caractéristiques : une violence organisée (et donc à l'inverse, non spontanée), justifiée par une cause politique au sens large, visant à déstabiliser un ennemi: *Dario Battistella /Franck Petiteville/Marie-Claude Smouts/Pascal Vennesson*, Dictionnaire des relations internationales, Paris, Dalloz, 3ème éd., 2012, 540.

La fonction de contrôle est en effet aux fondements du parlementarisme, elle est 'la fonction parlementaire par excellence'.[6] La révision constitutionnelle du 23 juillet 2008 s'est d'ailleurs inscrite dans cette logique en modifiant l'article 24 de la Constitution pour prévoir désormais que 'Le Parlement vote la loi. Il contrôle l'action du Gouvernement. Il évalue les politiques publiques'.

La lutte contre le terrorisme marque donc un retour en force du Parlement, ce qui permet d'affirmer que, dans cette hypothèse particulière, les équilibres institutionnels de la Ve République ont été modifiés. La logique fut la suivante : en renforçant les pouvoirs de l'exécutif et en déplaçant le curseur vers la sécurité, le Parlement a veillé, en contrepartie, à accroître ses propres pouvoirs de contrôle. Le contrôle a ainsi été envisagé comme un moyen de légitimer[7] cette période d'exception. D'une certaine manière aussi, il a permis de 'panser' un mal qui ronge les institutions, celui de la 'crise de la représentation'. En effet, les parlementaires, en déployant un arsenal d'outils de contrôle approfondi et performant, a permis, à la fois de surveiller l'action de l'organe exécutif et précisément de consolider ses décisions (et ainsi, de le légitimer comme institution capable de résoudre les difficultés) mais aussi de légitimer leur propre rôle auprès de la Nation. Ils sont concrètement parvenus à s'unir ensemble autour d'une même cause et ont cherché à renforcer les liens avec les circonscriptions respectives. L'affirmation du Parlement en la matière est mesurable puisque c'est l'initiative de certains, soutenus par tous, qui a donné un véritable élan pour bâtir de toutes pièces, un contrôle exceptionnel pour une situation qui l'était tout autant. Chaque chambre, poursuivant cet objectif, a développé un contrôle à son image, adapté à la 'culture' de chacune d'elle. De la spécificité naît ainsi la complémentarité : l'Assemblée nationale et le Sénat, grâce à leurs différences, ont permis au contrôle de la mise en œuvre des mesures de lutte contre le terrorisme d'être le plus complet possible.

En définitive, la lutte contre le terrorisme a permis au Parlement de se replacer au cœur des institutions et de réaffirmer sa fonction de représentation. Il a su démontrer, n'en déplaisent à ses détracteurs, qu'il avait encore une utilité et un rôle à jouer. Il s'est appuyé sur ses prérogatives en matière législative pour fixer des limites aux réponses apportées par l'exécutif et renforcer ses capacités de contrôle (II.). Il

6 *Philippe Lauvaux*, Le contrôle, source du régime parlementaire, priorité du régime présidentiel, Pouvoirs, 2010, n° 134, 35.

7 'Le contrôle parlementaire s'est vite imposé comme un élément de la légitimité de cette période d'exception': Rapport d'information déposé en application de l'article 145 du Règlement, par la Commission des lois constitutionnelles, de la législation et de l'administration générale de la République, sur le contrôle parlementaire de l'état d'urgence; par *Dominique Raimbourg/Jean-Frédéric Poisson*; Doc. AN n° 4281; 6 décembre 2016, 9.

les alors pleinement mises en œuvre, permettant l'émergence concrète de la 'faculté de contrôler' (III.)

II. La Réaffirmation des Fonctions du Parlement: le Parlement Législateur au Service du Parlement Contrôleur

En 1962, alors que la Constitution a tenté juridiquement d'asservir le Parlement, c'est un fait politique, le fait majoritaire, qui l'a durablement affaibli. En 2015, alors que quelques années plus tôt le constituant a cherché à rééquilibrer les pouvoirs en sa faveur, c'est un contexte de terrorisme qui lui a permis de se replacer au cœur des institutions et même de s'imposer face au législateur gouvernemental. L'acceptation de la prééminence du législateur gouvernemental dans l'adoption des mesures de lutte contre le terrorisme (1.) a alors trouvé sa contrepartie dans la mise en place d'un contrôle exceptionnel de ces mesures (2.).

1. La Préservation de l'Unité Nationale Législative: la Prééminence Admise du Législateur Gouvernemental en matière de Lutte contre le Terrorisme

Si la lutte contre le terrorisme est un enjeu majeur dans toutes les démocraties contemporaines, elle est devenue en France une priorité après les attentats de janvier 2015 qui ont visé le journal satirique Charlie Hebdo et le magasin Hyper Cacher de la Porte de Vincennes. Les institutions, et plus largement la démocratie, ont immédiatement été mises sous pression. Les pouvoirs publics ont alors cherché à apporter une réponse rapide et adéquate sans toutefois sortir du cadre de l'État de droit. Dans le discours qu'il prononce en hommage aux victimes des attentats le 13 janvier 2015 devant l'Assemblée nationale, le Premier ministre Manuel Valls exprime clairement cette idée : „À une situation exceptionnelle doivent répondre des mesures exceptionnelles. Mais je le dis avec la même force : jamais des mesures d'exception qui dérogeraient au principe du droit et des valeurs".[8] Une série de mesures ont ainsi été adoptées,[9] les principales visant à renforcer les services de renseignement. La loi sur

8 Hommage aux victimes des attentats, *J.O* AN, *Débats*, 1ère séance du 13 janvier 2015, 11–12.

9 Parmi les mesures adoptées, on peut citer la surveillance des déplacements aériens des personnes suspectées d'activités criminelles, les mesures de suivi des personnes radicalisées (mise en place d'un numéro vert), la création d'un site internet d'information du public 'stop-djihadisme', la créa-

le renseignement est alors adoptée le 24 juillet 2015.[10] Son article 19 prévoit notamment la création d'un fichier pour les personnes condamnées pour des actes de terrorisme. L'heure de l'état d'urgence n'a donc pas encore sonné. Malgré les modifications qui ont été apportées au texte et la réunion de la commission mixte paritaire, le Parlement a soutenu le Gouvernement pour lui permettre d'apporter des réponses à la menace terroriste. La marche républicaine du 11 janvier 2015, qui a réuni plus d'un million cinq cent mille personnes dont plusieurs chefs d'État et de gouvernement, s'est donc transposée sur le terrain institutionnel. L'union a donc fait la force même si les assemblées parlementaires ont pris soin de maintenir 'l'équilibre entre la sauvegarde des intérêts fondamentaux de la Nation et la protection des droits et libertés constitutionnellement garantis'.[11] Si ce texte a été adopté par une large majorité dans les deux assemblées,[12] il a ainsi fait l'objet d'une triple saisine, ce qui est suffisamment rare pour être souligné, par le Président de la République, par le Président du Sénat et par soixante députés.[13] Cela confirme la volonté des pouvoirs publics d'apporter une réponse certes forte mais conforme aux exigences de la démocratie et de l'État de droit. On relèvera également que c'est à partir de ce projet de loi que le Gouvernement a décidé de rendre publics les avis rendus par le Conseil d'État sur les projets de loi. La publication de ces avis, qui sont de précieux outils pour éclairer les débats parlementaires et informer les citoyens, à partir de cette loi symbolique sur le renseignement, confirme la volonté d'offrir une réponse juridique au terrorisme dans un cadre transparent.

Après les attentats du 13 novembre 2015, une nouvelle étape est franchie. La réponse de l'État tente ainsi de s'adapter aux mutations du terrorisme.[14] Dès le 14 no-

tion de quartiers dédiés aux détenus radicalisés dans les prisons, le renforcement du plan Vigipirate, etc.

10 Loi n° 2015–912 du 24 juillet 2015 relative au renseignement, JORF, 26 juillet 2015, 12735.

11 Saisine du Président de la République sur la loi renseignement, disponible sur le site du Conseil constitutionnel, <http://www.conseil-constitutionnel.fr/conseil-constitutionnel/francais/les-decisions/acces-par-date/decisions-depuis-1959/2015/2015–713-dc/saisine-par-president-de-la-republique.144144.html>, consulté le 20 juillet 2018.

12 En première lecture au Sénat, 229 sénateurs sur 336 votants se sont prononcés en faveur du texte. À l'Assemblée nationale, sur 561 votants, ce sont 415 députés qui ont voté pour. Après la réunion de la commission mixte paritaire, 100 députés ont voté pour sur 115 votants, alors qu'au Sénat 244 sénateurs ont voté pour sur 339 votants.

13 Décision n° 2015–713 du 23 juillet 2015, Loi relative au renseignement, JORF, 26 juillet 2015, 12751.

14 Pour un article sur les mutations du terrorisme, voir notamment *Alain Bauer*, Les mutations du terrorisme, Pouvoirs, 2016, n° 158, 97–113.

vembre, le Président de la République mobilise la loi du 3 avril 1955 et décrète l'état d'urgence sur le territoire métropolitain et en Corse.[15] Conformément à cette loi, la prorogation de l'état d'urgence au-delà de douze jours ne peut être autorisée que par la loi.[16] Après les attentats de novembre 2015, l'état d'urgence a été prorogé à six reprises. Il est donc resté en vigueur du 14 novembre 2015 au 31 octobre 2017, soit 719 jours, au point que c'est la permanence qui a caractérisé l'état d'urgence. Ce régime, créé en 1955 en réponse à une vague d'attentats perpétrés par le Front de libération nationale algérien, a par ailleurs également été modifié pour permettre l'adoption de mesures susceptibles de lutter contre ce phénomène protéiforme et en constante évolution – assignations à résidence, perquisitions administratives, fermeture des lieux de culte. L'état d'urgence a finalement été remplacé par une nouvelle loi renforçant la sécurité intérieure et la lutte contre le terrorisme[17] qui intègre dans le droit commun certaines mesures de l'état d'urgence. Ce sont donc six textes qui ont été adoptés dans le cadre de l'état d'urgence depuis novembre 2015, huit si on compte la loi sur le renseignement et la nouvelle loi anti-terroriste depuis janvier 2015.[18] On constate alors que l'union institutionnelle, souhaitée par le Président de la République devant le Congrès, a trouvé un terrain de concrétisation avec la loi puisque tous les textes ont été votés à une très large majorité à l'Assemblée nationale comme au Sénat et qu'à une seule reprise, sur le projet de loi du 21 juillet 2016 adopté dans un nouveau contexte d'attentat terroriste massif, une commission mixte paritaire a été réunie. Les clivages politiques ont ainsi été dépassés et chaque parlementaire a quitté, le temps d'un texte, sa casquette politique pour remplir pleinement sa fonction de 'représentant de la Nation tout entière'. La logique collective, c'est-à-dire la logique de groupe, s'est ainsi effacée au profit d'une posture individuelle nationale. Les groupes parlementaires n'ont donc pas absorbé les individualités, ce qui, là aussi, est suffisamment rare pour être souligné. Finalement, le Parlement a facilement accepté la préé-

15 Décret n° 2015–1475 du 14 novembre 2015 portant application de la loi n° 55–385 du 3 avril 1955, JORF, 14 novembre 2015, 21297.

16 Article 2 de la loi n° 55–385 du 3 avril 1955 relatif à l'état d'urgence, avant sa modification en novembre 2015.

17 Loi n° 2017–1510 du 30 octobre 2017 renforçant la sécurité intérieure et la lutte contre le terrorisme, JORF, 31 octobre 2017.

18 Il s'agit des textes les plus importants car d'autres textes ont également complété ces dispositifs et notamment la loi renforçant la lutte contre le crime organisé et le terrorisme, promulguée le 3 juin 2016, Loi n° 2016–731 du 3 juin 2016 renforçant la lutte contre le crime organisé, le terrorisme et leur financement et améliorant l'efficacité et les garanties de la procédure pénale, JORF, 4 juin 2016.

minence de l'exécutif et du législateur gouvernemental pour adopter les mesures nécessaires à la lutte contre le terrorisme.

Cette union législative nationale a même été poussée jusqu'à ne pas saisir le Conseil constitutionnel. Cela démontre que si le terrorisme a évolué, la posture de l'État a changé également. Le même Premier ministre, qui en appelait à ne pas déroger au 'principe du droit' le 13 janvier 2015, déclare devant le Sénat le 20 novembre 2015 : „Je suis dubitatif sur l'idée de saisir le Conseil constitutionnel car il y a toujours un risque. Si le Conseil répondait que la loi révisée est inconstitutionnelle sur un certain nombre de points, cela peut faire tomber 786 perquisitions et 150 assignations à résidence déjà faites".[19] Si le Premier ministre n'est pas constitutionnellement le gardien de la Constitution, une telle déclaration ébranle néanmoins les principes de l'État de droit. Le Premier ministre, inquiet ou conscient des inconstitutionnalités contenues dans la loi, en appelle donc à la représentation nationale pour qu'elle ne saisisse pas le Conseil constitutionnel. Dès lors, malgré les références répétées à la juridiction constitutionnelle dans les débats parlementaires, aucune loi, après celle sur le renseignement, n'a fait l'objet d'une saisine pour examiner sa constitutionnalité. La possibilité, introduite par la révision constitutionnelle du 23 juillet 2008, pour le Conseil constitutionnel d'intervenir après la promulgation de la loi, pour faire respecter les droits et libertés garantis par la Constitution, a probablement facilité cette décision.[20] Cette préférence pour la question prioritaire de constitutionnalité présentait deux avantages au moins. D'une part, c'est une voie qui offre la possibilité au juge constitutionnel de moduler ses décisions dans le temps, qui peut donner au législateur le temps d'apporter une nouvelle réponse législative. D'autre part, cela a permis d'éviter que celui-ci ne se prononce sur certaines dispositions de la loi qui ne peuvent plus être invoquées dans le cadre du contrôle a posteriori. C'est le cas de celles, imposées par le Parlement, qui introduisent d'importants pouvoirs de contrôle, en dehors des instruments déjà prévus par la Constitution et les règlements des assemblées. Ces dispositions, qui ne visent pas les droits et libertés garantis par la Constitution, sont donc placées hors de portée du juge constitutionnel.

19 *J.O* Sénat, Débats, séance du vendredi 20 novembre 2015, 11148.

20 La loi sur l'état d'urgence a fait l'objet d'un contrôle a posteriori à plusieurs reprises et le Conseil constitutionnel a censuré certaines dispositions adoptées dans le cadre de l'état d'urgence. Pour des exemples récents, voir les décisions 2017–677 QPC du 1er décembre 2017 ou 2017–684 QPC du 11 janvier 2018.

2. Le Renforcement des Pouvoirs de Contrôle du Parlement dans la Loi: le Retour du Législateur Parlementaire

Les différentes législations anti-terroristes, adoptées depuis janvier 2015, ont démontré la persistance et la force du législateur parlementaire lorsqu'il décide de mettre en œuvre les droits dont il dispose. À travers la procédure législative, et donc avec sa casquette de Parlement législateur, il a imposé au Gouvernement des mesures en matière de contrôle que ce dernier ne souhaitait pas voir introduites. Cela témoigne de deux choses. D'une part, l'idée qu'exprimait *Guy Carcassonne* selon laquelle „ce qui manque au Parlement, ce ne sont pas des pouvoirs, mais plutôt des parlementaires pour les exercer",[21] a trouvé un contre-exemple avec l'adoption de ces différentes lois. Cela démontre, avec éclat, cette vérité du Parlement aujourd'hui. D'autre part, pour être fort, celui-ci doit accepter de jouer son rôle. Dans le domaine du contrôle notamment, il est essentiel que le Parlement tout entier, et non seulement l'opposition, assume cette fonction. En imposant le contrôle parlementaire dans la loi, au-delà des clivages politiques, le Parlement législateur a montré qu'il n'avait pas disparu et qu'il pouvait s'imposer, sur le terrain législatif, face au Gouvernement.

Au moment de l'élaboration de la loi du 20 novembre 2015, qui a prorogé pour la première fois l'état d'urgence, c'est un amendement du rapporteur *Jean-Jacques Urvoas*[22] qui a permis d'introduire l'article 4–1 aux termes duquel 'L'assemblée nationale et le Sénat sont informés sans délai des mesures prises par le Gouvernement pendant l'état d'urgence. Ils peuvent requérir toute information complémentaire dans le cadre du contrôle et de l'évaluation de ces mesures'. Cette surveillance n'était pas prévue par le projet de loi initialement déposé. Cet article a donc été introduit par voie d'amendement en commission et le Gouvernement ne l'a pas remis en cause en séance. De cette manière, les pouvoirs de contrôle du Parlement ont considérablement été renforcés, en dehors des instruments classiques déjà existants. Cette disposition reconnait en effet au Parlement un pouvoir d'injonction à l'égard du Gouvernement en lui permettant de requérir toute information qu'il estime nécessaire. Par ailleurs, au cours des débats parlementaires, un amendement du groupe UDI avait été déposé pour prévoir la création d'une commission de contrôle de l'état d'urgence.[23] La commission des lois, par la voix de son rapporteur, a émis un avis défavorable en insistant sur la nécessité de ne pas 'sous-traiter le contrôle de l'exécutif' alors que les

21 Le point, 20 septembre 1997.

22 Amendement CL 1 déposé par le rapporteur *Jean-Jacques Urvoas* et voté par la commission.

23 Amendement n° 58 soutenu par *Philippe Folliot*, J.O AN, Débats, séance du 19 novembre 2015, 9602.

commissions permanentes de l'Assemblée nationale et du Sénat peuvent déjà exercer ces prérogatives.[24] À travers cette disposition, le Parlement s'est donc affirmé en véritable contre-pouvoir face au Gouvernement. S'il a donc accepté la prééminence exécutive pour lutter contre le terrorisme, jouant ainsi la carte de l'union législative, il a aussi considéré que ce pouvoir ne pouvait s'exercer sans limites, des limites qu'il a su imposer au Gouvernement et qui sont indispensables dans un État de droit.

Lors de l'élaboration du la loi du 21 juillet 2016, qui proroge l'état d'urgence pour la quatrième fois, le Parlement a de nouveau utilisé la loi pour renforcer ses pouvoirs de contrôle dans le cadre de la mise en œuvre de l'état d'urgence. Le Président de la commission des lois constitutionnelles, de la législation et de l'administration générale de la République, *Dominique Raimbourg*, a proposé une modification de l'article 4–1 par l'adjonction suivante:[25] „Les autorités administratives leur transmettent sans délai copie de tous les actes qu'elles prennent en application de la présente loi". Le secrétaire d'État chargé des relations avec le Parlement, *Jean-Marie Le Guen*, a émis un avis défavorable sur cet amendement. Il considère en effet que le contrôle parlementaire s'exerce déjà dans des conditions satisfaisantes.[26] Le Gouvernement se montre ainsi très réticent à un nouveau renforcement du contrôle parlementaire des mesures de l'état d'urgence. En dépit de cet avis défavorable du Gouvernement, l'amendement a été adopté. En imposant aux autorités administratives de rendre des comptes au Parlement, cette disposition interroge donc l'article 20 de la Constitution aux termes duquel c'est le Gouvernement qui 'dispose de l'administration'.

Cette affirmation du législateur parlementaire a pu enfin une nouvelle fois être mesurée à l'occasion de l'examen de la loi «renforçant la sécurité intérieure et la lutte contre le terrorisme». Dans le débat, les parlementaires ont insisté sur la nécessité de transposer le contrôle imposé dans le cadre de l'état d'urgence à cette nouvelle loi dans la mesure où ses quatre premiers articles sont inspirés de l'état d'urgence. Les députés souhaitaient la mise en place d'un 'contrôle particulier', voire même de 'mesures de contrôle exceptionnelles' dans le cadre de la lutte contre le terrorisme.[27] L'article 5 de cette loi est le fruit de la collaboration de l'Assemblée nationale et du Sénat. Tandis que la seconde Chambre a veillé à ce que les mesures que peuvent prendre les autorités administratives (articles 1 à 4) soient temporaires (concrètement, applicables jusqu'au 31 décembre 2020), la première Chambre a quant à elle introduit un

24 Ibid.

25 Amendement n° 84, *J.*O AN, Débats, 2ème séance du 19 juillet 2016, 5503.

26 Ibid.

27 Voir en ce sens l'intervention du député *Olivier Dussopt* sur l'amendement n° 124, 1ère séance du 27 septembre 2017, 2622.

alinéa premier dont la rédaction est sensiblement similaire à celle de l'article 4–1 de la loi du 3 avril 1955 (cf. supra). Précisément à l'Assemblée nationale, faisant part d'un 'consensus pour mettre en place un contrôle parlementaire spécifique', le rapporteur *Raphaël Gauvain* émet un avis favorable, contrairement au Gouvernement, représentée par *Jacqueline Gourault*.[28] Cette dernière considère en effet que si, sous le régime de l'état d'urgence le Parlement dispose d'un niveau d'information et de contrôle très élevé, dupliquer un tel contrôle pour des mesures administratives de droit commun n'est pas justifié et est même contraire à la séparation des pouvoirs. Il ne faut pas que le Parlement devienne un organe de contrôle permanent de chacune des décisions prises par le Gouvernement. Ce dernier invite alors les membres du Parlement à se servir des instruments dont il dispose déjà pour exercer le contrôle et propose de retenir le principe d'un rapport annuel remis par le ministre de l'intérieur, doublé de statistiques trimestrielles et d'auditions. Le Gouvernement ne souhaitait donc pas que le contrôle exceptionnel applicable sous le régime de l'état d'urgence perdure après la fin de celui-ci. Le consensus des groupes politiques, qui a altéré le fait majoritaire, a conduit à l'adoption de cet amendement et à la mise en place d'un contrôle parlementaire renforcé contre l'avis ferme du Gouvernement.[29] Face à un législateur parlementaire bien décidé à défendre le contrôle parlementaire, le Gouvernement a donc été mis en minorité.

L'absence de saisine a priori du Conseil constitutionnel a permis l'introduction de ces mesures exceptionnelles de contrôle car dans les trois hypothèses qui viennent d'être évoquées, une censure était prévisible. Celui-ci s'obstine en effet à refuser toutes mesures d'injonctions du Parlement à l'égard du Gouvernement.[30] Il persiste également à assimiler le contrôle à la sanction alors qu'à l'évidence le contrôle-sanction s'est aujourd'hui effacé au profit du contrôle-information. Par ailleurs, l'article 20 pouvait également permettre de douter de la constitutionnalité de l'obligation faite aux autorités administratives de transmettre tous les actes pris en application de ces lois, le Parlement n'étant pas en position de supériorité hiérarchique à l'égard de l'administration. À défaut d'avoir pu sanctionner ces dispositions, le Conseil constitutionnel n'est désormais plus compétent pour les déclarer inconstitutionnelles, seules les dis-

28 Voir les discussions sur l'amendement n° 124, J.O AN, Débats, 1ère séance du 27 septembre 2017, 2621–2627.

29 121 députés sur 126 votants ont voté pour cet amendement.

30 Voir notamment la décision du Conseil constitutionnel n° 2009–581 DC du 25 juin 2009, Résolution modifiant le Règlement de l'Assemblée nationale, cons. 55 et 58, JO 28 juin 2009, 10867, Rec. 120.

positions portant atteinte aux droits et libertés garantis par la Constitution étant susceptibles de faire l'objet d'une question prioritaire de constitutionnalité.

Il faut également souligner que si la lutte contre le terrorisme a permis un retour remarqué du Parlement législateur, elle a aussi permis de rappeler l'importance du Parlement dans le processus de révision de la Constitution. Là encore, celui-ci s'est affirmé face à un exécutif indécis. A la suite des attentats du 13 novembre 2015, le Président de la République utilise l'article 18 de la Constitution, révisée en 2008, pour s'adresser au Congrès et faire part de sa volonté de réviser la Constitution. Il propose alors deux mesures: la constitutionnalisation de l'état d'urgence et de la déchéance de nationalité pour les binationaux, y compris ceux qui sont nés français.[31] Le projet de loi constitutionnelle est déposé le 23 décembre 2015 sur le bureau de l'Assemblée nationale. Il reprend les annonces du Président de la République. Alors que le projet de loi constitutionnelle n'accordait pas ou peu de place au Parlement, dès la première lecture, l'Assemblée nationale va chercher à se replacer au cœur du dispositif en imposant un contrôle parlementaire de l'état d'urgence. L'Assemblée nationale a donc modifié l'article relatif à l'état d'urgence pour prévoir que 'Pendant toute la durée de l'état d'urgence, le Parlement se réunit de plein droit. L'Assemblée nationale et le Sénat sont informés sans délai des mesures prises par le Gouvernement pendant l'état d'urgence. Ils peuvent requérir toute information complémentaire dans le cadre du contrôle et de l'évaluation de ces mesures. Les règlements des assemblées prévoient les conditions dans lesquelles le Parlement contrôle la mise en œuvre de l'état d'urgence'. Lors de l'examen du texte en première lecture au Sénat, celui-ci a encore cherché à renforcer l'obligation d'informations du Parlement en prévoyant que 'l'état d'urgence est décrété en conseil des ministres, après consultation des présidents des assemblées' et surtout en introduisant un nouveau droit de contrôle en faveur du Parlement: 'Pendant la durée de l'état d'urgence, une proposition de loi ou de résolution ou un débat relatifs à l'état d'urgence sont inscrits par priorité à l'ordre du jour à l'initiative de la conférence des présidents de chaque assemblée ou d'au moins deux groupes parlementaires pendant la session ordinaire ou une session extraordinaire ou, le cas échéant, pendant une réunion de plein droit du Parlement'. Dans le même article, il a également ajouté qu'à la demande de l'Assemblée nationale ou du Sénat 'le Gouvernement leur transmet toute information complémentaire relative [aux mesures prises au titre de l'état d'urgence]'.Si ce ne sont pas ces dispositions qui sont à l'origine de l'échec du projet de loi constitutionnelle,[32] cela confirme la volonté du Par-

31 Congrès du Parlement, J.O AN, Débats, séance du 16 novembre 2015, 5–6.

32 Les deux assemblées se sont opposées sur la question de la déchéance de nationalité. L'Assemblée nationale avait modifié le projet de loi constitutionnelle en introduisant la catégorie des dé-

lement d'imposer et d'assumer sa fonction de contrôle. Au-delà, cela démontre que le Parlement peut jouer un rôle important pour lutter contre le phénomène de décision émotionnelle, essentiel notamment lorsque l'on touche au texte fondamental.[33]

Face à la détermination du Parlement, le Gouvernement n'a donc pas été en mesure d'empêcher le vote des dispositions auxquelles il était pourtant opposé. Cela témoigne ainsi de la force du Parlement dès lors qu'il en prend conscience et qu'il a la volonté de faire jouer, au-delà des clivages partisans, ses prérogatives législatives traditionnelles : droit d'amendement et vote. Cela n'a donc été rendu possible que par un réinvestissement, par chaque parlementaire, de sa fonction de représentation de la Nation. Par ailleurs, au-delà des textes, cette réaffirmation du Parlement s'est concrétisée par l'exercice d'un contrôle diversifié, profond et complémentaire entre l'Assemblée nationale et le Sénat permettant de rendre possible l'émergence d'une réelle 'faculté de contrôler', incarnée par le Parlement français, capable de faire face à la 'faculté de statuer ou de gouverner'. La lutte contre le terrorisme permet de donner une lecture moderne de la séparation des pouvoirs, plus adaptée à la réalité politique d'aujourd'hui.

III. L'Émergence Concrète de la 'Faculté de Contrôler' Incarnée par le Parlement

À partir de la proclamation de l'état d'urgence, en novembre 2015, le Parlement français s'est donc progressivement 'réveillé'. Le Gouvernement, les observateurs attentifs de la vie parlementaire et même les citoyens intéressés n'ont pu que constater le rôle primordial qu'il a assumé dans une telle situation. Cette période a été l'occasion de constater, une fois de plus mais de façon éclatante à ce moment, que, lorsque le Parlement est déterminé et qu'il se saisit des outils à sa disposition, son action est réellement mesurable car des effets concrets sont perceptibles. Définitivement, les parlementaires n'ont pas besoin de plus de pouvoirs mais simplement de certains d'entre

lits et en supprimant la condition de la double nationalité alors que le Sénat a, sur ces questions, rétabli le projet initial du Gouvernement en supprimant la référence aux délits et en imposant de nouveau la question de la double nationalité. Voir le dossier législatif sur le site de l'Assemblée nationale, <http://www.assemblee-nationale.fr/14/dossiers/protection_nation.asp>, consulté le 20 juillet 2018.

33 Pour une analyse critique de la décision du Parlement de réviser la Constitution, voir notamment *Olivier Beaud*, L'échec de la révision constitutionnelle: leçons d'un fiasco présidentiel, JP Blog, 14 avril 2016, <http://blog.juspoliticum.com/2016/04/14/lechec-de-la-revision-constitutionnelle-lecons-dun-fiasco-presidentiel/>, consulté le 20 juillet 2018.

eux qui soient motivés et décidés à exploiter pleinement tout l'arsenal déjà existant. En droit constitutionnel, 'droit politique', la volonté des acteurs politiques est déterminante. Précisément, grâce à leurs initiatives, un dispositif de contrôle étoffé, a été pleinement exploité (1). De ce fait, le Parlement s'est vu renforcé au sein des institutions ; il est alors permis de penser que l'équilibre institutionnel, en matière de lutte contre le terrorisme, a été redessiné (2).

1. Des Outils de Contrôle pleinement Exploités: un Parlement Determiné

Le terrorisme, phénomène polymorphe, nécessite une réponse, mais celle-ci, nécessairement, est difficile à apporter. Une part d'innovation est alors permise. En matière de contrôle, les parlementaires ont fait preuve d'inventivité. S'ils ont classiquement usé des outils de droit commun (1.1.), ils ont donc aussi et surtout, mis en œuvre un contrôle exceptionnel (1.2.).

1.1. *La Mobilisation Remarquée du Dispositif de Droit Commun*

Outre des débats d'organisés[34] et des questions écrites de déposées[35] – procédés relativement classiques pour recueillir des informations –, des commissions d'enquête ont également été constituées. Ces dernières, consacrées par la Constitution seulement en 2008[36] permettent elles aussi de récolter des éléments utiles mais, également, de procéder à de véritables investigations. Si des auditions sont donc bien souvent réalisées (il faut rappeler que les personnes concernées sont tenues de déférer à la convocation qui leur a été adressée et qu'elles sont tenues de déposer, sous peine de sanctions pénales)[37], il est utile de se souvenir aussi que le rapporteur dispose de prérogatives importantes comme la possibilité de se faire communiquer de nom-

34 Par exemple, le 13 janvier 2016, un débat sur l'état d'urgence et la politique pénale a été organisé à l'Assemblée nationale (J.O AN, Débats, 1ère séance du 13 janvier 2016, 129–141). Au Sénat, deux débats d'initiative sénatoriale ont été tenus, l'un le 13 janvier 2015 (sur les attaques terroristes dont la France a été victimes, J.O Sénat, Débats, séance du 13 janvier 2015, 6–15) et l'autre le 13 décembre 2017 (sur le retour des djihadistes en France, J.O Sénat, Débats, séance du 13 décembre 2017, 9583–9596).

35 Question écrite n° 3392, posée le 2 décembre 2015 à l'Assemblée nationale, disponible au lien suivant <http://questions.assemblee-nationale.fr/q14/14-3392QG.htm>, consulté le 20 juillet 2018.

36 Création d'un nouvel article 51-2 C. par la loi constitutionnelle n° 2008-724 du 23 juillet 2008.

37 Article 6 de l'ordonnance n° 58-1100 du 17 novembre 1958 relative au fonctionnement des assemblées parlementaires.

breux documents et qu'il peut exercer ses missions sur pièces et sur place. Ainsi, en décembre 2014, la première Chambre a créé une commission d'enquête 'sur la surveillance des filières et des individus djihadistes' et, en 2016, une seconde 'relative aux moyens mis en œuvre par l'État pour lutter contre le terrorisme depuis le 7 janvier 2015', à la demande de l'opposition (UMP). Au Sénat, les thèmes abordés ont été sensiblement les mêmes: organisation et moyens de la lutte contre les réseaux djihadistes en France et en Europe dès le mois d'octobre 2014 et, en février 2018, organisation et moyens des services de l'État pour faire face à l'évolution de la menace terroriste après la chute de l'État islamique. Ces doublons sont critiquables de prime abord puisqu'ils sont générateurs d'une certaine inefficacité. Toutefois, cette liberté de constitution permet à chaque chambre de conduire ses travaux en toute indépendance et selon ses propres spécificités. L'un des intérêts du bicamérisme français réside ici : de la différence naît la complémentarité.

Même si l'on se situe toujours dans un cadre classique – celui du contrôle de droit commun –, quelques éléments plus innovants ont déjà à ce stade, été développés. Ainsi, la première commission d'enquête instaurée par le Sénat en octobre 2014 a vu ses conclusions débattues en hémicycle[38] (ce qui n'est pas toujours le cas), ce qui a donné aux travaux de l'organe, une visibilité remarquée. En outre, cette même instance n'a pas hésité à mobiliser les réseaux sociaux[39] pour augmenter la diffusion de ses travaux. À l'Assemblée nationale, les travaux de la commission d'enquête relative aux moyens mis en œuvre par l'État pour lutter contre le terrorisme depuis le 7 janvier 2015 ont eu un retentissement important dans la Presse.[40] L'investissement des députés membres de cette commission est aisément mesurable: 64 réunions ont été tenues pour une durée totale de plus de 133 heures et 193 personnes ont été auditionnées. Un rapport d'information «sur le suivi de la mise en œuvre des propositions de la commission d'enquête» a été déposé par le Président de la commission d'enquête

38 J.O Sénat, Débats, séance du 12 mai 2015, 4860–4876.

39 Ainsi, la Présidente de la commission d'enquête, la sénatrice Nathalie Goulet, après avoir tenu une Conférence de presse, a répondu aux questions des internautes sur Twitter, le 8 avril 2015.

40 La Presse s'en est emparée pour plusieurs raisons. Le sujet était médiatique, des carences de l'action gouvernementale ont été soulignées mais également des limites au contrôle parlementaire étaient apparues. Plusieurs journaux dont Le Monde et 20 minutes estimaient ainsi que les travaux étaient jugés 'partisans politiquement' et que les parlementaires n'avaient qu'une connaissance limitée des sujets techniques qu'ils avaient à traiter. Voir par exemple l'article publié au lien suivant <https://www.20minutes.fr/societe/1880367-20160704-attentats-2015-questions-cles-rapport-commission-enquete-parlementaire>, consulté le 20 juillet 2018.

et le rapporteur, plusieurs mois plus tard, le 21 février 2017.[41] Les auteurs du rapport ont pu ainsi vérifier ce qu'il était advenu de leurs propositions. Pour ce faire, ils ont ainsi auditionné les ministres concernés, interrogé leurs services, opéré des déplacements sur le terrain et donné la parole aux victimes et à leurs familles. De façon pédagogique, un état de mise en œuvre des propositions examinées a été annexé. Le rapport liste les propositions qui n'ont pas été mises en œuvre, celles qui sont en cours et celles qui sont déjà en vigueur. À ce titre, les rapporteurs soulignent que certaines de leurs préconisations ont été reprises dans des projets de lois, preuve en est des liens intrinsèques entre la fonction législative et la fonction de contrôle du Parlement.[42]

Le cadre des 'missions d'information' a lui aussi été exploité pleinement. Soit elles ont été créées par la Conférence des présidents[43] (comme celle relative aux moyens de Daech, à l'Assemblée nationale), soit par les commissions permanentes elles-mêmes[44], seules[45] ou à plusieurs.[46] Là aussi, les rapports qui ont été établis ont permis à la fois de glaner de l'information mais également de proposer des mesures qui pouvaient être reprises ensuite par le législateur.

Si ces organes de travail sont donc intéressants pour dynamiser le contrôle parlementaire, leur intérêt est parfois plus limité lorsqu'ils servent des considérations politiques individuelles. Les propositions de résolutions visant à les créer n'ont alors pas réellement vocation à aboutir.[47]

41 Rapport d'information déposé en application de l'article 145–8 du Règlement, par la Commission des lois constitutionnelles, de la législation et de l'administration générale de la République ; sur le suivi de la mise en œuvre des propositions de la commission d'enquête relative aux moyens mis en œuvre par l'État pour lutter contre le terrorisme depuis le 7 janvier 2015; par *Georges Fenech/* Sébastien Pietrasanta ; Doc. AN n° 4534 ; 21 février 2017.

42 Voir par exemple, 20, 43.

43 Art. 145, al. 4 RAN ; art. X IGB Sénat.

44 Art. 145, al. 2 RAN ; art. 21, al. 1 RS et article X IGB Sénat.

45 Par exemple, mission d'information sur le désendoctrinement et le désembrigadement et la réinsertion des djihadistes en France et en Europe, créée par la commission des lois du Sénat en 2016 ; mission d'information sur la lutte contre le financement du terrorisme international créée par la commission des affaires étrangères de l'Assemblée nationale en 2018.

46 Mission d'information sur la sécurité des transports terrestres face à la menace terroriste, créée par la commission de l'aménagement du territoire et du développement durable et de la commission des lois du Sénat, en 2015.

47 À titre d'illustration, *Valérie Boyer* est à l'origine d'une proposition de résolution visant à la création d'une commission d'enquête relative au versement des allocations sociales aux djihadistes français. Proposition de résolution n° 418 tendant à la création d'une commission d'enquête relative au versement des allocations familiales aux djihadistes français, enregistrée à la présidence de l'Assemblée nationale le 22 novembre 2017.

Pour terminer et souligner l'utilisation importante des moyens de contrôle par les parlementaires, il faut noter que le Sénat a adopté une résolution européenne, «relative à la lutte contre le terrorisme et tendant à l'adoption d'un Acte pour la sécurité intérieure de l'Union européenne»[48], le 1er avril 2015 pour appeler à la rédaction d'une législation antiterroriste commune.

Enfin, le Gouvernement lui-même a cherché à informer les parlementaires en organisant une déclaration suivie d'un débat sur le fondement de l'article 50–1 de la Constitution. En effet, elle a eu lieu les 15 et 16 mars 2016 au Sénat et à l'Assemblée nationale sur 'le rapport au Parlement relatif aux conditions d'emploi des forces armées sur le territoire national pour protéger la population'.[49]

Une étape supplémentaire a encore été franchie lorsqu'il s'est agi, plus précisément de prendre acte de la décision de l'organe exécutif de proclamer l'état d'urgence, et, ultérieurement, de le proroger.[50]

1.2. *L'Utilisation Remarquable du Dispositif Exceptionnel de Contrôle*

C'est donc à compter de la discussion de la loi du 3 avril 1955 «relative à l'état d'urgence»[51], dès le 18 novembre à l'Assemblée nationale et le 19 novembre 2015 au Sénat, que les parlementaires, pour donner suite aux 'attentats de Paris' ont mis en place un contrôle exceptionnel, pour une situation exceptionnelle. Parce que les pouvoirs des autorités administratives augmentent consécutivement pour tenter d'endiguer la situation de 'péril imminent résultant d'atteintes graves à l'ordre public', le Parlement devait s'ériger en un gardien vigilant des libertés car celles-ci risquaient d'être atteintes plus facilement. Il était particulièrement bien placé pour se positionner comme tel car il assure une fonction de représentation qui est dans cette hypothèse, particulièrement mobilisée. La constitution d'un arsenal de contrôle performant est l'œuvre du seul Parlement et non du 'législateur'. En effet, pour mémoire, le Gouvernement n'avait rien envisagé dans ses différents projets de lois et surtout, au cours des discussions législatives, il s'est prononcé contre les initiatives parlemen-

48 Résolution européenne n° 88 relative à la lutte contre le terrorisme et tendant à l'adoption d'un Acte pour la sécurité intérieure de l'Union européenne, Session ordinaire 2014–2015.

49 15 mars au Sénat, 16 mars à l'Assemblée nationale.

50 Il s'agit précisément d'étudier le contrôle parlementaire en période d'état d'urgence, mis en œuvre par la loi du 3 avril 1955 relative à l'état d'urgence (successivement modifiée par les lois de prorogation) et celle du 30 octobre 2017 renforçant la sécurité intérieure et la lutte contre le terrorisme qui visait notamment à 'sortir' de l'état d'urgence.

51 Loi n° 55–385 du 3 avril 1955 relative à l'état d'urgence, Version consolidée au 27 mars 2019.

taires. Techniquement, ces derniers, grâce à leur droit d'amendement, sont donc parvenus à établir un contrôle spécifique sans le soutien de l'organe exécutif.

En novembre 2015, quelques jours après le discours du chef de l'État à Versailles, une 'obligation explicite et constante d'information et de réponse' [52] (dans un cadre temporel plutôt strict) a donc été posée (cf. supra). Dès lors, le Parlement se positionne comme un organe déterminé capable de recevoir et de traiter des données essentielles pour surveiller concrètement l'application de l'état d'urgence. En conséquence, chaque assemblée a décidé de mettre en place un suivi de l'état d'urgence, sous des formes différentes mais spécifiques à leur identité. Le Sénat, précurseur souvent en matière de contrôle, institue en premier 'un comité de suivi de l'état d'urgence', constitué de six personnes représentant toutes les sensibilités politiques. L'Assemblée nationale, plutôt sous l'emprise des groupes et du phénomène de bipolarisation, assure ce suivi grâce à un binôme au sein de la commission des lois.[53]

Lorsqu'il présente le cadre du contrôle envisagé, le 2 décembre 2015 devant la commission des lois, Jean-Jacques Urvoas précise également que des restitutions régulières des informations obtenues seront effectuées auprès des autres membres de la commission des lois en premier chef, mais également aux autres députés ainsi qu'*à* toute personne intéressée grâce à des réunions ouvertes à la presse. Depuis les réformes de la Constitution du 23 juillet 2008 et de son Règlement, le 27 mai 2009, la première Chambre a été particulièrement attentive au développement de la publicité des réunions des commissions et de leurs travaux. La publicité des travaux de ce comité de suivi s'inscrit donc dans cette tendance et également celle, plus générale, de 'l'ouverture' du Parlement à l'ensemble de la société civile.

Au cours de cette même réunion, le Président de la commission des lois de l'Assemblée nationale a ensuite indiqué qu'il allait utiliser un article qui ne l'avait jamais été là-bas jusqu'alors: l'article 5 ter de l'ordonnance du 17 novembre 1958 'relative au fonctionnement des assemblées parlementaires'.[54] Cette disposition permet à une

52 Doc. AN n° 4281, (op. cit.), 23.

53 Un député appartenant à la majorité (en l'espèce à ce moment, le Président de la commission des lois) et un député appartenant à l'opposition. Ce binôme sera instauré jusqu'à la fin de la XIVème législature.

54 'Les commissions permanentes ou spéciales et les instances permanentes créées au sein de l'une des deux assemblées parlementaires pour contrôler l'action du Gouvernement ou évaluer des politiques publiques dont le champ dépasse le domaine de compétence d'une seule commission permanente peuvent demander à l'assemblée à laquelle elles appartiennent, pour une mission déterminée et une durée n'excédant pas six mois, de leur conférer, dans les conditions et limites prévues par cet article, les prérogatives attribuées aux commissions d'enquête par l'article 6 ci-dessous…' (Souligné par nous).

commission permanente de se voir doter des pouvoirs d'une commission d'enquête pour une durée de six mois. Cette initiative est très intéressante car, pour mémoire, les pouvoirs d'une commission d'enquête sont importants et, seconde raison, parce que la commission permanente, par nature, existe donc déjà. Nul besoin alors de constituer un organe ad hoc, ce qui n'est pas toujours évident.[55] Au contraire, la commission permanente, instance nommée depuis le début de la législature, 'fonctionne' déjà. Elle a sa propre 'culture', ses membres se connaissent et ils ont développé depuis plusieurs mois des relations avec les ministres responsables des textes rentrant dans leurs champs de compétence. La décision est donc originale car elle a le mérite d'allier un instrument classique qui produit généralement des résultats intéressants et un élément plus novateur, l'article en question n'ayant donc pas encore été utilisé là-bas jusqu'alors. Elle doit beaucoup au président de la commission des lois, juriste de formation, qui a su utiliser tous les outils à disposition avant d'en envisager de nouveaux. Concrètement, la commission des lois s'est vu doter de pouvoirs d'enquête à compter du 4 décembre 2015 pour trois mois et, au 4 mars 2016, pour une nouvelle durée de trois mois.

Au Sénat, la disposition avait déjà été utilisée à deux reprises au cours de la Ve République.[56] Il y recourt donc plus naturellement dès le 10 décembre 2015. Il y avait donc a priori, moins d'innovation du côté du Palais du Luxembourg. En réalité, il a été au contraire encore plus audacieux et a clairement contribué à pousser la fonction de contrôle en période d'état d'urgence. En effet, alors que la durée maximale de détention des pouvoirs d'enquête est de six mois, la commission des lois a pu en disposer successivement pour trois périodes de six mois et une période de quatre mois. Concrètement, à chaque demande, la commission des lois changeait l'intitulé de l'objet de sa demande[57] (suivi de l'état d'urgence, suivi de la loi de prorogation d'état d'urgence etc.), étirant donc au maximum l'effet de l'article 5 ter de l'ordonnance du 17 novembre 1958.

En juillet 2016, à la suite de l'attentat perpétré à Nice et alors même qu'il avait été envisagé de mettre fin prochainement à l'état d'urgence, le contrôle parlementaire s'est

55 En plus de prendre en compte les compétences des membres de l'assemblée en question, il faut aussi respecter des équilibres entre les groupes, entre les membres d'un même groupe etc.

56 À deux reprises, le Sénat avait déjà eu recours à cette disposition: en 1997 à la demande d'une mission d'information et en 2000 à la demande de la commission des finances.

57 Le 10 décembre 2015, le 28 septembre 2016, le 19 juillet 2017 puis le 20 juillet 2017, la commission des lois du Sénat s'est donc vue dotée des attributions des commissions d'enquête, respectivement pour le suivi de l'état d'urgence, pour le suivi de la loi de prorogation de l'état d'urgence du 21 juillet 2016, du 19 décembre 2016 et du 11 juillet 2017.

considérablement enrichi. L'article 4–1 de la loi du 3 avril 1955 est de nouveau modifié pour être encore plus explicite à l'attention des autorités administratives (cf. supra). Comme l'expliquent *Dominique Raimbourg* et *Jean-Frédéric Poisson*, auteurs du rapport d'information déposé au nom de la commission des lois de l'Assemblée nationale sur le contrôle parlementaire de l'état d'urgence, trois objectifs étaient alors poursuivis:[58] il fallait, en premier lieu, continuer d'assurer un contrôle étroit dès lors que le curseur visait toujours à se déplacer de la liberté vers la sécurité. En deuxième lieu, il était nécessaire de pérenniser l'existant après la fin des pouvoirs d'investigation des commissions des lois, lesquels, par nature, étaient limités dans le temps (cf. supra). En troisième et dernier lieu, il était utile d'améliorer le contrôle qui s'était révélé lacunaire à certains égards.[59]

En définitive, l'Assemblée nationale comme le Sénat a mis à disposition des internautes une page spécialement dédiée au contrôle parlementaire de l'état d'urgence. Des données chiffrées récentes étaient régulièrement publiées, des statistiques précises étaient établies ainsi que le suivi des courriers adressés au Gouvernement, présenté. Précisément étaient ainsi connus le nombre d'assignations à résidence en vigueur, le nombre de perquisitions administratives ordonnées ou encore la prise de mesures collectives comme les interdictions de manifestation. Des comptes rendus d'auditions étaient disponibles ainsi que des rapports d'information qui permettaient de faire le point sur la mise en œuvre de l'état d'urgence. En ce sens, les rapporteurs dans les deux assemblées effectuaient régulièrement des communications. Le Parlement a fait œuvre de pédagogie en la matière et a veillé à diffuser rapidement et en continu, les informations qu'il détenait.

Cette dynamique a été prolongée en 2017, lorsqu'il a fallu sortir de l'état d'urgence, grâce à l'adoption de la loi renforçant la sécurité intérieure et la lutte contre le terrorisme. Cette loi est d'ailleurs empreinte d'un certain paradoxe, mis en lumière par *Olivier le Bot*. Alors qu'il s'agit de mettre fin à l'état d'urgence, le texte a pour objet de pérenniser certaines des mesures en vigueur durant cette période.[60] De ce fait, les parlementaires ont souhaité que des éléments du contrôle précédent soient re-

58 Doc. AN n° 4281(op. cit.), 24–25.

59 C'était notamment le cas pour les mesures prises à l'échelon déconcentré, voir Doc. AN n° 4281 (op. cit.), 24–25.

60 Pour l'auteur, 'la mise en perspective de ces deux éléments (sortir de l'état d'urgence, tout en reprenant ses dispositions) frappe d'emblée le commentateur par le paradoxe apparent qu'elle recèle: la loi réalise-t-elle réellement une sortie de l'état d'urgence en reprenant dans la législation ordinaire les dispositions qui en sont issues? N'instaure-t-elle pas au contraire, pour reprendre une expression maintes fois utilisée, un état d'*urgence permanent*?' *Olivier Le Bot*, op. cit. (note 5), 1115.

pris. En conséquence, les deux assemblées ont de nouveau mis en œuvre un contrôle concret et continu, permettant de croire, en la matière, au développement d'une véritable culture du contrôle en matière de lutte contre le terrorisme. À l'Assemblée nationale, une page Internet spéciale est alors instituée.[61] Elle contient des données chiffrées, actualisées fréquemment. Le Sénat, qui a également dédié une page spéciale à ce contrôle,[62] a décidé de créer une mission pluraliste pour l'assurer et précisément de surveiller l'application des quatre premières dispositions contestées de ce texte, pour lesquelles le Parlement 'bénéfice d'un droit d'information renforcé' (cf. supra).[63]

En conséquence, l'organe exécutif 'gouverne', l'organe législatif 'contrôle'. Il est alors possible, même à la marge et de façon exceptionnelle, de modifier les équilibres institutionnels. Les implications de ce contrôle spécifique sont nombreuses.

2. Un Équilibre Institutionnel Redessiné: un Parlement Renforcé

Le fait de s'attarder longuement sur ce contrôle parlementaire exceptionnel en en vantant l'efficacité, démontre déjà d'une part qu'il n'est pas encore 'naturel' de nos jours, et, d'autre part, qu'il doit véritablement être 'poussé' grâce à certaines initiatives déterminées.

En effet, alors qu'elle devrait être sa 'seconde nature', force est de constater que la fonction de contrôle a toujours été, pour le Parlement, depuis l'instauration de la Ve République, une 'seconde option'. Sous les deux régimes précédents, la logique était pourtant tout autre.[64] Dès le départ, les parlementaires ne se sont pas saisis du contrôle pour des raisons stratégiques mais aussi juridiques. Tandis qu'ils tentaient péniblement d'investir leur rôle de législateur face à un texte constitutionnel qui encadrait rigoureusement toutes leurs initiatives, ils négligeaient du reste leur rôle de contrôleur, alors que la Constitution était à l'inverse, silencieuse. Les seules mentions du contrôle étaient situées à l'article 48 (une séance par semaine de questions) et à l'article 49 qui détaille les différents outils relatifs à la responsabilité du Gouvernement. Ce sont

61 <http://www2.assemblee-nationale.fr/15/commissions-permanentes/commission-des-lois/controle-parlementaire-silt/controle-parlementaire-de-la-loi-renforcant-la-securite-interieure-et-la-lutte-contre-le-terrorisme/(block)/45410>, consulté le 20 juillet 2018.

62 <http://www.senat.fr/commission/loi/missions_de_controle/mission_de_controle_et_de_suivi_de_la_mise_en_oeuvre_de_la_loi_renforcant_la_securite_interieure_et_la_lutte_contre_le_terrorisme.html>, consulté le 20 juillet 2018.

63 Ibid.

64 Pour mémoire, le Parlement avait instauré un contrôle très étroit de l'ensemble du Gouvernement grâce au vote 'de l'ordre du jour' ou encore grâce au découpage des champs de compétence des commissions permanentes, nombreuses, calqués sur le périmètre des portefeuilles ministériels.

les parlementaires eux-mêmes ensuite, sous la surveillance étroite du Conseil constitutionnel, qui ont défini quelques instruments dans leurs règlements (commissions d'enquête,[65] questions).[66] Le juge, dès 1959 avait d'ailleurs considérablement réduit le contrôle parlementaire à un 'contrôle-sanction', initié simplement pour engager la responsabilité du Gouvernement.[67] En conséquence, l'analogie était faite: contrôler c'est fragiliser le Gouvernement. La majorité ne s'est alors pas saisie de cette fonction et l'opposition, alors même qu'elle le souhaitait, ne pouvait pas le développer, en raison de l'application du fait majoritaire (particulièrement à l'Assemblée nationale). Le Sénat était un peu plus attentif à cet égard. Il faut attendre la grande réforme du 23 juillet 2008 pour marquer un retour symbolique et mesurable du contrôle. En effet, l'article 24 de la Constitution la consacre désormais véritablement au côté de la fonction législative (ce qui est symbolique), et des outils sont explicitement inscrits dans le marbre (les commissions d'enquête et des débats).[68] Dès lors, en 2015, lorsque les parlementaires constituent un arsenal étoffé pour encadrer la mise en œuvre puis les prorogations de l'état d'urgence, ils se situent dans un mouvement qui tend à (re)valoriser le contrôle parlementaire. Grâce à la quantité d'informations glanées, aux statistiques réalisées disponibles facilement, aux auditions et consultations menées, le Parlement s'est positionné comme un organe incontournable de surveillance et de contrôle et qui a, de surcroît favorisé, la 'continuité' (puisqu'il assurait toujours une

65 Sur ce point, c'est l'ordonnance du 17 novembre 1958 relative au fonctionnement des assemblées parlementaires qui a consacré l'existence des 'commissions d'enquête' et des 'commissions de contrôle' (article 6).

66 En 1974, c'est avec l'accord de l'organe exécutif, par 'convention' que naît une catégorie de questions orales les questions au Gouvernement.

67 'Dans la mesure où de telles propositions tendraient à orienter ou à contrôler l'action gouvernementale, leur pratique serait contraire aux dispositions de la Constitution qui, dans son article 20, en confiant au Gouvernement la détermination et la conduite de la politique de la Nation, ne prévoit la mise en cause de la responsabilité gouvernementale devant le Parlement que dans les conditions fixées par les articles 49 et 50'. Décisions du Conseil constitutionnel n° 59-2 DC du 24 juin 1959, Règlement de l'Assemblée nationale (Rec., 58) et n° 59-3 DC du 25 juin 1959, Règlement du Sénat (Rec., 61).

68 À l'article 35 de la Constitution, il est prévu que le 'Gouvernement informe le Parlement de sa décision de faire intervenir les forces armées à l'étranger, au plus tard trois jours après le début de l'intervention. Il précise les objectifs poursuivis. Cette information peut donner lieu à un débat qui n'est suivi d'aucun vote' et à l'article 50-1, que 'Devant l'une ou l'autre des assemblées, le Gouvernement peut, de sa propre initiative ou à la demande d'un groupe parlementaire au sens de l'article 51-1, faire, sur un sujet déterminé, une déclaration qui donne lieu à débat et peut, s'il le décide, faire l'objet d'un vote sans engager sa responsabilité '. (Souligné par nous).

veille)[69] et une 'transparence'. Celle-ci tempérait justement avec une certaine opacité qui entourait l'action des autorités administratives.

Les deux assemblées se sont réellement positionnées en des institutions capables de recevoir des informations complètes et de les diffuser. Elles étaient donc à la fois des réceptacles et des relais. À l'Assemblée nationale, concrètement, les députés, lorsqu'ils rencontraient des situations délicates sur le terrain, pouvaient les faire 'remonter'. Des courriers étaient alors adressés au ministre de l'Intérieur pour approfondir la question et un suivi était ensuite effectué. La fonction de représentants de la Nation a été à la fois visible et utile.

Enfin, la constitution de cet arsenal de contrôle et sa mise en œuvre ont été l'occasion pour le Parlement de glisser d'un contrôle-information à un vrai contrôle-surveillance, substitué lui-même à un contrôle-sanction. Les parlementaires n'ont jamais souhaité fragiliser l'organe exécutif. Au contraire, ils ont soutenu son action en surveillant les mesures qui étaient prises dans un contexte si particulier. Le Gouvernement et l'ensemble de l'administration qui lui est subordonné étaient donc chargés d'informer, de s'expliquer, dans la logique anglo-saxonne de l'accountability. C'est ce type de contrôle qui devrait être au quotidien mis en œuvre et devenir naturel pour l'ensemble des acteurs de la vie politique. Alors que la situation justifiant l'intervention du Parlement était dramatique – la surveillance de l'état d'urgence pour lutter contre le terrorisme –, des aspects positifs pour la revitalisation de la démocratie et du système représentatif sont tout de même parvenus à émerger.

69 Voir par exemple, un compte rendu effectué à la commission des lois du Sénat : http://www.senat.fr/compte-rendu-commissions/20151214/lois.html#toc9. L'Assemblée nationale publiait très fréquemment les données obtenues sur une page dédiée à cet effet <http://www2.assemblee-nationale.fr/14/commissions-permanentes/commission-des-lois/controle-parlementaire-de-l-etat-d-urgence/controle-parlementaire-de-l-etat-d-urgence>, consulté le 20 juillet 2018.

'Ceci n'est pas un état d'urgence' Analysis of the Belgian Legal Framework for the Fight against Terrorism

Xavier Miny and Quentin Pironnet

Abstract

The recent wave of attacks has sparked a debate in Europe on the implementation of a so-called 'state of emergency'. Belgium has not escaped this, particularly due to the attacks in Paris on 13 November 2015 and those in Brussels on 22 March 2016. The city of Brussels also experienced exceptional circumstances from 21 to 26 November 2015. During these days the maximum level of threat was declared on the territory of the capital and its surroundings. The threat of attack was deemed 'serious and imminent' by the Belgian Coordination Unit for Threat Analysis (CUTA). However, Belgian constitutional law does not explicitly enshrine a specific provision concerning a state of emergency. While Belgian constitutional law does indeed mention a 'state of war' in Article 167 of the Constitution, there is no temporary regime which could be described as a state of emergency and which would allow a restriction of fundamental rights. The objective of the study is to present the current constitutional framework, as well as initiatives already advanced to reform. Our reflection will then focus on a critical approach to the absence of a 'state of emergency' in Belgium and the process of perpetuating exceptional counter-terrorism measures in ordinary legislation.

Introduction

Europe experienced a series of unprecedented terrorist attacks in the past five years and they have put the spotlight on the classical tensions between the concept of national security, state practices involving intrusive surveillance and the rule of law.[1] As always, the terrorist threat is a practical and important test for democracy[2] and human rights.[3]

1 *Ludovic Hennebel/Hélène Tigoudria*, Le juge, le terroriste et l'État de droit, in: *Ludovic Hennbel/Damien Vandermeersch (ed.)*, Juger le terrorisme dans l'État de droit, Brussels, Bruylant, 2009, at 61.

2 *Marc Verdussen*, Les tentations des sociétés démocratiques dans la lutte contre le terrorisme, Annuaire international des droits de l'homme, 2007, at 345; *Pierre Klein*, Le droit international à l'épreuve du terrorisme, Recueil des Cours – Collected Courses of the Hague Academy of International Law, Leiden/Boston, Brill, 2007, 209, at 411.

3 *Emilie M. Hafner-Burton/Laurence R. Helfer/Christopher J. Fariss*, Emergency and escape: explaining derogations from human rights treaties, International Organization, 2011, at 673.

Belgium is one of the most affected States by the recent wave of terrorism in Europe, as these attacks are the deadliest Belgium has experienced for decades. Furthermore, several perpetrators of the various attacks were linked to Belgium, in one way or another. Indeed, the country sadly holds the record for highest number of nationals joining Islamist armed groups per capita of any nation in Western Europe.

Before the recent wave of attacks, Belgium had been spared the horrors associated with modern terrorism for an extended period.[4] Some terrorist acts were perpetrated, but most of them were carried out in the 1980's, either by extreme left-wing terrorist groups, the Combating Communist Cells, or by a local criminal gang, the 'Brabant killers'.[5] Apart from these specific cases, and some other isolated attacks, the country remained relatively peaceful until the recent spark of terrorist assaults brought a number of failures and deficiencies to light. Following the mass-killings and bombings, Belgium was heavily criticised around the world, mostly based on its allegedly weak security policies[6] and its complex institutional structure, to the point the harshest critics dubbed the country a 'failed state'.[7] These attacks have also underlined Belgium's apparent difficulties in providing a quick response when faced with obvious, current, and imminent danger.

This paper aims to study the impact of terrorist attacks on Belgian public law. More specifically, it addresses the interactions between the fight against terrorism and the concept of a state of emergency in Belgium. It is structured in four chapters.

The recent wave of attacks has indeed sparked a debate in Europe regarding the establishment of a so-called state of emergency. However, Belgian constitutional law does not explicitly enshrine a specific provision concerning a state of emergency. While Article 167 of the Belgian Constitution does indeed mention the existence of a 'state of war', there is no temporary regime which could be described as a state of emergency and which would allow a restriction of fundamental rights or a derogation of the allocation of powers between the federal government and the federated entities

4 *Elke Devroe/Paul Ponsaers*, Terrorism and Governance Strategies in Brussels, Forensic Research & Criminology International Journal, 2018; available at <http://medcraveonline.com/FRCIJ/FRCIJ-06-00178.pdf>.

5 *Jos Vander Velpen*, De CCC – Het terrorisme en de Staat, Antwerp, EPO, 1986; *Jean Mottard/René Haquin*, Les tueries du Brabant. Enquête parlementaire sur la manière dont la lutte contre le banditisme et le terrorisme est organisée, Brussels, Complexe, 1990.

6 Belgium's security problem – No Poirots, Belgian police are flummoxed by IS, The Economist, 2 April 2016; available at <https://www.economist.com/europe/2016/04/02/no-poirots>.

7 *Tim King*, Belgium is a failed state – Brussels' nest of radicalism is just one of the failings of a divided, dysfunctional country, Politico, 12 February 2015.

in peace time (Chapter 1). In other words, security management must be deployed in accordance with the usual constitutional and legal requirements.

The events of the last five years have profoundly changed the paradigm (Chapter 2) by placing the Belgian State at the forefront of the fight (and the prevention) against terrorism. Faced with an emergency situation, but in the absence of a *sui generis* legal framework, the public authorities demonstrated pragmatism in managing the risk of armed actions, relying in part on the goodwill of the various actors who sometimes came under different levels of power in the Belgian federal structure.

The federal authorities in charge of the fight against terrorism finally acted in two ways. Firstly, in order to stem the problem immediately, they used the legal means at their disposal, which already allowed a rapid and effective response to the phenomenon (Chapter 3). At the same time, the ordinary legal environment was disrupted. Then, and in a fairly short period of time, a series of (more or less) *ad hoc* laws and regulations were adopted in order to further adapt the Belgian legislation to the particularities and importance of the contemporary terrorist threat (Chapter 4).

I. A Notable Constitutional Absence

It was during the eighteenth and nineteenth centuries that the European constitutions began to introduce the concept of state of emergency. What should be understood by 'state of emergency' or 'state of exception', is a situation in which a State, when confronted with a severe, imminent and deadly threat, directed towards the State itself and its people, responds by taking actions that would never be acceptable under normal circumstances, given the constitutional principles of that State. It refers to 'an exceptional situation of crisis or emergency which affects the whole population and constitutes a threat to the organised life of the community of which the State is composed'.[8] The state of exception is activated – generally by the government – when the State is facing a challenge so intense and so exceptional that it leads the state to derogate from its own constitutional principles, among which civil liberties and institutional rules, for the sake of self-preservation.[9] The need to declare a state of emergency may arise from situations as diverse as an armed action against the State by internal or external elements, a natural disaster, civil unrest, an epidemic or a financial or economic crisis.

8 See ECtHR, 1st July 1961, *Lawless v. Irlande case.*

9 *Kim L. Scheppele,* Law in a time of emergency: states of exception and the temptations of 9/11, University of Pennsylvania Journal of Constitutional Law, 2004, 1001, at 1004.

It could seem paradoxical to suspend the enjoyment of fundamental rights and key principles of a State in order to protect it.[10] The State, however, has the responsibility and duty to safeguard its independence, territorial integrity, continuity and to preserve the constitution. Whereas emergency management tends to focus on collective needs[11], States are granted, in limited time, space, and scope, wider powers to restore a state of a normalcy under which its citizens can fully exercise their freedoms in a democratic system. This system is considered 'a system that lays down absolute limits for the unfailing observance of certain essential human rights'.[12]

As the terrorist threat within Europe is increasing, as shown by the number of recent terrorist attacks, the debate regarding the possibility to implement such a state of emergency has been re-opened in several EU countries. The day after the coordinated terrorist attack across Paris on 13 November 2015, the French president François Hollande declared the first national state of emergency in France since 1961 and, via three decrees, activated Law No. 55–385 of 3 April 1955, which defines the contents of the emergency measures.[13] In contrast, in Belgium, such a system does not exist.[14]

Article 187 of the Constitution (former Article 130) provides that '[t]he Constitution cannot be wholly or partially suspended'.[15] Thus, it forbids in plain and intelligible language all emergency situations. For historical and philosophical reasons, the constituent feared that such mechanism would have left open the possibility of

10 *John Ferejohn/Pasquale Pasquino*, Law of exception: A typology of emergency powers, The International Journal of Constitutional Law, 2004, at 210.

11 *Jan Velaers*, Les principes généraux du droit à 'valeur constitutionnelle': des incontournables de notre ordre constitutionnel, in: Isabelle Hachez/Yves Cartuyvels/Hugues Dumont/Philippe Gérard/François Ost/Michel van de Kerchove (ed.), Les sources du droit revisitées, vol. 1 – Normes internationales et constitutionnelles, Limal, Anthemis, 2012, 530, at 559.

12 Report by the UN Special Rapporteur, Mr. Leandro Despouy, on the Question of Human Rights and State of Emergency, 23 July 1997.

13 Decrees No. 2015–1475; No. 2015–1476 and No. 2015–1478 of 14 November 2015. Cf. *Stéphanie Hennette Vauchez*, La France sous état d'urgence (14 novembre 2015–1er novembre 2017), Revue trimestrielle des droits de l'homme, 2018, at 347. See also the contributions of *Audrey de Montis* and *Priscilla Jensel-Monge* as well as of *Olivier le Bot* in this volume.

14 See *Geert Van Haegenborg/Willem, Verrijdt* De noodtoestand in het Belgische publiekrecht, Preadviezen van de Vereniging voor de Vergelijkende studie van het recht van België en Nederland, La Haye, Boom, 2016, 11 and *Sébastien Van Drooghenbroeck*, L'article 187 de la Constitution, Revue belge de Droit constitutionnel, 2006, 293.

15 Art. 187 : 'La Constitution ne peut être suspendue en tout ni en partie". See the text of the Belgian Constitution as updated following the sixth institutional reform <https://www.lachambre.be/kvvcr/pdf_sections/publications/constitution/GrondwetUK.pdf>.

abuse.[16] The words of Professors *Francis Delpérée and Marc Verdussen* encapsulate the nature of the framers concerns and set them in their wider context: the constitution is based on a 'postulat libéral de confiance'[17].

Article 187 was not included in the first draft of the Constitutional Commission. During the Congress debate of 5 February 1831, a member of Congress, *Van Snick*, proposed a constitutional clause inspired by the French author Benjamin Constant[18]: 'The constitutional powers only exist by virtue of the Constitution. They cannot, in whichever case or under whichever pretexted, suspend its action'.[19] To support this amendment, *Van Snick* referred to the French political instability where every regime violated and suspended the constitutions of its predecessors:

> "Vous le savez, messieurs, tous les pouvoirs qui se sont succédés en France ont tour à tour violé et suspendu les constitutions qui devaient régir immuablement ce pays, et ce, en invoquant chaque fois la grande loi : *Salus populi suprema lex esto*. Comme si le salut du peuple n'était pas toujours attaché à l'inflexible exécution des lois, et surtout de la loi fondomentale."[20]

Constant was still fresh in the constituent mind. In his comments on the Belgian Constitution, a former member of Congress, *Thonissen* considered the Article 187 as a guarantee against the floodgates to despotism:

> "Les ministres téméraires qui se permettent de violer la Constitution déguisent ordinairement leurs projets sous l'apparence du désir de sauver les institutions nationales, menaces, disent-ils, par la violence des passions politique. 'Ils s'écrient, dit Benjamin Constant, qu'une Constitution est une citadelle, et que, lorsqu'une citadelle est blo-

16 Cf. *Charles Huberlant*, État de siège et légalité d'exception en Belgique, in: Licéité en droit positif et références légales aux valeurs. Contribution à l'étude juridique du règlement des conflits de valeurs en droit pénal, public et international, Brussels, Bruylant, 1982, at 401.

17 *Francis Delpérée/Marc Verdussen*, Table ronde – Lutte contre le terrorisme et protection des droits fondamentaux: Belgique, Annuaire international de Justice constitutionnelle, vol. XVIII, 2003, at 96.

18 *Eric Van Hooydonck*, Het Artikel 130 van de Grondwet als algemene grondslag van het bestendigheidsbeginsel in het administratief recht, Tijdschrift voor Bestuurswetenschappen en Publiekrecht, 1992, at 81.

19 'Les pouvoirs constitutionnels n'existant que par la constitution, ils ne peuvent dans aucun cas ni sous aucun prétexte, en suspendre l'action'. For the translation, cf. *Brecht Deseure*, Constitutional precedence and the genesis of the Belgian Constitution of 1831, in: Ulrike Müßig (ed.), Reconsidering Constitutional Formation II: Decisive Constitutional Normativity – From Old Liberties to New Precedence, Cham, Springer, 2017, at 243.

20 *Emile Huyttens*, Discussions du Congrès National de Belgique 1830–1831, II, Brussels, Société typographique Belge, 1844, at 464.

> quée, la garnison peut en sortir pour disperser les assiégeants qui la bloquent'. Mais l'histoire de la France moderne répond victorieusement à ces sophismes ; elle nous a fait connaître les effets inévitables de cette étrange politique constitutionnelle qui conduit en droite ligne au despotisme. Ce n'est pas en anéantissant les formes tutélaires de la liberté et de l'ordre que les gouvernements peuvent espérer de se maintenir; ils sont déjà perdus lorsqu'il ne leur reste d'autres ressources que les mesures illégales et vexatoires".[21]

A discussion took place over its formulation[22], but the proposal was eventually approved. Article 187 became one of the few explicit cross-chapter clauses of the Belgian Constitution.[23] It should be noted that this did not go unnoticed by *Carl Schmitt* the German jurist and Nazi legal theorist, who analysed that:

> '[...] [the liberal representatives of the bourgeois Rechtsstaat] contemptuously rejected the state of exception, state of war, state of siege, etc., when they were unsatisfied with the example of the model land of bourgeois freedom, England, where indeed even the Habeas Corpus Act of 27 May 1679 is suspended during domestic unrest. The American federal constitution of 1787 provides for the possibility of a suspension of the Habeas Corpus Act in Art. 1, paragraph IX, 2. The French constitution of the 22 Frimaire VIII (Consular Constitution of 13 December 1799) contains the first example of the suspension of a "constitution". According to Art. 92, the constitution can be suspended for all areas in which armed uprising threaten the security of the state. That was termed "suspension de l'empire de la constitution". The manner of expression is explicable from the fact that one designated as the constitution only the bourgeois Rechtsstaat component (basic rights and separation of powers) [...] and identified it with the constitution in general. It is thus also the case with Art. [187] of the 1831 Belgian constitution.'[24]

21 *Jean J. Thonissen*, La Constitution belge annotée, Brussels/Paris, Bruylant/Librairie A. Marescq, 2nd edition, 1876, at 391.

22 *Emile Huyttens*, op. cit. (see note 20), at 465.

23 *Eva Brems*, Vers des clauses transversales en matière de libertés dans la Constitution belge?, Revue Trimestrielle des Droits Homme, 2007, at 351–383.

24 *Carl Schmitt*, Constitutional Theory (translated and edited by Jeffrey Seitzer), Durham/London, Duke University Press, 2008, at 156–157.

However, this excessively optimistic[25] 'peace-time' constitution[26] did not survive the passage of time.[27] On 8 August 1831, facing the invasion of Belgium by the Dutch army, *King Leopold the 1st* asked for the help of the French army without parliament's consent, even though Article 185 (former Article 121) of the Constitution forbade it.[28]

It was mainly during the two World Wars that the constitutional rules had to conform to the state of necessity. First, the 'arrêtés-lois' (legal executive orders or Decree-law) were adopted in time of war[29] and given the same legislative status as law, despite the fact that they were enacted without the assistance of the Parliamentary Assembly, which couldn't be gathered.[30] These Decree-laws were adopted by:

- *King Albert the 1st* and the de Broqueville Cabinet (during the First World War);
- *King Leopold the 3rd* and the Pierlot Cabinet (at the beginning of the Second World War);
- The Ministers meeting within the Council during the *King Leopold the 3rd's* impossibility of reigning (during the Second World War).

In its judgements *Geubelle* of 11 February 1919[31], and *Leemans* of 11 December 1944[32], the Court of Cassation recognized the legislative nature of these acts. We can read in the Court's opinions that the King, as the third branch of the legislative power, had taken the necessary legal measures required to defend the territorial and the vital interests of the Belgian Nation.

25 *Alicia Pastor y Camarasa*, Constitution et lutte antiterroriste: le cas belge, Annuaire international de Justice constitutionnelle, Vol. XXXII, 2017, 29, at 31; See also *Francis Delpérée/Marc Verdussen*, op. cit. (note 17), 91.

26 *André Buttgenbach*, L'extension des pouvoirs de l'exécutif en temps de guerre et la révision de la Constitution belge, Belgique judiciaire, 1935, at 394.

27 *Rusen Ergec*, L'état de nécessité en droit constitutionnel belge, Le nouveau droit constitutionnel, Brussels, Bruylant, 1987, 143, at 145.

28 *Yves Lejeune*, Article 185, in: Marc Verdussen (ed.), La Constitution belge – Lignes & entrelignes, Brussels, Le Cri, 2004, at 422.

29 See *Christian Behrendt*, Excursion à l'orée de la chasse gardée du juge constitutionnel – La Cour constitutionnelle et le contrôle de la constitutionnalité des arrêtés-lois de temps de guerre, des arrêtés-lois de pouvoirs extraordinaires et des décrets du Congrès national, Revue de Droit de l'ULg, 2007, at 537.

30 Voy. *Jan De Meyer*, Over de legitimiteit van de besluitwetten van de oorlogsregeringen in 1914–1918 en in 1940–1944, in: Liber Amicorum August De Schryver, minister van Staat, Gent, 1968, at 296.

31 Pasicrisie 1919, I, at 9.

32 Pasicrisie 1945, I, at 65.

Secondly, the Decree-law of 11 October 1916[33] on the state of war and the state of siege restricts essential rights, as it allows prior censorship, violation of the principle of confidentiality of correspondence, and so on. Furthermore, the Decree-Law of 12 October 1918[34] empowers the Minister of Justice to intern persons suspected of relations with the enemy.[35] Last time the Decree-law was implemented was during World War II. The state of war was declared in Belgium on 27 August 1939 and lifted on 1 June 1949. The state of siege was imposed on the Kingdom on 11 May 1940 and repealed on 25 January 1946. Furthermore, during World War II, the King was vested with extraordinary powers to issue decrees for maintaining the security of the State and public peace in conditions of war.

All these legal mechanisms gave rise to a lively and stormy debate about its compatibility with Article 187. Some argued that Article 187 only covered the hypothesis of a voluntary suspension of the Constitution[36], not the case of *force majeure*[37] or external aggressions[38]. Other authors have declared that the measures could be justified by the state of necessity.[39]According to case law and the 'advisory case-law' of the Belgian Council of State, a distinction should be made, in the context of war, between unconstitutional acts and extra-constitutional acts.[40] Moreover, the Court of Cassation referred to evidence that the constituent's intent was to grant a security right and

33 Belgian Official Gazette (hereafter B. O. G.), Arrêté-loi relatif à l'état de guerre et à l'état de siege, 15 October 1916.

34 B. O. G., 13 October 1918.

35 Doc. parl. Ch., sess. 2004–2005, 20 February 2006, No 2304/001.

36 Cf. *Francis Delpérée*, Droit constitutionnel, II, Le système constitutionnel. Les procédures de crise, Brussels, Larcier, 1989, at 460; *Louis Wodon*, Sur le rôle du Roi comme chef de l'État dans les cas de défaillances constitutionnelles, Bulletin de la Classe des lettres et des sciences politiques et sociales, 1941, 207, at 217–218.

37 *Oscar Orban*, Droit constitutionnel de la Belgique, I, Liège/Paris, H. Dessain/Giard & Brière, 1906, at 334–335.

38 *Rusen Ergec/Sandrine Watthée*, Les dérogations aux droits constitutionnels, in: Marc Verdussen/ Nicolas Bonbled (ed.), Les droits constitutionnels en Belgique: les enseignements jurisprudentiels de la Cour Constitutionnelle, du Conseil d'État et de la Cour de cassation, I, Brussels, Bruylant, 2011, 395, at 405–406.

39 See *Frédéric Dumon*, Over enkele grondwettelijke problemen gerezen tijdens de tweede wereldoorlog, Mededelingen van de koninklijke academie voor wetenschappen, letteren en schone kunsten van België, Klasse der letteren, 1983, at 47.

40 Cass., 4 March 1940, Pasicrisie, 1946, I, at 493 and the conclusion of the Attorney General Raoul Hayoit de Termicourt.

to ensure the continuity of the State.[41] This view was confirmed afterwards.[42] Therefore, the Council of State ruled that the laws granting extraordinary powers:

> 'cannot be accused of being unconstitutional because they are based on the need to safeguard, in abnormal circumstances, the existence of the Nation, even at the cost of exceptional provisions derogating from ordinary law. The state of necessity would thus justify these laws that we usually call 'extraconstitutional laws' (our translation).[43]

The situation is, however, radically different when the public institutions are unable to work as the country is occupied by a foreign force. There is no case-law to support the plea that the Constitution could be suspended in the hypothesis of either insecurity or terrorist threat.[44] However, during the 60's, proposals were made to establish a state of emergency in case of internal crisis:

> "At first sight, a not-expressly-provided-by-the-Constitution state of exception may seem unconstitutional. The exercise of powers granted by the Constitution is an obligation for the authorities it designates. These powers cannot, in principle, be exercised in any other way than that provided for in the Constitution; but that is to give too much importance to the formal aspect of things and to sacrifice the spirit of the Constitution. Above all, it wants to safeguard the survival and permanence of the State, the supreme guarantee of the common good and safeguarding the general interest" (our translation).[45]

41 Cass., February 11, 1919, Pasicrisie, 1919, I, at 9.

42 Cass., 10 January 1950, Pasicrisie, 1950, I, at 304; Cass., 8 January 1952, Pasicrisie, 1952, I, at 244.

43 'Ces lois ne peuvent [...] être taxées d'inconstitutionnalité parce qu'elles ont trouvé leur fondement dans la nécessité de sauvegarder, dans des circonstances anormales, l'existence de la Nation, même au prix de dispositions exceptionnelles et dérogatoires au droit commun. L'état de nécessité justifierait ainsi ces lois que l'on a coutume de qualifier 'lois extraconstitutionneles''. Draft law on the attribution to the King of extraordinary powers in time of war, Opinion of the Council of State (9 June 1952), Doc. Parl., Ch. repr., sess. 1952–1953, 4 February 1953, at 11.

44 *Nicolas Bonbled*, Les aspects contemporains de la continuité de l'État: l'exception, l'urgence et la transition, Journal des Tribunaux, 2014, at 643.

45 'A première vue, un état d'exception, non expressément prévu par la Constitution, peut paraître anticonstitutionnel. L'exercice des pouvoirs attribués par la Constitution est une obligation pour les autorités qu'elle désigne. Ces pouvoirs ne peuvent, en principe, pas être exercés d'une autre manière que celle que prévoit la Constitution. Mais, c'est là s'attacher trop à l'aspect formel des choses et y sacrifier l'esprit de la Constitution. Celui-ci veut, par-dessus tout, sauvegarder la survivance et la permanence de l'État, garantie suprême du bien commun et sauvegarde de l'intérêt général.' Law proposal on installation of a state of emergency, Doc. parl., Senate, 31 January 1962, 105, at 7.

The aforementioned proposal ignores one of the fundamental rules of the Constitution and can be criticized on many counts, especially since the establishment of the Constitutional Court.[46]

Under our constitutional system, in all circumstances, including the fight against terrorism, the public institutions must keep functioning normally and the exercise of fundamental human rights and freedoms can only be limited within the constraints of ordinary law.[47]

In our mind, a real emergency state could only be implemented by following the constitutional amendment procedure provided by Article 195 of the Constitution, which is particularly cumbersome.[48] Moreover, Article 187 is currently not declared as revisable.[49]

For lack of better tools, however, the parliament may, in accordance with Article 105, have recourse to the 'special powers' laws[50], delegate specific and wide powers to the executive[51], including the ability to amend the law with the *a posteriori* concurrence of the Parliament. That being said, on the one side, this 'special powers' mechanism was never used in the matter of security breach and cannot be confused with a state of emergency. On the other side, when used, it does not relieve the executive power from its obligation to respect the fundamental rights.

46 See *Sébastien Van Drooghenbroeck*, op. cit. (note 14), at 293–297; *Walter Ganshof van der Meersch*, Sécurité de l'État et liberté individuelle en droit comparé, in: Rapports généraux, Ve congrès international de droit comparé, Brussels, Bruylant, 1960, at 693; contra: *Rusen Ergec/Sandrine Wathée*, op. cit. (note 38), at 406.

47 *Francis Delpérée/Marc Verdussen*, op. cit. (note 17), at 98; *Olivier Mouton*, Pourquoi l'état d'urgence est impossible en Belgique, Le Vif, 27 November 2015 available at < https://www.levif.be/actualite/belgique/pourquoi-l-etat-d-urgence-est-impossible-en-belgique/article-normal-436991.html>.

48 Firstly, Parliament and the King must adopt a list of constitutional provisions, which are declared revisable. Then the Parliament is dissolved. After the elections, the freshly composed Parliament has the power to modify the constitutional provisions, which were declared open to revision, and only them. For this last step, two thirds of the members of each Chamber of Parliament ought to be present and two thirds of the present members must approve the amendment.

49 Declaration of revision of the Constitution of 20 May 2019, B. O. G., 23 May 2019.

50 *Yves Lejeune*, Droit constitutionnel belge: fondements et institutions, Brussels, Larcier, 2nd ed., 2014, § 58.

51 Opinion of the Council of State, Doc. parl., Ch., sess. 95–96, 7 June 1996, No 609/1.

It can be noted from the aforementioned paragraphs that the national Constitution is more protective than international conventions[52], which provide, in a controlled manner, derogation provisions, particularly Article 4 of the International Covenant on Civil and Political Rights and Article 15 of the European Convention on Human Rights. The two articles are similar, as both allow State Parties to 'take measures derogating from their obligations under the present Covenant to the extent strictly required by the exigencies of the situation.'[53] Both conventions provide a list of rights, that can never be derogated from, even in cases of emergencies.

Significant and thoughtful constitutional reform proposals have been made on the basis of these international conventions over the past ten years, in light of the new threat posed by terrorist groups.[54]

II. A Fundamental Change of Paradigm – A Clear and Present Terrorist Danger

One of the most significant issues that has had an impact on the coexistence and security of the citizens in Europe and Belgium is the threat of international terrorism. Shortly after the 9/11 attacks, fingers were pointed at the lack of a provision for a 'state of emergency' in Belgium constitutional law. After the Paris attacks, almost fifteen years later, this issue has been taken over by the politicians, who wish to take the current emergency measures a step further. Such measures must indeed nevertheless be taken in accordance with both the fundamental freedoms of the Kingdom[55] and the federal structure of the country.

52 *Nicolas Bonbled/Céline Romainville,* États d'exceptions et crises humaines ambigües: débat recent autour du terrorisme et des nouvelles formes de crise, Annuaire international de justice constitutionnelle, 2008, at 429.

53 ECtHR, Grand Chamber, 19 February 2009, *A. e.a v. the United Kingdom case.*

54 *Stefan Sottiaux,* Terrorism and the Limitation of Rights: The ECHR and the US Constitution, Oxford/Portland, Hart Publishing, 2008, at 30.

55 *Greta De Braeckeleer/Laurine Mys/Katja Van Aelst/Paulien Vande Velde-Van Rumst, Jurgen Goossens/Sien Devriendt,* Nood aan noodtoestand in België?, Belgian Constitutional Law Blog, 21 February, 2017; available at <https://belconlawblog.com/2017/02/21/nood-aan-noodtoestand-belgie/>.

1. 2006 – A Recent Concrete Proposal

Based on the case law of the European Court of Human Rights in relation to terrorism[56], legal experts who participated in a parliamentary working group specialising in fundamental rights suggested the inclusion of a derogatory clause.[57] Such a provision would have allowed the adoption of exceptional measures within a clearly defined constitutional framework, which would strengthen the principles of the rule of law.[58] This recommendation has not been acted so far.

2. The State of Emergency back on the Table

Even when the federal government proudly announced that the establishment of a state of emergency was not on the agenda[59], there were serious discussions about the opportunity to implement state of emergency powers[60], mainly after the Paris attacks.[61] The 'most far-reaching security measures'[62] were the security plans of the Flemish political party N-VA, presented in September 2016, as 'Niveau V. Verandering voor veiligheid' ('Niveau V. Change for security). This security plan project provides a state of emergency declared by the National Security Council. This situation would allow preventive detentions and the establishment of separate courts dealing

56 ECtHR, 26 May 1993, *Brannigan and McBride v. the United Kingdom case.*

57 Doc. parl., Ch., sess. 2004–2005, 20 February 2006, No 2304/001. Cf. *Eva Brems*, op. cit. (note 23), at 367–368.

58 Venice Commission, Les pouvoirs d'exception, Strasbourg, Sciences et technique de la démocratie, no 12, CDL-STD(1995)02; cf. also *John Ferejohn/Pasquale Pasquino*, op. cit. (note 10), at 158–173 and *Dominic McGoldrick*, The Interface of public emergency power and international law, International Journal of Constitutional Law, 2004, 380.

59 See *Vincent Souty*, Les dérogations en cas de circonstances exceptionnelles: un régime en demi-teinte, Revue trimestrielle des droits de l'homme, 2017, at 90. On 22 March 2016, the Minister of the Interior stated to RTBF that he did not want to think about the special powers Acts: "Ce n'est pas dans la culture de notre démocratie. Je ne sais pas ce que ça rapporte. On a pris beaucoup de mesures [...]. Je pense qu'on doit rester cool, vraiment maîtriser la situation et voir si on doit ajouter des mesures"; available at <https://www.rtbf.be/info/dossier/explosions-a-brussels-airport/detail_jan-jambon-la-volonte-de-revenir-au-plus-vite-a-une-vie-normale?id=9249331>.

60 *Lode Vanoost*, Noodtoestand in Frankrijk, kan het in België ook?, DeWereldMorgen.be, 17 November 2015.

61 *Martin Buxant*, Le gouvernement étudie la possibilité d'un couvre-feu en cas d'état d'urgence, L'Echo, 21 January 2016, 4.

62 *Patricia Popelier/Werner Vandenbruwaene*, Niveau V. Verandering voor veiligheid (Level V. Change for safety), Osservatorio sulle fonti/ Observatory on Sources of Law, January 2017; available at <https://www.osservatoriosullefonti.it/rubriche/sources-of-law-in-the-european-union-member-states/belgium>).

with terrorism cases. The National Security Council and municipalities would be able to deploy troops, to forbid public meetings, to control internal borders, to give house arrest, to filter social media and put websites offline. This state of emergency would be endorsed by the Parliament within five days and be valid for three months.

According to the N-VA, this plan still remains within the limits of the Constitution, according to the Supreme Court's case law on state of war. Referring to Attorney general *Hayoit de Termicourt's* reasoning[63], the Flemish nationalists argued that the necessity to safeguard national sovereignty and the continuity of government power have supra-constitutional value, allowing for extra-constitutional measures when State's institutions or the country's existence as a civil community are imperilled.

However, many scholars pointed out the legal weakness of such reasoning, regarding Article 187 and Article 146[64] of the Constitution[65].

When asked specifically about this issue, the Belgian Prime Minister answered that:

> "it can be necessary, in certain cases and in accordance with the fundamental principles, for the Government, for a limited period and under the control of the Parliament, to take a number of measures to ensure the strengthening of security public" (our translation)[66].

He added that:

> "To be honest, I'm not very inspired by the French model because I think it is going much too far. The notion of administrative search is, for example, a model that does not made me enthusiastic. I hope that the Government can continue the work undertaken since the end of last year, in other words: to try to see how we can adjust our legislative and regulatory framework, if it appears that it is necessary, in order to successfully combine the necessity of guaranteeing the right to security in a time when

63 Pasicrisie, 1946, at 493.

64 Art. 146 : 'Nul tribunal, nulle juridiction contentieuse ne peut être établi qu'en vertu d'une loi. Il ne peut être créé de commissions ni de tribunaux extraordinaires, sous quelque dénomination que ce soit'; 'A court and a body capable of rendering judgment can only be established by virtue of a law. No extraordinary courts or commissions may be created, no matter under which designation."

65 *Patricia Popelier/Werner Vandenbruwaene*, op. cit. (note 62).

66 '[...] il peut être nécessaire, dans certains cas et de manière cadrée au regard des principes fondamentaux, que le Gouvernement, pour une période limitée et sous le contrôle du Parlement, puisse prendre un certain nombre de mesures afin de garantir le renforcement de la sécurité publique'. Question No. 8839 by *Raoul Hedebouw*, MP, 26 January 2016, sess. 2015–2016, CRIV 54 COM 317, at 19.

> we face new types of threat, while guaranteeing these fundamental rights and personal freedoms we hold dear" (our translation)[67].

3. A Pragmatic Response to Major Emergencies

From 21 November to 25 November 2015, the federal government of Belgium imposed a security lockdown on Brussels due to information about potential terrorist attacks in the wake of the series of coordinated terrorist attacks in Paris by the Islamic State. During this period, the threat level was increased by the Coordination Unit for Threat Assessment (CUTA) to 4 (on a scale of four) for the Brussels region. As we will explain later, CUTA has been, since 2006, the official Belgian public authority that coordinates the police and intelligence services and that assesses whether Belgium is a target of terrorist and extremist threats.

Following a National Security Council to which the Communities (federated entities) chiefs of governments were invited, the Prime Minister took some measures and recommended others. The Brussels subway, public transport, schools, universities and restaurants were closed and some events, such as football games, were cancelled. The communes and provinces were invited to cancel events in their territories. The communication was rather confused and, as the journalist *Bertrand Henne* said:

> 'In a few days, Belgium and especially Brussels' reputation has been tainted as ever. In a nutshell, the federal government has not been up to the task, and the regions and communities stayed in the background'(our translation).[68]

It must be acknowledged that the institutional structure of Belgium does not help the centralisation of capacity decisions. Belgium is a federal State composed of two kinds of federated entities: the Regions and the Communities. The Federal authority, the Communities and the Regions are on an equal footing but have powers and responsibilities for different fields. At a lower level, the provinces are supervised by

67 'Pour tout vous dire, je ne suis pas très inspiré par le modèle français car je trouve qu'il va beaucoup trop loin. La notion de perquisition administrative est par exemple un modèle qui ne m'enthousiasme pas beaucoup. Je souhaite que le Gouvernement puisse poursuivre le travail entrepris depuis la fin de l'an dernier, c'est-à-dire tenter de voir de quelle manière on peut ajuster notre cadre législatif et réglementaire, s'il apparaît que c'est nécessaire, afin de réussir à conjuguer cette nécessité de garantir le droit à la sécurité dans un moment où nous sommes confrontés à de nouveaux types de menace, tout en garantissant ces droits fondamentaux et ces libertés personnelles qui nous tiennent à coeur'.

68 *Bertrand Henne*, Les Coulisses des Pouvoirs – 13 Novembre: la Belgique à la limite, Rtbf, 14 November 2016.

higher government authorities, in the context of the federal, community or regional powers. At the bottom of the pyramid, we find the communes (or municipalities).

Among other things, the federal government is responsible for for security, home affairs and justice. It is hard to get a centrally-controlled decision-making because of this fragmented authority. Moreover, the Brussels region is comprised of 19 municipalities, each with its own mayor and institutions. At the same time, these 19 municipalities are covered by six different police zones. Summing up, the federal structure of the country and the multitude of decision-making layers easily leads to paralysis. That is also the case in fighting terrorism. "A coherent anti-terrorism policy goes against the federal logic of Belgium" (our translation)[69], said *Marc Hooghe*, professor at the KUL[70].

Inevitably, this has prompted the question of whether public authorities could react in case of direct terrorist threat.

III. A Reaction by an Ordinary Legislative Arsenal[71]

Despite the absence of an institutionalised state of emergency – or state of exception – in Belgium, the Belgian government had to face a scourge of an inconsiderate scale. On 24 May 2014, the date of the attack on the Jewish Museum in Brussels, Belgium adapted, via an ordinary legislative arsenal, to the new terrorist threat.

In a brief retrospective of the resources deployed over the last five years, the aim of this Chapter will be to assess the impact, in practice, of the absence of a state of emergency in Belgium. Of course, it is not for us to evaluate the relevance of the action of the government of the Kingdom during these difficult moments but to examine the general structure of action in the field of the fight against terrorism.

Firstly, it is important to state that, following the attacks in Brussels on 22 March 2016, a parliamentary inquiry committee was set up to clarify the way in which these tragic events took place and were dealt with, as well as to reveal any political responsibilities. This committee, which has worked for several months, benefited from a significant asset, namely the access to a series of confidential documents.[72] For this particular reason, we shall take the liberty of referring to the committee's intermediate reports.

69 'Een samenhangend antiterreurbeleid gaat in tegen de federale logica van België'.

70 *Caspar Cillekens*, De tragiek van Belgistan, De Limburger, 3 April 2016.

71 From this page, all quotations have been translated by us from French or Dutch.

72 Indeed, according to art. 4 of the statutes of the inquiry committee, the latter 'may hear any person whom it deems necessary to bring before it and may have at its disposal all the documents it deems necessary for the performance of its duties'. Furthermore, it 'may at any time decide to

The Belgian legal system does not lack the legal means to deal with an emergency situation, such as with terrorist threats. The Royal Regulation of 16 February 2006 defines the emergency situation (Article 6, § 2) as follows:

> 'any event which causes or is likely to cause harmful consequences for social life, such as a serious disorder of public security, a serious threat to the life or health of individuals and/or to important material interests, and which requires the coordination of disciplines in order to eliminate the threat or limit the harmful consequences'.[73]

Because of this emergency, several reactions have been put in place following the attacks of recent years, especially in Paris and Brussels. We will discuss successively the emergency plans (1.), the role of the Coordination Unit for Threat Analysis (CUTA) (2.) and the Operation Vigilant Guardian (3.).

1. Emergency Plans

March 22 was the first time one was able to count on the existence of emergency planning. Emergency planning in Belgium consists of three types of plans: multidisciplinary emergency and response plans, developed by local authorities, monodisciplinary response plans, which local authorities checked against certain criteria, and internal emergency plans of companies and institutions at risk, that local authorities take into account in developing their own emergency planning.

The whole has four phases.[74] Phases one and two are coordinated at the municipal (local) level, while phase three involves coordination by the governor at the provincial level. Phase four, used during the terrorist attacks, is coordinated by the Minister of Home Affairs at the federal level.[75] The national alert or 'phase four alert' is

meet in closed session" (art. 7). Cf. Proposal to set up a parliamentary inquiry committee to examine the circumstances leading to the terrorist attacks of 22 March 2016 at Brussels National Airport and the Maelbeek underground station in Brussels, including the development and management of the fight against radicalism and the terrorist threat, Doc. parl., Ch., sess. 2015–2016, 11 April 2016, No. 54 1752/001, 11–12.

73 Royal Regulation of 16 February 2006 on emergency and intervention plans, B. O. G., 15 March 2006.

74 Royal Regulation of 31 January 2003 establishing the emergency plan for events and crisis situations requiring coordination or management at national level, B. O. G., 21 February 2003.

75 Parliamentary inquiry to examine the circumstances leading to the terrorist attacks of 22 March 2016 at Brussels National Airport and Maelbeek underground station in Brussels, including the development and management of the fight against radicalism and the terrorist threat – Intermediate and provisional report on the 'assistance and relief' aspect, Doc. parl., Ch., sess. 2015–2016, 3 August 2016, No. 54 1752/006, 27.

triggered by the Minister of Home Affairs and may be preceded by an early warning phase (Crisis Centre).[76]

In addition to these emergency plans, there may be other emergency and contingency plans, specific to particular areas, which are, in principle, confidential. Thus, in the documents given as a confidential document to the members of the parliamentary inquiry committee relating to the attacks in Brussels were the emergency plan for Zaventem Airport as well as the emergency plan of the STIB (Brussels public transport company).

The committee's intermediate report recounts the first moments following the attack in Brussels:

> 'On March 22, 2016, the federal phase took time to begin. Very quickly (after a few minutes), it had already become clear on the ground that the explosions in Zaventem were the work of terrorists.
> Very quickly a series of measures were taken from the Crisis Centre. At 08:45, the CUTA announces the passage to threat level 4 for the whole territory, with particular attention for international stations, regional airports, all means of public transport, nuclear power stations and the port of Antwerp. Notification to all intended recipients is made by fax at 09:04.
> Following this evaluation, a number of specific actions were taken at the coordination meeting that started in the meantime.
> The federal crisis management phase was only triggered at 09:03, and the 'coordination meeting' became a 'crisis unit' in accordance with the Royal Regulation of 31 January 2003. This decision was not clear on the ground and some witnesses stated that they were aware of the activation of this federal phase before that time. In the meantime, several meetings of the National Security Council have been held with the aim of taking general measures within the framework of threat level 4'[77]

Despite this apparent preparation, the analysis of the inquiry committee was not very optimistic: 'distressing observation on information management: lack of over-

76 Parliamentary inquiry to examine the circumstances leading to the terrorist attacks of 22 March 2016 at Brussels National Airport and Maelbeek underground station in Brussels, including the development and management of the fight against radicalism and the terrorist threat – Intermediate and provisional report on the 'assistance and relief' aspect, Doc. parl., Ch., sess. 2015–2016, 3 August 2016, No. 54 1752/006, 27.

77 Parliamentary inquiry to examine the circumstances leading to the terrorist attacks of 22 March 2016 at Brussels National Airport and Maelbeek underground station in Brussels, including the development and management of the fight against radicalism and the terrorist threat – Intermediate and provisional report on the 'assistance and relief' aspect, Doc. parl., Ch., sess. 2015–2016, 3 August 2016, No. 54 1752/006, 37.

all vision and strategy; increased information overload; abundance of data banks; insufficient analytical capacity; compartmentalization and, consequently, insufficient sharing; inefficient and outdated processing processes'. It also stressed that 'the fragmentation of information is aggravated by two dividing lines: between the judicial and administrative aspects; between the federal police and the local police'. We will come back to this.[78]

2. The Role and Functioning of the CUTA

The Coordination Unit for Threat Analysis, CUTA, is a body established by law of 10 July 2006 and is responsible for threat assessment.[79] After a little less than ten years of relatively peaceful existence, the CUTA has become, during the wave of attacks perpetrated on Belgian soil, an essential institution. At the time, its existence was revealed to the broad public, a host of questions were asked about its legitimacy and way of functioning. It is therefore up to us to first paint a brief portrait of this body.

The CUTA succeeded the Inter-Agency Group against Terrorism (GIA) and is placed under the joint authority of the Ministers of Justice and of Home Affairs (Article 5 of the Law). In addition to its directors, it is composed of experts and specialized analysts (art. 7). Its tasks are to carry out periodically a joint strategic assessment to evaluate whether threats may arise or how they are evolving, to carry out a joint assessment on an *ad hoc* basis and to ensure specific international relations with foreign or international counterparts (art. 8). The CUTA is also the receptacle of a whole series of intelligence and police information, enabling it to carry out its missions successfully.

The CUTA is not exempt from parliamentary oversight since it is subject to the oversight of both the Standing Committee on the Oversight of Police Services (P Committee) and the Standing Committee on the Oversight of Intelligence and Security Services (R Committee). The Circular FTF of 21 August 2015 sets out the responsibilities and tasks of the CUTA, which is also responsible for the exchange of information on hate preachers.[80]

78 Parliamentary inquiry to examine the circumstances leading to the terrorist attacks of 22 March 2016 at Brussels National Airport and Maelbeek underground station in Brussels, including the development and management of the fight against radicalism and the terrorist threat – Third interim report, on the 'security architecture' aspect, Doc. parl., Ch., sess. 2015–2016, 3 August 2016, No. 54 1752/008, 55.

79 Act of 10 July 2006 on threat analysis, B. O. G., 20 July 2006.

80 Circular of 18 July 2016 on the exchange of information and follow-up of hate preachers.

Its most important prerogative is certainly to assess the threat and determine its level. According to Article 11 (6) of the Royal Regulation on the CUTA[81], there are four levels of threat: level one or low; level two or medium; level three or serious and level four or very serious. Threat assessments are intended for different political, administrative or judicial authorities with any security responsibilities. It is important to recall, at this stage, that these very authorities must ultimately take appropriate measures to counter a possible threat as soon as it is detected.

On 22 March 2016, the CUTA stated that it had assessed the threat level at four, very serious. Almost automatically, the government seized the information and declared the lockdown on the city of Brussels. Thereafter, the CUTA's statements was examined in an unprecedented way.

At this stage, it is important to make an observation on the functioning of the CUTA, which marks a first illustration of the 'administrativisation' of the treatment of the terrorist threat, on which we will look further below. Indeed, this semi-independent body of experts has taken on considerable importance in the fight against terrorism and more particularly in legitimizing political decisions. There is, in fact, a kind of transfer of responsibility for the decision on exceptional measures taken during or after the attacks, of which this direct quote from the inquiry committee's report on the 22 March 2016 attacks is a perfect illustration:

> 'Some confusion and dissatisfaction was sometimes expressed about maintaining level 3 while some occupational categories (e. g. police) had already moved to level 2. These reactions illustrate that subjectivity and self-interest are still often dominant in the services concerned, which sometimes have difficulty accepting CUTA decisions'.[82]

Thus, the use of the terms 'accepting CUTA decisions' induces the idea of automaticity between the CUTA's opinion on a possible level of threat and the government's decision to take it into account and act accordingly. This is all the more striking as the CUTA does not carry out a risk analysis but only a threat analysis. In the same way, the Minister of Home Affairs himself has, on the occasion of a Flemish television

81 Royal Regulation of 28 November 2006 implementing the Law of 10 July 2006 on threat analysis, B. O. G., 1st December 2006.

82 Parliamentary inquiry to examine the circumstances leading to the terrorist attacks of 22 March 2016 at Brussels National Airport and Maelbeek underground station in Brussels, including the development and management of the fight against radicalism and the terrorist threat – Third interim report, on the 'security architecture' aspect, Doc. parl., Ch., sess. 2015–2016, 3 August 2016, No. 54 1752/008, 44.

programme, said that the CUTA determines the level of threat and that the government 'prend acte' of it[83], which basically means that he does not have a say about it.

In reality, it is the *CGCCR* that evaluates the effects related to the level of threat set by the CUTA. If necessary, the NSC provides for additional measures.[84] The *CGCCR* (Strategic Intelligence and Security Committee) submits proposals to the NSC (National Security Committee), which has sole decision-making authority. This is logical, as the latter is a purely governmental body, and is chaired by the Prime Minister and composed of the Deputy Prime Ministers and the Ministers of Justice, Defence, Foreign Affairs and Home Affairs.

While this is only of *de facto* importance, the CUTA is also taking on a new importance, since its reasoned opinion has become a formal obligation on the faculty to refuse to issue an identity card, provided for in the new Article 6 of the Law of 19 July 1991 on population registers.[85] We will come back to that.

3. Operation Vigilant Guardian

Following the attacks on Charlie Hebdo's editorial staff in Paris in early 2015, the Belgian government was able to set up a major operation, which was already legally possible for several decades. This operation allowed for the presence of soldiers on the streets.

On 17 January 2015, a Memorandum of Understanding was approved by the Council of Ministers and concluded between the Home Affairs and Defence Ministers.[86] It sets up 'Operation Vigilant Guardian', a huge operation of occupation of the public space by the military, not seen in peacetime Belgium for decades. Two types

83 Cf. the reference to it in the course of a parliamentary question, Doc., Question No. 199 by *Raoul Hedebouw*, MP, 13 February 2015 (DO 2014201501718), sess. 2014–2015, No. QRVA 54 017, 19.

84 Parliamentary inquiry to examine the circumstances leading to the terrorist attacks of 22 March 2016 at Brussels National Airport and Maelbeek underground station in Brussels, including the development and management of the fight against radicalism and the terrorist threat – Third interim report, on the 'security architecture' aspect, Doc. parl., Ch., sess. 2015–2016, 3 August 2016, No. 54 1752/008, 153.

85 Law of 9 November 2015 on various provisions of the Interior, B. O. G., 30 November 2015. See also *Marie-Aude Beernaert*, Renforcement de l'arsenal législatif anti-terroriste: entre symboles et prévention, Journal des Tribunaux, 2015, No. 6626, 833, at 835 and *Véronique Lafarque*, Terrorisme: impact sur la délivrance des cartes d'identité, Bulletin social & juridique, 2015, No. 549, 16.

86 It should be noted that this Memorandum of Understanding remains, for obvious reasons, classified. At most, we can capture bits of it by indirect means. The authors of this article have therefore not been able to become aware of it.

of missions are possible for the military: patrols or fixed posts. Street patrols provide protection for all users of public space. As for fixed posts such as in buildings, they are used in sensitive places. In this case, the aim is to provide protection for people working in these locations. These measures are further reinforced in Brussels, where the terrorist threat is higher than in the rest of the country. The number of military personnel mobilized has increased throughout the years. There were 1.800 soldiers on the streets in the wake of the 22 March attacks.[87]

Legally, everything already existed to rapidly deploy such an operation. A law as well as a Royal Regulation of 1994 mark out these missions.[88] Thus, the military, whether on the basis of a memorandum of understanding or a requisition[89] – i. e. without having to seek parliamentary approval –, may be assigned to a police support mission, provided that the police services' resources are not sufficient to maintain public order.[90] Under article 7/5 of the Law on the Police Function, however, the direction of operations remains the exclusive prerogative of a police officer.[91]

IV. A New Criminal Framework

The terrorist attacks in Paris in January and November 2015 and in Brussels in March 2016 prompted Belgian authorities to announce two sets of measures to fight terrorism. The first is a package of 12 counterterrorism measures, released in January 2015. The second set of 18 measures was announced in the days following the Paris terrorist attacks of 13 November 2015.[92] From the very first pages of its report, the parlia-

87 Motion for a resolution to disengage the Defence from Operation Vigilant Guardian in favour of a specific police force, Doc. parl., Ch., sess. 2016–2017, 16 November 2016, No 54 2156/001, 4.

88 Law of 20 May 1994 on the periods and positions of military personnel in the reserve framework and on the implementation and conditioning of the Armed Forces, *B. O.G*, 21 June 1994 ; Royal Regulation determining the forms of operational engagement and preparatory activities for the implementation of the Armed Forces, B. O. G., 20 July 1994.

89 Article 6/2 of the Royal Regulation of 6 July 1994 determining the forms of operational engagement and preparatory activities for the implementation of the armed forces, B. O. G., 20 July 1994.

90 Article 43 of the Law of 7 December 1998 organising an integrated police service, structured at two levels, B. O. G., 5 January 1999.

91 *Nicolas Lagasse*, L'emploi de la force sur le territoire national par les militaires en dehors des situations régies par le droit des conflits armés, Revue belge de Droit constitutionnel, 2013, No. 1, 3, at 35.

92 *Sophie André/Vincent Seron*, 30 measures against terrorism: penal populism between expected efficiency and potential collateral damage, in: Thomas Renard (ed.) Counterterrorism in Belgium: key challenges and policy options, Egmont Paper 89, Brussels, 2016, 10–22.

mentary inquiry committee wrote that 'Belgium, like other countries, has shown a willingness to strengthen the legislative arsenal available to the services in the fight against terrorism'.[93] Here we leave immediate action, facing an emergency situation as described above, to focus on delayed action. The main difference is the intervention, to this end, of the legislator alongside the executive branch.

There are two ways of dealing with the terrorist phenomenon through legislative action. On the one hand, it involves adopting new laws or amending existing laws in order to create a special regime for terrorist offences and persons suspected of terrorism or dangerous radicalisation (1.). This first aspect is marked by the pre-eminence of the judiciary in the treatment and evaluation of these situations deemed dangerous. On the other hand, it raises a question of regulating the public space, most of the time through Royal Regulations (2.). The actors put forward are no longer the judges but the administration and the police, who act by the notion of public order. We can see in it a movement of 'administrativisation' of the terrorist and jihadist phenomenon.

1. Legislative Amendments in Criminal Matters/Power to the Judge

Several ordinary legislative changes have taken place since the first attack on the Jewish Museum in Brussels in 2014.[94] Among these, several will be of interest to us, namely the law of 20 July 2015 to strengthen the fight against terrorism[95]; the law of 27 April 2016 on complementary measures to combat terrorism (1)[96], the law of 2 August 2016 containing various provisions on combating terrorism (III) (1)[97]; the law of 14 December 2016 amending the Criminal Code as regards the suppression of terrorism (1)[98]; and the law of 17 May 2017 amending the Code of Criminal Procedure with a view to promoting the fight against terrorism (1).[99]

93 Proposal to set up a parliamentary inquiry committee to examine the circumstances leading to the terrorist attacks of 22 March 2016 at Brussels National Airport and Maelbeek underground station in Brussels, including the evolution and management of the fight against radicalism and the terrorist threat, *Doc. parl.*, Ch., sess. 2015–2016, 11 April 2016, No. 54 1752/001, 5.

94 *Jan Roelandt*, De strijd tegen het terrorisme: een overzicht van de recente wetgevende ingrepen in het straf(proces)recht, Nullum Crimen, 2017, Vol. 12, 10.

95 B. O. G., 5 August 2015.

96 B. O. G., 9 May 2016.

97 B. O. G., 11 August 2016.

98 B. O. G., 22 December 2016.

99 B. O. G., 3 July 2017.

Of course, most of these laws are more or less an extension of existing terrorism legislation. Thus, the inclusion in ordinary legislation of a new offence relating to travel abroad for terrorist purposes in Article 140 *sexies* of the Criminal Code by the law of 20 July 2015 should first be highlighted. As the doctrine emphasizes, 'this will certainly raise important evidentiary problems, especially since the conduct will be punishable 'regardless of whether or not the terrorist offence is committed'.'[100] Indeed, it is no longer the commission itself that is punishable, but the intention of the alleged jihadist. While the punishment of intent already exists to some extent in the Criminal Code, it is taken to its extreme here in that it presupposes a particularly thorough faculty of investigation. Consequently, the 'ambiguous dimension' of this new legislation is bound to arise.[101]

Secondly, but not least, the legislator has extended the possibility of using 'particular research methods' to terrorist offences. With the amendment of a single article of the Code of Criminal Procedure – 90*ter* –, a large number of criminal procedure locks are being broken, like a chain reaction.[102] From now on, a wide range of measures may be authorised in the context of search for terrorist offences, including private telecommunications surveillance measures, proactive investigations, temporary freezing of bank accounts, discreet visual checks, infiltration, observation in a home, full anonymous testimony, telephone tracing or even the protection of threatened witnesses, in short, a whole series of mechanisms which derogate from ordinary law and which, *a priori*, do not respect the principle of adversarial proceedings and the right of defence.

Thirdly, Belgium has extended the possibility of revoking Belgian nationality for dual nationals. Although anecdotal, this measure is certainly marked by an important symbolic weight, as we have seen during the debates on its adoption in the French Republic. Under Belgian law, the Nationality Code has been amended for this purpose. It should be noted that the main novelty in relation to the possibility of forfeiture of existing nationality is the abolition of any time limit. Thus, regardless of how long has elapsed since the commission of the terrorist offence, the judge will be able to order forfeiture. According to the legislator, this can be explained by the fact that terrorism 'can be interpreted as a form of rejection of the country, its institutions

100 *Marie-Aude Beernaert*, op. cit. (see note 85), at 834. See also *Jan Velaers*, La lutte contre le terrorisme et les droits de l'homme: développements récents en Belgique, in: Pierre d'Argent/David Renders/Marc Verdussen, Les visages de l'État, Brussels, 2017, 775–792, at 788.

101 *Christian de Valkeneer*, Les réponses face au terrorisme: les glissements du judiciaire vers l'administratif, Journal des Tribunaux, 2017, No. 6706, 707, at 709.

102 *Marie-Aude Beernaert*, op. cit. (note 85), at 834.

and its values'.[103] The Constitutional Court has endorsed this reform.[104] Nevertheless, some questions remain.[105]

The legislator is not the only one to have acted during this recent period. Indeed, the Constituent itself intervened to revise an article that had remained unchanged since the birth of the Kingdom in 1831, namely Article 12. The latter enshrines the maximum time limit for police arrest – the 'garde-à-vue' – of 24 hours before having to obtain a warrant from an investigating judge. On 24 October 2017, the Constitution was revised to increase this period to 48 hours.[106] The constitutional amendment is different from the interventions dealt with so far in that it affects all citizens for, *a priori*, all types of offences. However, 'the reading of parliamentary documents gives rise to this feeling that the 'Salduz' case law was only a pretext for the Constituent Assembly which, to tell the truth, was more concerned about the fight against terrorism'.[107]

2. The 'Administrativisation' of the Fight against Terrorism / Power to the Executive

The terrorist threat is a global phenomenon and must be understood both *a priori* and *a posteriori*. 'Our country has many more foreign fighters going to Syria and Iraq than other countries. This worrying observation requires that we look for the causes', stresses the inquiry committee.[108] It is from this premise that the federal authorities have started to adopt a series of measures that more or less infringe public freedoms in order to prevent the commission of terrorist attacks but above all in order to stem the radicalisation of young people. In this context, it is usually the Belgian government that is at work. Moreover, it is above all a question of giving more power of action to the authorities on the ground, most often local, whether they are administrative or police.

103 *Doc. parl.*, Ch., sess. 2014–2015, No. 54 1198/001, 8.

104 Constitutional court, case No. 85/2009 of 14 May 2009.

105 *Patrick Wautelet*, Priver les djihadistes de leur nationalité belge: les garde-fous à respecter, Journal des Tribunaux, 2015, No. 6593, 183.

106 Revision of 24 October 2017 of Article 12 of the Constitution, B. O. G., 29 November 2017.

107 *Marc Verdussen*, Révision de la Constitution: le délai maximal d'arrestation judiciaire est doublé, Journal des Tribunaux, 2018, No. 6730, 385, at 388.

108 Proposal to set up a parliamentary inquiry committee to examine the circumstances leading to the terrorist attacks of 22 March 2016 at Brussels National Airport and Maelbeek underground station in Brussels, including the evolution and management of the fight against radicalism and the terrorist threat, *Doc. parl.*, Ch., sess. 2015–2016, 11 April 2016, No. 54 1752/001, 7.

First, a 2017 law amended the Communal Law in order to allow the mayor of a commune, the first administrative chief of his locality as well as the chief of the local police, to order the closure of establishments suspected of harbouring terrorist activities.[109] This new prerogative of the mayor, which offends *a priori* the constitutional freedoms of assembly and association, offers him an important power on his territory.

Second, a law adopted the same month aims at relaxing the obligation of professional secrecy which weighs on certain professionals.[110] From now on, agents of the Public Social Action Centres will be required to inform 'immediately' the Public Prosecutor's Office of any information that may constitute 'serious evidence' of a terrorist offence. Although stemming from a legitimate desire to benefit from the best possible information in order to thwart possible attacks, the law does not completely reassure in that it places in the hands of these agents the responsibility to evaluate themselves the quality of the confidences received and their possible dangerousness.[111] It should be noted that this law has been challenged before the Belgian Constitutional Court for violation of the right to privacy. After months of proceedings, the Court finally found a violation and therefore annulled the law on 14 March 2019[112]. This shows a slight inflection in our thesis, since the Court, in the end, can still act within the ordinary guidelines of its control. However, we will see later that the Constitutional Court, in general, is more flexible in terrorist matters.

In another vein, in March 2017, the Council of Ministers reached an agreement to extend the competences of private security organisations: installation of surveillance cameras, use of flying/mobile camera systems, carrying weapons and searching.[113] One year later, a law was adopted to extend the possibility of using surveillance

109 Law of 13 May 2017 inserting an article 134septies in the New Communal Law in order to allow the Mayor to close down establishments suspected of harbouring terrorist activities, B. O. G., 16 June 2017.

110 Law of 17 May 2017 amending the Code of Criminal Procedure with a view to promoting the fight against terrorism, B. O. G., 3 July 2017.

111 In all honesty, it should be pointed out that there is a Circular dated 20 July 2017 relating to this law which states that staff members may, in any event, seek advice from their immediate superior. However, this only places the problem raised above on another person.

112 Const. Court, 14 March 2019, nr. 44/2019 (available on http://www.const-court.be).

113 Parliamentary inquiry to examine the circumstances leading to the terrorist attacks of 22 March 2016 at Brussels National Airport and Maelbeek underground station in Brussels, including the development and management of the fight against radicalism and the terrorist threat – Third interim report, on the 'security architecture' aspect, Doc. parl., Ch., sess. 2015–2016, 3 August 2016, No. 54 1752/008, 113–114.

cameras, supplemented by a Royal Regulation.[114] The adoption of these new provisions is very clearly motivated by the desire to combat terrorism, although the new legislation applies indiscriminately. For example, the new law now allows intelligence services (State Security (VSSE) and the General Intelligence and Security Service (SGRS)) to consult live police surveillance footage, what they were previously unable to do.

Still in the administrative field, it is now up to the Minister of Home Affairs or his delegates to refuse to issue an identity card or to decide to withdraw the same card from a person suspected of wanting to carry out terrorist activity abroad.[115] Two clarifications should be noted. On the one hand, as we have already seen, the new legislation closely associates the CUTA with this decision, since its opinion is necessary to pronounce the measure. On the other hand, it should be noted that the measure 'may also apply to minors as well as adults'.[116] This also illustrates the administrativisation of the handling of the terrorist phenomenon with the new power to refuse to issue identity documents or to withdraw them, although this legislative amendment is largely the result of the implementation of a United Nations Security Council resolution.[117]

Among the many other Royal Regulations adopted with a view to strengthening the power of the executive and the administration, we should mention: the Royal Regulation of 2 June 2015 establishing the Strategic Committee and the Intelligence and Security Coordination Committee[118]; the Royal Regulation of 1 May 2016 establishing a national emergency plan for the approach of a terrorist hostage or terrorist attack[119]; the Royal Regulation of 21 July 2016 on the joint Foreign Terrorist Fighters database and implementing certain provisions of Chapter 1*bis* 'Information Management' of Chapter IV of the Law of the Police Functions[120]; the Royal Regulation

114 Law of 21 March 2018 amending the Law on the police function, in order to regulate the use of cameras by police services, and amending the Law of 21 March 2007 regulating the installation and use of surveillance cameras, the Law of 30 November 1998 organic intelligence and security services and the Law of 2 October 2017 regulating private and private security, B. O. G., 16 April 2018 and the Royal Regulation on the Declarations on the Installation and Use of Surveillance Cameras and the Register of Camera Image Processing Activities, B. O. G., 23 May 2018.

115 Law of 10 August 2015 amending the Law of 19 July 1991 on population registers, identity cards, foreigner's cards and residence documents and amending the Law of 8 August 1983 organising a national register of natural persons, B. O. G., 31 August 2015.

116 *Marie-Aude Beernaert*, op. cit. (see note 85), at 835.

117 Resolution No. 2178 of the United Nations Security Council, § 6, a).

118 B. O. G., 5 June 2015.

119 B. O. G., 18 May 2016.

120 B. O. G., 22 September 2016.

of 16 February 2017 laying down the procedure according to which the King may recognize an act of terrorism within the meaning of article 42*bis* of the law of 1 August 1985.[121]

Criticisms from the judicial world were not long in coming.[122] This 'shift from the judicial to the administration'[123], denounced by the Prosecutor General Christian de Valkeneer, is certainly one of the constants to be underlined since the beginning of the recent wave of attacks in Europe. For the author, the current model gives an increasing place to the administrative police and the concept of public security to the detriment of the criminal approach to the phenomenon. The Attorney-General considers this movement dangerous as it provides important prerogatives to the administrative authorities.[124]

Conclusion

'I would prefer, actually, that we have a state of emergency 'à la française' than we touch the core of our criminal law because it would threaten the rule of law and the situation of all citizens', said *Christophe Marchand*, a Belgian attorney.[125] By definition, the 'state of emergency' entails a modification in the protection of fundamental rights and in the balance between the state powers, as it grants mainly the executive with wider powers to effectively overthrow a terrorist threat or a crisis situation. However, due to the lack of such mechanism, there is no specific measures in Belgium that could be activated only in the hypothesis of specific circumstances such as a clear and present risk for the State. Of course, that does not mean there is no action in that cases, but the constitutional control would be the same as other acts.

Recent events have clearly required stronger measures to fight terrorists. From the different examples highlighted, we can see the incredible range of legislation and regulations available to the authorities, both administrative and judicial, to deal both with emergencies relating to terrorism and with the more global phenomenon of rad-

121 B. O. G., 3 March 2017.

122 *K. Van Cauwenberghe*, Kan terrorisme de rechtsstaat onderuit halen?, Juristenkrant, 2015, at 13.

123 *Christian de Valkeneer*, op. cit. (note 101), at 707–711.

124 *Christian de Valkeneer*, op. cit. (note 101), at 710.

125 'Je préférerais, à tout prendre, qu'on ait un état d'urgence à la française, plutôt que de toucher au corps même de notre droit pénal, car cela menace l'Etat de droit et donc la situation de l'ensemble des citoyens', *Jean Quatremer*, La Belgique aimerait résister à la tentation de l'état d'urgence, Libération, 23 march 2016.

icalism. However, no exceptional regime has been used to exercise these existing prerogatives. How, then, can we explain that the advocates of the creation of an institutionalised 'state of emergency' in Belgium still exist, as we have seen in the first part of our article? To answer this question, it is necessary to define the way in which the Belgian system functions in the field of terrorism and to compare it with the main salient features of a 'classic' state of emergency.

Belgium functions, as we have seen, by amending or creating ordinary legislation, although often limited to the terrorist field. It is important to ask what separates the Belgian way of dealing with the terrorist phenomenon, without a 'state of emergency', from the way used by countries in a state of emergency. Is it only, as Jan Velaers has pointed out[126], the restriction of the scope of the measures to terrorist offences and the failure to transfer the means of action to the executive branch that separate the two systems? Let us examine these two aspects.

On the one hand, the restriction of the scope of the newly created measures to terrorist offences would be an important difference with the state of emergency. While most of the measures adopted by the federal authority are aimed exclusively at terrorist offences, some are not. Thus, amending the Constitution to extend the period of police custody potentially concerns any person and any offence. Beyond this remark, it is a chimera to think that the scope of terrorist offences constitutes a homogeneous and determined whole. Moreover, although normally circumscribed, the interpretation of these new criminal measures very often constitutes an open door to the arbitrariness of the judge (or the administration) since they have an eminently subjective scope, by wanting to incriminate intentionality. This explains why some see in this 'legislative frenzy [...] a subjectification of criminal law'.[127]

On the other hand, the lack of transfer of the means of action to the executive power would be an important difference with the state of emergency. Here too, this statement needs to be challenged. Admittedly, broad powers have not been given temporarily to the Belgian government as it may have been the case in France or in other states under a state of emergency. Nevertheless, important decisions on action to prevent and suppress terrorism and potentially violate individual and collective human rights can be taken by governmental or executive actors. One example is certainly the preponderance of the federal prosecutor's office in this matter, marked

126 *Jan Velaers,* op. cit. (note 100), at 791.

127 *Jean-Claude Paye,* État d'exception sans état d'urgence, La Libre Belgique, 22 December 2016.

by its subordination to the executive power.[128] One can also mention the role of the mayors or the CUTA, seen above.

We would tend to think that the difference does not necessarily lie in these two criteria, but, more insidiously for the Belgian system, in its permanence, contrary to the state of emergency marked by its temporary character. Indeed, the presence of soldiers in the streets is not linked to an exceptional power that the executive should 'return' at the end of a given time since its possibility is provided for in permanent legislation. Similarly, the list of Foreign Terrorist Fighters and the power to detain or refuse to issue identity papers are not linked to the existence of the Islamic state but will remain in force until they are repealed by a new parliamentary majority.

At the end, we will object that a final difference may lie in the severity of the measures, that are supposed to be more flexible in the Belgian system since they must respect the Constitution, which has not been suspended by a possible state of emergency. According to *Jan Velaers*, the use of ordinary legislative amendments to deal with the terrorist phenomenon has at least one advantage, namely that it remains within the scope of respect for the fundamental rights enshrined both in the Belgian Constitution and in international conventions.[129] Thus, if one examines the various measures taken by the Belgian legislator after the attacks on the Jewish Museum in Brussels, they were subject to *a priori* control by the Council of State, as well as *a posteriori* by the Constitutional Court, in particular as to their compatibility with a series of fundamental rights including the freedom of expression, the prohibition of deprivation of liberty or the freedom of movement. Here again, the border is porous. Indeed, the Constitutional Court tends to be more lenient with repressive texts justified by the fight against terrorism.[130] On the basis of these reflections, some do not hesitate to assimilate the state of emergency and the repressive system specific to terrorism in Belgium. For example, *J.-C. Paye* considers that 'this type of legislation, by generalising exception procedures at all stages of the criminal procedure, puts us in

128 *Jean-Claude Paye*, Belgique: une 'lutte antiterroriste" ordinaire, Pyramides (La régularisation éthique dans les administrations publiques), 2012, No. 16/1, 1, at 3.

129 *Jan Velaers*, op. cit. (note 100), at 791.

130 An older example than the current period is striking in this respect. Following the attacks of 11 September, a Law of 6 January 2003 on special research methods was adopted by parliament. Following an annulment by the Constitutional Court – at this time the Court of Arbitration – for failure to respect fundamental rights, the legislator revised its copy and adopted a new version of the law, almost identical to the previous one, the Law of 27 December 2005, but this time insisting on the framework of the fight against terrorism. The Court approved. *See Jean-Claude Paye*, op. cit. (note 126), 1, at 8.

a permanent state of exception, in which what was the rule, the guarantee of certain constitutional rights, is constantly violated'.[131]

At this stage, we will lend an ear to some authors. 'When a State is confronted with a serious threat, such as terrorism, it may be tempted to proceed with what *Mireille Delmas-Marty* calls a 'circumvention of the rule of law', by 'a duplication of the criminal system between a common law that respects the principles and a parallel circuit that is gradually freed from them by a tightening of procedural and substantive rules,'.[132] The conclusions of part of the Belgian legal doctrine are unequivocal. They see in these reforms 'a concern to intervene ever more upstream', to 'play on the register of symbols', with, in the end, a risk of 'being counterproductive'.[133]

In conclusion, we must ask ourselves the question of the relevance of introducing a state of emergency in Belgium since the government already enjoys broad powers in this area, helped by the administrative movement to combat terrorism, the relative consensus within parliament in this area and the leniency of the Constitutional Court when it comes to defending fundamental rights in this particular field. In short, we will say with another author that while the fight against terrorism is undoubtedly the challenge of contemporary European societies, 'the rule of law does not enshrine the principle that the end justifies the means'.[134]

131 *Jean-Claude Paye*, op. cit. (note 126), at 6.

132 *Mireille Delmas-Marty*, Aux quatre vents du monde – Petit guide de navigation sur l'océan de la mondialisation, Paris, 2016, 29, quoted by *Marc Verdussen*, Révision de la Constitution: le délai maximal d'arrestation judiciaire est doublé, Journal des Tribunaux, 2018, No. 6730, 385, at 388.

133 *Marie-Aude Beernaert*, op. cit. (note 85), at 836.

134 *Jan Velaers*, op. cit. (note 100), at 791.

When 5×4 is not a Winning Majority: Judicial Decision-making on Unconstitutional Constitutional Amendments

Rubens Beçak and Jairo Lima

Abstract

The main democratic critiques of strong judicial review tend to disregard constitutional amendments as a mechanism to mitigate judicial supremacy. The main reason for this lies in the requirements of supermajority rules to amend a constitution. Supermajority rules do not offer equal treatment to those who will take part in the decision-making process, as this rule favors the maintenance of the status quo by making changes more difficult. Underlying this assertion is the belief that in democracy political equality depends on a decision-making process in which all opinions have the same value, mainly through simple majority. Moreover, the distrust of constitutional amendments as an instrument of dialogue is justified by the existence of judicial review on constitutional amendments. However, both constitutional courts and constitutional amendments are part of the majority of the democratic societies, therefore, we demonstrate how judicial review can be compatible with the democratic potential of constitutional amendments. This is done through the use of supermajority rules in the constitutional courts deliberation, because, unlike what happens in parliaments, the maintenance of the status quo that it represents is advantageous for the presumption of constitutionality of constitutional amendments and does not mean violation of equal treatment since the democratic status of the courts does not come from the representativeness of their members.

I. Introduction

Contemporary constitutional theory has focused on the role that constitutional courts play in guaranteeing fundamental rights in democratic societies. Several authors have analyzed the negative implications of this phenomenon, such as *Jeremy Waldron, Richard Bellamy, Mark Tushnet,* and *Larry Kramer.*[1] However, they are not part of a homogeneous group. They come from distinct philosophical traditions: liberal in *Waldron,* republican in *Bellamy* and popular-democratic in *Tushnet* and *Kramer.* Nevertheless, it can be said that they represent the political constitutionalism perspective, since they have in common the search for the restoration of the political aspect of constitutionalism.

1 See *Jeremy Waldron,* Law and Disagreement, Oxford University Press 1999; *Richard Bellamy,* Political Constitutionalism, United Kingdom, Cambridge University Press 2007; *Mark Tushnet,* Taking the Constitution Away from the Courts, 1999; *Larry Kramer,* The People Themselves: Popular Constitutionalism and Judicial Review, 2004.

Differently from an inquiry on the legitimacy of judicial review, the starting point of this article is the presence of constitutional courts in different constitutional systems throughout the world. From that fact, the paper is directed towards a reconstruction of judicial review from the criticism of *Waldron* and *Bellamy,* to demonstrate ways of optimizing it democratically. For this reason, it questions: to what extent can judicial review, especially of constitutional amendment, be exercised with the inclusion of criticisms made by the political constitutionalists *Jeremy Waldron* and *Richard Bellamy*?

The development of the argument starts with item 2 presenting the main criticisms on judicial review, from *Waldron* and *Bellamy,* with special emphasis on the political equality of the majority rule, as well as the theoretical gap surrounding the constitutional amendment for these authors. Item 3 highlights the democratic elements in the amendment power and its distinct nature in relation to the original constituent power and the constituted powers. Finally, item 4 addresses the issue of unconstitutional constitutional amendments and the supermajority decision method.

II. Political Constitutionalism and Constitutional Amendments

In the debate on the legitimacy of judicial review, *Jeremy Waldron* and *Richard Bellamy* presume that we live in a complex and plural society in which people disagree about the sense of justice and the content of fundamental rights. These disagreements do not mean that we must abandon the need to define a common vision in society. On the contrary, one must examine the political activity of collective decision-making inserted in the context of disagreements. From this starting point, these authors question which institution should be responsible for ending these disagreements.[2]

The problem that concerns *Jeremy Waldron* lies in the secondary importance of legislation compared to judicial review. He believes one of the reasons why the legitimacy of judicial review has reached widespread acceptance is precisely the revelation of failures in parliamentary majority decision. It so happens that constitutional courts, despite justifications, also use the same decision-making method. For this reason, the difference between courts and parliaments would be in the electoral origin of the latter and not in their methods of decision-making. Thus, the judicial review would be only a second round of decisions made by members without electoral legitimacy.[3]

Both *Waldron* and *Bellamy* argue that in Parliament the majority rule adds moral respectability to the task of choosing from different options. This is because it has the advantage of giving equal weight to the opinions of each member of the decision-

2 *Jeremy Waldron,* op. cit.; Richard Bellamy, op. cit.

3 *Waldron,* op. cit., *at* 90 f.

making process, making every opinion decisive for the outcome.[4] *Ronald Dworkin*[5] disagrees with *Waldron*, as he believes that the majority rule is not a general principle of justice regardless of context. In contrast to *Dworkin's* criticism, *Waldron* acknowledges that the majority method can also be used in undemocratic circumstances.[6]

It should be noted that the majority rule indicated by the authors is the bare majority, in which the '50 % plus 1 decision' becomes binding for all. Under the perspective of the political constitutionalism, the qualified majority (supermajority) does not have the same merits of the bare majority, as it disrespects the idea of equal treatment of opinions by granting more weight to those who support the maintenance of the status quo, requiring opponents' votes to be greater than '50 % plus 1'.

Because of the importance that the majority rule plays in the decision-making process of parliaments, it is often associated with the idea of tyranny of the majority. *Waldron* and *Bellamy* do not deny that the tyranny of the majority is possible, but it is not necessarily the result of a disagreement between the rights decided by the majority rule. Decisions that do not protect fundamental rights are a substantive concept, that is, both parliament and court can make mistakes. The problem lies in the fact that if parliament is wrong there would be a court to correct the mistake. But what happens when the court also fails? There is no procedure to ensure that the courts will necessarily decide in favor of protecting fundamental rights, particularly of minorities.[7] Therefore, *Waldron* and *Bellamy* reject judicial review because there is no such guarantee of minorities' protection by the courts.

In addition, there are several laws that are not the result of a homogeneous majority imposing its will upon a consistent minority. On the contrary, laws often correspond to a series of compromises mediated by coalitions of different minority groups, especially in proportional and multiparty systems. There is no arbitrariness when a government has a legislative majority to approve its programs, which won a free and fair election. For *Waldron* and *Bellamy*, the arbitrariness would be in considering the vision of some individuals who were not elected as having more weight than that of elected officials, as in judicial review. Losing a majority decision is not the same as being part of a minority that does not have the minimum legal protection.[8]

4 *Bellamy*, op. cit., *at* 38.

5 *Ronald Dworkin*, Response. Boston University Law Review, v. 90:1059, 2010, at 1085.

6 *Jeremy Waldron*, A majority in the lifeboat. . Boston University Law Review, v. 90:1043, 2010, 1044/1050.

7 *Jeremy Waldron*, The Core of the Case Against Judicial Review, The Yale Law Journal, 115:1346, 2006, 1396–1399; *Bellamy*, op. cit., at 37 f.

8 *Bellamy*, op. cit., at 241–255.

Despite these criticisms, *Jeremy Waldron's* position cannot be understood as totally excluding judicial review, since his texts after 'Law and Disagreement' presented a more specific delimitation of the scope of his criticism, including the stipulation of conditions for judicial review to be accepted. This theoretical movement can also be observed in *Richard Bellamy*. In this case, the author pointed out possible interactions between British political constitutionalism and the emergence of the Constitutional Court after the Human Rights Act and the European Court of Human Rights. Currently, both authors acknowledge the performance of the constitutional courts under the scope of weak judicial review, in which the judicial interpretation of the constitution is not final and binding on other branches.[9]

In weak judicial review 'courts are given the opportunity to explain why a challenged statute is unconstitutional. Having done so, they step aside and let the legislature respond. To the extent that courts have some advantage over legislatures in constitutional interpretation, and that legislators recognize the existence of such an advantage, the legislative deliberations will be informed but not controlled by what the courts have said. But, in the end, if enough legislators believe that the court's constitutional interpretation is not as good as their own, weak-form review allows the legislators to have their way-putting the people in a position to govern themselves while simultaneously operating within the bounds set by the constitution.'[10]

In general terms, political constitutionalism puts the debate of the content of fundamental rights under an ordinary political process, that is, by disregarding the existence of different moments in the context of democratic politics: a constituent and a constituted (in *Joseph Sieyès'* perspective), or a normal and a constitutional (in *Bruce Ackerman's* view).[11] For political constitutionalism, the constituent process is continuous and occurs within the circumstances of social disagreement. Accordingly, the political constitution is created and amended in the day-to-day of politics.[12]

For this reason, a reflection focused on a constitutional moment fixed in time is absent from the discussions around political constitutionalism. According to *Marco*

9 For a judicial supremacy concept, see *Stephen Gardbaum,* Reassessing the new Commonwealth model of constitutionalism, International Journal of Constitutional Law, v. 8, No. 2, 2010, 173.

10 *Mark Tushnet,* Weak-Form Judicial Review and 'Core' Civil Liberties, Harvard Civil Rights-Civil Liberties Law Review, v. 41, 2006, 10.

11 *Joseph Sieyès,* What is the Third Estate? Frederick Praeger Publisher 1963; *Bruce Ackerman,* We the People: Foundations, Harvard University Press 1993.

12 *Graham Gee* and *Grégoire Webber,* What is a political constitution? Oxford Journal of Legal Studies, v. 30 No. 2, 2010, 288–289.

Goldoni,[13] this statement reveals the main weakness of the political constitutionalists' political conception, for they understand that politics arises in a context without limitations, that is, without any external forces (constituent power) to generate it. Political institutions, however, do not operate in a vacuum and do not come out of nowhere. Political constitutionalism fails to consider how fragile the political context is in which action takes place. The mundane characteristic of political action imposes an extended conception of time that provides a 'before' and an 'after'. Part of the purpose of political action is the maintenance and renewal of the world shared by humans. Therefore, avoiding this aspect of reality means idealizing the circumstances of politics.

Therefore, because of the rejection of the dualist politics idea (constituent and constituted powers), political constitutionalism does not discuss the role of constitutional amendments. However, considering that political constitutionalism recognizes the legitimacy of constitutional courts in weak judicial review, it would be expected some attention to constitutional amendments because they work as mechanisms for legislative responses.

Rosalind Dixon and *Adrienne Stone*[14] present three reasons why political constitutionalism rejects constitutional amendments as an appropriate mechanism to promote interaction with the legislature: a) practical impossibility due to the demanding requirements of the amendment approval process; b) disregard of majority rule when a qualified quorum is required for the approval of the amendment; and, finally, c) the idea that constitutional amendments contribute to the prolixity of the constitutional text.

It can be said that *Jeremy Waldron* represents the argument of practical impossibility, since his criticisms focus on the American constitutional reality, in which the process of adding amendments to the Constitution is quite demanding. This practical difficulty prevents the constitutional amendment from being a frequent and continuous legislative response, since its adoption requires great national commitments.[15] Regarding *Richard Bellamy*, it should be pointed out that his arguments start off from the British political-constitutional context, in which he is immersed. Thus, his proposal for political constitutionalism does not encompass the duality between origi-

13 *Marco Goldoni*, Two internal critiques of political constitutionalism, International Journal of Constitutional Law, v. 10, No. 4, 2012, 943–946.

14 *Rosalind Dixon* and *Adrienne Stone*, Constitutional Amendment and Political Constitutionalism: a Philosophical and Comparative Reflection, Melbourne Legal Studies Research Paper, No. 703, 2014, 9.

15 *Dixon* and *Stone*, op. cit., at 10.

nal constituent power and derived constituent power, since the constitution would be the continuous and ordinary political process itself. Because of that, it would be unjustifiable to alter the interpretation of the constitution by means of qualified majorities, since its interpretation occurs in the day-to-day of the political process, depending more on political than on legal-procedural barriers.

Therefore, from the internal perspective of political constitutionalism, constitutional amendments cannot mitigate the weaknesses that this critical approach sees in the strong judicial review. However, we believe that it is important to develop an analysis of the constitutional amendment, since the pertinence of political constitutionalism criticism goes beyond the geographical context envisaged by *Waldron* and *Bellamy*.

III. Towards a Democratic Amending Power

The constituent power, as a foundational moment of a new constitutional order, represents a historical concept of written constitutions in the post-revolutions period of the late Eighteenth century. This is not to say that there had not been any representation of that idea before. According to *Martin Loughlin*, the concept of constituent power was already present during the British revolutionary debates of the Seventeenth century. However, the idea lost its legal meaning from the monarchical restoration and the gradual institutionalization of parliamentary government.[16]

Nowadays, the idea of constituent power is associated with popular sovereignty, because of its own semantic value, meaning 'to institute together'. The verb 'to constitute' originates from the Latin word 'constituere', which, in turn, is formed from the prefix 'co' (company, society, concomitance) added to the verb "instituere" (to establish), generating the meaning of joint establishment. Unlike the sovereignty understood as supreme individualized command, the constituent power demands an intersubjective and cooperative engagement, which happens through democratic procedures.

For that reason, the legitimacy of a constitution depends on the condition of meeting, through the act of creation, the principles of participation and inclusion, that is,

16 *Martin Loughlin,* Constituent power subverted: from English constitutional argument to British constitutional practice; in: Loughlin, Martin and Walker, Neil (Eds.), The Paradox of Constitutionalism – Constituent Power and Constitutional Form, United Kingdom, Oxford University Press, 2007, 27.

the normative prescriptions of its semantic meaning.[17] In the process of emergence of constituent power, the sharing of democratic values is much more interesting than verifying formal procedures.

Both freedom of decision and popular participation are essential elements for a democratic conception of constituent power able to contribute to constitutional legitimacy. However, it should be noted that this freedom does not entail the exclusion of the foundation of the exercise from this faculty itself. 'Like democracy, constituent power destroys itself when it violates the conditions that make it possible'.[18]

Constitutions created from a broad public and participatory debate can better promote common knowledge about the content of the text, and therefore tend to have more compliance by individuals and other political actors. "Constitution-making processes that are highly opened and inclusionary (or at least appear to be so) increase citizens' awareness and regard for the document as well as their confidence that other citizens have developed the same awareness and respect".[19]

For *Joel Colón-Ríos*,[20] the democratic character of constituent power is not exhausted in the goal of legitimizing a new constitutional text, but it is also present in the ways in which constitutions are amended, since the amending power derives from this original constituent power. However, the amending power is not in the same category as the original constituent power nor of the constituted powers.

It is not originally constituent because it is limited in its form of expression (procedural) and in the scope of its changes (substantive), that is, it loses the legal unconditionality traditionally associated with original constituent power. In addition, it is not enough to qualify the amending power as constituted when taking into consideration the fact that constitutional amendments are an act of creating new constitutional norms, which broaden or restrict the scope of the constitution (e.g. creation of a new fundamental right). Moreover, when compared with ordinary law, amending power not only involves a procedure with more deliberative potential, but it may

17 *Andreas Kalyvas*, Popular Sovereignty, Democracy, and the Constituent Power, Constellations, v. 12, nº 2, 2005, 235–239.

18 *Joel Colón-Ríos*, Weak constitutionalism: democratic legitimacy and the question of constituent power, Routledge 2012, 118.

19 *Zachary Elkins*, *Tom Ginsburg* and *James Melton*, The Endurance of National Constitutions, Cambridge University Press, 2009, 97.

20 Op. cit., at 139.

also indicate the participation of different agents of the ordinary Legislative branch, when for example it requires the ratification of the amendment by referendum.[21]

Hereupon, it follows some examples of popular participation in the adoption of constitutional amendments: the United States (when ratification takes place through the Constitutional Convention in the Member States); France (Art. 89); Austria (Art. 44 – in situations of total revision); Spain (Art. 166); Italy (Art. 138 – in the case of a specific requirement); Denmark (Section 88); Ireland (Art. 46); Japan (Art. 96); Chile (Art. 128 – when there is disagreement between the President of the Republic and the National Congress on the terms of the amendment); Colombia (Art. 377); among others.

The amending power of the constitution must be analyzed according to its proximity to the original constituent power, without being confused with it, however. The amending power is consubstantiated in a division of the constituent power, which would be identified as original when it creates a new constitution, and derived when it only changes the text of the constitution. The main characteristic that differentiates these two powers lies in the relation of subordination of the derived constituent power in relation to the original constituent power, which is expressed through the limits imposed on the amending power.

Therefore, the amending power corresponds to a delegation of competence granted by the constituent subject. 'The amendment power is a delegated power exercised by special constitutional agents. When the amendment power amends the constitution, it thus acts per procurationem of *the people*, as their agents'.[22] In other words, the amending power is granted by the original constituent and, therefore, is heteronomous. Thus, the one delegating may limit the scope of powers of the derived constituent power. This denotes a hierarchical relationship between the original constituent power and the amending power, since the former is the source of legitimacy of the latter.

We take it as established then that the amending power stands out from the original constituent power from the delegating-delegated relationship, since it exercises constitutional powers within the limits imposed by the constitutional foundation. It is, therefore, a faculty located in an intermediate point between the initial creation and the ordinary execution, that is, between the original constituent power and the constituted powers. It is thus included in the category of constituent power (in its derived viewpoint), since it can amend the instrument of delegation of powers, pro-

21 *Yaniv Roznai*, Unconstitutional Constitutional Amendments: the limits of amendment powers, Oxford University Press, 2017, 112.

22 *Roznai*, op. cit., at 118.

vided it follows procedural and substantive limits. Despite the existence of a hierarchical dynamic between original constituent power and derived constituent power, from an outside point of view there is no break in the unity of the constitution, since the constituted powers are equally subordinated to constitutional norms, regardless of whether they originate from the original text or from an amendment.

Understanding the identification of the specificity of the amending power is indispensable to indicate its proximity to the manifestation of popular sovereignty from its constituent viewpoint. Recognizing both the creation and the modification of the constitution as a right belonging to the people, was already defended by Hamilton in the Federalist paper nº 78. Thus, this approach will also inform how constitutional amendments should be interpreted in the scope of its judicial review, an issue analyzed in the next chapter.

IV. Supermajority Rule in Judicial Review of Constitutional Amendments

The democratic potentials of the amending power does not cease in its constituent and responsive nature since it depends on the analysis of a judicial decisional process that does not end at the promulgation of the constitutional change. Despite the exteriorization of a constitutional interpretation by means of a constitutional amendment, that activity is dynamic, because a specific constitutional reasoning does not perpetuate itself from the idea of 'final word', either from parliaments or constitutional courts.

Although derived constituent power has manifested itself as a legislative response, constitutional change can be re-assessed by a judicial institution. From the perspective of political constitutionalism, this faculty removes any justification for the defense of constitutional amendments as instruments to attenuate criticisms of the judicial review, since amendments would also be subject to review by constitutional courts. For a constitutional amendment to be recognized as unconstitutional, there must be a violation of some normatively superior restriction to the amendment act. It is only from the prediction of limits to the amending power that one can inquire about the appropriate mechanisms to sanction eventual violations.

The procedural limits to the amending power are justified insofar as they serve to differentiate the production of the constitutional norm from ordinary law (e.g. a quorum greater than the simple majority for approval, requirement of more than one round of deliberation, manifestation of federative entities, popular participation through a referendum, interval between votes). In addition, some constitutions also require obedience to substantive limits to amending power (e. g. democracy (Turkey, Art. 4), Republic (Italy, Art. 139), secularism (Portugal, Art. 288, b), fundamental rights (Brazil, Art. 60, paragraph 4, IV), human dignity (Angola, Art. 236, a), territorial integrity (Cape Verde, Art. 285), official language (Bahrain, Art. 120, c), and national flag (East Timor, Art. 156, i).[23]

In general, constitutional orders that seek to sanction noncompliance with the limits of the exercise of the amending power use the justice system, especially constitutional courts, to repair unconstitutional deviations. However, when constitutional courts assume responsibility for the exercise of judicial review of constitutional amendments (e. g. Germany, India, Colombia, Brazil), the debate about democratic deficiencies in this institutional arrangement, already presented in the first item, resurfaces, now with increased democratic difficulties because it is a review of a constitutional norm and not an ordinary law.

This distinction imposes a specific understanding regarding judicial review of constitutional amendments, since the object of judicial evaluation carries with it a democratic potential superior to the ordinary law. Given this scenario, the democratic tension present in judicial review in general is enhanced when the constitutional amendment is the object of judicial evaluation. According to *David Landau,* the doctrine of unconstitutional constitutional amendments seems to be the most extreme act of counter-majoritarianism.[24]

Faced with this extreme counter-majoritarian measure, judicial review of constitutional amendments require a more demanding commitment to the democratic principles of the amending power. In view of the wide presence of constitutional courts in contemporary democracies, we adopt the perspective that seeks to constrain or hinder judicial review of constitutional amendments without postulating its complete elimination.

Internal and external constraints may be included among the possible ways to redefine the extent and scope of judicial review in favor of its democratic enhancement. In the first case, we find the different methods of constitutional interpretation that moderate judicial interference in the construction of the normative content of the

23 See *Mark Tushnet,* Peasants with pitchforks, and toilers with Twitter: constitutional revolutions and the constituent power, International Journal of Constitutional Law, v. 13, No. 3, 2015, 640, and *Melissa Schwartzberg,* Democracy and Legal Change, Cambridge University Press, 2007, 201.

24 *David Landau,* Abusive constitutionalism, University of California Davis Law Review, v. 47, 2013, 232.

rights.[25] The external constraints are those imposed by other actors on constitutional courts, e. g.: supermajority requirement to strike down a constitutional amendment. They do not depend, therefore, on a self-deference to parliamentary work.[26] It is on this type of constraint that we will analyze from now on.

1. Majority Rule Decision-making

Majority rule, as a method for resolving issues when members of a community disagree, is considered the most important tool for making electoral and legislative decisions. This importance has to do with the fact that it is the last source of democratic legitimacy.[27] Thus, this statement recognizes the rule of majority as the democratic method par excellence.[28]

However, this rule does not necessarily imply that democracy is understood as popular sovereignty, since it can be used in different contexts of democratic or electoral institutions. Moreover, democracy does not peremptorily follow the majority rule, since in its Greek origins the democratic method used was the lottery.[29]

According to *John Heinberg*, the majority rule can be seen from three different moments.[30] In the first one, the majority method is based on the idea of force of the greatest number of wills over the minority force, such as the body movement in Physics. In the second option, the foundation of the majority finds support in the theorization of natural law by Contractualism, especially in John Locke, which developed the idea of government as consent of the governed along with the political equality contained in the expression "one man, one vote". Finally, the third aspect of the majority rule encompasses the concern about the abuses of this method regarding minorities and the incursion into the mechanisms that a constitutional government should use to review decisions made exclusively by majoritarian criteria, such as the judicial review.

These perspectives are restricted to the idea of majority in its most simple version, that is, to the concept of '50 % + 1'. The widespread presence of this rule in different

25 See, e. g., the presumption of constitutionality in *Edwart Dawson*, Adjusting the presumption of constitutionality based on margin of statutory passage, Journal of Constitutional Law, v. 16:1, 2013, 107/113.

26 *Robert Justin Lipkin*, Which Constitution? Who decides? The problem of judicial supremacy and the interbranch solution, Cardozo Law Review, v. 23:3, 2006, 1110–1112.

27 *Claus Offe*, Political legitimation through majority rule? Social Research, v. 50, No. 4, 1983, 719.

28 *John Gilbert Heinberg*, Theories of majority rule, The American Political Science Review, 452, 1932, 452.

29 *Stéphanie Novak*, Majority Rule, Philosophy Compass, 9/10, 2014, 682.

30 Id. at 453–465.

spheres of contemporary political decision-making stems from the fact that it is the only voting mechanism that is: a) decisive, since, for a pair of alternatives, it generates a single result; b) equalitarian/anonymous: if the vote of two people is changed, the final result is not changed; c) neutral: it does not favor any of the alternatives; and d) positively responsive: the votes cannot be counted in the opposite way.[31]

However, the simple majority rule involves some degree of institutional instability, since alterations depend only on changing the composition of the majority. This characteristic, from the perspective of political constitutionalism, represents an advantage, since the democratic note of this decision-making method resides in the possibility that political questions be ordinarily resolved, with equalitarian treatment of all members of the decision-making body.

In addition, simple majority does not have incentives to consult the minority or to consider its interests, since it does not depend on it to implement its political choices.[32] Consequently, there would be a greater threat of violation of minorities' rights, and thus mechanisms that would provide some form of protection against these actions from the majority would be indispensable.

On the other hand, decisions made by qualified majorities would be less likely to harm minority rights, since they depend on a numerically greater coalescence of wills, that is, the interests of a greater number of people are important for reaching the quorum of approval. In this way, institutions and procedures protecting minorities become less indispensable regarding decisions derived from the supermajority rule, such as constitutional amendments.

However, the rule of supermajority, or qualified majority (requirement of a percentage greater than 50 % + 1) does not satisfy the neutrality condition of the simple majority rule. When a qualified quorum is required for the approval of a decision, the opinion of those who want the approval of the change depends on a greater number of supporters than the simple half plus 1. On the other hand, those who want to maintain the situation and are against the proposal can block it by a group smaller than 50 % minus 1 (depending on the chosen proportion). In this type of arrangement, the "approval" and "non-approval" options do not receive the same treatment, since a greater number of supporters is required for the first alternative in comparison to the second. Therefore, the maintenance of the *status quo* is privileged.

31 *Kenneth May,* A set of independent necessary and sufficient conditions for simple majority decision, Econometrica, v. 20, No. 4, 1952, 680–682.

32 *Melissa Schwartzberg,* Counting the many: the origins and limits of supermajority rule, Cambridge University Press, 2014, 4.

Historically, the oldest document ever found that mandated a supermajority rule refers to the Lex Acilia Repetundarum, from Ancient Rome, dating approximately between 123 and 122 BC. Other remote examples of using the supermajority rule are found in the Third Council of the Lateran (1179), which required a 2/3 majority for the election of the Pope, and in the Florentine Republic, with the use of this instrument for the approval of candidates for magistrates.[33]

In her research, *Melissa Schwartzberg*[34] identified that the consolidation of the supermajority rule started in the Modern Age because it represented an alternative method of decision to unanimity. Clerical decisions based on the spiritual unity of the members of a group did not account for the disagreements that occurred in the definition of those responsible to emanate this consensus. Moreover, with the claim of same status among cardinals, the majoritarian aggregative method was the option that avoided a discussion about the individual merits of each voter. However, this element of equal treatment was not enough to explain the adoption of a supermajority rule, since there was still a commitment to the idea of unanimity, which is indispensable for the legitimacy of results. Thus, the supermajority rule was adopted as an intermediate level to accommodate the requirements of equal treatment, while still maintaining the influence of a unanimous consensus.

In the same sense, *James Buchanan* and *Gordon Tullock*[35] defended the supermajority rule by arguing that it is the second-best option to limit the tyranny of the majority. For these authors, the best protection of the distribution of rights occurs through unanimity, as it is the only way that guarantees an economically efficient result, since it is not possible to improve one's condition without worsening that of another.[36] The only preference-aggregation process that can result in zero externality is the consensus. However, the high costs of a unanimous decision-making process make it impossible to execute. For this reason, the supermajority rule would be the second-best option to protect minorities after the unanimity. According to this reasoning, a simple 51 % majority could confiscate the other 49 % of the members of the group, whereas in a supermajority of 75 %, for example, tyrannical action would occur only on 25 %

33 *Schwartzberg*, op. cit., at 45–46 and 50–62.

34 Id., at 50–58.

35 *James Buchanan* and *Gordon Tullock*, The Calculus of Consent: logical foundations of constitutional democracy, Indianapolis: Liberty Fund, 1962.

36 For critiques to *Buchanan* and *Tullock* approach, see *John Bradbury* and *Joseph Johnson*, Do supermajority rules limit or enhance majority tyranny? Evidence from the US States, 1960–1997, Public Choice, 127, 2006, 438.

of the voters.[37] It should be noted that this arithmetical argument simply diminishes the effects of a tyrannical action, without completely neutralizing it, which would only occur by unanimity.

Regardless of the merits and difficulties from each of the majority rules, it is important to emphasize that the theoretical tradition that developed the topic is mainly associated with electoral and parliamentary decision-making procedures. However, since constitutional courts also use the same majority method (mainly simple majority), there is an explanatory gap regarding the use of this rule in judicial systems. According to *Jeremy Waldron*, therefore, people see the use of the majority rule as obvious, without paying attention to the fact that this is an institution without the same electoral credentials as parliamentary bodies.[38]

2. Supermajority in Constitutional Courts

Akhil Amar[39] points out 4 key factors that explain the adoption of the bare majority rule by the US courts. First, the bare majority has specific mathematical properties that makes it the obvious answer when there are two alternatives. Second, from *John Locke's* influence on the founders of the American nation, the bare majority is considered the basic principle of every assembly. Third, the US Constitution incorporates the majority premise, albeit implicitly, as it specifies in the text when the decision method will not be bare majority.[40] Thus, if the exception is a qualified majority, the rule would be the bare majority. Finally, the bare majority rule was used in the promulgation of the US Constitution, because, although not foreseen, ratifications occurred by bare majorities, thus indicating a self-evidence of this decision-method.

However, the alleged self-evidence of the US Supreme Court's bare majority rule was challenged as early as 1823, when the first constitutional amendment was proposed to raise the Supreme Court's quorum to unanimity. According to *Evan Caminker*, the most recent similar proposition came in 1981 with the proposal re-

37 *Bradbury* and *Johnson*, op. cit., at 439.

38 *Jeremy Waldron*, Five to four: why do bare majorities rule on courts? The Yale Law Journal, 123:1692, 2014, 1695. *Mark Tushnet* belives that court simple majority rulings are part of the substance of US courts, in: How different is writing small from writing large. The Good Society, v. 18, No. 1, 2009, 16.

39 *Akhil Amar*, America's unwritten Constitution: the precedents and principles we live by, New York: Basic Books 2012, 357–360.

40 Examples of supermajorities: art. I, § 3, cl. 6; art. I, § 5, cl. 2; art. I, § 7, cl. 2; art. II, § 2, cl. 2; art. V; XIV amendment, § 3; XXV amendment, § 4.

quiring 7 favorable votes to strike down a law as unconstitutional.[41] It should be noted that at the state level, Ohio adopted, in 1912, a constitutional amendment stipulating a supermajority quorum for declarations of unconstitutionality (which was not maintained after an amendment in 1968), as well as North Dakota and Nebraska.[42]

In the US, therefore, decisions made by the Supreme Court with a difference of 5×4[43] bother those who see this situation as a violation of the doctrine of reasonable doubt, which states that legislative acts should be presumed as constitutional by the courts until their unconstitutionality is demonstrated beyond any reasonable doubt, as in the presumption of innocence. *Robert Cushman* also points out that there is no necessary connection between the doctrine of reasonable doubt and the unanimity rule, since, like the presumption of innocence, the decision-making of the jury does not always happen through unanimity.[44]

On the other hand, there are other constitutional courts that use the supermajority method in very specific situations, such as the Constitutional Court of Chile, which, as a rule, makes decisions through the bare majority (Art. 92 of the Chilean Constitution) but requires the favorable manifestation of 8 of the 10 members of the Constitutional Court in the abstract declaration of unconstitutionality of a law previously declared unconstitutional in a specific case (Art. 93, paragraph 7 of the Chilean Constitution).[45]

In Peru, the Constitutional Court is composed of 7 judges and adopts the bare majority rule, except to resolve the inadmissibility of an unconstitutionality claim or to declare the unconstitutionality of a norm, with a hierarchy of law, where 5 judges are required to agree. If a qualified majority is not reached, the Court declares the unconstitutionality claim unfounded, in accordance with Art. 10 of its rules of procedure.

The Constitutional Court of the Czech Republic consists of 15 judges and, in cases of judicial review of infra-constitutional law, as well as of judicial review of in-

41 *Evan Caminker*. Thayerian deference to Congress and Supreme Court supermajority rules: lessons from the past, Indiana Law Journal, v. 78, 2003, 88.

42 For the historical context of these amendments, see: *Sandra Zellmer* and *Kathleen Miller*, The fallacy of judicial supermajority clauses in state constitutions; available at: <https://papers.ssrn.com/sol3/papers.cfm?abstract_id=2725234>.

43 See *Robert Riggs*, When every vote counts: 5–4 decisions in the United States Supreme Court, 1900–90, Hofstra Law Review, v. 21, No. 3, 1993.

44 *Robert Cushman*, Constitutional decisions by a bare majority of the court, Michigan Law Review, v. 19, nº 8, 1921, 772, 781 and 791.

45 See *Humberto Nogueira Alcalá*, Le sentencia del Tribunal Constitucional en Chile: análisis y reflexiones jurídicas, Estudios Constitucionales, a. 8, No. 1, 2010, 80.

ternational treaties, it requires the positive manifestation of 9 judges (paragraph 13 of the Constitutional Court).

In Brazil, the declaration of unconstitutionality of a law depends on the bare majority of the 11 judges. However, there are three exceptions that institute a supermajority of 2/3 for issues related to the refusal of admissibility of general repercussions of extraordinary appeals; approval of a binding precedent; and modulation of temporal effects from judicial review rulings.

According to Art. 190 of the Organic Law of judicial guarantees and judicial review of Ecuador, the quorum for deliberation of the full Constitutional Court is the bare majority of all 9 judges. The exception to this rule are cases of dismissal of judges of the Court, by 2/3 of the members. Similarly, the Federal Constitutional Court of Germany applies the supermajority rule of 2/3 for the procedure of early retirement or removal from office of a court judge, in accordance with paragraph 105 of the Federal Constitutional Court Act.

Finally, Turkey is an example of a supermajority requirement exclusively in relation to the judicial review of constitutional amendments, by imposing the concurrence of 2/3 of the members of its Constitutional Court (Art. 149 of the Turkish Constitution).

It should be noted that the adoption of the majority rule, be it simple or qualified, can be present in courts structured as 'seriatim' or as 'per curiam'. In the first case, the court's ruling is reached according to the decision of each member of the court; in the second case, the court issues a single decision. The reason for this independent relationship is that the rules around unanimity, qualified majority or simple majority are instruments of internal decision-making. On the other hand, the seriatim or per curiam structure is a post-decision element related to the way the internal division of previously made decisions will be publicized. For this reason, it is possible for a court to make a decision using the rule of majority of its members in a closed session and then make a public statement by means of a per curiam opinion so as not to divulge the internal division of the judges and strengthen the collegial character of the decision.[46] Finally, the discussion of the majority rule only makes sense in constitutional courts that adopt aggregate forms of individual opinions.

Taking the criticisms to judicial review perpetrated by political constitutionalism as a starting point, it can be said that the rule of supermajority for judicial review of constitutional amendments has the advantage of creating a formal decision-making instrument that makes the amendment more difficult to be removed, since it makes

46 *Conrado Mendes*, Constitutional Courts and Deliberative Democracy, United Kingdom: Oxford University Press, 2013. 168.

the decision dependent on the concurrence of more court members. As a result, the supermajority rule is a mechanism of deference to legislative activity.

In the scope of judicial review of constitutional amendments, the restriction of judicial activity is justified because the object of revision is a norm from the derived constituent power, that is, from that power that differs from the constituted powers, since it has the possibility of extending constitutional protection. This characteristic imposes higher democratic demands on this amending power, which are not present in constituted powers. Thus, in the scope of strong judicial review, the attenuation of democratic criticism to this way of acting can be fulfilled by adopting the rule of supermajority for decisions on the judicial review of constitutional amendments.

The stipulation of the supermajority rule in judicial review of constitutional amendment also contributes to the stability of judicial decisions in comparison to the bare majority rule,[47] since both creation and overruling a precedent will depend on a more demanding commitment regarding the support for approval. In the judicial branch, maintaining the status quo meets the demand for stability of decisions, especially regarding constitutional courts, responsible for the uniformity of constitutional interpretation.

From the moment the rule of supermajority makes more expensive to approve a decision, it favors the preservation of the status quo, since a minoritarian group with less than 50 % minus 1 can veto the proposal being discussed. The application of this rule in a constitutional amendment proposal, for example, means the presumption of maintenance of the current constitutional text, which, to be amended, is costlier than the approval of 50 % plus 1 of the group members. On the other hand, when the supermajority rule is transferred to the judicial review, there is no way to dissociate itself from this presumption of conservation of the questioned act, in this case, the amendment. However, this presumption of maintaining the status *quo* of the supermajority rule is in favor of judicial deference to the legislative act and meets the demand for democratization of judicial review.

Unlike parliamentary deliberations, the presumption, by giving different weights for 'constitutionality' vs. 'unconstitutionality' at the beginning of the judicial decision, does not violate the idea of equal treatment between the decision makers. This is because the political equality that political constitutionalists believe is violated by the rule of supermajority concerns the lack of equal consideration between the opinions of political representatives, that is, of individuals acting on behalf of the collectivity. At this point, the allegation of a violation of equal treatment makes sense, since

47 *Jed Handelsman Shugerman,* A six-three rule: reviving consensus and deference on the Supreme Court, Georgia Law Review, v. 37, 2003, 949.

political equality among legislators is a corollary of adherence to political equality among citizens.[48]

On the other hand, constitutional courts act based on reasons independent from their being representative institutions. The courts are criticized precisely due to the absence of a direct democratic connection that exists in parliaments. Jeremy Waldron points out that the use of majority rule in electoral and parliamentary contexts is justified by the aggregation of a majority of interests; in the judicial sphere, to add votes means to count justifiable interpretations based on a legal argument. Therefore, one must be cautious when transferring the reasons that surround the majority rule in the parliamentary context to the judicial branch.[49]

It should also be noted that the argumentative line developed in this research does not necessarily defend the adoption of the supermajority rule in the judicial review of infra-constitutional law. This is because the premise for the supermajority rule only when dealing with the review of amendments is based on the diverse nature of the constitutional amendment in relation to the infra-constitutional law. Both are not fruits of the same source of power, they act on hierarchically distinct norms and their demands of democratic engagement are different. For that reason, they need non-identitarian judicial review, that is, a form of judicial review that somehow considers these differences constitutive.[50]

A judicial review in which the level of judicial interference on the amendment and the infra-constitutional law is the same would ignore all the different presuppositions between these norms. For this reason, the rule of supermajority in the judicial review of amendments does not cover the extension of the argument to the review of infra-constitutional law if this entails adopting the same supermajority quorum for both norms.

V. Concluding Remarks

From these arguments, it is evident that the case for adopting the rule of supermajority necessarily depends on the institutional context in which it will be inserted, since, as shown, it cannot be disassociated from its preservationist nature. This ele-

48 *Waldron,* (note 37, at 1722.

49 Id., op. cit., at 1708–1709.

50 See *Carlos Bernal,* Unconstitutional constitutional amendments in the case study of Colombia: an analysis of the justification and meaning of the constitutional replacement doctrine, International Journal of Constitutional Law, v. 11, No. 2, 2013.

ment, however, is not dispensable in all political arenas where there is aggregation of votes, under the justification of unequal treatment of the eligible options.

First, because the egalitarian treatment demanded by the democratic process is directly related to the representation of citizens, who have the right to see their opinions being treated with the same opportunity and weight by the parliamentary representatives. However, when the majority rule is transposed to the judicial branch, the representative element and its corollaries are not carried along.

Second, even if democracy involves the idea of opening decisions to constant changes due to social disagreements, one has to consider that, among the different decision-making arenas, some require a degree of stability greater than others. Constitutional jurisdiction, for example, is built, both by the nature of its members and by its institutional arrangement, with the aim of ensuring the consistency of judicial decisions that interpret the constitution. In this sense, where there are strong reasons for the presumption of maintenance of the decision, be it parliamentary or judicial, the supermajority rule satisfies this requirement.

Finally, although the legitimacy of amendment judicial review may not be accepted by political constitutionalism, at least it can be said that the supermajoritary method in the constitutional courts meets the general demands for legislative deference. In this sense, *Jeremy Waldron* had already expressed the possibility of establishing supermajority for judicial review.[51] Moreover, in a recent speech, *Waldron* stated that the possibility supermajority rule in courts deserves to be considered, even as an experiment, 'we might see a supermajoritarian requirement as a salutary institutional expression of a presumption in favor of the legislature, and as a device to ensure that the striking down of legislation takes place only when its unconstitutionality is beyond question'.[52]

51 *Waldron* (note 37), at 1730.

52 *Jeremy Waldron*, Judicial review and political legitimacy, Text of his speech at Colombian Constitutional Court in 8/4/17, 13–14.

Act of Ill-gotten Political Party Assets in Taiwan: A Bill of Attainder in the Name of Transitional Justice

David KC Huang

Abstract

Taiwan's congress enacted the Act of Political Party Assets in the name of transitional justice in 2016. However, the Act has stirred up debates surrounding constitutionality, because only the Chinese Nationalist Party is *de facto* subject to the Act, which means that the Act may constitute a bill of attainder *in abstracto*. Meanwhile, supporters of the Act have firmly claimed that the Act is part of Taiwan's transitional justice project, and that this justifies the Act. They claim that justice stands for the restitution of ill-gotten assets howsoever they were acquired by whoever acquired them. Based on these arguments, this article begins by examining the Act according to the concept of the bill of attainder, then goes on to analyse the Act via the principles of justice, peace and the rule of law in order to discover the true spirit of transitional justice in Taiwan.

I. Introduction

Transitional justice came to the world's attention with Germany's unconditional surrender[1] at the end of WWII and the Nuremberg Trials.[2] Nowadays it is usually more associated with the third wave of democratisation.[3] It is defined as 'the range of judicial and non-judicial mechanisms aimed at dealing with a legacy of large-scale abuses of human rights and/or violations of international humanitarian law',[4] the mechanisms of which are designed 'to address the need for accountability, to provide justice and to foster reconciliation in societies in transition from authoritarian to democratic rule or from war to peace'.[5] Most importantly, '[t]he aim of transitional [...]

1 *Cf. Jeffrey K. Olick*, In the House of the Hangman: The Agonies of German Defeat, 1943–1949, Chicago 2005, 17–19.

2 See generally *Sanya Romeike*, Transitional Justice in Germany after 1945 and after 1990, Occasional Paper No.1, International Nuremberg Principles Academy 2016, 1, at 8–9.

3 *Joanna R. Quinn*, The Development of Transitional Justice, in C. Lawther, L. Moffett and D. Jacobs (eds.), Research Handbook on Transitional Justice, Cheltenham 2017, 11–33, at 14–15.

4 *Rachel Kerr* and *Eirin Mobekk*, Peace and Justice: Seeking Accountability after War, Cambridge 2007, 3.

5 *Kerr* and *Mobekk*, l. c.

justice […] is to contribute to sustainable peace and the rebuilding of a society based on the rule of law'.[6]

We have learnt from *Rachel Kerr* and *Eirin Mobekk* that transitional justice is associated with three key terms: justice, peace and the rule of law.[7] This means we need to think about the logic extension of transitional justice in accordance with its intension,[8] which in turn means that it must be subject to the principles of justice, peace and the rule of law, or else it cannot achieve its specific goals. For example, transitional justice cannot be conducted by enacting a bill of attainder[9] because legislative vengeance[10] is deemed unconstitutional[11] and unjust under any circumstances. Moreover, it cannot contradict the principles of the rule of law[12] *per se*, or it will provide no 'sustainable peace'[13] and will only trigger another demand for transitional justice at some point in the future. In other words, the extension of transitional justice logically limits its means of implementation, that no violations of legal principles whatsoever shall be deemed constitutional, even they are enacted in the name of transitional justice.

This article will analyse Taiwan's Act Governing the Handling of Ill-gotten Properties by Political Parties and Their Affiliate Organizations (further: Act of Political Party Assets) accordingly – as an Act promulgated by Taiwan's supreme legislative body, the Legislative Yuan, in 2016 which set off fierce debates surrounding its constitutionality. The Act was proposed by the congressmen and congresswomen of the ruling Democratic Progressive Party, whose political opponents in the Chinese Nationalist Party protested that they would be the only political entity that would be subject to the Act. This article will therefore begin by examining whether or not the Act constitutes an act of attainder[14] in the first instance and will continually check

6 *Kerr* and *Mobekk*, l. c.

7 *Kerr* and *Mobekk*, l. c.

8 See generally *Patrick J. Hurley*, A Concise Introduction to Logic, Boston 2012, 88–92.

9 See generally *David F. Forte* and *Matthew Spalding* (eds.), The Heritage Guide to the Constitution: Fully Revised Second Edition, Washington D. C. 2014, 202.

10 Compare *Terence Kilburn* and *Anthony Milton*, The Public Context of the Trial and Execution of Strafford, in: J. F. Merritt (ed.), The Political World of Thomas Wentworth, Earl of Strafford, 1621–1641, Cambridge 1996, 230–251, at 235, with *Kenneth Pickthorn*, Early Tudor Government: Henry VII, Cambridge 1934, 119.

11 *Alexander Hamilton, John Jay* and *James Madison*, The Federalist, Indianapolis 1788/2001, 232.

12 *T. R. S. Allan*, Constitutional Justice: A Liberal Theory of the Rule of Law, New York 2001, 148.

13 *Kerr* and *Mobekk*, op. cit. (note 4), at 3.

14 See generally *Forte and Spalding* (note 9), at 202.

the constitutionality of the Act in accordance with the principles of the rule of law. In particular it will examine the burden of proof[15] and *ex post facto*[16] laws in contrast to German examples. The article will conclude that the Act is indeed nothing more than an act of attainder masquerading as transitional justice, and that its enactment will only trigger off another demand for transitional justice in the future.

II. Act or Bill of Attainder?

> "In common law, bills of attainder were legislative acts that, without trial, condemned specifically designated persons or groups to death. Bills of attainder also required the 'corruption of blood'; that is, they denied the right to the condemned's heirs to inherit the guilty party's estate. Bills of pains and penalties, in contrast, singled out designated persons or groups for punishment less than death, such as banishment or disenfranchisement".[17]

According to *T. R. S. Allan*, 'the act or 'bill' of attainder is the paradigmatic example of legislation whose violation of the principles of equality and due process contravenes the rule of law', because '[i]t denies the separation of powers between legislature and judiciary, and the related distinction between legislative and judicial process, and so removes the protection that law is meant to provide from governmental hostility and arbitrary power'.[18] Punishments under an act of attainder 'may not only be for past acts, but it also may be triggered whenever the person engages in any future prohibited acts'.[19] Hence, *James Madison* reiterates in The Federalist that '[b]ills of attainder, *ex post facto* laws ... are contrary to ... every principle of sound legislation ... additional fences against these dangers ought not to be omitted'.[20] The US Constitution therefore stipulates that '[n]o Bill of Attainder or *ex post facto* Law shall be passed'.[21]

Historically, 'the victor of any political confrontation' in England could enact an act of attainder because of the political need 'to pronounce penalties on the hard core

15 See generally *Mojtaba Kazazi*, Burden of Proof and Related Issues: A Study on Evidence Before International Tribunals, The Hague 1996, 58; *Andrew Stumer*, The Presumption of Innocence: Evidential and Human Rights Perspectives, Oxford 2010, 190–191.

16 See generally *Hamilton, Jay* and *Madison*, l. c.

17 *Forte* and *Spalding* (note 9), at 202.

18 *Allan*, op. cit. (note 12), at 148.

19 *Forte* and *Spalding*, l. c.

20 *Hamilton, Jay* and *Madison*, op. cit. (note 11), at 232.

21 U. S. Const. art. I § 9, cl. 3.

of the vanquished. Initially the punishment was part of the judgement in parliament but after Richard II's revenge against Gloucester, Arundel and Warwick … the judicial process almost disappeared and the pronouncement of penalty came to stand by itself'.[22] Hence, attainder in England became an act of Parliament 'which was itself the result of a battle or a revolution', so that '[i]t is not surprising if the accused had no guarantee of judicial treatment and if the procedure was summary and undefined', because it represented the 'occasion when 'ther was many gentlemen agaynst it, but it wold not be, for it was the Kings pleasure'.[23] Moreover, England's bill of attainder was not just the 'Kings pleasure',[24] it also represented Parliament's abuse of power. One of the most notorious cases of attainder in England was that of *Thomas Wentworth*, the First Earl of Strafford, who was sentenced to death by Parliament in 1641. When Parliament realised that 'the Lords were unlikely to vote for Strafford's impeachment', it directly enacted an act of attainder instead and executed Strafford accordingly '[b]efore the Lords could reach their judgement'.[25]

We normally identify an act as a bill of attainder by looking at it from the perspective of due process.[26] In the 1890 Kentucky Constitutional Convention, *C. T. Allen* stood on this perspective[27] and held that '[a] legislature passes an act robbing me of my life for an alleged crime, I not hearing the witnesses, having no jury, not being allowed to face what witnesses they have, and deprived of the privilege to cross-examine them, robbing me of my life and sending me to my grave. That is a Bill of Attainder, as I understand it'.[28] However, the case of *Thomas Wentworth* provides us with another perspective, that of purpose, for understanding the nature of the bill of attainder. That is, when a person or a group is deemed guilty by a legislature for whatever reason, as was the case with *Thomas Wentworth*,[29] an act can be enacted purposively under which a crime is tailored to the accused.[30] That, by its very purpose, is still a bill of attainder as I, too, understand it. In other words, our question is: can we

22 *J. G. Bellamy*, The Law of Treason in England in Later Middle Ages, Cambridge 1970, 177.

23 *Pickthorn*, op. cit. (note 10), at 119.

24 *Pickthorn*, l. c.

25 *Kilburn* and *Milton*, op. cit. (note 10), at 235.

26 *Thomas J. Gardner* and *Terry M. Anderson*, Criminal Law, Boston 2016, 18; *Suri Ratnapala*, Jurisprudence, Singapore 2017, 400–409; see also *United States v. Brown*, 381 U. S. 437 (1965).

27 Ky. Const. Conv., Convention Record, 1 Kentucky Constitutional Convention 1890, 1, at 13–27.

28 Ky. Const. Conv., l. c., at 21.

29 See *Kilburn* and *Milton*, op. cit. (note 10), at 235.

30 See *W. Cleon Skousen*, The Making of America: The Substance and Meaning of the Constitution, Washington D. C. 1985, 475.

tailor or design a specific crime to a particular person or political group under the name of democracy? The US Constitution says we cannot,[31] as does the Canadian parliament,[32] but Taiwan's Act Governing the Handling of Ill-gotten Properties by Political Parties and Their Affiliate Organizations promulgated on 10 August 2016 obviously says that we can:

> Assets remain at the time of the promulgation of this Act those that are defined as having been acquired by the [defined] political party and [its] affiliate organisations, or consigned or transferred to the trustees, or registered under the name of the trustees by the defined since 15 August 1945. Such asset shall be deemed ill-gotten property unless it is proved to be part of the membership due, party funding, donations to political campaigns, government grants or interest thereon.
> Assets acquired by the [defined] political party and affiliate organisations since 15 August 1945 without charge, or if the charge was disproportional *per se*, unless it is proved to be part of membership dues, party funding, donation for political campaigns, government grants or interest thereon, shall be deemed ill-gotten property even it is no longer possessed by the defined party or its trustees at the time of the promulgation of this Act.[33]

Article 5 of the Act of Political Party Assets (2016) defines ill-gotten property[34] by the rule of *expressio unius est exclusio alterius*.[35] Hence, all assets of defined political parties and their affiliate organisations since 15 August 1945 that were not obtained in accordance with the Article can only be defined as ill-gotten properties.[36] The burden of proof[37] is placed upon the political parties and their affiliate organisations[38] *per se*, because assets that are not categorised under the waivers in accordance with Article 5 of the Act will be deemed ill-gotten property.[39] Article 5 of the Act, and even the Act in its entirety, '[sets] out its purposes in some detail and to which reference

31 U. S. Const. art. I § 9, cl. 3.

32 E. g., Canadian HC Deb 14 May 1984, vol 3, 3683–3684 (debating on the Act Respecting the Execution of Clifford Robert Olson and held that the bill of attainder is 'unacceptable' in Canada because it was 'a proceeding at one time employed by the British Parliament to convict and condemn an individual of a high crime by Act of Parliament').

33 Act of Political Party Assets § 5 (2016) (Author's translation).

34 Ibid.

35 See generally *Tempest v. Kilner* (1846) 3 CB 249.

36 Act of Political Party Assets § 5 (2016).

37 See generally *Kazazi*, op. cit. (note 15), 57–64.

38 Compare Act of Political Party Assets § 5 (2016), with Act of Political Party Assets § 8 (2016).

39 Act of Political Party Assets § 5 (2016).

could be made for purposes of interpretation'[40] according to the intrinsic aid rule of legal interpretation.[41] Moreover, only the defined political parties and their affiliate organisations will be motivated to apply the waivers in reality, so how should the Ill-gotten Party Assets Settlement Committee prove any disputed asset claims?

In other words, the Act violates the rule of burden of proof as we normally understand it; 'that is, the party which is making affirmative allegations regarding a disputed fact or issue bears the burden of proving such a fact or issue throughout the case'.[42] Furthermore, how can this Act be enacted if the defined political parties and affiliate organisations are not deemed guilty in the eyes of the legislature? If this is the case, how can this Act, in accordance with its legislative purpose or intrinsic aid,[43] not be identified as an act of attainder? In my opinion, this 'is a Bill of Attainder, as I understand it',[44] especially when we read the definition of the political party provided by Article 4, Clause 1, of the Act:

> Political party refers to one established and registered in accordance with the Civil Associations Act for the Period of the Communist Rebellion before 15 July 1987.[45]

15 July 1987 was the day of the lifting[46] of Taiwanese Martial Law,[47] which means that there are only two political parties that are beyond the reach of the Article, even though both were established before 15 July 1987: the Democratic Progressive Party, whose congressmen and women enacted this Act, and the Chinese Communist Party, which successfully led that armed rebellion against the Republic of China. Neither party was 'registered in accordance with the Civil Associations Act for the Period of Communist Rebellion',[48] in fact no record of the registration of the Democratic Progressive Party has been found[49] in accordance with information provided by the ROC

40 *Gary Slapper* and *David Kelly*, English Law, Abingdon 2010, 38.

41 See generally *Mark Thomas* and *Claire McGourlay*, English Legal System Concentrate, Oxford 2017, 46–47.

42 *Kazazi*, op. cit. (note 15), at 58.

43 See generally *Slapper and Kelly*, l. c., at 38; *Thomas* and *McGourlay*, l. c., 46–47.

44 Ky. Const. Conv., op. cit. (note 27), at 17.

45 Act of Political Party Assets § 4 (1) (2016) (Author's translation).

46 Presidential Order 1987, President Gazette 4794 (14 July 1987).

47 Taiwan Garrison Command Martial Law Order No.1 (19 May 1949).

48 Act of Political Party Assets § 4(1) (2016).

49 See generally *Shelley Rigger*, From Opposite to Power: Taiwan's Democratic Progressive Party, Boulder 2001, 15–36; *Denny Roy*, Taiwan: A Political History, Ithaca 2003, 152–182.

Ministry of the Interior,[50] and it is impossible that the Chinese Communist Party had registered itself *per se*.[51] This meant that the Chinese Nationalist Party was *de facto* the only political party[52] that is covered by the definition[53] provided by the Act, because it is *de jure* the only party established and registered before the date that has sufficient assets for 'robbing'.[54] This explains why the Control Yuan, an independent branch which exercises the power of impeachment on behalf of the Republic of China,[55] has filed a constitutional litigation against the Ill-gotten Party Assets Settlement Committee in March 2017,[56] expressing publicly that the entire Act is unconstitutional in the eyes of the Control Yuan because it 'presumes that KMT [Nationalist Party] assets were illicitly obtained and places the burden of proof on the KMT… The act also authorizes the committee to freeze KMT assets without a court order'.[57] In fact, the Chinese Nationalist Party is the only possible 'prey' of the Ill-gotten Party Assets Settlement Committee; and if this Act is not deemed a bill of attainder by law as well as by fact, what exactly defines a bill of attainder to which James Madison was strongly opposed[58] in *The Federalist*?

In a nutshell, no legislature in the world would consider itself to be in the wrong when its legislators pass a bill of attainder, including the English Parliament when it sentenced *Thomas Wentworth* to death.[59] No politician in the world will retaliate against his or her political enemies under the name of 'the power of the dark side'.[60]

50 ROC Ministry of the Interior = Ministry of Interior, Republic of China. The Website of Parties and National Political Associations, available at <https://party.moi.gov.tw/pgms/politics/party!detail.action?id=16>.

51 Cf. *Lung-Chu Chen*, The U.S.-Taiwan-China Relationship in International Law and Policy, New York 2016, 15–16; see generally Judicial Yuan Interpretation No.644 [2008] (holding that the ROC Constitution provides no ban against communism or the partition of the nation).

52 See generally *Jake Chung*, Legislature Approves Law on Ill-gotten Party Assets, available at <http://www.taipeitimes.com/News/front/archives/2016/07/26/2003651800>.

53 Compare Act of Political Party Assets § 4(1) (2016), with Act of Political Party Assets § 5 (2016).

54 Ky. Const. Conv., op. cit. (note 27), at 21.

55 See generally *ROC Control Yuan*, Our History, available at <https://www.cy.gov.tw/ct.asp?xItem=6036&CtNode=989&mp=21>.

56 *Wei-Han Chen*, Control Yuan Queries Party Assets Law, available at <http://www.taipeitimes.com/News/front/archives/2017/03/29/2003667669>.

57 *Chen*, l. c.

58 *Hamilton, Jay* and *Madison*, op. cit. (note 11), at 232.

59 *Kilburn and Milton*, op. cit. (note 10), at 235.

60 Star Wars: Return to the Jedi (1983).

That is why *James Madison* was unconditionally opposed to all forms of bills of attainder in *The Federalist,*[61] and that is what we can learn from Thomas Wentworth's death.

III. Transitional Justice or Transitional Injustice

He who comes to equity must come with clean hands.[62]

Perhaps the clean hands doctrine of English equity[63] can help us to realise exactly what justice[64] is supposed to be, and from there we can learn what transitional justice[65] is supposed to be. If a lion accuses a tiger of being brutal because a tiger hunts its prey, will the lion's claim sound just? By the same logic if a legislature unconstitutionally passes a bill of attainder under the name of transitional justice, violating the principles of due process and procedural fairness[66] in order to convict the 'devil' of unconstitutionality, will this bill of attainder really bring transitional justice to us, or will it will only trigger off another claim to transitional justice in the future? In other words, transitional justice is applied to 'deal with an unjust or atrocious past', which implies that it can only be applied under just, equal and constitutional processes, or else there will be another 'unjust or atrocious past'[67] sooner or later, meaning that a repetition of wrongdoing is another wrongdoing, instead of transitional justice, and those who seek transitional justice must act judiciously.[68]

Few people in the world would consider giving up the pursuit of justice, but what is supposed to be 'constitutional justice is defined, in large part, by an accu-

61 *Hamilton, Jay* and *Madison,* op. cit. (note 11), at 232.

62 *Alastair Hudson,* Equity and Trust, Abingdon 2017, 24.

63 See generally *Paul S. Davies* and *Graham Virgo,* Equity & Trust: Text, Cases, and Materials, Oxford 2016, 16–18; *Hudson,* l. c., at 24.

64 I am aware that there is no direct connection between English equity and transitional justice; however, law and legal theories are surrounded by the concept of justice *per se,* and I attempt to highlight the need of clean hands if one aims at transitional justice – it is obviously absurd when a butcher claims transitional justice against another butcher.

65 *Claudio Corradetti,* Philosophical Issues in Transitional Justice Theory: A (Provisional) Balance, 2/2013 Politica & Società 2013, 185, 185–220.

66 *Jeremy Olivier,* How to Achieve Transitional Justice in Taiwan, available at <https://sentinel.tw/transitional-justice-taiwan/>.

67 *Anja Mihr,* An Introduction to Transitional Justice, in O. Simić (ed.), An Introduction to Transitional Justice, Abingdon 2017, 1–27, at 3.*Mihr,* op. cit. (note 74), 3.

68 Cf. *Davies* and *Virgo,* l. c., 15–16 (rephrasing the legal maxim of English equity, 'those who seek equity must do equity').

rate understanding of the legal tradition',[69] instead of foreign legal tradition, under which anything that presumes to be just governance can be determined accordingly.[70] For example, the German Basic Law mirrors the dreadful failure of the Weimar Constitution,[71] so that it can embrace the concept of *streitbare Demokratie*[72] promoted by *Karl Löwenstein*,[73] a militant democracy[74] or defensive (*wehrhafte*[75]) democracy, authorising the Bundesverfassungsgericht,[76] the German constitutional court, to strike down '[a]ssociations whose aims or activities contravene criminal laws, or are directed against the constitutional order or the concept of international understanding'.[77] Moreover, political parties in Germany are constitutionally obliged to 'publicly account for their assets and for the sources and use of their funds'.[78] This means that political parties in Germany are unconstitutional in the eyes of the Bundesverfassungsgericht and the German Basic Law unless and until they 'publicly account for their assets and for the sources and use of their funds',[79] which is the constitutional justice that originated in the German legal tradition in response to Nazism,[80] that he who comes to German politics must come with clean hands.[81]

69 *T. R. S. Allan*, Constitutional Justice and the Concept of Law, in G. Huscroft (ed.), Expounding the Constitution: Essays in Constitutional Theory, New York 2008, 219–244, at 241.

70 Cf. *Allan* op. cit. (note 69), at 241.

71 *Svetlana Tyulkina*, Militant Democracy: Undemocratic Political Parties and Beyond, Abingdon 2015, 66.

72 See generally *Hans-Gerd Jaschke*, Die Zukunft der 'streitbaren Demokratie', 1(1) Totalitarismus und Demokratie 2004, 109, at 111–117.

73 See generally *Karl Löwenstein*, Militant Democracy and Fundamental Rights, I, 31(3) Am. Political Sci. Rev. 1937, 417, at 417–432; *Karl Löwenstein*, Militant Democracy and Fundamental Rights, II, 31(4) Am. Political Sci. Rev. 1937, 638, at 638–658.

74 See generally *Shlomo Avineri*, Introduction, in A. Sajó (ed.), Militant Democracy, Utrecht 2004, 1–14, 1–14.

75 *Jaschke*, op. cit., at 109.

76 German Basic Law § 21 (4) (1949/2017) (providing that 'Über die Frage der Verfassungswidrigkeit nach Absatz 2 sowie über den Ausschluss von staatlicher Finanzierung nach Absatz 3 entscheidet das Bundesverfassungsgericht').

77 German Basic Law § 9 (2) (1949).

78 German Basic Law § 21 (1) (1949/2017) (providing that 'Sie müssen über die Herkunft und Verwendung ihrer Mittel sowie über ihr Vermögen öffentlich Rechenschaft geben').

79 Ibid.

80 See *Roman David*, Transitional Injustice? Criteria for Conformity of Lustration to the Right to Political Expression, 56(6) Eur.-Asia Stud. 2004, 789, at 798.

81 Cf. *Hudson*, op. cit. (note 62), 24 (rephrasing the legal maxim of English equity, 'he who comes to equity must come with clean hands').

As far as this article is concerned, it is difficult to conclude that German transitional justice regarding political party assets constitutes a bill of attainder against the NSDAP and the Socialist Union Party, the Sozialistische Einheitspartei Deutschlands, or SED. It is undoubtedly a constitutional obligation of the Federal Republic of Germany that anyone who comes to German politics must come with clean hands,[82] an obligation with which all parties in Germany must comply, including the NSDAP and the SED[83] if they intend to engage in political activities within the country. In the case of the SED the declaration of assets is not so much the pursuit of transitional justice[84] as the fulfilment of German constitutional obligations,[85] despite the fact that a pursuit of transitional justice against the SED has been conducted.[86] As far as the NSDAP is concerned, the party is not compatible with the constitutional framework of the Federal Republic of Germany[87] at all, so its very existence is simply unconstitutional.[88]

However, there is no such constitutional obligation embodied in the ROC Constitution of 1947. More precisely, political parties within Taiwan are constitutionally prohibited only from '[making] use of armed forces as an instrument in a struggle for political powers'[89] in accordance with the main text of the Constitution. Such parties may be dissolved by the Judicial Yuan if their 'goals or activities endanger the existence of the Republic of China or the nation's free and democratic constitutional order'[90] in accordance with the Additional Articles of the Constitution. This means that both the ROC Constitution and German Basic Law embrace the idea[91] of mil-

82 *Hudson*, l. c.

83 Cf. *Gábor Halmai*, The Role of Constitutionalism in Transitional Justice Processes in Central Europe, Research Report, International Center for Transitional Justice 2017, 1, at 13 (reporting that transitional justice regarding the SED has been conducted under the framework of the German Basic Law instead of the East German 'indigenous process of coming to terms with the past', by which many East Germans believe that they were conquered by the West).

84 Cf. *Halmai*, l. c.

85 German Basic Law § 21 (1) (1949/2017).

86 See generally Romeike, op. cit. (note 2), 43–63.

87 German Basic Law § 9 (2) (1949).

88 Compare German Basic Law § 9 (2) (1949), with German Basic Law § 18 (1949), *and* German Basic Law § 21 (4) (1949/2017); see also BverfGE 2, 1 (SRP-Verbot, 1952); but see BverfGE 2 BvB 1/13 (NPD-Verbot, 2017, holding that the NPD is incapable of doing what it has promoted in politics.

89 Constitution of R. O. C. § 139 (1947).

90 Constitution of R. O. C. amend. § 5V (1992/2005).

91 Compare Constitution of R. O. C. amend. § 5V (1992/2005), with German Basic Law § 9 (2) (1949).

itant democracy,[92] but with different focuses originating from different legal traditions[93] in response to different incidents. Political parties in the ROC are burdened with disarmament[94] and those in Germany are burdened with property declaration.[95] In contrast to the German Basic Law, which gives clear constitutional authorisation regarding the assets of political parties,[96] it is impossible to conclude that the ROC Constitution has the intention of doing the same thing because it is extremely difficult to imagine why the Nationalist Party's assets would 'endanger the existence of the Republic of China or the nation's free and democratic constitutional order'.[97] Moreover, it is undoubtedly unconstitutional to enact an *ex post facto*[98] act regarding political party assets without the authorisation of the constitution, and such an act cannot be considered as transitional justice if it is unconstitutional *in abstracto*.

There is no doubt that ill-gotten assets should be reimbursed,[99] but this does not justify an act that presumes all the Nationalist Party's assets are illegal.[100] Regardless of transitional justice,[101] criminal justice is based upon the presumption of innocence,[102] that *ei incumbit probatio qui dicit, non qui negat*,[103] because it is about proving a universal negative, and '[p]hilosophy and logic will tell you that a universal negative is impossible to prove'.[104] This means that justice, including transitional justice if it asserts to be just, should stand in defence of a person who is accused of holding ill-gotten assets, that 'the accuser ought to prove the case against him, and the accused should

92 See generally Löwenstein, op. cit. (note 73–1), 417–432; *Löwenstein*, (note 73–2), 638–658.

93 Cf. *Mihr*, op. cit. (note 67), at 3.

94 Constitution of R. O. C. § 139 (1947).

95 German Basic Law § 21 (1) (1949/2017).

96 Ibid.

97 Constitution of R. O. C. amend. § 5V (1992/2005).

98 *Hamilton*, *Jay* and *Madison*, op. cit. (note 13), at 232.

99 E. g., *A. James McAdams*, Transitional Justice after 1989: Is Germany So Different?, 33 GHI Bulletin 2003, 53, at 56 (reporting that German 'courts reviewed competing claims for thousands of houses, dachas, parcels of land, and other forms of property lost under the old dictatorship' ever since the 1990 unification); *see also Romeike* (note 2), 57–59.

100 E. g., Act of Political Party Assets § 5 (2016).

101 See generally *Corradetti*, (note 72), 185–220; *McAdams*, op. cit. (note 107), 53–64.

102 See *Stumer*, op. cit. (note 17), 190–191.

103 *Adolf Berger*, Encyclopedic Dictionary of Roman Law, Philadelphia 1953/1991, 652.

104 *Paul A. Schichner*, Prepared to Answer: A Christian's Guide to Today's Spiritual Questions, Grand Rapids 1978, 12; see also *Francis Garden*, A Dictionary of English Philosophical Terms, London 1878, 115–117.

be in no way bound to prove the negative'[105] because '[i]t would be unjust were he required to do so, for the law presumes all men to be innocent till they are proved guilty'.[106] The case of SED is different, because its lawful position relies on the fulfilment of German constitutional obligation,[107] to 'publicly account for their assets and for the sources and use of their funds'.[108] However, we cannot find such a constitutional obligation within the ROC Constitution.[109] In other words, I have no doubt that ill-gotten assets possessed by the Nationalist Party should be reimbursed,[110] but I have every doubt about the presumption against the accused's innocence[111] unless the constitution burdens all[112] political parties with clean hands.[113]

As far as restitution after the collapse of the Third Reich was concerned, *Sanya Romeike,* on behalf of the International Nuremberg Principles Academy, states that the Federal Restitution Act (1957) is rooted in the restitution laws enacted by the Western powers before the foundation of the Federal Republic of Germany.[114] '[T]he Act obliged the Federal Republic to pay compensation for assets which had been stolen by the Nazi party or state authorities'.[115] This means that denazification was associated with the Allied powers,[116] by which many Germans simply regarded it as 'Siegerjustiz',[117] or 'victor's justice'.[118] In other words, the collapse of the Third Re-

105 *Victoria Institute* (ed.), Journal of the Transactions of the Victoria Institute, or Philosophical Society of Great Britain: Volume V, London 1871, 178.

106 *Victoria Institute,* l. c.

107 German Basic Law § 21I (1949/2017).

108 Ibid.

109 Compare Constitution of R.O.C. § 139 (1947), with Constitution of R.O.C. amend. § 5V (1992/2005).

110 Cf. *Dafydd Fell,* Party Politics in Taiwan: Party Change and the Democratic Evolution of Taiwan, 1991–2004, Abingdon 2005, 77–78.

111 E.g., Act of Political Party Assets § 5 (2016).

112 Contra Act of Political Party Assets § 4(1) (2016) (providing by implication that the promoter, the Democratic Progressive Party, is beyond the reach of this Act).

113 E.g., German Basic Law § 21I (1949/2017).

114 *Romeike,* op. cit. (note 2), at 30.

115 *Romeike,* op. cit. (note 2), at 30.

116 See *David A. Messenger* and *Katrin Paehler,* Introduction, in D.A. Messenger and K. Paehler (eds.), A Nazi Past: Recasting German Identity in Postwar Europe, Lexington 2015, 1–14, at 1–14.

117 See generally *Horst Meier,* Protestfreie Zonen? Variationen über Bürgerrechte und Politik, Berlin 2012, 245–254.

118 *Messenger* and *Paehler,* l. c., at 3.

ich and the establishment of the Allied Supreme Powers[119] provided the legal framework[120] for transitional justice against the NSDAP, but the same framework cannot be applied to Taiwan simply because the Republic of China still exists. Under the same constitutional peace, enacting an *ex post facto* law[121] brings more legal and constitutional problems, disturbing the constitutional peace that has already been settled.[122] If this is really something that must be done, then as far as this article is concerned it can only be done by amending the constitution, instead of through ordinary legislation,[123] altering the constitutional peace through the constitution.[124]

IV. Conclusion

When *Nigel N. T. Li* explained the distinction between revenge and justice in his 1998 class of constitutional law, he told a personal story in which his wife challenged him with a dilemma.[125] If *Li* loved his wife and if she were murdered, *Li* should revenge himself on her murderer; or else he had never really loved her. In order to please her, *Li* replied strategically, saying: 'I will kill this man in person if you wish me to, but I still insist that my revenge is not justified'.

119 See *Gert-Joachim Glaessner*, German Democracy: From Post-World War II to the Present Day, Oxford 2005, 3.

120 *Cf. Glaessner*, l. c. (explaining that the sovereignty of Germany was replaced by the supreme power of the four Allies after the collapse of the Third Reich, and that 'some 'reserve powers' of the four Allies concerning Berlin and the future of Germany remained' even after the foundation of the two German states).

121 *Hamilton, Jay* and *Madison*, op. cit. (note 11), at 232.

122 Cf. *Paul C. Roberts* and *Lawrence M. Stratton*, The Tyranny of Good Intentions: How Prosecutors and Law Enforcement Are Trampling the Constitution in the Name of Justice, New York 2000/2008, 65–78.

123 For example, if a political party is not prohibited from operating a business, it implies that it is legal to do so until it is banned in accordance with law. However, if the law retrospectively punishes this political party for operating a business, I doubt that it is beyond the reach of the legislative power because the legislature has disturbed the settled constitutional peace. I further doubt the constitutionality of an *ex post facto* constitutional amendment, but it is surely more acceptable than an ordinary *ex post facto* law enacted by the legislature. Compare German Basic Law § 20 (3) (1949), with German Basic Law § 79 (3) (1949).

124 But cf. German Basic Law § 79 (3) (1949), providing that not all the constitutional peace can be altered even by amending the constitution.

125 See generally *Richard B. Angell*, Reasoning and Logic, New York 1964, 151–152.

People retaliate against their enemies in the name of justice.[126] Even the Parliament that executed *Thomas Wentworth* by enacting an act of attainder[127] would surely insist that it was just to do so. As to the approach to justice, if it were 'contrary to … every principle of sound legislation',[128] this would represent the last resort. However, these excuses just convert the victims of previous wrongdoings into the new wrongdoers, and all we see is a butcher claiming transitional justice against another butcher.[129] We simply prove *Herman W. Göring* right when he said '[t]he victor will always be the judge and the vanquished the accused'[130] after receiving his indictment at Nuremberg, meaning that there is no transitional justice but only 'Siegerjustiz' masquerading as transitional justice.[131]

When we resort to any possible means to make sure that the Nationalist Party is condemned,[132] our foregone conclusion that the accused must be guilty is directly exposed, and the supporting legislative act constitutes no more than a bill of attainder.[133] When this bill of attainder is seen as a form of legislative revenge,[134] '[v]engeance is not justice'[135] at all. How can we believe that injustice will bring out justice? As far as this article is concerned, it will only trigger off another request for transitional justice at some future point, and transitional justice will never end in Taiwan. In a nutshell, there is no doubt that ill-gotten assets possessed by the Nationalist Party must be reimbursed, but not by this means.[136]

126 See *Russell Cropanzano, Jordan H. Stein* and *Thierry Nadisic*, Social Justice and the Experience of Emotion, New York 2011, 95.

127 *Kilburn* and *Milton*, op. cit. (note 12), at 235.

128 *Hamilton, Jay* and *Madison*, op. cit. (note 11), at 232.

129 Cf. *Karl Simms*, Paul Ricoeur, London 2003, at 116 (holding that 'we must overcome the desire of vengeance. Vengeance is not justice… 'An eye for an eye' is not justice, it is vengeance').

130 *Kingsley C. Moghalu*, Global Justice: The Politics of War Crimes Trials, Westport 2006, 30.

131 Cf. *Moghalu*, l. c., quoting Barry Gewen who comments that 'Nuremberg was in the end a political trial with a foregone conclusion'.

132 Act of Political Party Assets § 5 (2016).

133 Cf. *Kilburn* and *Milton*, op. cit. (note 10), at 235.

134 *Kilburn and Milton*, l. c.

135 *Simms*, l. c., at 116.

136 Cf. Constitution of R. O. C. § 23 (1947) (providing the proportionality principle by which no law shall be deemed constitutional unless it is proportional by purpose and by means).

The Challenges of Constitutional Reforms in Democratizing States in Sub-Saharan Africa: Is it a 'Mission Impossible' for Nigeria?*

Oyelowo Oyewo

'Sustainable fundamental change is premised on constitutional reforms that succeed in catalysing the emergence of stable, democratic nations. Such constitutional reforms have to contend with more than merely formally designing institutions; they also need to balance the competing short-term interests of key political actors and the long-term public good.'[1]

Abstract

The 'third wave' of democratization that swept through the African continent in the 1990 s has been followed by the phenomenon of 'fourth wave' of democratization and constitutional reforms, as such, a case study of Nigeria's constitutional reforms attempts of the 1999 Constitution (as amended) and the fostering of its constitutional democracy, epitomizes the struggles of a democratizing state that is battling not only the forces working against the deepening of democracy and democratic governance, but entrenched mistrust and suspicions amongst the major ethnic and religious groupings in the country. This work critically interrogates the impact of the wave of democratization and the factors driving the constitutional reforms and the counter-forces against it. Some of the specific procedures for achieving constitutional reforms and the distances gone along such procedural path will be examined. What are the dynamics and trajectories of constitutional reforms in strengthening and deepening democratic governance in sub-Saharan state? The likelihood of success or failure of such constitutional reforms in Nigeria specifically, and the implications of the successes or failures of constitutional reforms on democratization in the sub-Saharan Africa generally, is the focus of this work.

* This work is dedicated to the memories of my brother *Samson Oyerinde* Oyewo who passed on 7th May, 2018, and my brother-in-law and mentor Professor *Olaide Akanni Oluboyede* who passed on 30th May 2018.

1 Cf. *Martin van Vliet/Winluck Wahiu/Augustine Magolowondo,* Constitutional Reform Processes and Political Parties: Principles for Practice, Publication of Netherlands Institute for Multiparty Democracy (NIMD)/ International Institute for Democracy and Electoral Assistance (International IDEA)/African Studies Centre (ASC), 13, available at<https://nimd.org/wp-content/uploads/2015/02/Constitutional-reform-processes.pdf>, accessed on 20th March, 2018.

I. Introduction

The 'third wave' of democratization that swept through the African continent in the 1990 s[2] has been followed by the phenomenon of 'fourth wave' of democratization[3] and constitutional reforms,[4] such that by 2016, at least 12 of the 16 member states of the Economic Community of West African States (ECOWAS) either floated talks about constitutional reform or effectively engaged in some form of constitutional change.[5]

These include: Gambia (President *Barrow* promised reforms to the country's 1997 Constitution);[6] Togo (opposition members of parliament continue to push for amendments to the 1992 Constitution);[7] Guinea Bissau (political rivals also

2 *Jørgen Møller/Svend-Erik Skaaning,* The Third Wave: Inside the numbers, Journal of Democracy, Vol. 24, No. 4, 2013, 97–109 at 102–103; *Samuel P. Huntington,* Democracy's Third Wave, Journal of Democracy Vol.2. No.2 Spring 1991, 12–34.

3 *Muhamad Olimat,* The Fourth Wave: Revolution and Democratization in the Arab Middle East, Journal of International Women Studies, Volume 12 Issue 3, 2011, 1–6; *Shaheen Mozaffar,* Democratic Transitions in Africa, Bridgewater Review Vol. 16 Issue 2 1997, 7–10.

4 *Stephanie M. Burchard,* Democracy Trends in Sub-Saharan Africa, 1990 to 2014, Institute of Defence Analysis (IDA) Publication Document NS D-5303, 2014, 1–14; *Charles Manga Fombad,*'Constitutional Reforms and Constitutionalism in Africa: Reflections on Some Current Challenges and Future Prospects, Buffalo Law Review, Vol. 59, 2011, 1007–1108; *H. Kwasi Prempeh,* Africa's 'Constitutionalism Revival': False Start or New Dawn?, International Journal of Constitutional Law, Vol. 5, Issue 3, 1 2007, Pages 469–506.

5 *Yuhniwo Ngenge,* Deconstructing West Africa's fourth wave of constitutional change, in: Annual Review of Constitution-Building Processes: 2016, International Institute for Democracy and Electoral Assistance (International (IDEA)), 2017, 76–95; available at <https://www.idea.int/sites/default/files/publications/annual-review-of-constitution-building-processes-2016.pdf>.

6 Gambia's Road to Democratic Reform, the Africa Center for Strategic Studies, 24 April, 2018; available at <https://africacenter.org/spotlight/gambia-road-to-democratic-reform>; accessed on 30 April, 2018. The pillars of Gambia's reform program are outlined in its 2018–2021National Development Plan (NDP), which was the result of extensive consultations with stakeholders from local government, civil society organizations, the private sector, and international partners. Adopted by Barrow in January 2018, this plan seeks to restore the rule of law, deepen democracy, advance transitional justice, and transform the security sector. The plan is broad in its ambition, reflecting the weak starting point of Gambia's institutions after two decades of autocratic rule. Cf. also *Seedy Drammeh,* Perspective on New Gambia, 2018, published the Centre for Media and Development Research in Africa (CENMENDRA).

7 Togo's popular protests and demands for constitutional reform, available at <https://www.constitutionnet.org/news/togos-popular-protests-and-demands-constitutional-reform>, accessed on March 20, 2018; Togo's political crisis; A ray of hope, available at <https://www.ghanaweb.com/GhanaHomePage/NewsArchive/Togo-s-political-crisis-A-ray-of-hope-631130>, accessed on 30 April, 2018.

agreed to a roadmap for a new constitution as part of efforts to resolve the country's political crisis);[8] Senegal (voters approved changes to the existing Constitution in a referendum);[9] Côte d'Ivoire (voters involved in adopting a completely new constitution);[10] Ghana (a Supreme Court decision to throw out a legal challenge that had delayed reforms initiated a few years before paved the way for the process to resume);[11] and Nigeria (constitutional amendment processes to reform the 1999 Constitution were being undertaken by the National Assembly).[12] In other member states, constitutional commissions were established to consider either wholesale

8 Significant decisions adopted to ensure the resolution of the protracted political crisis in Guinea Bissau, 16/04/18; available at <http://www.ecowas.int/significant-decisions-adopted-to-ensure-the-resolution-of-the-protracted-political-crisis-in-guinea-bissau/>, accessed on 25 April, 2018; cf. *Habibu Yaya Bappah*, Why Peace Fails in Guinea Bissau? A Political Economy Analysis of the ECOWAS-brokered Conakry Accord, 2017 Friedrich-Ebert-Stiftung Peace and Security Centre of Competence Sub-Saharan Africa, 16–35.

9 *J. Peter Pham*, Senegal Consolidates Its Constitutional Democracy, 29 March, 2016, available at <http://www.atlanticcouncil.org/blogs/africasource/senegal-consolidates-its-constitutional-democracy>, accessed on 20 March, 2018; *Eric Pichon*, Constitutional referendum in Senegal Shorter Presidential Term: A Half-Kept Promise', European Parliamentary Research Service; available at <http://www.europarl.europa.eu/RegData/etudes/ATAG/2016/579087/EPRS_ATA(2016)579087_EN.pdf>, accessed on 20 March, 2018.

10 Côte d'Ivoire: New Constitution Adopted, Global Legal Monitor, available at <http://www.loc.gov/law/foreign-news/article/cte-divoire-new-constitution-adopted/>, accessed on 20 March, 2018.

11 A legal challenge to the process in 2012 disrupted and stalled the government set up of a five-member Constitutional Review Implementation Committee's (CRIC) work, but the Supreme Court rejected the challenge in a 2015 decision *Asare v Attorney General* (Writ No. J1/15/2015 delivered on 15 October 2015, available at <https://cdn.modernghana.com/images/content/report_content/asare_v_ag_2015_crc_decision.pdf>, accessed on 20 March, 2018, paving the way for the process to resume. In *Asare v Attorney General*, the plaintiff challenged the constitutionality of the process and asked the Supreme Court to declare it null and void on the grounds that only parliament, under the Constitution, had the authority to initiate a constitutional amendment process; cf. *Yuhniwo Ngenge*, op. cit. (note 6), at 81, 95; cf. *Lydia Apori Nkansah*, Dispute Resolution and Electoral Justice in Africa: The Way Forward, Africa Development, Vol. XLI, No. 2, 2016, pp. 97–131.

12 On June 8, 2018, the sets of Acts to amend the 1999 Constitution (to be known as the 4th Alteration) were assented to and made public by the Presidency in Nigeria. Hitherto 1999 Constitution had experienced three alterations (1st to 3rd Alterations) mainly relating to electoral matters (1st and 2nd Alterations) and the constitutional recognition of the National Industrial Court (3rd Alteration). Festus Owete, 'Analysis: Constitutional Amendment: Next steps after Senate, House Approvals', *Premium Times*, July 28, 2017, available at <https://www.premiumtimesng.com/author/festus>, accessed on March 20, 2018; cf. *Ilias B. Lawal*, The review of the constitutional amendment procedure and presidential assent in Nigeria, Journal of Law and Conflict *Resolution*, (2015) 7(5) pp. 26–30.

constitutional replacements (Burkina Faso) or amendments (Benin, Mali, Liberia, Sierra Leone), and even in Mauritania (the only West African country outside ECOWAS) constitutional reforms have also been part of the political agenda of President *Mohamed Ould Abdel Azziz.*[13]

The dynamic phenomenon of constitutional reforms varies from country to country, in the form of: constitutional amendments; alterations; revisions; reviews; remaking; constitutional conference; constitutional debates; referendum and plebiscite, inter alia.[14] The undertow pulling at the wave of democratization have also bedevilled these constitutional reforms with various challenges, politically, constitutionally, socio-culturally, ethno-religiously, trust and other issues.

As a case study, Nigeria's constitutional reforms attempts of the 1999 Constitution (as amended) and the established constitutional democracy, epitomizes the struggles of a democratizing state that is battling not only the forces working against the deepening of democracy and democratic governance, but entrenched mistrust and suspicions amongst the major ethnic and religious groupings in the country.[15] With an acknowledged deficient Constitution[16] that was labelled 'a document that lies against itself',[17] the legitimacy of the constitution has always been questioned. Thus at the inception of democratization, the were unsurprising strident calls for a sovereign national conference and fundamental constitutional reforms (like that of neighbouring Benin Republic), however, they were side-stepped with the convening of a National Political

13 *Yuhniwo Ngenge*, l. c., at 76–95.

14 *Eleanor Thompson*, What Constitutional Review Processes in West Africa Tell Us, Pambazuka News, June 18, 2014, available at <https://www.pambazuka.org/printmail/89687>, accessed on 21 March, 2018.

15 *Oyelowo Oyewo*, Constitutional Law in Nigeria, 2019, Wolters Kluwer, 30–33; *Oyelowo Oyewo*, Nigeria: What Manner of Federation is this? Inaugural Lecture delivered on March 20 2019, University of Lagos Press, 34–81.

16 *Marietu Tenuche*, Revisiting the National Political Reform Conference (NPRC) (2005) and the National Question in Nigeria, International Review of Social Sciences and Humanities Vol. 2, No. 1 (2011), 37–48; national Conference, Final Draft of Conference Report 2014, August 2014; available at <www.premiumtimesng.com>, accessed on 20 March, 2018.

17 *Chief Fredrick Rotimi Williams* (SAN) described the Constitution as 'a document that lies against itself'. Cf. *John Rawls'* Political Liberalism: Implications for Nigeria's Democracy, Submitted by *Ekiyor Welson*, to the University of Exeter as a Thesis for the degree of Doctor of Philosophy in Sociology in May 2011, 48–49; available at: <https://ore.exeter.ac.uk/repository/bitstream/handle/10036/3213/WelsonE.pdf?sequence=1&isAllowed=y >, accessed on 22 March, 2018. Basically, because the preamble to the 1999 Constitution asserts that 'We the people...' made the constitution, when in fact the public participation in the making of the Constitution was severely limited to some hand-picked scholars, the contradiction meant that the Constitution lied against itself.

Reforms Conference (NPRC) 2005 under President Olusegun Obasanjo's Administration. Albeit, the implementation of the Report of the Conference was aborted when the ploy to use it for a third term agenda was unearthed by the Senate of the National Assembly.[18] A subsequent attempt at addressing calls for constitutional reforms also took the form of the convening of another National Conference (Confab) under President *Goodluck Jonathan,* and interestingly, the highly exorbitant Confab's Report 2014,[19] especially its observations and recommendations for constitutional reforms, were not adopted by the 8th National Assembly in the 4th Alteration process.

Even with the experience of Nigeria's party alternation and change of ruling party in 2015, from the Peoples' Democratic Party (PDP), that ruled from 1999, to the All Progressive Congress (APC) which rode on the mantra of 'Change' and 'Restructuring' to power, the hope of fundamental constitutional reforms has presently been deferred. As the question of constitutional reforms became enmeshed in ethnic conflicts as follows: the separatist/secessionist agitations from the Igbo people of the south-eastern Nigeria; the restructuring agitations of the 'True Federalist' agitators of the south-western and middle-belt Nigeria; national insecurity caused by extreme fundamentalist terrorist sect (Boko Haram) waging war in the north-eastern and middle-belt Nigeria; the bloody rampaging killing fields all over the middle-belt and north-eastern Nigeria between pastoralists herdsmen and agrarian farmers; and the seeming push-back against constitutional reforms by the majority ruling ethnic group of Hausa/Fulani. The exercise of the powers of the National Assembly to amend the 1999 Constitution, including the most recent 4th Alteration to the 1999 Constitution, have always fallen short of delivering major constitutional reforms that will address the fundamental issues of the Nigerian federation and assuage the various interests groupings, for the fostering of deepened and sustainable democratic governance/democracy.[20] Raising the question, whether constitutional reforms in

18 *Marietu Tenuche*, Revisiting the National Political Reform Conference (NPRC) (2005) and the National Question in Nigeria, International Review of Social Sciences and Humanities Vol. 2, No. 1 (2011), 37–48.

19 National Conference, Final Draft of Conference Report 2014, August 2014; available at: <www.premiumtimesng.com>, accessed on March 20, 2018.

20 The Fourth Alteration as proposed by the 8th National Assembly, (four of such proposal by way of Acts of the National Assembly have been assented to by the President and came into effect as the 4th Alteration to the 1999 Constitution on 8th June 2018) failed to address the major issues of restructuring, resource management and control, political powers, policing powers, security and peace, social injustice and the expansion of rights of citizens to include economic social and cultural rights, public participation in constitutionalism, existential challenges including poverty, among other fundamental issues known as the 'National Question'. Cf. *Oyelowo Oyewo*, l. c., 34–81.

Nigeria has become a 'mission impossible? And if so, its implication(s) for sub-Saharan democratizing states.

The paper will therefore critically interrogate the impact of the wave of democratization and the factors driving the constitutional reforms and the counter-forces against it. Some of the specific procedures for achieving constitutional reforms and the distances gone along such procedural path will be examined. What are the dynamics and trajectories of constitutional reforms in strengthening and deepening democratic governance in sub-Saharan state? The likelihood of success or failure of such constitutional reforms, and the implications of the successes or failures of constitutional reforms on democratization in the sub-Saharan Africa, will also be discussed.

The paper is divided into three parts: Part I examines constitutional reforms in the transition from the 'third wave' into the 'fourth wave' of democratization in the sub-Saharan Africa, using Nigeria's experience as a focal point; Part II interrogates the procedures, challenges, obstacles and barriers to constitutional reforms; Part III connects the dots into the future by proffering observations and recommendations on the whole phenomenon before the conclusion.

The methodology to be employed is the use of primary and secondary materials, case law, and other relevant materials, in critically analysing the issues. A comparative approach will also be employed to measure and critique the constitutional reforms in Nigeria. A definite outcome that one can foresee from this work is that the fundamentals of democratization brought about by the 'third wave' of democratization have changed, hence the imperative of constitutional reforms of the 'fourth wave' of democratization for alternative realities and the sustainability of democracy in Nigeria and other the sub-Saharan African states.

II. Constitutional Reforms in Democratization in the Sub-Saharan Africa

1. Understanding the Wave of Democratization in the Sub-Saharan Africa

Although there are many definitions and meaning attached to democracy,[21] however, it is the modern accepted system of governance that can deliver the most pos-

21 *Harvard Strand/Harvard Hegre/Scott Gates/Marianne Dahl*, Democratic Waves? Global Patterns of Democratization, 1816–2008, January 6, 2012, Paper prepared for the 3rd *International Conference on Democracy as Idea and Practice*, Oslo, 12–13 January 2012, 1–9.

sible sets of freedoms and foster development in any country. Whilst there are conflicting views as to the suitability of democracy for Africa,[22] democracy has become the mantra for governance in sub-Saharan Africa, and more and more, other alternatives such as autocracy, monarchism, communism, socialism, and military rule, have all become unpopular and archaic on the continent.[23]

One cannot concoct democracy using a formula. Three interrelated elements are, however, essential to any democracy. One element, of course, is elections. Democratic elections are one of the important milestones on the long journey of democratization. But a free election is not a fair election if in the run-up to Election Day the playing field is not level because the political process is manipulated and basic rights are undermined. A second element must be present for democracy to work: good governance, including the rule of law. And the third essential element in a democracy is a robust civil society that can keep government honest, keep citizens engaged and keep democracy-building on track. In a fully functioning democracy anywhere in the world, all three elements must be present: electoral, institutional and societal.[24] These theoretical expositions on principles of liberal democracy have been applied in the various constitutions of the democratizing sub-Saharan African countries.[25] Suffice to say that the process of democratisation entails not only a transition to formal liberal democracy, but also the consolidation of such a democratic system as an enduring value of the state.

Whilst the first wave of democratization was a non-issue for the African continent due mainly to colonialism, the shedding of the shackles of colonialism through independence engulfed the continent in the second wave of democratization.[26] Although

22 *Gavin Williams,* Democracy as idea and democracy as process in Africa, 2000: available at <www. Jstor.org/stable>.

23 '...democracy is the only model of government with any broad ideological legitimacy and appeal in the world', Larry Diamond, Colonial Legacy & Post-colonial Experience in Nigeria, in: Larry Diamond, Jaun Linz, and Seymour Lipset, (eds.) Democracy in developing Countries,), London 1988, Lynne Reiner Publishers Inc; *Adrian Leftwich,* Governance, Democracy and Development in the Third World, Third World Quarterly, 1993, 605–624; *Cyril Obe,* No Choice, But Democracy: Prising the People out of Politics in Africa? Claude Ake Memorial Papers No. 2, 2008, Universitetstryckeriet, Uppsala, Sweden, 15–17.

24 *Barry Lowenkron,* Assistant Secretary of State for Democracy Africa, Democracy in Sub-Saharan, Testimony Before the Senate Foreign Relations Subcommittee on African Affairs Washington, DC July 17, 2007; avaiable at <https://2001–2009.state.gov/g/drl/rls/rm/2007/88617.htm>.

25 African Constitutions, African Studies Centre Leiden, available at: <https://www.ascleiden.nl/content/webdossiers/african-constitutions>, accessed on 22 March, 2018.

26 *Carolyn Chisadza* and *Manoel Bittencourt,* Is Democracy Eluding Sub-Saharan Africa? University of Pretoria Working Paper: 2014–03 January 2014, 3–4.

most sub-Saharan countries experienced independence that were accompanied by multi-party constitutional governance but, it did not take long for most of them to descend into one-party autocracy, or coup d'état, or civil wars, thereby deconstructing constitutional democracy.[27] The 'third wave' of democratization[28] that swept over most African countries from 1989 was therefore seen as the needed 'breath of fresh air' into the expiring or expired democratic governments in general, and democracy in particular. Most countries did not only establish constitutional democracy but held elections, legalized multi-party systems, introduced term limits for their leaders, and enhanced respect for human rights,[29] in the democratization processes.

Democratization, generally refers to the transformation process from a nondemocratic regime to a procedural democracy on the way to a substantive democracy, either as the first government in a newly independent country or by replacing an authoritarian system in an older one. It is important to note that a country may stagnate or stop altogether at some intermediate step in the democratization process and that the transformation to a substantive democracy may take years, decades, or never be completed.[30] Countries like Benin, Ghana, Nigeria and Gambia fit this categorization because they involved a 'top down' transition in which a well-established military regime ceded power to a civilian led-government. While countries like Kenya, and Senegal, that always had a civilian led-government, transformed from a dictatorial dominant de-facto one-party state into a multi-party democracy. Some other countries like South Africa came out of an apartheid regime into the democratization process. Still some countries transited from civil war-torn countries into the democratic pro-

27 *Stephen Brown* and *Paul Kaiser*, Democratisations in Africa: Attempts, Hindrances and Prospects, Third World Quarterly, Vol. 28, No. 6, September 2007, 1–9.

28 A wave of democratisation, originating in Portugal and Spain in the 1970 s, swept across the developing world in the 1980 s and 1990 s. This so-called 'Third Wave' moved across Latin America and Eastern Europe, and later Asia and Africa. The transformation in the nature of political regimes was remarkable: while in 1974 there were 41 democracies among the existing 150 states, by 2003 about three-fifths of all the world's states were considered formal democracies, however imperfect they might be. Cf. *Samuel Huntington*, The Third Wave: Democratization in the Late Twentieth Century, 1991, University of Oklahoma Press; *Larry Diamond*, Is the Third Wave Over?, Journal of Democracy 7, July 2006, 20–37; *J Møller* and *SE* Skaaning (note 3), at 102–103; *Samuel Huntington*, Democracy's Third Wave, Journal of Democracy Vol.2. No.2 Spring 1991, 12–34.

29 *Kehinde Olayode*, Contemporary Challenges of Democratisation and Development in Africa, European Scientific Journal October, Vol. 12, No. 28, 2016, 146, at 151–155.

30 *Bingham Powell*, Jr. and *Eleanor Powell*, Democratization: A Briefing Paper for AP Comparative Government and Politics, 2005, PP. 2–3; available at <apcentral.collegeboard.com>, accessed on 22 March, 2018.

cess, like Liberia and Cote d'voir.[31] The democratizing sub-Saharan African countries were categorized into three by Freedom House: free; partly free; and not free, as shown in Table 1 below.

Table 1 Sub-Saharan Africa Freedom House Designations

Designation	Countries
Free	Benin, Botswana, Cape Verde, Ghana, Mali, Mauritius, Namibia, Sao Tome & Principe, South Africa
Partly Free	Burkina Faso, Burundi, Central African Republic, Comoros, Ethiopia, Gambia, Guinea-Bissau Kenya, Lesotho, Liberia, Madagascar, Malawi, Mozambique, Niger, Nigeria, Senegal, Seychelles, Togo, Uganda, United Republic of Tanzania, Zambia
Not Free	Angola, Cameroon, Chad, Congo, Côte d'Ivoire, Democratic Republic of the Congo, Equatorial Guinea, Eritrea, Gabon, Guinea, Rwanda, Sierra Leone, Somalia, Swaziland, Zimbabwe

Source: Freedom House: Freedom in the World 2010

From Table 1 we can deduce the varying degree of progress and quality of democratization going on in most of the sub-Saharan countries. Countries designated as free are not merely democratizing through regular elections, but allow the general public to participate directly in political decision making, with developed political institutions and political process, including respect for human rights. Partly free designation covers the majority of democratizing countries, that have experienced regime change into constitutional governance accompanied by elections and semblance of democratic governance,[32] but have not evolved democratic institutions or practices that can be said to be deepening democracy. Not free designation covers the countries that are yet to even embark on democratization or establish institutions or practice for democratic governance, including regular free and fair elections or respect for human rights.

Be that as it may, nearly 80 percent of Africans express support for democracy—up from 65 percent a decade ago—and the proportion of those that reject alterna-

31 *Ashley Munetsi,* Democratization in Sub-Saharan Africa: The Good, the Bad, and the Ugly, 2011, CMC Senior Paper 115; available at <http://scholarship.claremont.edu/cmc_theses/115>.

32 *JSHola Omotola,* The African Union and the Promotion of Democratic Values in Africa: An Electoral Perspective, *Occasional Paper* No. 185, Governance and APRM Programme, May 2014, South African Institute of International Affairs, 5–35.

tive forms of authoritarian rule has risen by 15 percentage points in the past 10 years to 51 percent, according to a reputable US-based poll taken in 2015 in 37 countries.[33]

Beyond the third wave of democratization in most of the sub-Saharan countries, are the challenges of fostering, deepening and sustaining democratic governance and full democracy, resulting in the push for constitutional reforms in the majority of them, that is perceived to be part of the ripple effect of the 'fourth wave' of democratization that swept through North African countries of Algeria, Tunisia, Egypt, Morocco and Libya.[34] However, in this work the constitutional reforms phenomenon is categorized as logical part of the 'third wave' of democratization, as the process of securing the constitutional instrument for the democratization were often viewed as a means to an end (like the proverbial 'bull in china shop' where the emphasis is to get rid of the bull to save the china and fix the shop).[35] The flawed constitution-making process for the constitutional instrument that serves as the legal substratum upon which the democratic governance are to be practiced, impacts negatively on the democratization to full democracy, hence the need for constitutional reforms.[36]

A new constitution usually heralds the transition from the old authoritarian or dominant regime to the new or return to constitutional multi-party democracy, to set the tone for democratic governance or set down the rules of engagement for all constitutional and political actors.[37] What therefore appears to be a common constitutional law theory of democratizing countries of sub-Saharan Africa is that, reforming the constitution or making a new constitution to establish the framework for regular conduct of elections through multi-party political system, will engender constitutional democracy.[38] Sub-Saharan Africa experienced a decade and a half of

33 Sub-Saharan Africa: Pitched Contests for Democratization through 2022, A Global Trends Paper, February 2018, A Publication of the National Intelligence Council, p. 1; available at <www.dni.gov/nic/globaltrends>, accessed on 22 March 2018.

34 *Yuhniwo Ngenge*, op. cit. (note 6), 76–95. See also *Usman Tar*, The challenges of democracy and democratisation in Africa and Middle East, *Information, Society and Justice*, Vol. 3 No. 2, July 2010, 81–94.

35 Strengthening Democracy in Uncertain Times, 21st Forum 2000 Conference, 8–10 October, 2017, 7.

36 *Abrak Saati*, Participation – to unveil a myth, in Public Participation in: Tania Abbiate/Markus Böckenförde/Veronica Federico (eds.), African Constitutionalism, 2018 (Routeledge), 13–24.

37 *Michele Brandt/Jill Cottrell/Yash Ghai/Anthony Regan*, Constitution-making and Reforms: Options for the Process, 2011, Interpeace, 13–14.

38 *Charles Manga Fombad*, Constitutional Reforms and Constitutionalism in Africa: Reflections on Some Current Challenges and Future Prospects, Buffalo Law Review, Vol. 59, 1007 at 1009–1010. The Constitution-making processes in the countries under study, such as: Benin, Ghana, and Sen-

growing democracy, through 2005. Since then, the region has experienced 10 years of democratic backsliding,[39] leaving sub-Saharan Africa with the same levels of freedom as in 2001, except for the recent burst of democratization in Gambia, Liberia, Sierra Leone, Tanzania, and Zimbabwe. The democratic backsliding has plagued such countries like Senegal, Benin, Togo, Nigeria, Kenya, Burkina Faso, Burundi, Mozambique, and Uganda.[40]

A more recent Freedom House Report on 'Democratic Governance in Africa: Three Key Trends'[41] revealed key trends of stagnation and declining progression in democratization in sub-Saharan Africa, particularly with east and central African countries having poorer ratings than the west and southern African countries. It was stated in the Report that, the

> 'growing gap between East and West Africa is particularly striking…… the average rate of change for Freedom in the World ratings in East and West African countries, with democratic governance stagnating or declining in every country in East Africa over the last 12 years, while much of coastal West Africa improved (though some Sahel countries declined)'.

These recent trends in democratization in sub-Saharan Africa is heightened by demands for reforms by the African people for more public participation, inclusivity, and accountability, thereby engendering more phenomenon of 'fourth wave' of democratization or volatility in the polity.[42] The sub-Saharan Regime Types is presented and summarized below.

egal involved the referendum procedure, while the Nigeria's 1999 Constitution came into force without going through a referendum procedure.

39 *Adeolu Durotoye*, Resurgent Backsliding and Democracy in Africa, International Journal of African and Asian Studies, Vol.18, 2016, 39–46.

40 Ibid.

41 *John Temin* and *Daniel Summers*, Democratic Governance in Africa: Three Key Trends, May 10, 2018; available at <https://freedomhouse.org/blog/democratic-governance-africa-three-key-trends>.

42 *Alexis Smallridge et al.* Trends in Democratization in sub-Saharan Africa', May 23, 2018, Center for Strategic and International Studies; available at <https://www.csis.org/events/trends-democratization-sub-saharan-africa>.

Sub-Saharan Africa: Regime Types, 1991-2016

Full democracy: The chief executive and national legislators are held accountable by and secure office through competitive elections, and political participation is open and well institutionalized.

Partial democracy: The chief executive and national legislators are held accountable by and secure office through largely inclusive and competitive elections, and political participation is broad but may exhibit weak, dysfunctional, or factional party systems that compromise citizen participation. Alternatively, partial democracies may hold elections that are not fully fair or free but are nonetheless not predetermined by electoral irregularities.

Partial autocracy: The chief executive or national legislators secure office in a manner other than inclusive and competitive multiparty elections, despite allowing some political competition, or political participation is substantially repressed.

Full autocracy: The chief executive or national legislators secure office in a manner other than inclusive and competitive elections and suppress nearly all political competition.

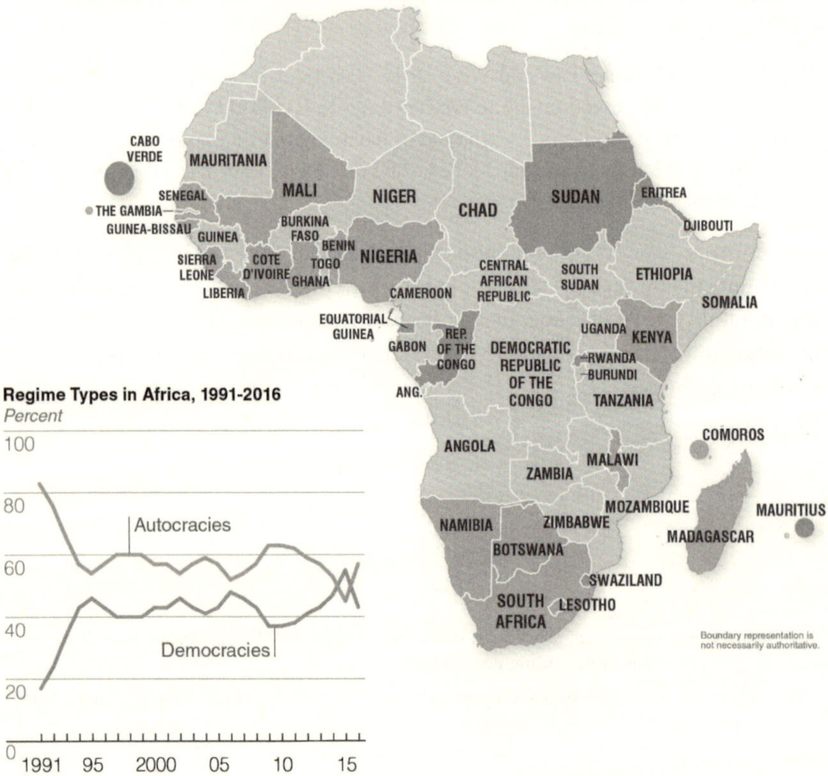

Source: Sub-Saharan Africa: Pitched Contests for Democratization through 2022, A Global Trends Paper, February 2018, A Publication of the National Intelligence Council

The characterization of democratization in sub-Sahara Africa in a global trends paper published by the National Intelligence Council, in February 2018 (Sub-Saharan Africa: Regime Types 1991–2016, above), typified the sub-Saharan countries into four from the spectrum of: Full Democracy ⇒ Partial Democracy ⇒ Partial Autocracy ⇒ Full Autocracy. Unfortunately, as at 2016 there were more sub-Saharan regimes typified as Partial Autocracy than Partial Democracy and Full Democracy put together. The recent trends in the categorization of democratization as shown, lend credence to the research and writings of proponents of receding or backsliding democratization phenomenon on the African Continent in general.[43]

There is no doubt that the democratization waves have impacted sub-Saharan Africa positively, although, recent years have seen backsliding among both the top performers, such as South Africa, and the more repressive countries, such as Cameroun and Ethiopia, albeit, recent developments in Gambia, Liberia, Sierra Leone, and Zimbabwe, are clear indications or the relentlessness of the dynamic force of democratization against autocratic regimes. Undoubtedly, lack of adherence to the rule of law, infringements on the fundamental freedoms, such as, right to life and liberty, freedoms of expression and association, discrimination against women and minorities, and widespread corruption, remain serious problems in many democratizing countries.[44] The push for constitutional and political reforms will therefore engage the democratization processes of the various sub-Saharan countries, in the years to come if democracy is to take root and flourish on the African continent.

2. Contextualizing Constitutional Reforms

A basic problem of democratization in Africa is the inadequacy/ineffectiveness of the constitution in sufficiently addressing the fundamental problems and transitional issues of the state. As a key ingredient of democratization, the making of the constitution (basic norm and the *fons et origo* of all other norms) must not only address legal and political matters, but also address issues of social justice, public participation, inclusivity, and economic development of the state. Hence it has been observed that the constitution provides much more than an overarching legal framework for society. It regulates political power and strongly affects relations between society and the state. Thus, a constitution can play an important role in forging a common identity

43 *Larry Diamond*, op. cit. (note 29), 20–37; Adeolu Durotoye, Resurgent Backsliding and Democracy in Africa, International Journal of African and Asian Studies, Vol.18, 2016, 39–46.

44 Freedom House Report, available at <https://freedomhouse.org/regions/sub-saharan-africa>, accessed on 30 May, 2018.

and creating institutional spaces where citizens interact on an equal basis with their leaders. From this perspective, as recognised by Justice Ismail Mahomed, a former Chief Justice of South Africa and the Supreme Court of Namibia, a constitution is nothing less than a 'mirror reflecting the national soul'.[45]

The constitution-making processes that therefore accompanied the third wave of democratization were often characterized by overall approaches that marked departures from the independence constitutions or post-military-rule constitution models that were undemocratic. Commenting on the hitherto undemocratic constitution making in sub-Saharan Africa, James Tully stated that constitution making is the single activity in 'modern politics that has not been democratized over the last century.[46] Constitution making in many African countries has witnessed a change from the Tully criticised approach to participatory constitution making process, as in the cases of South Africa, Kenya, Tanzania, Rwanda, Ethiopia, Uganda, Benin, among others.

The processes by which constitutions are reviewed or amended or altered or rewritten or remade come under the rubric of constitutional reform,[47] which are taking on increasing importance, not just the formal procedures used but also the degree of engagement and participation by various stakeholders or interest groupings and civil society in the country. Constitutional reforms in the democratization processes may therefore take the form of piecemeal or incremental amendments or alterations as is the case in Nigeria, with the most recent 4th Alteration coming into force on 7th June 2018. In some cases, the old Constitution is used to substantially effect fundamental reforms as was the case in South Africa. The Benin constitutional reform experience of sovereign national conference uniquely involved public participation and procedure that superseded the old constitution. Indeed, public participation in constitu-

45 *Martin van Vliet/Winluck Wahiu/Augustine Magolowondo*, op. cit. (note 2), at 12. Constitutions perform several roles, including: the basic and fundamental law; as political and social charter; as symbols and values of the society; as a social contract among the people or peoples or between the people and their elected representatives; as a power map; as the ground rules of engagement between all competing interests and stakeholders.

46 James Tully, Strange Multiplicity: Constitutionalism in an Age of Diversity, 1995 Cambridge University Press, 28; *Abrak Saati*, Participation – to unveil a myth, in Public Participation in African Constitutionalism, *Tania Abbiate/Markus Böckenförde/Veronica Federico* (eds.), op. cit. (note 37), 13–24.

47 Morris Kiwinda Mbondenyi and Tom Ojienda, Constitutionalism and Democratic Governance in Africa: Contemporary Perspectives from Sub-Saharan Africa, 2013, Pretoria University Law Press, 23–24.

tional reform has been identified as a key requirement not only for legitimacy of the constitution but also for its effectiveness.[48]

Constitutional reforms have become key feature of democratization and the main political activity in most African states. In Angola, Algeria, Egypt, Kenya, Swaziland, Zimbabwe, and Nigeria to mention a few, constitutions are either being reformed or there are very intensive contestations on the need for reforms. Without doubt, these agitations for reforms and on-going reviews of existing constitutions are precipitates of the changing character of national, regional, and global politics.[49] Most recently, in a national address on Wednesday, February 7, 2018, Mozambican President *Filipe Nyusi* announced changes for the country's constitution, changes which will increase the likelihood of striking a peace deal with the country's largest opposition group, the Mozambican National Resistance (the armed wing of which is known as Renamo). Renamo previously fought the government during the 16-year civil war that ended in 1992 and was involved in the fighting between 2013–2016.[50]

The push for constitutional reforms can therefore be seen as a key feature of democratization in sub-Sahara Africa, and where constitutional reforms demands are suppressed or unheeded by the established ruling class then the inevitability of violent conflict and the backsliding of democracy becomes real.[51]

3. The Nigerian Case Study

Often referred to as the giant of Africa due its population, resources, diversity, and strategic influence and role on the continent, Nigeria, is an epitome of a sub-Saharan state grappling with democratization, hence its significance as a case-study from which lessons of great value can be learnt by other sub-Saharan countries experiencing the wave of democratization on the African continent.

48 At least five reasons have been advanced by the advocates of public participation, viz: i. legitimacy of the constitution; ii. Educational exercise in democracy; iii. Building of social capital; iv. Reconciliation of former adversaries of violent conflict; and v. leading to higher levels of democracy – *Abrak Saati*, Participation – to unveil a myth, in Public Participation in African Constitutionalism, *Tania Abbiate/Markus Böckenförde/Veronica Federico* (eds.), op. cit. (note 37), 14–15.

49 *Julius Ihonvbere*, Politics of Constitutional Reforms and Democratization in Africa, *International Journal of Comparative Sociology*, Vol. 41, No. 1, 2000. 9–25.

50 Cf. <https://www.brookings.edu/blog/africa-in-focus/2018/02/09/africa-in-the-news-mozambiques-constitutional-reforms-in-dakars-education-funding-summit-and-u-s-sanctions-on-south-sudan-and-drc/>, accessed on 25 March, 2018.

51 Sub-Saharan Africa: Pitched Contests for Democratization through 2022, A Global Trends Paper, February 2018, A Publication of the National Intelligence Council, 1–2; available at <www.dni.gov/nic/globaltrends>, accessed on 22 March, 2018.

A creation of British Colonial rule that gained independence in 1960, in the course of the 'second wave' of democratization that swept through the continent, however, the promise of establishing democratic governance has eluded the country. The military coup of 1st January, 1966, forcefully terminated the fledgling democracy to plunge the country into autocratic military dictatorship that was punctuated by return to democracy on 1st October 1979 and subsequent overthrow by yet another military coup in 1984 (led by the current president General Muhammadu Buhari). Agitations for transition to democracy experienced start and stop malady, with the Draft 1989 Constitution (under General Ibrahim Badamosi Babangida) followed by the June 12 1992 elections, acclaimed to have been won by late MKO Abiola, but annulled and the whole process terminated. Subsequently, the 1995 Constitution (under General Sanni Abacha) was terminated by the death of General Abacha, and his successor General Abdulsalami Abubakar, who became military Head of State on 9th June 1998 handed over to a civilian democratic government, established by the 1999 Constitution (which was stated to be a necessary amendment of the 1979 Constitution). Hence, the 1999 Constitution was not a product of consensus building or public participation process, rather it was a product of military decree, Constitution of the Federal Republic of Nigeria (Promulgation) Decree No. 24 of 1999, which restored democratic rule on 29th May, 1999.[52]

The 1999 Constitution's democratic rule is perceived as part of the third wave of democratization, which has witnessed what has been termed 'elections democracy'[53] as regular elections have held every four years without fail till date, with party alternation being experienced during the 2015 elections, unfortunately, democracy is yet to be fostered or deepened, as attested to by the poorly conducted MArch/April 2019 Presidential and State Houses of Assembly Elections.[54] Agitations for sovereign national conference and constitutional reforms have been rife, due to the obvious defects of the 1999 Constitution which failed to address the structural imbalance, inequitable distribution of resources and lack of inclusivity in power sharing within

52 *Oyelowo Oyewo*, Constitutional Law (note 16), *Oyelowo Oyewo*, Nigeria (note 16) 34–81.

53 Emerging Trends and Challenges of Electoral Democracy in Africa International IDEA Policy Dialogue 25–27 May 2016 Abuja, Nigeria, available at <https://www.idea.int/sites/default/files/publications/emerging-trends-and-challenges-of-electoral-democracy-in-africa.pdf> accessed on 20 March 2018.

54 Free and fair elections still elude Nigerian democracy, as elections are still violent and highly rigged. Abuse of human rights is on the increase according to Amnesty International. Good governance is absent, in the face of systemic and endemic corruption. Insecurity and conflicts, ethnic and religious, are on the increase. The dividends of democracy are still being awaited by the general populace.

the Nigerian federation, apart from, social injustice, ethnic and religious conflicts, and rabid corruption.

Interestingly, the first amendment through the Constitution of the Federal Republic of Nigeria (First Alteration) Act, 2010, and the second amendment through the Constitution of the Federal Republic of Nigeria (Second Alteration) Act 2010, published in 2011, dealt mainly with electoral reforms. While the Constitution of the Federal Republic of Nigeria (Third Alteration) Act 2010, published in 2011, dealt with the elevation of the National Industrial Court unto the status of constitutionally established and recognised courts of the federation. These constitutional amendments have been perceived as constitutional reviews with little or no reform objectives that can deal with the major flaws of the 1999 Constitution, as they did not address any of the major issues raised by the National Question, such as restructuring, social injustice and roots of internal conflicts.[55] Most importantly, they were strictly proposals from the executive that were passed through the legislature, the National Assembly, and the State legislatures, State Houses of Assembly, in accordance with the constitution alteration provisions.[56]

Attempts at constitutional reforms in response to strident demands for the convocation of sovereign national conference to remake or drastically reform the constitution have only resulted in the convening of political conferences by former Presidents Obasanjo and Jonathan, although the Reports and recommendations of these political conferences have not been accepted for purposes of constitutional reforms by the National Assembly. The most recent constitutional review exercise initiated by the 7th National Assembly, the product of which was vetoed by President Goodluck Jonathan, have been pushed through by the 8th National Assembly, which forwarded 33 Bills to President Muhammadu Buhari, who has assented to 4 Bills into Acts constituting the Fourth Alteration of the 1999 Constitution.

The Fourth Alteration consists of Acts of the National Assembly that seek to alter the 1999 Constitution as follows: i)amendment which reduced the age requirement to contest for elective positions, commonly referred to as the #NotTooYoungToRun; ii) amendment which bars presidents and governors from being sworn into office more than twice, in effect, any second-in-command, who has been sworn in to complete the tenure of an elected president or governor, cannot do more than a sin-

55 Nigeria's Stability: Constitutional Reform and Beyond, Brussels, 11 June 2012 Observatoire de l'Afrique Africa Briefing Report, by Damien Helly, available at <https://www.iss.europa.eu/sites/default/files/EUISSFiles/Nigeria's-Stability-Constitutional-Reform-and-Beyond-1.pdf>, accessed on 23 March 2018.

56 Section 9 of the 1999 Constitution (as altered).

gle fresh term; iii) amendment granting financial autonomy to states' judiciary and state houses of assembly into law, which will reduce the overbearing influence of state governors on other arms of government, thereby deepening values of democracy in the 36 states of the federation; and iv)amendment that seeks to provide for the funding of the House of Assembly of States and the judiciary directly from the Consolidated Revenue Fund of the state.[57]

It can be seen from the constitutional reforms approach adopted by the political leadership in Nigerian that incremental review and amendments of the 1999 Constitution, is preferred to wholesale reforms. It remains to be seen whether the country will ever experience fundamental constitutional reforms to address the National Question issues of federalism, security and peace, respect for human rights, social justice, equity, inclusivity and justice for all, or the desired constitutional reforms will remain a mission impossible?[58] Especially, as the forces demanding for constitutional reforms are getting impatient and wont to resort to violence, as we have seen with struggles of the Indigenous People of Biafra (IPOB), Niger-Delta Militants, the Islamic Fundamentalist in the Northern part of Nigeria, and other ethno-religious groupings in Nigeria. Assuredly, the struggle for constitutional reforms will continue, as we have not yet seen the end of this latent struggle.

III. The Anatomy of Constitutional Reforms

1. Constitutional Reforms Processes and Procedures

The term, constitutional reforms, is used in this context as the processes and procedures that are taken to review, revise, amend, alter, or even remake the constitution after it has come into force whether or not the reform is undertaken in consonance with the amendment provisions of the extant constitution. This can be distinguished from constitution-making that involves the crafting, writing, creating of a new or fresh constitution. Our focus is therefore on constitutions upon democratization. This phenomenon of constitutional engineering is geared towards fine-tuning or recalibrating the basic legal norm to accommodate the exigencies of democratization and define the collective values of the state. Indeed, it has been posited that, the proponents of constitutional reform are increasingly observing that fundamental societal change

57 *Oyelowo Oyewo*, Constitutional Law (note 16), 30–33; *Oyelowo Oyewo*, Nigeria (note 16), 34–81; cf. <https://leadership.ng/2018/06/16/correcting-misnomers-in-1999-constitution/>.

58 *Oyelowo Oyewo*, l. c. (Nigeria).

will only emerge from constitution reforms that successfully catalyse changes in political culture in favour of shared values, constitutionalism, respect for the rights of citizens and the rule of law.[59] These constitutional reform processes are therefore aimed at much more than designing new laws and institutions, as they are processes concerning questions of the nature of the state, its political culture, social justice, equitable management of national resources, and balancing of the internal forces, for stability, development and progress.

There is much variety in the amendment procedures used from on country to the other, with different institutional actors and steps involved.[60] Generally, the constitutional reforms procedures are specified in the constitution, and this include, first the initiation of constitutional reform proposals (as an executive bill, member's bill, report of special political conference, reforms commissions, constitution drafting committee, private bill, or as a civil society initiative, among others) with great relevance to the nature and substance of the reforms.[61] In almost all the constitution of the democratizing states, the Parliament has the constitutional authority to initiate and process constitutional reforms proposal, such as the constitutions of South Africa, Ghana, Senegal, Nigeria, Kenya, and Benin. The proposals are then passed through parliamentary proceedings that must fulfil constitutionally specified requirements for the legality of the constitutional reforms, including the requisite majority votes necessary to pass such constitutional reforms into force. Thus, in Ghana and Nigeria, constitutional reforms processes have been challenged, unsuccessfully in the former, but successfully in the latter.[62]

59 *Martin van Vliet/ Winluck Wahiu/Augustine Magolowondo*, op. cit. (note 2), 9–11.

60 *Tom Ginsburg* and *James Melton*, Does Constitutional Amendment Rule Matter at All? Amendment Cultures and the challenges of measuring amendment difficulty, International Journal of Constitutional Law, Vol. 3 Issue 3, 2015, 686 – 713.

61 Bénin recently reaffirmed its position as a regional beacon of democracy when, President *Patrice Talon* – who won the March 2016 election with a promise of 'change' against *Boni Yayi's* prime minister and heir apparent *Lionel Zinsou* – followed through on a campaign promise and appointed a 35-member commission to propose political and institutional reforms, including the option of limiting presidential terms to a single seven-year mandate. The commission, chaired by justice minister *Joseph Djognénou*, submitted its report at the end of June 2017; available at <:https://presidential-power.com/?p=5160>, accessed on 23 March, 2018.

62 In *Prof. Stephen Kwaku Asare v Attorney –General* a seven-member Supreme Court panel has dismissed a case brought by US-based Ghanaian lawyer challenging the constitutionality of the Constitution review process. Prof. *Asare* was contending amongst others that the President under the Constitution, does not have the power to set up a commission to review the country's supreme law, the 1992 Constitution; available at <https://www.ghanaweb.com/GhanaHomePage/NewsArchive/Supreme-Court-dismisses-case-against-review-of-Constitution-387658> While in *Olisa Agbakoba vs. Attorney General of the Federation & National Assembly* Suit No. FHC/L/

Beyond the Parliament, there are some other constitutionally specified institutional requirement involved in the process of validating the reforms, including majority votes of state legislatures, approval or affirmation by the constitutional court[63] or supreme court, referendum,[64] plebiscites,[65] and presidential assent/veto, these provisions in one form or the other are contained in the constitutions of these democratizing states, including Nigeria, Benin, Senegal, South Africa.[66] These constitution amendment procedures may chill the whole reform process, especially as executive and parliamentary tenures are fixed, and it may not be possible for the whole reform process to be started and finished during one tenure, as has been experienced most recently by Nigeria where the 7th National Assembly's efforts that was trumped by the court's invalidation, was picked up and continued by the 8th Assembly to se-

CS/545/2014, the National Assembly was held to be in violation of section 9 (on alteration of the constitution) of the 1999 Constitution.

63 Curiously, in Benin, the Constitutional Court ruled in October 2011 that presidential term limits could not be changed by way of referendum. The court considered it a violation of the decision of Bénin's National Conference of February 1990 to declare certain constitutional articles unchangeable, including Article 42, which stipulates a limit of two five-year terms; available at <https://presidential-power.com/?p=5160>, accessed on 23 March, 2018.

64 In March 2016 voters in Senegal through a constitutional referendum approved by 62 % of the votes cast, changes to the existing Constitution, cf. International Foundation for Electoral Systems (IFES) 2016; cf. also *Yuhniwo Ngenge*, op. cit. (note 6), 76–77; La Croix, Referendum au Sénégal: Oui ou non au Président Sall, 20 March 2016; available at <https://www.la-croix.com/Monde/Referendum-Senegal-president-Macky-Sall-2016-03-20-1300747836>.

65 Voters in Senegal were asked in a March 20, 2016 referendum to not only reaffirm the two-term limit on the presidency, but also cut the length of terms themselves down to five years from the current seven years. Altogether, the fifteen constitutional amendments approved by nearly two-thirds of the citizens who took part in the plebiscite consolidate the already significant progress made by the West African country in terms of democratic governance and make it something of a model for the region – *J. Peter Pham,* Senegal Consolidates Its Constitutional Democracy; available at <https://www.atlanticcouncil.org/blogs/africasource/senegal-consolidates-its-constitutional-democracy>.

66 The South African Constitutional Court was required to review the entire text of constitutional in detail and pass a certification judgement in the form of a unanimous decision of all eleven judges or by a clear majority. The certification hearings began on 1 July 1996, and on 6 September, the court unanimously ruled that the text adopted in May 1996 could not be certified because it did not fully satisfy the principles and conditions agreed in the multi-party talks. The court also rejected eight of its clauses. This forced the CA to reconvene and address the issues in the ruling. On 7 October, the CA compromised and voted for a new text, with one party (the IFP) voting against it. On 11th October, the new text was presented to the Constitutional Court, which granted its unanimous approval on 4 December. This text became the Constitution of South Africa, which President *Nelson Mandela* signed into law on 10 December 1996. Cf. *Martin van Vliet/Winluck Wahiu/Augustine Magolowondo*, op. cit. (note 2), at 43.

cure the assent of President Muhammadu Buhari, in the form of the Fourth Alteration in June 2018. There lies the dilemma and frustration of advocates of fundamental constitutional reforms that may only be filled through the remaking of the constitution, especially, where the ruling executive and its majority in Parliament are not disposed towards achieving the ends of the fundamental reforms by advocates of constitutional reforms. Can they go along with an incremental constitutional review approach or force an extra-constitutional reform approach like the sovereign national conference, or go the way of revolutionary reforms through violent change, which is undemocratic?[67] It can be seen therefore that the push for constitutional reforms will always be a dynamic force of 'change' in democratizing states, particularly, where the ruling executives are not inclined towards fundamental changes that will deepen democracy in Africa.[68]

2. Challenges, Obstacles and Barriers to Constitutional Reforms

The first challenge of constitutional reforms is setting the agenda for reforms. Main issues such as, needed reforms of institutions and political process to engender free and fair elections, strong and virile political parties and democratic institutions,[69] rule of law, good governance, independence of the judiciary, guarantee of human rights and social justice, restructuring the state for equitable development and inclusivity, do not easily lend themselves to consensus building amongst constitutional reforms advocates. These issues are often unpopular with the political leadership and the ruling class, as they view them as threat to the 'African ruler-ship' and the perquisites of office.[70] Constitutional reforms that deal with such fundamental issues are bound to strengthen democracy and sustainable development in the State. The South African Constitution[71] in Chapter 9 provides for State institutions supporting constitutional

67 *Tom Ginsburg* and *James Melton* (note 61), 686 – 713.

68 'We judge that Sub-Saharan Africa is entering a period of heightened competition between governments and their citizens over the nature of democratic governance that is likely to breed persistent volatility through 2022.' – Sub-Saharan Africa: Pitched Contests for Democratization through 2022, A Global Trends Paper, February 2018, A Publication of the National Intelligence Council; available at <www.dni.gov/nic/globaltrends>, accessed on 22 March, 2018.

69 *Martin van Vliet/ Winluck Wahiu/Augustine Magolowondo* (note 2), 14–24.

70 *Mac-Ogonor/ Paul Eke/Ngboawaji Daniel Nte,* The challenge of globalization and democratization to the African Union: The case of Togo Crisis, International Journal of Human Sciences, Vol. 6 Issue 1, 2009, 758–772.

71 Available at <https://www.gov.za/documents/constitution-republic-south-africa-1996>.

democracy that ensure transparency, accountability and constitutionalism.[72] This exemplary reform ought to be adapted by sub-Saharan constitutional reforms processes to ensure implementation of the reformed constitution to effectuate democratization and establishment of democracy. Countries like Ghana and Botswana have evolved institutions and political processes that by and large engender free and fair elections, transparency and accountability through independence of the judiciary.

A prevalent challenge to democratization in Africa is unlimited tenure of office that in the past saw African Presidents ruling for decades and even until death.[73] Constitutional reforms must aim at certainty of tenure and limitation of period for re-election, so as not to substitute the old autocratic one-party Presidents with multi-party despots, who will even change the constitution to elongate their tenure.[74] Unfortunately, the challenges of tenure limitation and tenure elongation are rife even in democratizing states as, Uganda, Togo, Gambia, Benin, Senegal, Nigeria, and Zambia.

Related to tenure limitation is the phenomenon of tenure elongation through succession by the Vice-President due to the death of an incumbent President. Ghana and Nigeria, experienced this after the death of Presidents *Atta Mills* and *Umaru Yar'Adua* respectively. While Ghana's constitutional practice handled the transition smoothly, it heightened the fragility of the democratization process in Nigeria, fortunately, the Fourth Alteration has now resolved the issue so as to limit the successor to an additional re-election to put certainty to the uncertainty of the event of the death of the President. What usually transpire when African Presidents become critically ill has been well captured in a cartoon[75].

72 The Constitution of the Republic of South Africa 1996, section 181 (1) regulates: 'The following state institutions strengthen constitutional democracy in the Republic: (a) The Public Protector, (b) The South African Human Rights Commission, (c) The Commission for the Promotion and Protection of the Rights of Cultural, Religious and Linguistic Communities, (d) The Commission for Gender Equality, (e) The Auditor-General, (f) The Electoral Commission.' These institutional safeguards are designed to strengthen and deepen democracy. However, the question is, do these provisions safeguard the deepening of democracy in practice?

73 *Christian Roby*, Democracy in Africa Marches Forward Unevenly, Global Views, Democracy Governance, 13 July 2018; available at <https://www.devex.com/news/democracy-in-africa-marches-forward-unevenly-92968>; *Denis M. Tull/Claudia Simons*, The Institutionalisation of Power Reaccessed': Presidential Term Limits in Africa, Africa Spectrum 2017 52. 2, 79–102; *Adrienne Lebas*, Term Limits and Beyond: Africa's Democratic Hurdles, Current History, 2016, 169–174.

74 The attempt by former President *Olusegun Obasanjo* to propose constitutional reforms for tenure elongation through the National Political Reforms Conference met with opposition from the National Assembly, the Senate of which voted to reject in totality the Recommendations of that Conference because of the ploy to introduce tenure elongation through the Recommendation.

75 Gado Cartoons 8 Apr 2012; available at <https://twitter.com/igaddo/status/188961850183004160>, accessed June 2019.

The challenge of autonomy of the other arms of government, the legislature and the judiciary in relation to the executive ought to be addressed, as the concentration of powers in the executive and the overbearing propensity of the executive in relation to the other two branches of government, has been a carry-over of one-party autocracy, and prolonged military rule coupled with the phenomenon of retired military Heads of State returning to rule as civilian Presidents, a characteristic feature of Nigeria, Ghana, Togo, Benin, Ghana, Liberia, Gambia and Guinea. President *Buhari's* unilateral suspension of the Chief Justice of Nigeria, *Walter Onnenghen* (CJN), upon filing of charges against the CJN before the Code of Conduct Tribunal, and the use of Department State Security (DSS) to conduct dramatic 'sting' operations against some Justices of the Supreme Court of Nigeria, have all called to question the powers of the executive in relation to the judiciary, and the practice of rule of law and separation of powers under the present constitutional democracy in Nigeria.

Indeed, there are several obstacles and barriers to constitutional reforms, including lack of effective public participation in the reform process.[76] The importance of public participation cannot be over-emphasised, even were the majority of the populace in democratizing states are perceived as being uneducated illiterates, as that does not mean that they are incapable of participating in reforms that pertains to their present and future well-being. Indeed, the era of ICT, social media and artificial intelligence have made the world to become a global village, and every person ought to have access to information that will help him/her to make informed decisions and choices. Another obstacle to constitutional reforms in sub-Saharan Africa is religious/ethnic prejudices and conflicts that hinder consensus-building in pushing ahead with major constitutional reforms. Nigeria offers a case study of the negative role of ethno-religious conflicts in the democratization process, as the predominantly Muslim North agenda, including the adoption of Sharia legal system is antithetical to the secular status of the Nigerian State as provided in section 10 of the 1999 Constitution. Worst still is religious extremism and fundamentalism that breeds terrorism and armed conflict, such as the Boko Haram Terrorist sect that is waging war against Nigeria, Niger, Chad and Cameroun; and the Al-Shabaab Terrorist sect that is waging terrorist war against Kenya, and Tanzania.

Despotic or poor governance and corruption presents obstacles in the form of counter-forces to constitutional reforms on the one hand, and wanting to manipulate the reform process to further entrench the executive to the detriment of demo-

76 *Morris Kiwinda Mbondenyi/Tom Ojienda*, Constitutionalism and Democratic Governance in Africa: Contemporary Perspectives from Sub-Saharan Africa, 2013, Pretoria University Law Press, 191–241.

cratic development, on the other hand. The actions of such despotic leadership can even become constitutional coups, whereby the 'constitutional reforms' are actually deployed to subvert democratization and entrench authoritarian rule.[77] President *Pierre Nkurunziza* of Burundi's push for a third term in 2015 led to political instability, followed by a failed military coup, before he subsequently emerged victorious in an election marred by violence and intimidation in 2015. In 2015, President Denis *Sassou Nguesso* of Congo wanted to extend his 32-year stay in power and announced a referendum to change the constitution to allow him to contest the election. This was met with mass protest, with people proclaiming that the 'Congo does not belong to Nguesso'. However, inn 2016 he won at the polls amid tight security measures and a communications black out. Burkina Faso's *Blaise Compaoré* was forced to flee following widespread protests against his bid to extend his 27-year rule in 2014.[78] Algeria's President *Abdelaziz Bouteflika* two-decade rule is now facing a constitutional crisis of elongation, as Algerians are now revolting against his continuing in power.[79]

Interestingly, attempts to manipulate constitutional reforms processes may incur sanctions by the African Union under Article 23(5) of the African Charter on Democracy, Elections and Governance (ACDEG), whereby amendment or revision of the constitution or legal instruments in a way that infringes on the principles of democratic change of government constitutes an 'illegal means of accessing or maintaining power' and is subject to sanctions on the offending state. Moreover, one the legal instruments that bind members of the Economic Community of West African States

77 Threats to democracy from those in power constitute some of the gravest affronts to the global state of democracy today as leaders manage to increase their political power by manipulating electoral norms, restricting dissent and freedom of speech, and reforming the constitution to extend their terms in office—all within the legal framework of the democratic system. Most alarming, these actions have a ripple effect on the functioning of institutions beyond those directly targeted, and affect people's safety, wellbeing and livelihoods. Some countries have diverted from this dangerous path towards authoritarianism, – *Catalina Uribe Burcher* and *Sumit Bisarya*, Threats from within: democracy's resilience to backsliding, Chapter 3, Global State of Democracy: Exploring Democracy's Resilience, 2017, International IDEA Publication, 70–87, at 70. Cf. also *Kamissa Camara*, Here's how African Leaders Stage 'Unconstitutional Coups': They tweak the Constitution to stay in Power, 2016, available at <https://www.washingtonpost.com/news/monkey-cage/wp/2016/09/16/heres-how-african-leaders-stage-constitutional-coups-they-tweak-the-constitution-to-stay-in power/?noredirect=on&utm_term=.2fedec4ca410>; *Morris Kiwinda Mbondenyi* and *Tom Ojienda*, l. c., 331–335.

78 Joleen Steyn Kotze, Africa Faces a New Threat to Constitutional Democracy: The Constitutional Coup, The Conversation, February 8, 2017.

79 *Lamine Chikhi/Hamid Ould Ahmed*, Bouteflika's key allies back army plan to oust him, World News, Reuters, 27 March, 2019, available at <https://www.reuters.com/article/us-algeria-protests/algeria-awaits-constitutional-signal-on-bouteflikas-fate-idUSKCN1R80K1>.

(ECOWAS), and further reinforce the democratic values they have pledged to uphold through continental and national laws, is the Protocol on Democracy and Good Governance, Supplementary to the ECOWAS Protocol relating to the Mechanism for Conflict Prevention, Management, Resolution, Peacekeeping and Security. Among the constitutional maxims declared in Article 1 of the protocol, as being shared by all ECOWAS member states, is separation of powers within a government and 'zero tolerance for power obtained or maintained by unconstitutional means'. This ECOWAS instrument must have come into play in the Community's Members' role in the recent transition in Gambia.[80]

IV. The Future Prospects of Constitutional Reforms and Democratization in Sub-Saharan Africa

1. Trajectories and Prospects of Constitutional Reforms

As earlier postulated, constitutional reforms will continue to be a dynamic phenomenon for re-engineering, and infusing continuous momentum into democratization process, and fostering and deepening democracy on the continent. Constitutional reforms process, however, is not an end, but a means to an end. For democracy in much of Africa, has been observed to be constrained from delivering on its development potential for three reasons: first, governance capacity is lacking; second, the quality of electoral democracy is thin; and finally, neopatrimonialism undermines electoral democracy in Africa.[81] And ample evidence exists that the problem of democratization in sub-Saharan Africa is not solely premised on the short-comings of the constitution itself but rather the failure to implement the constitutions, as has been the case in states like Nigeria, Kenya, Senegal and Uganda.

The constitutional reforms process must therefore be preserved from abuse or overuse by political leaders so as not to lose its legitimacy and effectiveness. As earlier noted, consensus-building in setting the most fundamental issues for inclusion in the reforms becomes key and germane. One of the flaws of the Constitutional Conference Report and recommendations for implementation in Nigeria, is broadness and the mundaneness most of its recommendations that covers agriculture, economy, politics, social justice, restructuring of the federation and powers of the federating

80 E Thompson, op. cit. (note 15).

81 *Jakkie Cilliers,* The future of democracy in Africa, African Future, Paper 19, October 2016, available at <https://issafrica.s3.amazonaws.com/site/uploads/af19.pdf>.

units, employment, national values, social justice, indigeneity and so many other reforms proposals![82] The 15-point constitutional amendment agenda of the March 20, 2016, of Senegal's referendum stand in contrast to the Nigeria's Political Conference Report and recommendations of 2014.

Constitutional reforms should not become frivolous, superfluous or mundane or ordinary, as the constitution being the basic law, often safeguarded by special amendment provisions must not lose its essence, so that the constitution would not also lose its fundamental nature and coherence. Constitutional reforms proposal must be harmonized with existing provisions to enhance their effectiveness and not to bring discordance with such provisions. For instance, a number of the issues that are being sought to be legislated upon through the constitutional review process, such as a national dress code in Liberia or whether political parties in Senegal can receive public funding, would be better left to complementary legislation. Rather, the nature and purpose of the constitutional reform process is to agree on common basic principles of government and fundamental issues that will benefit all citizens and persons regardless of party affiliation. Insistence on inclusion of extraneous provisions or those that reflect a narrow ethno-religious ideology will not achieve the goals of the constitution reforms process and will likely only result in suspicions, distrust, divisions, deadlocks, and conflicts.[83]

Public participation in the constitution reforms process has been argued to galvanize support, legitimacy and effectiveness for the product of the process. However, clarity of distinction has been urged in participation, typified as false participation, symbolic participation, limited participation, consultative participation and substantial participation. The nature of participation ought to be substantial, for as has been observed eloquently, 'participation is not always exercised with the same amount of influence for participants, rather significant differences appear between cases.'[84] The public buy-in through public participation must be substantial and valuable and not false or symbolic participation. The essence of public participation in constitution reforms process was considered by the Kenyan Court in *Njoya & Ors. v Attorney Gen-*

82 National Conference, Final Draft of Conference Report 2014, August 2014, available at <www.premiumtimesng.com>, accessed on 20 March, 2018.

83 *Eleanor Thompson,* What Constitutional Review Processes in West Africa Tell Us, Pambazuka News, June 18, 2014, available at <https://www.pambazuka.org/printmail/89687>, accessed on 21 March, 2018.

84 *Abrak Saati,* Participation – to unveil a myth, in Public Participation in African Constitutionalism, in: Tania Abbiate/Markus Böckenförde/Veronica Federico (eds.), op. cit. (note 37), 19–24.

eral & Ors[85], where a constitutional reform process that produced a draft Constitution was held to be in violation of the rights of the Kenyan people to be involved in the making of a new constitution as provided by the extant constitution, hence the none involvement of the Kenyan people in the making of the draft Constitution rendered it null and void.

2. Prognosis

The demands for constitutional reforms is on the increase, irrespective of the fact that some of the democratization process in sub-Saharan states are on the decline and democracy appears to be receding from the African continent. Incumbent African regimes have become adept at interfering in the electoral process, as recently seen in Zimbabwe, Uganda, Ethiopia, Kenya, Angola, Mozambique, Nigeria and elsewhere. Leaders in these countries invest significant resources in ensuring a favourable electoral outcome by constraining the democratic space.[86] The most recent elections of March and April 2019 in Nigeria were roundly condemned by International Observers, Civil Society, and Opposition parties, as being poorly conducted and marred by rigging, falsification of results, ballot-snatching and violence, and a backward step for democracy in Nigeria.[87] Agitation for constitutional reforms will therefore continue to be the possible means for the advancement of democratic governance and development in democratising countries of sub-Sahara Africa.

Nigeria's recently passed Fourth Alteration to the 1999 Constitution while offering hope that constitutional reforms may not after all be mission impossible, at the same time reveals the politics and manipulations of constitutional reforms process by the political leadership, as the main agenda of restructuring the federation, resource management and equitable allocation, guarantee of economic and social rights, and autonomy of local government system of administration, are largely left out of the process for now. Hence, the call for restructuring and constitutional reforms will continue to ring out until when some reasonable consensus can be reached in achieving the desired constitutional reforms in the country. This offers hope for all the democratizing states that if the regimes are being pushed, through consensus and concerted efforts

85 2004 1 KLR 232, at 249. For a full discussion of the relevant portion of the report case cf. Public Participation in African Constitutionalism cf. Tania Abbiate/Markus Böckenförde/Veronica Federico (eds.), op. cit. (note 37), 29–31.

86 *Jakkie Cilliers* (note 81).

87 *Claire Wilmot*, After Elections, Important Questions Remain for Nigeria's Democracy, Reliefweb, International Peace Institute, 19 March, 2019; available at <https://reliefweb.int/report/nigeria/after-elections-important-questions-remain-nigeria-s-democracy>.

of the civil society for constitutional reforms, incremental advancement towards democracy will be achieved, at the minimum. But where these reforms are persistently resisted the regimes leave no option than for violent change which will also inevitable involve constitutional reforms.[88]

V. Recommendations and Conclusion

1. Recommendations

1.1 The first recommendation is to employ the Freedom House designation of democratizing countries as a basis for advocating the degree or intensity of collaborative initiation and implementation of constitutional reforms in the 'Not free states' -Angola, Cameroon, Chad, Congo, Côte d'Ivoire, Democratic Republic of the Congo, Equatorial Guinea, Eritrea, Gabon, Guinea, Rwanda, Sierra Leone, Somalia, Swaziland, Zimbabwe; 'Partly free states' -Burkina Faso, Burundi, Central African Republic, Comoros, Ethiopia, Gambia, Guinea-Bissau Kenya, Lesotho, Liberia, Madagascar, Malawi, Mozambique, Niger, Nigeria, Senegal, Seychelles, Togo, Uganda, United Republic of Tanzania, Zambia; 'Free States' – Benin, Botswana, Cape Verde, Ghana, Mali, Mauritius, Namibia, Sao Tome & Principe, South Africa. The civil society, the opposition parties working with regional organisation of African Union, and sub-regional bodies, e.g. ECOWAS, to achieve some consensus building for agenda, procedures, and effectual implementation of constitutional reforms.

1.2 Reforms must be substantively targeted at addressing the fundamental defects of the constitution and democratic governance, such as reforming the political parties, elections, election management bodies, and electoral system to guarantee free and fair elections, autonomy of the other arms of government while curtailing the excesses of the executive, to ensure good governance, design constitutions that will guarantee and enforce the protection of human rights including economic and social rights. Partly free countries such as Nigeria, Kenya, Uganda, Senegal, Tanzania, Zambia, among others, ought to have their civil society engaging in consensus building to achieve these ends.

1.3 Thorough analysis of all aspects of constitutional reforms processes become imperative for their effectiveness of involvement of public participation that will substantially engage the populace in the processes so as to confer not only legitimacy and ef-

88 *Eleanor Thompson* (note 15); Sub-Saharan Africa (note 69); *Yuhniwo Ngenge*, op. cit. (note 6).

fectiveness to the democratization process, but for the constitution to gain the respect and loyalty of the people in their commitment to its observance and implementation.

1.4 Since the ruling governments are, especially in countries designated as 'Not Free', have the propensity to manipulate constitutional reforms process for their selfish objectives of tenure elongation and weakening of the democratic process, constitutional reforms process must be protected from abuse by the civil society and AU and sub-regional bodies.

1.5 The United Nations, the AU, and sub-regional bodies must collaborate to have targeted interventions at the democratization and constitution reform processes of African states. The recent Gambian experience in collaborative intervention by Member States of the ECOWAS, demonstrates the usefulness of such intervention that could have been deployed in some countries like Zimbabwe, The Congo, Burundi, Uganda, and Kenya. These international, regional and sub-regional interventions will expedite the democratization process on the African continent and galvanize good governance and development.

2. Conclusion

The reality of the waning wave of democratization clearly presents the constitutional reforms process as bridging avenue for achieving the continuing engagement of mainly electoral multi-party regimes such as -Burkina Faso, Burundi, Central African Republic, Comoros, Ethiopia, Gambia, Guinea-Bissau Kenya, Lesotho, Liberia, Madagascar, Malawi, Mozambique, Niger, Nigeria, Senegal, Seychelles, Togo, Uganda, United Republic of Tanzania, Zambia, that are designated as 'Partly Free' states – in fostering democratic governance. Even in states designated as 'Not Free', constitutional reforms must be vigilantly pursued so as to democratize them and guide them towards genuine democratic governance for good governance and development.

Democratization without well designed and crafted constitutional instrument to deal with all the issues in the transition to democracy, can mire the process in the doldrums of electoral multi-partyism without genuine progression towards democracy. The Nigerian democratization process with all the potentials for positive changes, will become a mission impossible without the needed constitutional reforms toward fostering and establishment good governance, constitutionalism, rule of law, social justice, equality and inclusivity, equity and justice, in short democracy!

Les Réponses Infra-Constitutionnelles à une Crise de Nature Constitutionnelle: Cas de la Résolution de la 'Crise Anglophone' au Cameroun

Paul Zibi

Abstract

Regardless its nature, a crisis is always a time of upheaval that can lead to the change of a State constitutional organisation. Facing crisis, some States resort to infra-constitutional responses where constitutional changes might be advocated. Those responses generally have legislative, regulatory or political nature. It is the choice that has been made by the government of Cameroon which – facing the Anglophone crisis since October 2016 – attempted to resolve this latter by bringing forthfront infra-constitutional responses in a crisis which basically has constitutional origins. These responses pertain to the reaffirmation and the non-negotiable character of the unitary form of the State and the consolidation of constitutional acquis, namely the bilingualism and the decentralisation. The first ones target the delegitimisation of any speech questioning the unitary form of the State and the annihilation of any aspiration to federalism and secessionism. As for the second ones, they aim to strengthen the perfectible bilingualism and to enhance the decentralisation process.

Résumé

Quelle que soit sa nature, une crise est toujours un moment de bouleversement qui peut entraîner la mutation de l'organisation constitutionnelle d'un Etat. Confrontés aux crises, certains Etats optent plutôt pour des réponses infra-constitutionnelles, là où des changements constitutionnels devraient être recommandés. Ces réponses sont généralement de nature législative, réglementaire ou même politique. C'est le choix qu'a opéré le gouvernement camerounais qui – confronté à la crise anglophone depuis octobre 2016 – a essayé de résoudre celle-ci en apportant des réponses infra-constitutionnelles à une crise dont les origines sont fondamentalement constitutionnelles. Ces réponses tiennent globalement en la réaffirmation et au caractère non négociable de la forme unitaire de l'Etat et en la consolidation des acquis constitutionnels que sont le bilinguisme et la décentralisation. Les premières visent la délégitimation du discours de remise en cause de la forme unitaire de l'Etat et la néantisation des velléités fédéralistes et sécessionnistes. Les secondes quant à elles s'emploient à promouvoir le bilinguisme jusque-là imparfait et à accélérer le processus de décentralisation.

I. Introduction

La survenance d'une crise identitaire à l'instar de celle que traverse actuellement le Cameroun requiert que l'on interroge ses causes profondes. La 'crise anglophone' –

puisque c'est ainsi qu'il est désormais convenu de l'appeler[1] – a pris des proportions telles que l'on semble plus que jamais plonger aujourd'hui dans l'incertitude des lendemains[2]. Cette crise que l'on pourrait qualifier dans le contexte actuel de crise de la citoyenneté duale[3] puise ses racines dans l'histoire coloniale du Cameroun, mais surtout dans son histoire constitutionnelle. En effet, il n'est point de doute que les rémanences de la domination coloniale ont façonné l'écriture des premières Constitutions africaines,[4] tant et si bien qu'elles se lisent encore aujourd'hui dans certains aspects des dispositifs constitutionnels en vigueur. La Constitution camerounaise est une illustration parfaite de ces réminiscences du passé impérialiste. En vérité, cette Constitution porte encore en elle les germes de la division héritée de la bipartition des peuples qui avaient en commun leur culture.

Pour le comprendre, il convient de revisiter sommairement l'histoire coloniale du Cameroun. Protectorat allemand de 1884 à 1916, le Cameroun est placé sous mandat par la Société des Nations (SdN) et administré par l'Angleterre et la France.[5] Ces puissances devaient assurer le maintien de la paix, de l'ordre, de la bonne gouvernance du territoire, la promotion du bien-être matériel et moral ainsi que le progrès social des populations de ce territoire.[6] Elles exécutent ce mandat de 1922 à 1945. Leur domination est prorogée lorsqu'à l'issue de la seconde guerre mondiale, le pays est placé sous la tutelle de l'Organisation des Nations Unies (ONU) entre 1945 et 1960. La double appartenance linguistique[7] qui résulte de ces deux périodes et qui fait aujourd'hui du

1 *International Crisis Group,* Cameroun: la crise anglophone à la croisée des chemins, Rapport Afrique, n° 250, 2 août 2017, 38.

2 Cette crise a débuté en novembre 2016 par des revendications corporatistes des avocats et des enseignants dans les deux régions anglophones du nord-ouest et du sud-ouest du Cameroun.

3 En référence au sentiment de plus en plus exacerbé d'appartenance et de repli linguistiques que certains Camerounais des deux langues développent depuis le début de la crise, lire: *International Crisis Group,* Cameroun : l'aggravation de la crise anglophone requiert des mesures fortes, Crisis Group Briefing Afrique, n° 130, Nairobi/Bruxelles, 19 octobre 2017, 7–8.

4 *G. Hesseling,* La réception du droit constitutionnel en Afrique trente ans après: quoi de neuf?, in: Carla M. Zoéthout et al, Constitutionnalism in Africa, a quest of autochtonous principles, Sanders Institut, Gonda Quint-Deventer, 1996, 33–47.

5 V. J. *Ngoh,* Southern Cameroons, 1922–1961: A constitutional history, Aldershot, England: Ashgate Publishing Ltd, 2001, 2, 1.

6 V. l'article 2 de l'Accord de mandat.

7 Aujourd'hui encore le Cameroun fait partie des pays du 'outer circle', c'est-à-dire des pays dans lesquels les langues officielles, héritées de la colonisation, ont le statut de langues étrangères, J.-G. *Mboudjeke,* Bilinguisme, politiques et attitudes linguistiques au Cameroun et au Canada, Revue électronique de sciences du langage sudlangues, n° 6, 152.

Cameroun un pays bilingue[8], aboutira à la division de l'ancien protectorat allemand en deux entités, à savoir le Cameroun oriental administré par la France, d'une part; et d'autre part, le Cameroun septentrional britannique (Northern Cameroon) et le Cameroun méridional britannique (Southern Cameroon).

Si le Cameroun oriental acquiert son indépendance le 1er janvier 1960, le référendum organisé le 11 février 1961 dans la partie britannique conduira au rattachement du Cameroun septentrional britannique au Nigéria et à la réunification le 1er octobre 1961 du Cameroun méridional britannique au Cameroun oriental.[9] Depuis lors, cette union des deux anciennes entités n'a cessé de nourrir une histoire constitutionnelle qui a expérimenté le fédéralisme entre 1961 et 1972 et depuis lors a choisi l'option unitaire comme forme de l'Etat.

Toutefois, cette option unitaire n'a pas suffi à dissiper les différences aux plans culturel et linguistique des peuples qui le composent. En effet, la majorité francophone, représentant 83 % de la population, exerce une domination sociopolitique[10] et presque naturelle sur une minorité anglophone présente dans deux régions sur dix[11] et comprenant seulement 17 % de la population. Celle-ci à tort ou à raison s'est toujours estimée lésée. Les frustrations qu'elle exprime depuis la réunification de 1961 ont atteint un point culminant en octobre 2016 lorsque les enseignants et les avocats des deux régions anglophones ont décidé de porter à l'attention du gouvernement, par une grève généralisée, des revendications socio-corporatistes. Celles-ci portent globalement sur la restauration de la langue anglaise et la prise en compte de la culture de la common law qu'ils estiment en déperdition dans ces régions à cause de la propagation de la langue française et de la généralisation du droit romano-germanique de tradition civiliste héritée de la France.[12]

8 *G. T. Foumena*, Considérations sur le bilinguisme et les normes juridiques au Cameroun, Revue Africaine de Droit et de Science Politique (RADSP), Vol. V, n° 10, Juil.-Déc. 2017, 98.

9 Sur l'histoire de la réunification lire: *V. J. Ngoh*, Les Dessous de la réunification au Cameroun: De 1955 à 1961, Presprint Limbe, Cameroun, 2011, 111.

10 *J.-G. Mboudjeke*, l. c., at 158.

11 Le Cameroun compte dix régions constituant en même temps des circonscriptions administratives et des collectivités territoriales décentralisées.

12 Sur le bilinguisme et le droit, lire: *C. Manga Fombad*, Managing legal diversity: Cameroonian bijuralism at a critical croosroads, Law Explorer, 19 mars 2016, disponible au lien suivant <https://lawexplores.com/managing-legal-diversity-cameroonian-bijuralism-at-a-critical-crossroads/>, consulté le 21 mars 2018; *G. T. Foumena*, op. cit., 97–121; *Y. S. Nkoulou*, Langue et droit au Cameroun : Linéaments de la problématique de l'unification du droit dans un contexte bilingue, RIDC, n° 3, 2015, 695–726.

Pourtant, depuis l'accession à l'indépendance et le rattachement en 1961 du Cameroun méridional au Cameroun oriental, la question anglophone[13] ne semble avoir été tranchée ni avec la réunification encore moins avec l'Etat unitaire intervenu en 1972.[14] Elle a toujours constitué l'antichambre de la revendication identitaire prévalant aujourd'hui. Depuis lors en effet, une certaine frange anglophone a entrepris de saper cette union dès les premières lueurs de la réunification des deux Cameroun.[15] Aujourd'hui, l'on se rend bien compte que les revendications corporatistes des avocats et des enseignants enclenchées ont non seulement attisé les flammes dormantes d'une crise qui couve depuis plusieurs décennies. Elles ont aussi facilité son expansion et sa radicalisation comme jamais auparavant. S'il peut sembler évident que les origines de cette crise sont consubstantiellement liées à l'histoire coloniale du Cameroun, l'on ne saurait cependant disculper les premiers constituants lorsqu'il a fallu que le pays accède à sa pleine souveraineté.

En effet, cette crise a remis au goût du jour le débat constitutionnel sur la forme de l'Etat qui cache en réalité un 'débat identitaire de redéfinition de la cohabitation entre les composantes francophone et anglophone du Cameroun situés respectivement dans l'ex-Cameroun oriental pour la première et dans l'ex-Cameroun occidental pour la seconde[16]'. Si la forme de l'Etat est réputée intangible en vertu de la Con-

13 Il existe une abondante littérature sur la question: A.-*D. Olinga,* La question anglophone aujourd'hui, Revue Juridique et Politique, Indépendance et Coopération (R.J.P.I.C), 1994, 293–308 ; *M. Aboya Endong,* La question anglophone au Cameroun: entre menaces sécessionnistes et revendications identitaires, R.J.P.E.F., numéro 1, janvier-mars, 2005, 115–116 ; *E.H. Nfobin* and *Nchotu V. Nchang,* The Cameroon anglophone question in international law, African Journal of International and Comparative Law, 22.2, 2004, Edinburg University Press, 234–257.

14 La Constitution du 2 juin 1972 marque la naissance de la forme unitaire de l'Etat. Son article 1er indique que: 'La République fédérale du Cameroun, formée de l'Etat du Cameroun oriental et de l'Etat du Cameroun occidental devient à compter de l'entrée en vigueur de la présente Constitution, un Etat unitaire sous la domination de la République unie du Cameroun».

15 Le 1er octobre a toujours marqué la date symbolique des revendications à l'autodétermination et pour cette cause on a vu naître des mouvements se nourrissant des velléités sécessionnistes tels que le Southern Cameroon National Council (SCNC), Southern Cameroon People's Organisation (SCAPO), le Cameroon Anglophone Movement (CAM), le Free West Cameroon Movement (FWM), le Southern Cameroons Restoration Movement *(SCRM),* et l'Ambazonia Movement, etc., *International Crisis Group,* Cameroun: la crise anglophone à la croisée des chemins (note 1), 7.

16 *L. Sindjoun,* Identité nationale et ''révision constitutionnelle'' du 18 janvier 1996: Comment constitutionnalise-t-on le ''nous'' au Cameroun dans l'Etat post-unitaire?. », in : Polis, Vol. 1, Spécial, Février 1996, consulté sur <http://www.poliq.sciencespobordeaux.fr/vol1 ns/article2.html>.

stitution[17] et qu'il y est consacrée l'égale valeur du français et de l'anglais[18] – ce qui au regard du respect de la norme fondamentale clorait tout débat sur ces deux questions – il reste que la crise actuelle interroge aussi le modèle de gouvernance locale qui est pourtant encadré par la technique de décentralisation.[19] Toute crise qui naîtrait donc de ces trois questions éminemment constitutionnelles devrait appeler des réponses de même nature.

Or, dans sa volonté de mettre fin à la crise anglophone qui prévaut actuellement, le gouvernement a pris un certain nombre de mesures. L'examen minutieux de celles-ci permet de constater qu'elles sont essentiellement infra-constitutionnelles dans ce sens qu'elles n'ont, pour certaines, qu'une portée réglementaire, et pour d'autres, un caractère politique qui influe cependant sur le dispositif constitutionnel existant. Il ne reste pas moins que les mesures prises semblent plutôt révélatrices d'une esquive volontaire du gouvernement à saisir la nature véritable de la crise, se prévalant plutôt de mesures infra-constitutionnelles pour des questions qui sont matériellement constitutionnelles ou dont la résolution met en exergue l'habilitation constitutionnelle en matière réglementaire. Il se pose donc la question de l'opportunité des réponses infra-constitutionnelles pour résoudre une crise dont les causes sont fondamentalement constitutionnelles.

En effet, le nœud de la crise qui se déroule actuellement et du conflit désormais armé qui chaque jour prend de l'ampleur trouve un fondement constitutionnel ; tant et si bien que les réponses à apporter devraient être revêtues d'une forme constitutionnelle qui redéfinirait la forme de l'Etat, le statut réel des langues officielles que sont l'anglais et le français et le modèle de gouvernance des collectivités locales. Elle doit provoquer pour ainsi dire des réformes qui s'enracinent dans l'ordre constitutionnel. Au contraire, les actes pris par le gouvernement s'avèrent plutôt être des changements périphériques du dispositif constitutionnel, c'est-à-dire des changements qui portent non pas sur la Constitution elle-même, mais qui l'affectent indirectement. Toutefois, le fait que la crise anglophone soulève des questions éminemment constitutionnelles ne saurait dissoudre la prééminence naturelle du pouvoir exécutif en temps de crise. En effet, l'action de l'exécutif prime sur celle des autres organes étatiques et se trouve par

17 L'article 64 de la loi constitutionnelle du 18 janvier 1964 précise qu'aucune révision portant sur la forme républicaine, à l'unité et à l'intégrité du territoire ne peut être retenue.

18 *G. T. Foumena* , (note 8), 99.

19 Sur cette question lire utilement: *C. M. Ngo Tong,* Le modèle camerounais de décentralisation, in E. Batchom, (dir.), L'Etat ailleurs, Entre logiques de case et dynamiques du village global, Hommage à Luc Sindjoun, L'Harmattan, Paris, 2018, 41–64.

conséquent en bien meilleure posture en temps de crise[20]. C'est cette prééminence de l'exécutif en temps de crise qui dicte le choix du discriminant principal du thème de cette étude qui est, non pas la notion d'amendement, mais plutôt celle de 'réponses', plus appropriée pour qualifier les mesures prises par le gouvernement.

Bien plus, la raison pour laquelle le présent article évitera de faire mention du terme 'amendement'[21] – vocable auquel l'on fait généralement recours pour qualifier des modifications d'un dispositif constitutionnel – est que l'usage de cette notion serait juridiquement inapproprié. Il est en effet difficile de parler d'amendement pour des mesures qui ne portent pas directement sur le dispositif constitutionnel. Qui plus est, l'on ne parle généralement d'amendement que pour qualifier une proposition de modification d'un texte de loi au cours de discussion parlementaire;[22] le cas échéant une proposition de modification d'un texte constitutionnel. Or, en aucun cas la crise actuelle n'a fait l'objet jusqu'à date d'une proposition ou d'un projet de loi qui ait donné lieu à une discussion devant une assemblée constituante. Elle a plutôt eu droit à des réponses[23] d'ordre réglementaire et politique qui tournent néanmoins autour des questions aménagées par la Constitution dans le but de résoudre une crise de nature constitutionnelle.

En s'appuyant exclusivement sur les différentes mesures prises par le gouvernement, le présent article se propose de présenter la démarche qui consiste à vouloir résoudre une crise dont les causes remontent à la Constitution originaire du 2 juin 1972[24], d'une part, par des réponses dont le but affiché se décline en la réaffirmation de la forme unitaire de l'Etat (I); d'autre part, par celles dont l'objectif est la consolidation des acquis constitutionnels que sont le bilinguisme et la décentralisation (II).

20 *Leroy*, L'organisation constitutionnelle et les crises, Paris, LGDJ, 1966, 31.

21 Le terme 'amendement» aurait sans doute été plus approprié puisque le présent article est la résultante de la communication présentée à l'atelier intitulé ' Amendements constitutionnels en période de crise » à l'occasion du 10ème Congrès mondial de droit constitutionnel qui s'est tenu à Séoul en Corée du Sud du 18 au 22 juin 2018.

22 *S. Guinchard* (Sous la dir.), Lexique des termes juridiques 2017–2018, 25e éd., Dalloz, Paris, 2017, 156.

23 Terme plus approprié pour désigner la recherche de solutions à une crise.

24 La Constitution du Cameroun est – si l'on s'en tient à la lettre de la loi et que l'on sorte de l'analyse juridique positiviste – celle du 2 juin 1972, puisque celle supposée actuellement vigueur se lit comme suit: la loi n° 96/06 du 18 janvier 1996 portant révision de la Constitution du 2 juin 1972, modifiée et complétée par la loi n° 2008/001 du 14 avril 2008. Ceci est d'autant vrai que cette Constitution de 1972 procède de la souveraineté constituante du peuple, alors la révision de 1996 est l'œuvre du pouvoir constituant institué ou dérivé. Son article Premier met fin à la République fédérale instituée en 1961 en consacrant l'unification – remise en cause aujourd'hui par la crise actuelle – entre 'l'Etat du Cameroun oriental et l'Etat du Cameroun occidental'.

II. La Réaffirmation de la Forme Unitaire de l'État

La crise anglophone a éventré une réalité ancienne qui veut qu'au Cameroun certaines questions de nature constitutionnelle, notamment celles concernant la forme de l'Etat, ne soient jamais débattues dans un cadre formel de discussion sur la loi fondamentale.[25] Or, il est établi qu'en temps de crise l'amendement de l'organisation constitutionnelle, quel qu'il soit, se justifie par l'état de nécessité afin d'apporter des solutions qui vont s'insérer, au-delà de ce temps, à l'ordonnancement constitutionnel[26]. Pour résoudre la crise actuelle, les réponses apportées pour réaffirmer la forme unitaire de l'Etat se font hors de tout cadre d'amendement constitutionnel. Elles sont apportées soit sur le terrain politique, soit par des actes réglementaires réaffirmant la forme unitaire de l'Etat (1) et visant à anéantir les velléités fédéralistes et sécessionnistes (2).

1. La Délégitimation de la Remise en Cause de la Forme Unitaire de l'État

Si l'intérêt de la réforme de la Constitution du 2 juin 1972 fut suscité par les soubresauts politiques du début des années 1990[27] et ont abouti à la loi constitutionnelle du 18 janvier 1996, la crise anglophone actuelle, en dépit de sa radicalisation,[28] n'a encore donné lieu à un début de discussion sur un changement de nature constitutionnelle. Elle est confrontée sur ce plan à la clause d'intangibilité sur la forme unitaire de l'Etat (1.1.) et à l'irréductibilité du gouvernement à ouvrir un dialogue sur celle-ci (1.2.).

1.1. La Clause d'Intangibilité sur la Forme Unitaire de l'État

L'ensemble des mesures prises[29] depuis l'éclatement de la crise dite anglophone convergent toutes vers un dénominateur commun qui est celui de la réaffirmation

25 De toutes les révisions constitutionnelles qui sont intervenues depuis la Constitution du 2 juin 1972, aucune n'a effectivement jamais porté sur la forme de l'Etat en dépit des revendications à l'autodétermination de certains ressortissants anglophones.

26 *Leroy* (note 20), 12.

27 *A. Ondoua* (dir), Rapport introductif, in: La Constitution camerounaise du 18 janvier 1996: Bilan et perspectives, Afrédit 2007, 12.

28 Lorsque la crise déclenche en octobre 2016, personne n'aurait pensé que, deux ans après, l'on serait englué aujourd'hui dans une guerre ouverte entre, d'une part, les forces de défense et de sécurité loyalistes, et d'autre part, les groupes de sécessionnistes armés. Depuis quelques mois, des morts dans les deux camps se comptent par dizaines.

29 V. *infra*. Quelques mesures essentiellement réglementaires et politiques, prises dans le cadre de la résolution de la crise, seront égrenées plus bas.

du principe intangible de la forme républicaine et unitaire de l'Etat. Le fondement de ce principe se trouve à l'article 64 de la loi constitutionnelle du 18 janvier 1996 qui précise qu': 'Aucune procédure de révision ne peut être retenue si elle porte atteinte à la forme républicaine, à l'unité et à l'intégrité territoriale de l'Etat et aux principes démocratiques qui régissent la République'. Cette formulation prend elle-même son fondement de l'article 1er alinéa 2 qui fait du Cameroun un 'Etat unitaire et décentralisé', une République 'une et indivisible'. Il s'agit là d'un héritage de l'histoire constitutionnelle française qui a inséré dans la Constitution de 1875 la clause de l'intangibilité de la forme de l'Etat; celle-là même que Yaniv Roznai indique fort à propos en parlant de: 'The original French unamendability of the republic form of government,'[30] C'est cette clause éternelle qui fonde la position du gouvernement aujourd'hui à ne consentir à aucune forme de négociation avec une quelconque partie en vue ne serait-ce que réfléchir sur l'éventualité d'une réforme constitutionnelle qui remettrait en cause la forme actuelle de l'Etat. Il ne s'agit pas cependant d'un phénomène nouveau, car il en va de l'existence même du Cameroun en tant qu'une nation avec son identité singulière.

En effet, la structuration géo-linguistique de l'identité nationale[31] peut être lue à travers l'évolution même de la loi fondamentale camerounaise qui est très souvent étroitement liée à la question de la structuration et de l'organisation de l'Etat.[32] Questionner cette identité géo-linguistique serait donc remettre en cause le caractère unitaire de l'Etat, considéré comme un verrou contre toute prétention au séparatisme identitaire dans un pays qui compte deux cent quatre-vingt-trois ethnies ou communautés de langage.[33] La multiplicité linguistique et ethnique n'a pas eu pour effet de décomposer l'Etat en autant de strates possibles, mais plutôt de construire une unité qui se nourrit de cette diversité. Celle-ci étant alors considérée comme le fondement de l'unité. Le préambule de la Constitution révisée en 1996 donne le ton dès son premier énoncé en indiquant que le peuple camerounais: 'Fier de sa diversité linguistique et culturelle, élément de sa personnalité nationale qu'elle contribue à enrichir,

30 L'auteur parle de l'intangibilité originaire de la forme républicaine du gouvernement en France, *Y. Roznai*, Unconstitutional constitutional amendments: A study of the nature and the limits of constitutional amendment powers, A thesis submitted to the Department of Law of the London School of Economics for the degree of Doctor of Philosophy. London, February 2014, 112.

31 *L. Sindjoun* (note 16), 5.

32 *A. Ondoua*, l .c.

33 Selon la Société Internationale de Linguistique (SIL), le Cameroun compte 283 langues officiellement recensées parmi lesquelles 277 langues vivantes et 6 langues éteintes, disponible au lien suivant <www.silcam.org>, consulté le 18 mai 2018.

mais profondément conscient de la nécessité impérieuse de parfaire son unité, proclame solennellement qu'il constitue une seule et même nation (…)'.

Si l'argument sur le caractère intangible de la forme de l'Etat – bien que considéré comme une clause éternelle – est donc souvent avancé comme argument politique d'unité nationale, il ne résiste cependant pas à l'analyse. Il faut justement indiquer que les autres formes de l'Etat autres que l'Etat unitaire ne sont pas incompatibles avec l'idéal d'unité. Le fédéralisme par exemple souhaité aujourd'hui par une bonne frange des Camerounais originaires des régions anglophones et certains francophones,[34] est un courant centripète qui signifie fédérer, unir[35] ou encore un efficace instrument d'unification et de centralisation[36], au point où un auteur se demandait si 'accepter le fédéralisme, ce n'est pas, implicitement, consentir à la centralisation?'.[37] C'est dire que l'unité ne se conçoit que dans la volonté de s'unir et ne saurait être tributaire d'une forme exclusive d'Etat.

Cette posture sur la non-négociabilité de la forme de l'Etat tirant sa substance dans un principe intangible justifie l'absence de changement formel du dispositif constitutionnel qui effleurerait cette question. C'est elle qui fonde par ailleurs la position du gouvernement à n'ouvrir aucun dialogue sur cette problématique dans le cadre de la crise actuelle.

1.2. *L'Irréductibilité Gouvernementale au Dialogue sur la Forme de l'État*

Depuis le début de la crise, le gouvernement s'est toujours interdit d'ouvrir un dialogue qui porterait sur la forme de l'Etat, l'objectif étant de 'maintenir le statu quo'.[38] La première réponse apportée fut la création par arrêté du Premier Ministre d'un Comité Interministériel Ad Hoc chargé d'examiner les revendications des enseignants. Officiellement, le Comité ad hoc devait mener au départ des négociations avec les syndicats des enseignants anglophones, mais les discussions auront finalement lieu avec le Cameroon Anglophone Civil Society Consortium (CASCC, 'le Consortium'). Il s'agit d'une organisation composée de quatre associations d'avocats et de plusieurs syndicats d'enseignants formée pour constituer la partie interlocutrice qui doit discu-

34 *International Crisis Group*, Cameroun (note 15), 19.

35 *D. Turpin*, Droit constitutionnel, Paris, PUF, 4e éd., 1999, 68.

36 Ibid., 59.

37 *J. Rivero*, Fédéralisme et décentralisation : harmonie ou contradiction?, Pages de doctrine, 1980, t. I, 213.

38 *International Crisis Group* (note 1), 11.

ter avec le gouvernement.[39] Dans un premier temps, le gouvernement semble soupçonner le Consortium d'être porteur des revendications autres que celles concernant le système éducatif, juridique et judiciaire, mais acceptera néanmoins d'ouvrir des pourparlers avec celui-ci. Le préalable posé était cependant que les discussions devaient être limitées aux revendications corporatistes et devaient éviter toutes les prétentions qui ont un rapport avec la structuration actuelle de l'Etat ou qui remettrait en cause l'intégrité du territoire et l'unité nationale.[40] Ce préalable affiche l'intransigeance du gouvernement sur ce point précis.

Les onze (11) revendications formulées au départ par le Consortium passeront, à la grande surprise du gouvernement, à vingt-et-cinq (25) entre novembre 2016 et janvier 2017. Sur ces 25 revendications, le gouvernement apportera des réponses à vingt-et-un (21), estimant que celles restantes remettent en cause le préalable posé dès l'entame des discussions. En fait, les discussions achopperont parce que le gouvernement estime que les revendications sur le système éducatif, juridique et judiciaire ne servent que de paravent aux membres du Consortium qui auraient un agenda caché visant la sécession.[41]

Capitalisant sur cet imbroglio, le gouvernement, à travers ses représentants locaux en l'occurrence les gouverneurs des régions du Nord-Ouest et du Sud-Ouest, va prendre des mesures drastiques. La première de ces mesures est l'arrestation des leaders du Consortium qui ont rompu les pourparlers au prétexte des violences orchestrées par les forces de l'ordre sur la population. Puis, on assistera à la coupure et la limitation pendant trois mois de l'accès à internet. Enfin, le Ministre de l'administration territoriale et de la décentralisation[42] va prendre un arrêté en date du 17 janvier 2017 pour interdire les activités de la CACSC, le consortium, et de la SCNC. L'article 1er de l'arrêté indique à cet effet que: 'Sont nuls et de nul effet pour objet et activité contraire à la Constitution et de nature à porter atteinte à la sécurité de l'Etat, l'intégrité du territoire, à l'unité nationale et à l'intégration nationale, les groupements dénommés Southern Cameroon National Council (SCNC) et Cameroon Anglophone Civil Society Consortium (CACSC)'.

Le référence à l''objet et activité contraire à la Constitution' indique clairement les doutes du gouvernement sur les intentions réelles des membres du Consortium et de

39 Ibid.

40 Sur l'historique des rencontres entre le Comité interministériel ad hoc, les syndicats des enseignants et officieusement avec le Consortium, lire: *International Crisis Group*, (note 1), 11 et suivants.

41 Ibid., 12.

42 L'équivalent au Cameroun du Ministre de l'intérieur.

la sincérité des revendications qu'ils ont soulevées au départ. Au demeurant, ces intentions – réelles ou supposées – se heurtent à son irréductibilité à ne céder parcelle à aucune discussion qui remettrait en cause la forme actuelle de l'Etat et par voie de conséquence prêterait le flanc à la sécession.

2. La Néantisation des Velléités Fédéralistes et Sécessionnistes

Sur la forme de l'Etat, le langage des sourds continue entre le gouvernement et certains activistes anglophones qui souhaitent voir une autre forme que celle proclamée dans la Constitution depuis 1972. En dépit de toutes les mesures édictées par le gouvernement depuis le début de la crise, il ne transparaît aucune volonté de négocier sur les termes qui porteraient sur la remise en cause du caractère unitaire de l'Etat. Certaines de ces mesures sont prises dans l'objectif de dissuader les velléités, d'une part, de la frange radicale qui souhaite la sécession et appelle de ses vœux l'instauration de l'Etat d''Ambazonie'[43] (1) ; d'autre part, du bord plus modéré réclamant le fédéralisme comme solution à la crise actuelle (2).

2.1. Les Choix Institutionnels de Dénégation du Fédéralisme

Pour le gouvernement, les revendications des enseignants et des avocats n'ont jamais eu une autre finalité que d'asseoir une division de fait qui – même si une solution était trouvée à chacune d'entre elles – remettrait tôt ou tard au goût du jour le débat sur la forme unitaire de l'Etat. Elles servent de prémices à ce que devrait être plus tard un Etat composé de plusieurs autres Etats où les systèmes juridique et éducatif seraient différents les uns des autres. Ce n'est d'ailleurs pas la première fois, depuis la réunification de la République du Cameroun et de la Southern Cameroon en 1972, que 'l'anglophonie rebelle[44]' use de prétextes savamment orchestrés dans le but d'essayer de remettre en cause cette union qui n'a pas été acquise de manière parfaite.[45]

43 Nom que les sécessionnistes donnent à leur Etat fictif.

44 *L. Sindjoun* (note 16), 5.

45 *V. J. Ngoh*, Les dessous de la réunification du Cameroun : De 1995 à 1961, Presprint, Limbé, 2011, 47. L'auteur fait par exemple observer que lors du référendum pour la réunification qu'une bonne partie de l'électorat du Cameroun méridional a cru que l'option de la réunification avait été remplacée par la sécession et l'indépendance.

En 1994 déjà la Southern Cameroon Peoples Council[46] avait exprimé, à la suite de la convocation par le Président de la République du Comité consultatif de révision de la Constitution de 1972, la volonté de prendre les décisions qui concernent les anglophones dans le cadre d'une Constitution qui ne leur est pas imposée.[47] Autrement dit, le désir était celui d'un retour à l'Etat fédéral qui leur permettrait d'acquérir une certaine autonomie que ne garantissait pas l'instauration de l'Etat unitaire depuis 1972. C'est aussi fort de ces soupçons au séparatisme que le gouvernement, par la voix du ministre de la communication,[48] a opposé une fin de non-recevoir à l'initiative des chefs religieux de convoquer une conférence générale anglophone qui devait se tenir le 29 août 2018 dans le but d'apporter une solution à la crise.[49]

De la même manière, depuis le début de la crise actuelle en octobre 2016, les mouvements pour la défense des intérêts des Anglophones, dont les visées *a priori* sont généralement inavouées, usent des revendications corporatistes liées aux questions d'éducation et du droit appliqué pour étendre leur action au fédéralisme pour les plus modérés. Bien entendu, le gouvernement reste de marbre face à ces velléités. Toutefois, celui-ci valide, à travers quelques-unes de ses actions, certaines spécificités de ce que pourrait être un Etat fédéral. On le voit par exemple avec la création depuis l'année académique 2017 d'une Section de la Common Law à l'Ecole d'Administration et de Magistrature (ENAM). Il s'agit de l'une des mesures instruites par le Président de la République au gouvernement afin d'apporter des réponses aux revendications exprimées par les avocats anglophones en ce qui concerne le fonctionnement du système judiciaire. Or, à l'observation du système judiciaire camerounais, il est facile de constater que cette mesure concerne uniquement les magistrats qui serviront dans les tribunaux pratiquant la Common Law dont on sait pertinemment que leur ressort territorial se trouve être les deux régions anglophones du Nord-Ouest et du Sud-Ouest. On peut classer dans le même ordre d'idées, la création d'une Section de la Common Law au sein de la Chambre judiciaire de la Cour Suprême ou encore la création par arrêté du Ministre de l'Enseignement Supérieur de départements d'English Law dans

46 Nouvelle dénomination à partir de 1994 de la 'All Anglophone Conference' qui est un mouvement dont le but est de défendre les intérêts des anglophones dans le cadre du débat constitutionnel commencé en 1993 et qui allait aboutir la Constitution du 18 janvier 1996.

47 *L. Sindjoun* (note 16), 6.

48 Dans une adresse du ministre de la communication à l'occasion du point de presse du 27 juillet 2018.

49 Les organisateurs qui ont à leur tête le Cardinal *Christian Tumi* parlent néanmoins d'un report aux dates du 21 et 22 novembre 2018 bien que le gouvernement n'a pas encore approuvé la tenue d'une telle conférence.

les Universités d'Etat dans lesquelles la formation est fondamentalement axée sur la droit romano-germanique (Douala, Dschang, Maroua, Ngaoundéré)[50]. Et inversement, la création de départements de French Private Law[51] dans les deux Universités d'Etat de Buea et Bamenda se trouvant dans les deux régions anglophones du pays.

Ces mesures dont l'acte juridique de naissance est difficilement identifiable pour certaines, peuvent néanmoins être complétées par la signature de décrets du Président de la République octroyant à certaines élites anglophones de postes d'envergure.[52] Il s'agit là d'autant de réponses apportées par le Président de la République à travers son gouvernement afin de trouver de solutions aux revendications des Anglophones. Il le fait sur le fondement des pouvoirs larges que lui confère l'article 5 de la Constitution en utilisant notamment celle-ci comme un acte d'habilitation qui le pose aussi comme le garant de l'intégrité du territoire.

2.2. *Les Options Sécuritaires de Réprobation de la Sécession*

L'enlisement actuel de la crise est rendu facile par la posture radicale des mouvements prônant la sécession[53] des deux régions anglophones et la création d'un Etat dont les limites ne seraient autres que celles de l'Etat fédéré du Cameroun occidental entre 1961 et 1972. La menace de la sécession qui n'est pas un phénomène nouveau[54] a toujours été brandie par la branche radicale anglophone comme une arme au soutien des revendications politiques et sociales.[55] Aujourd'hui encore plus qu'hier, les mesures prises par le gouvernement pour contrecarrer les velléités d'auto-détermination se situent pour l'essentiel sur le champ sécuritaire de la répression. Pas bien surprenant, surtout lorsqu'on sait que la sécession est considérée comme un crime à la

50 Un tel département existait déjà à l'Université de Yaoundé II, lire aussi dans ce sens: *G. T. Foumena* (note 8), 118.

51 La précision de 'French Private Law' n'est pas anodine. Elle témoigne, d'une part, de l'existence d'un droit public sans bords qui serait commun ; et d'autre part, de l'existence de deux sous-systèmes juridiques s'appuyant, d'un côté, sur le droit civil d'obédience française, et de l'autre, sur la Common Law d'inspiration anglo-saxonne. Chaque sous-système devant être incorporé à l'autre dans le souci d'harmonisation d'un droit camerounais.

52 C'était déjà le cas en 1992 avec notamment l'octroi jusqu'aujourd'hui du Poste de Premier Ministre à un originaire de la partie anglophone, lire: *C. M. Ngo Tong* (note 19), 50.

53 On dénombre aujourd'hui plus d'une dizaine de groupuscules sécessionnistes, lire: *International Crisis Group, Cameroun* (note 3), 4.

54 *M. Aboya Endong* (note 13).

55 *L. Sindjoun* (note 16), 5.

sûreté de l'Etat et par conséquent sévèrement réprimée par le Code pénal[56]. En effet, celui-ci dispose en son article 111 alinéas 1 et 2 qu' :'Est puni de l'emprisonnement à vie celui qui, en temps de paix, entreprend par quelque moyen que ce soit de porter atteinte à l'intégrité du territoire. En temps de guerre, d'état d'urgence ou d'exception, la peine est celle de la mort'.

Pour le gouvernement les appels à la sécession justifient l'escalade répressive à l'encontre de ceux qui y prétendent et ceux qui perpétuent des actes de violences sur les forces de défense et de sécurité[57] sur le prétexte de l'autodéfense.[58] Ainsi, après l'échec des négociations entre les syndicats d'enseignants et les avocats, le gouvernement va procéder à l'arrestation d'une dizaine de militants anglophones et va renforcer sa présence militaire dans les deux régions. Le plus grand coup sécuritaire reste sans doute l'arrestation le 5 janvier 2018 au Nigéria et leur déportation au Cameroun quelques jours plus tard, d'une trentaine de leaders séparatistes qui formaient le gouvernement intérimaire de leur Etat virtuel. Si ces actions opérationnelles de nature répressive constituent des réponses aux violations de l'unité de la nation et de l'intégrité du territoire, il convient de noter que ce sont les mesures prises par le gouvernement en termes d'organisation sécuritaire du territoire qui revêtent véritablement un caractère juridique.

C'est le cas de la réorganisation du commandement militaire territorial qui a fait l'objet d'un acte réglementaire[59] redessinant la nouvelle carte militaire qui ne correspond pas à la carte administrative du pays. Surtout, il s'agit d'une réorganisation qui répartit les régions militaires dans une configuration qui associe une région anglophone et une région francophone pour en faire une région militaire. Il s'agit notamment de la deuxième région militaire interarmées qui comprend désormais les régions du Littoral (francophone) et du Sud-Ouest (anglophone) et la cinquième région militaire interarmées dont le ressort territorial sera dorénavant la région de l'Ouest (francophone) et la région du Nord-Ouest (anglophone).[60]

56 Loi n° 2016/007 du 12 juillet 2016 portant Code pénal.

57 Selon le gouvernement, notamment par la voix de son ministre de la communication, on dénombre au mois d'août 2018, plus d'une centaine d'agents des forces de défense et de sécurité assassinés.

58 Les groupes sécessionnistes qui commettent des meurtres des agents des forces de défense et de sécurité évoquent comme argument la défense de leur territoire.

59 Décret n° 2018/148 du 21 février 2018 modifiant le décret n° 2014/308 du 14 août 2014 modifiant le décret n° 2001/180 du 25 juillet 2001 portant réorganisation du commandement militaire territorial.

60 Voir Article 3 (nouveau) du décret.

Cette configuration correspond curieusement à la répartition proposée par ceux qui réclament le retour à un Etat fédéral qui n'aurait plus uniquement deux Etats fédérés comme ce fut le cas entre 1961 et 1972. Ceux-là imaginent un fédéralisme qui tiendrait compte des grands équilibres sociologiques avec des Etats fédérés qui s'appuieront, non plus sur le soubassement sociologique de l'anglophonie et de la francophonie, mais plutôt sur des grandes aires culturelles du pays. On aurait ainsi un Etat fédéré qui comprendrait les ethnies géographiquement et culturellement proches des 'Grassfields' qui se trouvent aussi bien dans la région anglophone du Nord-Ouest que dans celle francophone de l'Ouest ou encore les 'Sawa', groupe ethnique que l'on rencontre aussi bien dans le Sud-Ouest (anglophone) que dans la région du Littoral (francophone).[61] Pour les autres, on aurait un Etat fédéré constitué de peuples de la zone équatoriale forestière peuplée des 'fang-beti' que l'on retrouve dans les régions du Centre, du Sud et de l'Est et un dernier qui serait formé des régions soudano-sahéliennes de l'Adamaoua, du Nord et de l'Extrême-Nord.

Toutefois, si cette option du fédéralisme se positionne aujourd'hui comme l'une des pistes de sortie de crise,[62] il n'existe actuellement aucun effort au niveau du gouvernement[63] à vouloir décomposer un Etat dont la vocation naturelle prédispose peut-être déjà à cette forme composée de l'Etat. Tout au contraire, le gouvernement à travers un ensemble de mesures qui réaffirment les principes constitutionnels directeurs – symboles de l'unité dans la diversité – que sont le bilinguisme et la décentralisation.

III. La Consolidation des Acquis Constitutionnels du Bilinguisme et de la Décentralisation

Les mesures prises par le gouvernement dans le but de résoudre la crise actuelle sont plus prégnants lorsqu'il s'agit de consolider les acquis constitutionnels que représentent le bilinguisme et la décentralisation. Ces acquis hérités de l'histoire constitutionnelle lointaine et récente qui posent justement problème, parce que mal implémentés pour certains et insuffisants pour d'autres. Ils constituent néanmoins

61 Lire aussi dans ce sens, *International Crisis Group* (note 3), 19–20.

62 *G. Dejo*, Le fédéralisme est-il porteur d'espoir? Cas du Cameroun, Nkafu Policy Institute, mai 2017; *A. Nkoyock*, Crise anglophone au Cameroun: le fédéralisme est-il porteur d'espoir ?, disponible au lien suivant <http://www.jeuneafrique.com/396895/politique/crise-anglophone-cameroun-federalisme-porteur-despoir/>, consulté le 24 Janvier 2017.

63 Face à la montée des revendications sécessionnistes, le Président de la République, lors de son adresse à la nation le 31 décembre 2016, n'avait laissé place à aucun doute en affirmant que: 'Le Cameroun est un et indivisible. Il le demeurera…».

aujourd'hui les meilleures armes dont dispose le gouvernement pour apporter des solutions à cette crise. Si le bilinguisme est intimement lié à l'histoire ancienne du Cameroun, notamment celle de l'unification du Cameroun oriental et du Cameroun occidental en 1961,[64] la volonté d'adopter la décentralisation apparaît quant à elle avec la Constitution du 18 janvier 1996 qui précise en son article 1er alinéa 2 que: 'Le Cameroun est un Etat unitaire décentralisé,'. Dans l'optique de résoudre la crise, ce sont ces deux acquis que le gouvernement nourrit, notamment à travers la promotion du bilinguisme (1) et l'accélération du processus de décentralisation (2).

1. La Promotion du Bilinguisme

La crise actuelle n'est pas simplement une crise de l'identité anglophone, elle est aussi une crise de l'identité camerounaise en ce sens qu'elle affecte le statut des deux langues officielles. Elle a remis au goût du jour le débat sur le statut égalitaire des deux langues officielles. Cette égalité qui ne tient pas compte du nombre de locuteurs,[65] mais de l'usage qui a été fait jusque-là du bilinguisme officiel. Le train de mesures prises depuis le début de la crise en ce sens suffit à confesser l'existence d'un problème que l'on tend aujourd'hui à résoudre à travers des mesures que l'on qualifierait d'affermissement du bilinguisme de manière générale et de valorisation de la langue anglaise en particulier.

1.1. L'Affermissement du Bilinguisme

Le bilinguisme officiel résulte de la réunification le 1er octobre 1961 de deux territoires anciennement sous la domination des Français et des Britanniques.[66] Il consacre l'existence de l'anglais et du français comme les deux langues officielles du Cameroun. Cependant, les deux Constitutions qui ont été adoptées après la réunification ont consacré une inégalité *de jure* entre les deux langues traduisant ainsi en acte juridique l'inégalité numérique entre les anglophones et les francophones. En effet, dans ses dispositions transitoires et spéciales, la Constitution fédérale du 1er septembre 1961 avait sciemment hiérarchisé les deux langues, faisant du français une langue supposée supérieure à l'anglais. L'article 59 de cette Constitution indiquait notamment que: 'La Constitution (...) sera publiée en français et en anglais, le texte en français faisant

64 La Constitution de la République fédérale du Cameroun du 1er septembre 1961 est celle qui introduit pour la première fois en son article 1er, l'existence de deux langues officielles à savoir l'anglais et le français.

65 *G. T. Foumena* (note 8), 99.

66 J.-*G. Mboudjeke* (note 7), 151.

foi'. Si l'option fédérale pouvait justifier une telle hérésie compte tenu du contexte politique d'alors marqué par la prééminence de la présence de la France et la démission des Britanniques après le rattachement du Cameroun méridional au Cameroun oriental,[67] l'on comprend moins pourquoi – une fois les deux Cameroun réunifiés le 20 mai 1972[68] – la Constitution du 2 juin de la même année instituant l'Etat unitaire va réintroduire *in extenso* en son article 39 cette inégalité.[69] C'est la loi constitutionnelle du 18 janvier 1996 qui viendra consacrer l'égale valeur des deux langues. A ce sujet, l'article 1er alinéa 3 précise que: 'La République du Cameroun adopte l'anglais et le français comme langues officielles d'égale valeur[70]'.

Cependant, l'habitude de la domination juridique d'une langue sur une autre s'étant installée pendant plus de trois décennies, à laquelle il faut adjoindre l'avantage numérique des populations de l'ancien Cameroun oriental sur celles de l'ex-Cameroun occidental, il s'est installé au fil des années une inégalité *de facto* entre les deux langues.[71] Il a donc fallu cette crise pour que ravive la flamme du bilinguisme intégral et que l'on se rende compte de cette inégalité. Des mesures correctives ont dès lors été prises. La première et sans doute la plus retentissante sur le plan de l'annonce politique est la création par décret du Président la République de la Commission Nationale pour la Promotion du Bilinguisme et du Multiculturalisme (CNPBM).[72] La tâche principale assignée à cette commission témoigne du caractère absolument résolutoire de cet acte juridique qui fait d'elle une instance dont la mission est 'd'œuvrer à la pro-

67 La Constitution du 1er septembre 1960 avait néanmoins essayé de trouver un justificatif à cette inégalité en rappelant en son article 60 les statistiques de l'ONU en ce qui concerne le nombre d'habitants, soit Cameroun oriental: 3.200.000 habitants et Cameroun occidental: 800.000 habitants.

68 Le 20 mai est la date de célébration de la fête nationale.

69 V. aussi dans ce sens, *G. T. Foumena* (note 8), 99.

70 Remarquons que dans les Constitutions précédentes en l'occurrence celles de 1961 et 1972, la mention 'français' venait toujours en première position, alors que la loi constitutionnelle de 1996 fait d'abord référence à l' 'anglais', respectant ainsi l'ordre alphabétique qui devrait prévaloir dans cette circonstance.

71 Plusieurs facteurs peuvent encore l'attester aujourd'hui: sur le sceau officiel du Cameroun, on peut voir que la mention 'Republic of Cameroon' est en plus petits caractères que la même mention écrite en français; la plupart des écriteaux sur des bâtiments publics, quand ils omettent pas purement et simplement l'anglais, sont reproduits de la sorte; il n'existe aucune correspondance anglaise officielle pour certains sigles et abréviations; toutes les insignes des forces armées et de police ont des écriteaux uniquement en français, etc.

72 Décret n° 2018/013 du 23 janvier 2018 portant création, organisation et fonctionnement de la Commission Nationale pour la Promotion du Bilinguisme et du Multiculturalisme, disponible au lien suivant <https://www.prc.cm/fr/multimedia/documents/5214-decret-n-2017-013-du-23-01-2017-creation-cnpbm-fr>.

motion du bilinguisme, du multiculturalisme au Cameroun, dans l'optique de maintenir la paix, consolider l'unité nationale du pays et de renforcer la volonté et la pratique quotidienne du vivre ensemble de ses populations.'[73]

Si l'intitulé du décret asserte en lui-même l'existence d'un bilinguisme imparfait au Cameroun, l'accolement du substantif 'multiculturalisme' à cette notion s'inscrit dans la posture du gouvernement à n'admettre que partiellement le problème anglophone. La référence au multiculturalisme s'affichant dès lors comme l'option des pouvoirs publics à ne pas voir le Cameroun sous le seul prisme de la bipolarité linguistique[74] héritée de l'histoire coloniale, mais aussi en tenant compte de la diversité linguistique et culturelle soulignée à la première phrase du préambule de la Constitution. Même si l'on peut interroger la capacité de cette commission à constituer une véritable option pour la résolution de la crise actuelle, elle a au moins pour mérite d'afficher la volonté du gouvernement à ne jamais concéder autre chose que l'unité nationale. Le bilinguisme ne devient à cet égard qu'un outil pour matérialiser le vivre ensemble.

C'est dans la même optique que l'on peut comprendre l'une des mesures visant à résoudre la crise faisant suite aux instructions du Président de la République à son gouvernement de procéder au recrutement de 1000 jeunes diplômes bilingues.[75] Cette mesure portait sur l'une des revendications des syndicats d'enseignants anglophones qui s'insurgeaient en réalité contre la francophonisation de leur système éducatif. Cependant, pour le gouvernement, il s'agissait officiellement de résorber le déficit d'enseignants dans les matières scientifiques et techniques dans les établissements d'enseignement secondaire à travers le pays. Là encore, il n'a été nullement question pour le gouvernement de donner l'impression d'apporter une réponse orientée vers la résolution de la crise dans la zone anglophone, mais plutôt d'offrir une réponse globale à une question nationale. Toutefois, cette mesure ne fait que cacher un bilinguisme aux relents de valorisation de la langue anglaise.

1.2. La Valorisation de la Langue Anglaise

La crise anglophone actuelle a suscité une prise de conscience nationale sur la place que devrait occuper la langue anglaise dans un Etat qui est supposé pratiquer un bilinguisme intégral et égalitaire. Si l'idée d'un 'fondement constitutionnel d'un bilin-

73 Article 3 alinéa 1 du décret.

74 *Y. S. Nkoulou* (note 12), 699.

75 V. Avis de recrutement du 22 juin 2017 du Ministère de la Fonction Publique et de la Réforme Administrative (MINFOPRA), disponible au lien suivant <www.minfopra.gov.cm>, consulté le 18 mai 2018.

guisme bancal' sur laquelle se fonde une certaine doctrine[76] peut être réfutée, il reste que le statut constitutionnel d'équipollence[77] de l'anglais et du français n'a pas dépassé le stade de sa proclamation. L'un et l'autre sont prédominamment utilisés selon que l'on se retrouve dans la partie anglophone ou francophone du pays. L'avantage numérique de la population francophone s'imposant par lui-même, il n'est donc pas surprenant que l'un des griefs portés par les défenseurs de la cause anglophone tourne autour de la condamnation de la francophonisation progressive des deux régions anglophones.[78] Depuis 1961 et l'adoption dans la Constitution du 1er septembre de la même année de l'anglais et du français comme langues officielles, le français est resté la langue administrative d'usage dans la plupart des administrations publiques. La crise actuelle n'a fait que mettre en lumière cette réalité qui, depuis quelques mois, tend néanmoins à s'estomper grâce à certaines actions entreprises par le gouvernement.

On a en effet assisté à quelques mesures qui, pour certaines, se faisaient déjà désirées quelques années avant la crise, à l'instar de la traduction en langue anglaise des actes uniformes OHADA.[79] Il s'agit d'une problématique qui a longtemps été soulevée par la doctrine[80] et qui a constitué l'une des revendications majeures portées par les avocats anglophones lorsqu'ils entament la grève en octobre 2016. Mais au-delà de la simple traduction en langue anglaise de ces textes, il se pose un problème de réception et d'adaptation dans le sous-système de la common law des textes non seulement rédigés en français, mais également fortement imprégnés du droit romano germanique.[81] Il y a lieu de craindre qu'il s'agit d'une mesure bien plus alambiquée que la simple traduction d'une langue à une autre. Elle est en effet très loin de la volonté d'harmonisation du droit camerounais. On peut en dire de même de la décision du ministère en charge de la fonction publique, sur instruction du Président de la République, de lancer depuis deux ans déjà un concours spécial réservé aux candidats

76 *Y. S. Nkoulou* (note 12), 702.

77 *G. T. Foumena* (note 8), 105.

78 *International Crisis Group* (note 1), Cameroun: la crise anglophone à la croisée des chemins, 25.

79 Organisation pour l'Harmonisation en Afrique du Droit des Affaires. Il s'agit d'une organisation interétatique d'intégration juridique comprenant 17 pays d'expression française qui, en dehors de la Guinée Equatoriale, pays hispanophone situé dans une sous-région essentiellement francophone, dont le but est de proposer un cadre juridique commun dans le domaine économique et du droit des affaires.

80 Lire par exemple: *J.-J. Ndongo,* Les actes uniformes de l'Ohada en traduction, in: Parallèles, n° 25, octobre 2013, 30–41. V. aussi l'abondante littérature recensée in: *G. T. Foumena* (note 8), 110.

81 *G. T. Foumena,* l. c.

d'expression anglaise[82] pour le recrutement des auditeurs de justice auprès de l'Ecole Nationale d'Administration et de Magistrature (ENAM).[83]

Une autre lecture de cette décision de lancer un concours spécial pour les candidats d'expression anglaise ne saurait d'ailleurs résister au reproche de l'inconstitutionnalité de celle-ci. Elle remet en effet en cause l'égale valeur entre les deux langues mentionnée dans la Constitution.[84] Si dans ce cas le principe constitutionnel d'égalité de langues peut volontairement être subordonné à une solution de crise, il n'en va pas de même de la technique constitutionnelle de décentralisation qui *a contrario* constitue bien une réponse à cette crise.

2. L'Accélération du Processus de Décentralisation

Pour tempérer le caractère centripète du pouvoir qui découlait de la Constitution du 2 juin 1972, 'fondatrice de l'Etat unitaire',[85] le constituant de 1996 avait associé la notion de décentralisation à l'expression 'Etat unitaire'. Au-delà de cette simple jonction de mots à forte dose de rhétorique, il faisait surtout de la République du Cameroun 'un Etat unitaire décentralisé'. Désormais, le découpage territorial laissait poindre les 'collectivités territoriales décentralisées'.[86] Cependant, la décentralisation ainsi enga-

82 V. Order n° 002857/MINFOPRA of 20 June 2017 to announce the competitive entrance examination for the recruitment of fifty-five (55) Legal Probationers into the judicial Division of the National School of Administration and Magistracy et Order n° 000601/MINFOPRA of 29 March 2018 to announce a competitive examination for the special recruitment of fifty (50) Pupil Magistrates of English expression into the Magistracy and Court registry Division of the National School of Administration and Magistracy. National School of Administration and Magistracy.

83 Ce concours sort du cadre habituel des concours administratifs lancés chaque année et qui concernent les candidats des deux langues.

84 Même si ce concours est ouvert à tous les candidats, indépendamment de leurs origines anglophone et francophone, pour peu qu'ils soient capables de concourir en anglais; il reste que l'acte juridique qui le créé constitue déjà en lui-même une contrariété à la Constitution qui consacre l'égale valeur des deux langues officielles.

85 *L. Sindjoun*, (note 16), 5.

86 Articles 55 et suivants de la loi constitutionnelle du 18 janvier 1996. Ces collectivités territoriales décentralisées constituées de régions et de communes seront mises place par les lois du 22 juillet 2004, notamment la loi n° 2004/017 du 22 juillet 2004 portant orientation de la décentralisation <http://www.cvuc-uccc.com/minat/textes/13.pdf>, la loi n° 2004/018 fixant les règles applicables aux communes <http://www.cvuc-uccc.com/minat/textes/12.pdf> et la loi n° 2004/019 fixant les règles applicables aux régions <http://www.cvuc-uccc.com/minat/textes/11.pdf>.D'autres lois viendront renforcer le dispositif, en l'occurrence la loi n° 2009/019 du 10 juillet 2009 portant régime financier des collectivités territoriales décentralisées <http://www.cvuc-uccc.com/minat/textes/204.pdf> et la loi du 15 décembre 2009 portant fiscalité locale <http://www.cvuc-uccc.com/minat/textes/192.pdf>.

gée reste peu effective parce qu'elle n'est pas appliquée rigoureusement.[87] Pour l'aile modérée de la cause anglophone, celle-ci reste à améliorer (2.1.).[88] C'est sans doute ce qui fonde les changements que le gouvernement a entrepris sur ce plan depuis le début de la crise (2.2.).

2.1. *La Décentralisation comme Alternative aux Prétentions Fédéralistes et Sécessionnistes*

La décentralisation qui est un processus d'aménagement et d'organisation de l'Etat unitaire[89] s'est imposée au Cameroun comme une alternative aux velléités de ceux qui voulaient voir autre chose que cette forme de l'Etat. En effet, à l'occasion des débats enclenchés en mai 1993[90] et qui allaient aboutir à la révision constitutionnelle du 18 janvier 1996, l'option de la forme unitaire de l'Etat avait déjà été remise en cause par les anglophones organisés autour de la 'All Anglophone Conference'. Ils réclamaient le retour au fédéralisme. Cependant, cette proposition avait été rejetée par le comité consultatif de révision au profit de la décentralisation[91] soutenue, quant à elle, par les membres du gouvernement qui insistaient sur l'impératif de conserver le caractère unitaire de l'Etat.[92] La crise actuelle expose le même schéma et n'a fait que raviver les revendications soit à l'auto-détermination, soit au fédéralisme. Pour certains activistes anglophones, le fédéralisme apparaît comme une stratégie de négociation maximaliste qu'ils mettent en exergue afin d'obtenir au moins une décentralisation effective.[93]. Ils réclament ainsi une vraie autonomie de gestion des dix régions actuelles, passant par l'amélioration et l'application intégrale des lois sur la décentralisation.[94]

Pour y parvenir, certains auteurs excipent clairement la nécessité d'en finir avec le modèle jacobin hérité de la Constitution française du 4 octobre 1958. C'est le cas de *Charles Manga Fombad* qui propose à ce sujet de dompter l'obsession gauloise à la centralisation des pouvoirs afin de désamorcer les tensions régionales qui existent

87 *International Crisis Group)* (note 1), ii.

88 Ibid., 20–21.

89 *C.M. Ngo Tong* (note 19), 41.

90 Création par le Chef de l'Etat d'un Comité d'experts en charge d'élaborer une nouvelle Constitution.

91 *International Crisis Group,* op. cit., 7.

92 *C.M. Ngo Tong,* op. cit., 47.

93 *International Crisis Group* (note 1), Cameroun : la crise anglophone à la croisée des chemins, op. cit., 19.

94 Ibid.

dans certains pays francophones aujourd'hui à l'instar du Cameroun.[95] Pour lui, on a besoin aujourd'hui de gouvernements locaux élus et pas simplement des administrations déconcentrées qui ne sont qu'une excroissance du pouvoir central en vigueur dans les pays avec une organisation constitutionnelle unitaire et hyper-centralisée.[96] La nécessité de revisiter le modèle de décentralisation[97] qui existe aujourd'hui au Cameroun s'impose donc au regard des revendications des populations locales de s'occuper de leurs propres affaires.

Si la décentralisation telle que prévue aujourd'hui par le dispositif constitutionnel et législatif peine à avoir des résultats probants, il ne serait pas inutile de penser un nouveau modèle de décentralisation qui offrirait plus d'autonomie dans la gestion des affaires locales. Pour ce faire, un changement constitutionnel qui ferait recours à un régionalisme plus accentué ne serait pas vain, parce qu'il faut bien le reconnaître, quelle que soit sa nature la crise nécessite toujours un bouleversement constitutionnel.[98] Il ne suffit pas parfois de se limiter aux changements d'ordre institutionnel.

2.2. La Décentralisation Institutionnelle comme Réponse à la Crise sur la Forme de l'État

Le gouvernement dans ses nombreuses tentatives de résolution de la présente crise anglophone n'a pas été avare de solutions spectaculaires. Si la forme unitaire de l'Etat n'est pas négociable, le gouvernement a cependant entrepris d'introduire une avancée majeure à travers la création par décret n° 2018/190 du 2 mars 2018 du Ministère de la Décentralisation et du Développement Local (MINDDEVEL).[99] Intervenue en pleine crise anglophone, la création de ce département ministériel ne peut pas échapper d'être perçue comme un effort de renforcement et d'application effective du processus de décentralisation enclenché depuis 1996. Il s'agit là d'offrir une réponse institutionnelle à la frange modérée d'activistes anglophones qui ne souhaitent

95 *C. Manga Fombad*, Constitutional reforms and constitutionalism in Africa: Reflections on some current challenges and future prospects, 59 Buffalo Law Review, 2011, 27.

96 Ibid.

97 Le modèle de décentralisation existant aujourd'hui est un modèle de 'dénégation de la forme fédérale de l'Etat', lire dans ce sens: *B.R. Guimdo Dongmo*, Le droit de la décentralisation à l'ère de la démocratisation au Cameroun, in: La politique de la décentralisation au Cameroun: Jeux, enjeux et perspectives, sous la coordination Technique de la Fondation Paul Ango Ela, Harmattan Cameroun, 2013, 38.

98 *Leroy* (note 20), 287.

99 Décret n° 2018/190 du 2 mars 2018 complétant certaines dispositions du décret n° 2011/408 du 9 décembre 2011 portant organisation du gouvernement.

pas voir le Cameroun se disloquer soit en micro Etats, soit en deux parties indépendantes l'une de l'autre. Les missions confiées à ce ministère démontrent à suffisance l'esprit d'ouverture du gouvernement désormais disposé à lâcher du lest en transférant véritablement les compétences et les moyens appropriés aux collectivités territoriales décentralisées.[100]

Entre autres missions, ce ministère est notamment chargé d'élaborer la législation et la réglementation relatives à l'organisation et au fonctionnement des collectivités territoriales décentralisées. Si cette formulation n'offre que très peu de doute sur l'abnégation du gouvernement à ne consentir à aucun changement d'ordre constitutionnel, elle offre néanmoins l'opportunité à celui-ci de proposer une législation méliorative du cadre juridique actuel de la décentralisation. Bien plus, le nouveau ministère en charge de la décentralisation[101], vient se positionner comme l'institution-pilote d'une politique qui jusque-là était partagée entre la multitude de départements ministériels qui exerçaient des compétences en matière de décentralisation. Il est aussi une institution de monitoring de la décentralisation en ce sens qu'il s'occupera désormais de l'évaluation et du suivi de la mise en œuvre de celle-ci, ainsi que du contrôle et du suivi des collectivités territoriales décentralisées ; en même temps qu'il assurera la tutelle de l'Etat sur celles-ci.[102]

Si l'on peut légitimement s'interroger sur le bien-fondé d'un tel ministère quand la tendance revendicatrice est plutôt au décentrement de l'action étatique, donc à l'autonomisation des collectivités locales, le raisonnement *a contrario* voudrait que l'on attende pour pouvoir juger de son efficacité. Toutefois, l'on est en droit de s'interroger si ce énième organe de prolongement de l'Etat central est la solution pour mettre en œuvre le processus de décentralisation. Celle-ci n'a-t-elle pas plus besoin d'institutions locales fortes choisies de manière libre par les populations, plutôt que d'organes étatiques dont la dimension tutélaire sera toujours plus pesante dans un pays au jacobinisme affirmé? La solution institutionnelle à ce problème est pourtant consacrée dans la loi constitutionnelle du 18 janvier 1996 puisque celle-ci prévoit la mise en

100 Article 2 alinéa 1 de la loi n° 2004/017 du 22 juillet 2004 portant orientation de la décentralisation.

101 C'est l'ancien Ministère de l'Administration Territoriale et de la Décentralisation (MINATD) qui a été divisée en deux ministères avec, d'une part, le Ministère de l'Administration Territoriale(MINAT); et d'autre part, le Ministère de la Décentralisation et du Développement Local (MINDDEVEL). Il s'agit de la volonté du gouvernement à vouloir désormais dissocier la déconcentration administrative de la décentralisation territoriale.

102 Sur les missions du nouveau ministère, lire l'article 8 alinéa 5-bis du décret n° 2018/190 du 2 mars 2018 complétant certaines dispositions du décret n° 2011/408 du 9 décembre 2011 portant organisation du gouvernement.

place des exécutifs régionaux[103] dans le cadre de l'institutionnalisation des régions en tant que collectivités territoriales décentralisées.

IV. Conclusion

Au demeurant, on peut reconnaître avec un auteur qu''une crise, même si elle ne suscite pas une mutation constitutionnelle immédiate, a une influence profonde de l'évolution constitutionnelle des régimes politiques'.[104] La crise anglophone actuelle amène peut-être à s'interroger sur cette assertion; tant elle influe d'ores et déjà sur le dispositif constitutionnel existant, notamment en questionnant la forme de l'Etat, en trahissant l'intégrité du territoire et en réorganisant les institutions étatiques. En effet, les mesures, pour la plupart infra-constitutionnelles parce que réglementaires, prises par le gouvernement depuis le déclenchement de cette crise emportent réflexion. Il y a effectivement lieu de s'interroger sur les mesures portant sur la forme de l'Etat unitaire qui – bien que réaffirmant la position du gouvernement à ne donner suite aux prétentions fédéralistes, encore moins sécessionnistes – traduisent néanmoins la gêne perpétuelle d'un pays naturellement composite. Au point où l'on se demanderait avec un auteur si le Cameroun n'est-il pas une fédération qui s'ignore ou un Etat régional inavoué? [105] Les options prises pour consolider le bilinguisme et renforcer la décentralisation, deux acquis constitutionnels, participent également de la remise en question du Cameroun sous sa forme actuelle. Il n'est donc pas sans intérêt de souligner au terme de cette réflexion le bien-fondé d'une réforme constitutionnelle en ce temps de crise, ainsi que l'obligation qui incombe à l'Etat, aujourd'hui plus que jamais en crise,[106] de déverrouiller les clauses constitutionnelles dites intangibles dans l'optique de la restauration de la paix sociale.

103 V. Article 57 alinéa 1.

104 *Leroy* (note 20), 287.

105 *B. R. Guimdo Dongmo* (note 97), 39.

106 Au moment où nous achevons la rédaction du présent article en août 2018, la crise dite anglophone a pris des proportions mortelles encore plus inquiétantes avec plus d'une centaine d'agents des forces de défense et de sécurité assassinés et un nombre indéterminé de séparatistes armés tués.

Which Proportionality Review Should be used for the Use of Lethal Force in Times of Crisis? An Analysis of the European Court of Human Rights' Judges' Prerogatives in the Light of the Right to Life.

Anne-Laure Youhnovski Sagon

Abstract

Harm to life in times of crisis requires a proportionality review to guarantee the lasting quality of the Rule of Law. Formal and substantial proportionality reviews are requested to verify the adequacy of the use of lethal forces. Nevertheless, States sovereignty sometimes alters the formal proportionality review, which must be renovated through international humanitarian law. With regard to substantial proportionality review, it must be carried out on the basis of positive and procedural obligations incumbent upon the State. Nevertheless, some judgments do not comply with these requirements, which undermines the effectiveness of the substantial proportionality review. To remain relevant, the proportionality review must be reformed in order to preserve the European Court of Human Rights' function, ensuring the balance of use of lethal force in times of crisis.

Introduction

Increases of texts dedicated to the fight against terrorism and the trivialization of the use of lethal weapons all reflect the deterioration of the security situation in Western countries. In this context, the European Court of Human Rights has to find a just balance to reconcile the use of lethal force with the right to the protection of life as enshrined in Art. 2 (1) of the European Convention on Human Rights (ECHR).[1] Indeed, respect for human life is not an absolute right. The European Convention on Human Rights provides for derogations in case of 'lawful acts of war',[2] and exempts the imposition of death from Art. 2 (1) for the use of force which is 'absolutely necessary'.[3]

1 ECHR, Art. 2 (1): Everyone's right to life is protected by law. Death cannot be inflicted on anyone intentionally except in execution of a capital sentence pronounced by a court in case the offense is punishable by the law.

2 ECHR, Art. 15 (2): The previous provision does not allow any derogation from the Art. 2, except in the case of death resulting from lawful acts of war.

3 ECHR, Art. 2 (2): Death is not considered to have been inflicted in violation of this article in cases where it would result from the use of force rendered absolutely necessary : a) to ensure the defense of any person against unlawful violence ; (b) to make a regular arrest or to prevent the es-

When it is necessary to assess the proportionality of the harm to life, the judges do not linger on the legal qualification of the conflict. They thus deny the distinction made by the ECHR between the derogation in Art. 15 (2), dedicated to 'acts of war', and the use of force in 'times of crisis', as mentioned by Art. 2 (2) of the Convention. From this jurisprudential trend to the standardization of different forms of conflict, the analysis will be based on 'times of crisis', at the crossroads of 'lawful acts of war', 'fight against terrorism', or 'state of emergency'.

As a precursor to a proportionality review of the harm to life in times of crisis, the case law *McCann v. United Kingdom* (27 September 1995) invites the judges to verify that the force used is '(…) strictly proportionate to the purposes referred in paragraph 2 of Art. 2'.[4] In that decision, a special unit of British forces in Gibraltar had to stop terrorists from the Irish Republican Army to perpetrate a car bombing. When security forces see the terrorists parked and see them leaving their cars, they wanted to stop them. Fearing an armed response, police shot them when in reality, no terrorist was armed and the car was not trapped. If the Court accepted to believe the police officers, who deeply thought that the arrested men were going to set off a bomb, the Court finds a violation of Art. 2 in view of failures in the preparation of the operation. Specifically, the instructions given to agents by the authorities were too approximate and not very detailed.

Since then, the decision *Camenzind v. Switzerland* (16 December 1997) specified the method of proportionality review to be carried out by judges.[5] In fact, the Court states that when carrying out a proportionality review, the Court '(…) is made, on the one hand, to ensure that the legislation and practice in this area offer individuals 'adequate and sufficient safeguards against abuses' (…)'[6]. The Court examines, on the other hand, the particular circumstances of each case in order to determine whether, *in concreto,* the interference litigious was proportionate to the aim pursued. First, the review of 'adequate safeguards against abuse' leads to a consideration of how to adopt the process that led to seeking the exemption or exception. This is the for-

cape of a person regularly detained; (c) to suppress, in accordance with the law, a riot or insurrection.

4 ECtHR, 27 September 1995, *McCann and Others v. United Kingdom,* No. 18984/91, § 149: In this respect, the use of the words 'absolutely necessary' in Art. 2 para. 2 (Art. 2–2) states that the force used must, in particular, be strictly proportional to the aims referred to in Art. 2, paragraph 2 (a), (b) and (c) (Art. 2–2-abc).

5 ECtHR, 16 December 1997, *Camenzind v. Switzerland,* No. 21353/93.

6 ECtHR, 16 December 1997, *Camenzind v. Switzerland,* No. 21353/93, § 45.

mal aspect of proportionality review.[7] Then, *in concreto,* the analysis of the result of the decision-making process leads to focus on the substantive aspect of proportionality review.[8] Censor of disproportionate impacts on life in times of crisis, the judges will see their jurisprudences analyzed through the specificities of the use of the lethal public force. We have to wonder if, even in times of crisis, the European Court of Human Rights is an effective guardian of the right to life.

First, the examination of formal proportionality remains objective, limited to structural review of the mode of adoption of the measure. Although it preserves the integrity of State's sovereignty,[9] the method of assessing the proportionality of the use of lethal force delivered in *McCann's* decision is no longer appropriate, and must be restored in light of international humanitarian law's methods (I).

Second, the substantive proportionality test is intended to be subjective, since an examination of the content of the measure involves an assessment of how the respondent State analyzed the circumstances of the case, at the time of the adoption of the lethal measure. Pronounced in the light of positive obligations inherent to the right to life, the State's sentence oscillates, according to the positive obligation mobilized. This preserves the State's margin of appreciation in the event of internal conflict resolution. The awkwardness of the Court harms the relevance of the substantive proportionality review, which has to be renewed if the lasting quality of the Rule of Law is to be guaranteed (II).

7 The formal aspect of proportionality involves verifying that the foreseeability of the measure is sufficient because of the existence of adequate standards, with sufficient guarantees through the possibility of bringing an action if the state goes beyond these normative bases. Moreover, the examination of formal proportionality implies an abstract review of the proportionate motivation of the internal authorities in the decision-making process. Cf. *Sébastien Van Drooghenbroeck,* La proportionnalité dans le droit de la convention des droits de l'homme. Prendre l'idée simple au sérieux, Bruxelles 2001, at 346 ; and *Gloria Gaggioli,* L'influence mutuelle entre les droits de l'homme et le droit international humanitaire à la lumière du droit à la vie, Paris 2013, at 345.

8 Substantive aspect of proportionality is divided into two branches. First, the examination of proportionality rule corresponds to 'all the substantive requirements that proportionality imposes on the state and its acts. This rule, stable and unique, would effectively impose the appropriation, necessity and proportionality in the strict sense or omission attributable to that State', cf.: *Sébastien Van Drooghenbroeck,* op. cit., at 173.

9 ECtHR, 20 December 2011, *Finogenov and o. v. Russia,* Nos 18299/03 and 27311/03; ECtHR, 13 April 2017, *Tagayeva v. Russia,* Nos 26562/07, 14755/08, 49339/08, 49380/08, 51313/08, 21294/11 and 37096/11.

I. The Formal Proportionality Review of Harm to Human Life: an Objective Control to be Renovated

The exercise of the formal proportionality review serves too often to the respect of the State's sovereignty, harming the efficiency of the jurisdictional sanction of the attack on human life (1). Using methods of humanitarian law would strengthen the effectiveness of the formal proportionality review (2).

1. The Formal Proportionality Review Serving the Respect of the State's Sovereignty

The formal proportionality review corresponds to the review of the process adopted that led to seek the exemption or exception. It involves checking two aspects. First, that the predictability of the measure is sufficient thanks to the existence of adequate standards, accompanied by sufficient guarantees[10] through the possibility of bringing an action against the State. Moreover, the examination of formal proportionality implies an abstract review of the proportionate motivation of the internal authorities in the decision-making process.[11]

First, the Court carries out a global analysis, considering 'all relevant circumstances',[12] which include the verification, the preparation of the operation, its progress, as well as the review and the quality of the normative framework.[13] Some examples illustrate the deficiencies of this formal proportionality check. For instance, during a military operation conducted by security forces near a construction site, a man who worked in this project as a night watchman was killed at the end of his guard by lost bullets. Here, the Court condemns the measure's lack of proportionality. Indeed, the execution of the contested operation was not 'absolutely necessary to defend others against unlawful violence or to arrest the victim'.[14] Similarly, in the decision *Ergi v. Turkey*, concerning the death of a civilian during a fight with armed opponents, the Court sentences Turkey for the lack of 'sufficient precautions (…) to

10 ECHR, 16 December 1997, *Camenzind v. Switzerland,* No. 21353/93.

11 *Sébastien Van Drooghenbroeck* and *Gloria Gaggioli*. l.c. (note 6).

12 ECtHR, 13 June 2002, *Anguelova v. Bulgaria,* No. 38361/9, § 110, quoted by *Jean-Manuel Larralde,* L'article 2 de la Convention européenne des droits de l'homme et la violence publique meurtrière, in: Michel Levinet (ed.), Le droit au respect de la vie au sens de la Convention européenne des droits de l'homme, Bruxelles 2010, 189–214, at 194.

13 *Jean-Manuel Larralde,* op. cit., at 195.

14 ECtHR, 20 May 1999, *Ogur* v. *Turkey,* No. 21594/93, §§ 82 and 84.

save the lives of the civilian population'.[15] Moreover, Bulgaria has been condemned by the Court for the unnecessary use of firearms, as well as inadequate training. Precisely, police forces had killed a person suspected of having committed a non-violent offense with no consequences to the lives of others.[16] Therefore, States have to firmly supervise 'legislatively and administratively, by means of precise instructions, the use of weapons by the security forces'.[17]

Here, and these examples confirm this point of view, we can understand that the review of formal proportionality, limited to the practical realization of the mortal act, is abstract. Therefore, it enables the European Court of Human Rights to comply with the principle of subsidiarity enshrined in the preamble of the Convention[18] and thereby preserves the Member State's sovereignty.[19] Also, concerning armed conflicts, historical and factual assessments of the Court is determinative of the scope and rigor on the proportionality review. In order to limit any historical subjectivity and to avoid any interference by the Court in 'States' management of their history',[20] the abstract review of proportionality, limited to the procedural framework's review, preserves the State's sovereignty. However, the lack of rigor of the undermines the effectiveness of formal proportionality review, which must be recast in the light of extra-conventional sources.

2. Humanitarian Law in Service of the Effectiveness of the Formal Proportionality Review

The formal proportionality review suffers from a lack of effectiveness. It is provoked by the erroneous qualification achieved by the judges about different times of crisis. Precisely, Art. 15 (2) refers to the harm of life only in times of armed conflict. Indeed this article allows lethal acts resulting from 'lawful acts of war'. This terminol-

15 ECtHR, 28 July 1998, *Ergi v.Turkey*, No. 23818/94, § 81.

16 ECtHR, 6 July 2005, *Nachova v. Bulgaria*, Nos 43577/98 and 43579/98, § 103. About the proportionality of the use of force, see § 95: 'when it is known that the person to be arrested poses no threat to the life or physical integrity of anyone and is not suspected of having committed a violent offense, even if it may result in impossibility of stopping the fugitive'.

17 *Rusen Ergec*, European and International Protection of Human Rights, Brussels 3rd ed. 2014, 241.

18 Protocol No. 15 amending the European Convention on Human rights, signed 24 June 2013.

19 ECHR, 20 December 2011, *Finogenov and o. v. Russia*, Nos 18299/03 and 27311/03; ECHR, 13 April 2017, *Tagayeva and o. v. Russia*, Nos 26562/07, 14755/08, 49339/08, 49380/08, 51313/08, 21294/11 and 37096/11.

20 *Jean-François Flauss*, L'Histoire dans la jurisprudence de la Cour européenne des droits de l'homme, 65 Revue trimestrielle des droits de l'homme (2006), 5, at 21–22.

ogy, which is specific to humanitarian law, imposes a formal proportionality review distinct from the one inherent to Art. 2 (2) of the Convention.

However, the judge neglects the different legal terminologies, leading to a proportionality review which is not adapted to the legal situation. The case law *McCann v. United Kingdom* recalled that no exception under Art. 2 (2) can be requested under Art. 15 (2) in time of peace.[21]

Some examples are relevant of this jurisprudential disharmony. In one case, in a context of armed operations carried out in Chechnya, a village's bombing killed the applicant's son. In the second case, a bombardment broke out on a convoy of civilians, and two of the applicant's children were killed. In both cases, the Court concluded in a breach of Art. 2 (2) of the Convention, after conducting a formal proportionality review following the method issued in the *McCann*'s decision. Therefore, the judges tried to verify whether the operation has been 'prepared and controlled by the authorities to minimize the use of lethal force'.[22] However, the *Mc Cann's* method of formal proportionality review was not adapted for these cases. In one case as in the other, it is striking weapons 'without discrimination'. These are acts of war representative to armed conflict, and can't be qualified as simple 'use of force' existing in times of peace, as provided in Art. 2 (2).[23]

It is true that the wording of Art. 2 (2) is no longer relevant to the current context. The 'use of force' is very often similar to what Art. 15 (2) called 'lawful acts of war'. Since there is no question of amending the redaction of Art. 2 of the Convention, it is necessary for the judge to standardize his review to the one operated in humanitarian law. Precisely, the European Court of Human Rights has already agreed to adapt its methods to humanitarian law's method, in particular in the decision *Varnava v. Turkey* (18 September 2009). For the first time, the Court specifies that Art. 2 must be interpreted in the light of international law's principles, 'including rules of international humanitarian law'.[24] However, this innovation should not be understood as an abdication of the proportionality review of Art. 2 of the Convention.

21 ECtHR, 27 September 1995, *McCann and a. v. United Kingdom,* No. 18984/91, § 147.

22 ECtHR, 24 February 2005, *Issayeva v. Russia,* No. 57950/00; ECtHR, 24 February 2005, *Issayeva, Youssoupouva and Bazayeva v. Russia,* Nos 57947/00, 7948/00 and 57949/00, §§ 190 and 199.

23 As implicitly stated in Art. 13 (2) of the Additional Protocol to the Geneva Conventions of 12 August 1949 on the Protection of Victims of Non-International Armed Conflicts, signed 8 June 1977: 'Neither the civilian population as such nor civilians should be the object of attacks. Violations or threats of violence the purpose of which main is to spread terror among the civilian population'.

24 ECtHR, Gr. Ch., 18 September 2009, *Varnava and a. v. Turkey,* Nos 16064/90, 16065/90, 16066/90, 16068/90, 16069/90, 16070/90, 16071/90, 16072 / 90 and 16073/90, § 185.

In sum, the formal proportionality review carried out by the judge can sometimes undermine the right to life's protection. Complementary to this formal proportionality review, the substantive proportionality review must be introspective so as to establish if it is sufficient to overcome the deficiencies evocated.

II. The Substantive Proportionality Review of Harm to Human Life: a Subjective Control to be Firmed up

The exercise of substantive proportionality review by the Court is quite complex. Indeed, the sanction of the disproportion will be pronounced on the basis of positive obligations imposed on each Member State. While substantive positive obligations impair the substantive proportionality review's efficiency (1), this is also the case for procedural positive obligations, instigators of its alteration (2).

1. Material Positive Obligations: Factors of Deficiency of the Substantive Proportionality Review

While formal proportionality review is an abstract review, substantive proportionality review is concrete. The judge must examine *in concreto* the result of the act that harmed life, and not only its mode of adoption. The judge needs to verify that the lethal act performed by the State was appropriate, proportionate and necessary to the exceptions provided in Art. 2 (2) of the Convention. At the end of the judge's substantive proportionality review, the State will necessarily be condemned, either on the basis of substantive positive obligations, or on the basis of procedural positive procedural obligations.[25] As a reminder, a positive obligation signifies that the Member State has to 'adopt reasonable and adequate measures to protect the rights contained in the European Convention on Human Rights'.

At first, we will focus on the substantive positive obligation. It corresponds to the State's obligation to implement effective measures to protect human life. The use of lethal force should therefore only be a last resort. However, the judge, if the result obtained is disproportionate to the menace, hardly condemns the State on the basis of substantive positive obligations. It proves that the judge wishes, once again, to

25 A positive obligation is the fact to 'adopt reasonable and adequate measures to protect the rights contained in the European Convention on Human Rights'. The use of the concept of positive obligation becomes recurrent from the ECtHR decision, 26 March 1985, *X. and Y. v. The Netherlands*, No. 8978/80; ECHR, 21 February 1990, *Powell and Rayner*, No. 8310/81, § 51.

preserve the State's national margin of appreciation.[26] One example is representative of this process. The decision *Finogenov v. Russia*[27] attests of the judge's reluctance to condemn the State on the basis on the substantive obligations inherent to Art. 2. Indeed, during a hostage taking at the Moscow's theatre, Moscow's police forces have used gas in the auditorium. The intervention brigade took the building by storm and killed all terrorists, as well as one hundred twenty five spectators. Very explicitly, the Court indicates that the judges recognize to Russia a certain national margin of appreciation 'with regard to the military and technical aspects of the situation'.[28] The European Court of Human Rights then condemns Russia, not for the use of gas in the auditorium but for the bad planning and implementation of the rescue operation.[29] We can notice here that we return to formal proportionality review, which is easier to perform for the judge than the substantive one.

It is clear that the Court does not wish to interfere in the state decision-making process when managing times of crisis. In order to overcome the substantive proportionality review's failure, it is on the basis on procedural positive obligations that the Court will rather choose to sanction a State.

2. Procedural Positive Obligations: Instigators of the Substantive Proportionality Review Alteration

The right to life's procedural aspect[30] includes the implementation of repressive and preventive legislation[31] about the protection of human life. It also carries out an effective investigation to sanction any violation of this right.[32] Also, the disproportion

26 *Dean Spielmann, En jouant sur les marges. La Cour européenne des droits de l'homme et la théorie de la marge d'appréciation nationale: abandon ou subsidiarité du contrôle européen ?* In: Institut grand-ducal, Actes de la Section des Sciences morales et politiques, Luxembourg vol. XIII 2010, 205: '*la marge d'appréciation nationale est une notion qui fait référence à la possibilité de manœuvre que la Cour européenne des droits de l'homme est disposée à reconnaître aux autorités nationales pour la mise en œuvre de leurs obligations au titre de la Convention européenne des droits de l'homme*'.

27 ECtHR, 20 December 2011, *Finogenov and o. v. Russia*, Nos 18299/03 and 27311/03.

28 ECtHR, 20 December 2011, *Finogenov and o. v. Russia*, Nos 18299/03 and 27311/03, § 213.

29 ECtHR, 20 December 2011, *Finogenov and o. v. Russia*, Nos 18299/03 and 27311/03.

30 Édouard Dubout, La procéduralisation des obligations relatives aux droits fondamentaux substantiels par la Cour européenne des droits de l'homme, 70 Revue trimestrielle des droits de l'homme (2007), 397, at 398.

31 ECtHR, Gr. Ch., 30 November 2004, *Öneryildiz v. Turkey*, No. 48939/99, § 89.

32 This positive procedural obligation derives in particular from principles 22 and 23 of the United Nations Principles on the Use of Force, adopted on 7 September 1990 by the Eighth United Nations Congress and Resolution 1989/65 of the Economic and Social Council of the United Nations,

of the result obtained by lethal acts will often be censured by invoking the absence of investigation or effective remedies. The disproportion will be more frequently pronounced on the light on the lack of investigation and effective remedies. In the decision *Tanrikulu v. Turkey,* the Court sentences Turkey on the basis of procedural obligations. Indeed, the authorities did not carry out a real investigation into the circumstances in which the victim died.[33]

At first glance, this contentious process allows the judge to respect the State's sovereignty. However, a contradiction arises when the substantive proportionality review reveals a disproportion of the using of armed forces, and that this disproportion is only repressed on the basis of procedural positive obligations. Indeed, this form of conviction is less 'infamous' and 'less dishonorable'[34] for the respondent State than being convicted on the basis of substantive obligations.

When observing some respondent State's convictions, we can doubt about the European Court's sincerity in its will to condemn right to life violations through the proportionality review. An author reveals that 'the political context cannot be neglected',[35] in view of the conflicting relations existing between certain members of the Council of Europe and the supranational court. Also, the author insinuates that the reluctance to State's conviction on the basis of substantive obligations inherent to right to life responds to political considerations. The aim is not to deteriorate the irreverence maintained by some Member States with regard to the Court.

Phlegmatic, the European Court of Human Rights' behavior leaves the observer doubtful: Do the European Court of Human rights' decisions weaken the proportionality review legitimacy in 'times of crisis'? In order to soften the equation considering the use of physical violence as a 'normal way of power',[36] the Court must act with probity concerning the jurisprudential regulation of the use of the murderous forces in any 'times of crisis'.

which provide for the establishment of independent investigation procedures in cases of public use of lethal force. See also *Laurent Sermet,* Le droit à la vie, valeur fondamentale des sociétés démocratiques, et le réalisme jurisprudentiel, 5 Revue française de droit administratif (1999),988, at 994.

33 ECtHR, 8 July 1999, *Tanrikulu v. Turkey,* No. 23763/94, § 110.

34 Édouard Dubout, op. cit., at 403.

35 *Olivier Cahn,* Obligations positives procédurales et droit à la vie, in : Geneviève Giudicelli-Delage, Stefano Manacorda, Juliette Tricot (dir.), Devoir de punir ? Le système pénal face à la protection international du droit à la vie, Paris 2013, 215–263, at 255.

36 *Max Weber,* Le savant et le politique, Paris 2002, 124.

Le Droit au Juge sous l'État d'Urgence (France)

Olivier Le Bot

Résumé

Les mesures prises sous le régime de l'état d'urgence génèrent d'importants effets pour les particuliers et sont de nature à créer d'importantes limitations aux droits fondamentaux. Pour cette raison, l'État de droit requière une intervention d'un juge pour exercer un contrôle. Cette question présente deux dimensions: d'un côté, le droit d'accéder à un juge constitutionnel, afin d'exercer un contrôle de constitutionnalité de la loi, d'un autre le droit de saisir un juge ordinaire chargé de contrôler les mesures individuelles prises en application de celle-ci.

Abstract

The measures taken under the State of emergency regime generate important effects for individuals and can create significant limitations of fundamental rights. Therefore, the rule of law implies the intervention of a judge to exercise a control. This issue has two dimensions: one the one hand, the right to a constitutional judge, in order to review the constitutionality of the law and, on the other hand, the right to get access to an ordinary court in order to review the applications of the legal provisions.

I. Introduction

Le droit français prévoit **trois régimes de crise** en présence de circonstances exceptionnelles. Leur mise en œuvre confère à l'autorité publique des pouvoirs renforcés pour réagir à une situation de crise. La coexistence de ces trois régimes correspond à l'idée d'une réaction graduée en fonction de la gravité de la menace :

- pleins pouvoirs du chef de l'État en cas de menace sur les institutions ou l'indépendance du pays (guerre, coup d'État), à travers le régime de l'article 16 de la Constitution ;
- transfert des pouvoirs de police de l'autorité civile à l'autorité militaire en cas d'état état de siège (mis en œuvre en cas de péril imminent résultant d'une guerre étrangère ou d'une insurrection armée) ;
- extension des pouvoirs de police de l'autorité administrative en cas d'état d'urgence.

Le régime de l'état d'urgence est fixé par la loi n° 55–385 du 3 avril 1955 relative à l'état d'urgence (modifiée à plusieurs reprises en 2015, 2016, 2017 et 2018).[1] L'état d'urgence peut être déclaré, sur tout ou partie du territoire, dans deux hypothèses : 'soit en cas de péril imminent résultant d'atteintes graves à l'ordre public, soit en cas d'événements présentant, par leur nature et leur gravité, le caractère de calamité publique' (art. 1er). Les conditions caractérisant l'état d'urgence rejoignent le sens donné à cette notion en droit européen[2]. La notion de 'péril imminent résultant d'atteintes graves à l'ordre public' a été regardée comme s'appliquant à l'hypothèse d'une menace terroriste.

Formellement, la déclaration de l'état d'urgence se fait en conseil des ministres. Sa prorogation au-delà de douze jours ne peut être autorisée que par une loi (art. 2). Celle-ci fixe alors la durée définitive de son application (art. 3). L'effet de ce régime est de conférer des pouvoirs spéciaux aux autorités civiles de l'État. Des mesures de police administrative qui seraient normalement illégales deviennent autorisées durant la période d'application de l'état d'urgence.

Le ministre de l'intérieur et le préfet disposent ainsi de la faculté de prendre les mesures suivantes :

- interdiction de la circulation des personnes ou des véhicules dans les lieux et à l'heure fixés par arrêté ;
- instauration de zones de protection ou de sécurité où le séjour des personnes est réglementé ;
- interdiction de séjour dans tout ou partie du département à toute personne cherchant à entraver, de quelque manière que ce soit, l'action des pouvoirs publics ;
- fermeture provisoire des salles de spectacle, débits de boissons et lieux de réunion de toute nature ;
- interdiction, à titre général ou particulier, des réunions de nature à provoquer ou entretenir le désordre ;

1 Loi n° 55–385 du 3 avril 1955 relative à l'état d'urgence, version consolidée au 27 mars 2019, disponible sur <https://www.legifrance.gouv.fr/affichTexte.do?cidTexte=JORFTEXT000000695350>.

2 Selon l'ancienne Commission européenne des Droits de l'Homme une situation relève d'une situation d'urgence si elle présente les caractéristiques suivantes: un danger réel ou imminent; des effets touchant l'ensemble de la nation; une menace sur la vie organisée de la communauté; une crise ou un danger exceptionnels, au sens où les mesures ou restrictions normales qu'autorise la Convention aux fins de la protection de la sûreté, de la santé et de l'ordre publics sont tout à fait insuffisantes; Com. EDH, affaire grecque, annuaire 12, volume 1, § 53, cité in 'Avis sur la protection des droits de l'homme dans les situations d'urgence', adopté par la Commission de Venise à sa 66e session plénière, Venise, 17–18 mars 2006) CDL-AD 2006, 015, n° 10.

- ordre de remettre des armes et les munitions correspondantes ;
- assignations à résidence ;
- perquisitions à domicile, de jour comme de nuit ;
- possibilité d'autoriser les agents de police, pour une durée maximale de 24 heures, à procéder à des contrôles d'identité, à la fouille et à l'inspection visuelle de bagages et à la fouille de véhicules.

En temps normal, c'est-à-dire hors période d'application de l'état d'urgence, les deux dernières mesures mentionnées ne peuvent être prises que par l'autorité judiciaire – le juge judiciaire dans pour les perquisitions, le ministère public pour les contrôles d'identité et fouilles de bagages et de véhicules.

Jusqu'en 2015, la loi du 3 avril 1955 sur l'état d'urgence n'avait fait l'objet que de peu d'**applications**. Elle a été mise en œuvre à trois reprises pendant la guerre d'Algérie, entre 1955 et 1962. Il a ensuite fallu attendre près d'un demi-siècle pour de nouvelles applications : trois en outre-mer, en Nouvelle-Calédonie en 1985, à Wallis-et-Futuna en 1986 et en Polynésie en 1987 – dans ces deux derniers cas, sans prolongation au-delà des 12 premiers jours; une en métropole, en 2005, circonscrite aux seules communes de la région parisienne confrontées à des situations de violences urbaines.

Suite aux attaques coordonnées du 13 novembre 2015 à Paris, le gouvernement, réuni en conseil des ministres dans la nuit du 13 au 14, a déclaré l'état d'urgence par le décret n° 2015–1475 du 14 novembre 2015 signé par le président de la République.[3] Six lois de prorogation se sont par la suite succédé, portant à deux ans la durée cumulée d'application de ce régime. Plusieurs de ces textes ont également procédé à une modification du régime applicable, soit pour en améliorer l'efficacité, soit pour en renforcer les garanties.

Son application a suscité un contentieux constitutionnel de l'état d'urgence particulièrement nourri, par le biais du droit au juge constitutionnel.

II. Le Droit au Juge Constitutionnel

Aucune loi prorogeant et modifiant l'état d'urgence n'a été déférée au Conseil constitutionnel au titre du contrôle *a priori* ouvert aux autorités politiques par l'article 61 de la Constitution.

3 Décret n° 2015–1475 du 14 novembre 2015 portant application de la loi n° 55–385 du 3 avril 1955, JORF n°0264 du 14 novembre 2015, page 21297, texte n° 44.

Il est même arrivé, à l'occasion de la première loi de prorogation, que le Premier ministre lui-même appelle les parlementaires à ne pas saisir le juge constitutionnel. Pour empêcher un contrôle, et le cas échéant une censure qui aurait mis en danger les procédures, le chef du gouvernement a demandé aux parlementaires de ne pas soumettre la loi au Conseil.[4]

> "À ce stade", indiquait-il, "je suis extrêmement dubitatif sur l'idée de saisir le Conseil constitutionnel. Parce que je souhaite que nous allions vite sur la mise en œuvre des dispositifs que nous venons, que nous allons, que vous allez voter, mais il y a toujours un risque à saisir le Conseil constitutionnel. Si le Conseil répondait que la loi révisée est inconstitutionnelle sur un certain nombre de points, sur un certain nombre de garanties apportées, cela peut faire tomber 786 perquisitions et 150 assignations à résidence déjà faites. Il y a y compris des mesures qui ont été votées hier à l'Assemblée nationale – je pense à celle sur le bracelet électronique, moi je suis dans la transparence – qui ont une fragilité constitutionnelle. Je sais bien qu'il peut y avoir une QPC mais je souhaite que nous allions vite parce que [...] nous souhaitons donner aux forces de l'ordre, aux forces de sécurité, à la justice, tous les moyens de poursuivre ce qui représente un danger pour la Nation, pour la République et pour les Français".[5]

L'objectif était ainsi d'aboutir à une promulgation immédiate de la loi sans examen, à ce stade, de sa constitutionnalité. L'argument d'efficacité mis en avant par le Premier ministre a été entendu par les parlementaires, qui ont choisi de ne pas exercer leur droit de saisine du Conseil constitutionnel. Fort heureusement pour notre État de droit, ce consensus politique a seulement eu pour effet de différer – et non d'empêcher – le contrôle de constitutionnalité. La loi, non examinée au titre du contrôle a priori, a vu plusieurs de ses dispositions être contestées par le biais du contrôle *a posteriori* de la question prioritaire de constitutionnalité (QPC).[6]

En effet, à l'occasion des recours formés contre les mesures prises au titre de l'état d'urgence, les requérants, par le biais de leur droit au juge constitutionnel, ont soulevé des questions prioritaires de constitutionnalité sur lesquelles le Conseil constitutionnel s'est prononcé dans une dizaine de décisions.[7]

4 Une saisine a priori du Conseil constitutionnel, avant la promulgation de la loi, peut être réalisée par 60 députés ou 60 sénateurs sur le fondement de l'article 61 de la Constitution.

5 M. Valls, Sénat, séance du 20 novembre 2015, compte-rendu intégral des séances, disponible au lien suivant <http://www.senat.fr/seances/s201511/s20151120/s20151120_mono.html>.

6 Art. 61-1 de la Constitution.

7 CC, décis. n° 2015-527 QPC du 22 décembre 2015 *M. Cédric D.* (Assignations à résidence dans le cadre de l'état d'urgence); n° 2016-535 QPC du 19 février 2016 *Ligue des droits de l'homme*

On retiendra de ces décisions trois enseignements principaux.

Premier enseignement: le Conseil constitutionnel a examiné les dispositions contestées en application des critères et conditions prévalant en temps normal. Il exige du législateur le même respect des règles et principes constitutionnels qu'en période ordinaire. S'il a pu être jugé que son appréciation se trouvait assouplie, la pratique révèle que le Conseil a conclu à la non-conformité totale ou partielle dans presque toutes les décisions (huit, sur les neuf qu'il a rendues).[8]

Deuxième enseignement: ces censures n'ont produit qu'un effet platonique pour le requérant. En effet, le Conseil constitutionnel a choisi, systématiquement, de ne pas prononcer l'annulation immédiate de la disposition reconnue inconstitutionnelle mais de reporter à une date d'ultérieure la prise d'effet de la déclaration d'inconstitutionnalité. Il privait ainsi l'auteur du recours du bénéfice de la déclaration d'inconstitutionnalité, et laissait au législateur un certain délai, 2 mois, 3 mois, pour revoir la loi et la rendre conforme à la Constitution. Cette modulation dans le temps de la portée des annulations a affaibli, sur le plan concret, l'intérêt du droit au juge constitutionnel pour les particuliers requérants.

Troisième enseignement: dans nombre de cas, le Conseil a conditionné la constitutionnalité des pouvoirs spéciaux conférés à l'autorité administrative pendant l'état d'urgence au contrôle exercé par le juge administratif sur leur mise en œuvre. L'existence de ce contrôle juridictionnel a largement conditionné la validation du dispositif législatif. Aussi est-il essentiel d'en apprécier l'effectivité.

(Police des réunions et des lieux publics dans le cadre de l'état d'urgence); n° 2016–536 QPC du 19 février 2016 *Ligue des droits de l'homme* (Perquisitions et saisies administratives dans le cadre de l'état d'urgence) ; n° 2016–567/568 QPC du 23 septembre 2016 *M. Georges F. et autre* (Perquisitions administratives dans le cadre de l'état d'urgence II); n° 2016–600 QPC du 2 décembre 2016 M. *Raïme A.* (Perquisitions administratives dans le cadre de l'état d'urgence III); n° 2017–624 QPC du 16 mars 2017 *M. Sofiyan I.* (Assignations à résidence dans le cadre de l'état d'urgence II); n° 2017–635 QPC du 9 juin 2017 M. *Émile L.* (Interdiction de séjour dans le cadre de l'état d'urgence); n° 2017–677 QPC du 1er décembre 2017 Ligue des droits de l'Homme (Contrôles d'identité, fouilles de bagages et visites de véhicules dans le cadre de l'état d'urgence); n° 2017–684 QPC du 11 janvier *2018 Associations La cabane juridique / Legal Shelter et autre* (Zones de protection ou de sécurité dans le cadre de l'état d'urgence). Toutes les décisions du Conseil constitutionnel peuvent être consultées sur son site internet: https://www.conseil-constitutionnel.fr/decisions/qpc.

8 CC, décis. n° 536 QPC, n° 567/568 QPC, n° 600 QPC, n° 624 QPC, n° 635 QPC, n° 677 QPC et n° 684 QPC.

III. Contrôle Juridictionnel des Mesures Prises: Quelle Efficacité?

Des données sur la mise en œuvre des pouvoirs spéciaux doivent d'abord être fournies. En deux années d'application de l'état d'urgence, les autorités ont ordonné 4.469 perquisitions administratives, 754 assignations à résidence, près de 600 interdictions de séjour, essentiellement pour interdire à des militants contestataires radicaux de se rendre à des manifestations, 19 fermetures de lieux de culte[9] et plus de 4.000 arrêtés autorisant pour une durée de 24 heures les fouilles de bagages, visite de véhicules et contrôle d'identité, l'autorisation étant le plus souvent reconduite chaque jour pour une durée de 24 heures.[10]

Il est évident que les mesures prises sont lourdes de conséquences pour les personnes qui en sont l'objet et portent une atteinte importante à des libertés fondamentales, liberté d'aller et venir, droit de propriété, liberté de réunion, inviolabilité du domicile. Aussi est-il impérieux qu'un juge puisse sanctionner ou s'opposer à une utilisation de celles-ci dans des cas qui ne le justifieraient pas.

Comme le relevait la Commission de Venise en 2006, dans son avis sur la protection des droits de l'homme dans les situations d'urgence, 'les dérogations ne peuvent être maintenues – et leur portée ne peut être définie – que 'dans la stricte mesure où la situation l'exige'. Leur nécessité et leur proportionnalité doivent faire l'objet d'un contrôle, aux niveaux national et international. Ce contrôle est d'une importance capitale, puisqu'il ressort de la pratique des États que les violations des droits de l'homme les plus graves tendent à se produire dans le contexte d'états d'urgence et que les États peuvent être tentés de tirer prétexte d'un état d'urgence pour utiliser leur pouvoir de prendre des mesures dérogatoires à d'autres fins ou d'une ampleur plus grande que la situation ne l'exige'.[11] Dans le même sens, le Comité des droits de l'homme des Nations unies a précisé en 2001: 'Même si les États parties peuvent, pendant un état d'urgence, apporter, dans la stricte mesure où la situation l'exige, des ajustements aux modalités concrètes de fonctionnement de leurs procédures relatives aux recours ju-

9 Disponible au lien suivant <https://www.interieur.gouv.fr/Espace-presse/Dossiers-de-presse/Sortie-de-l-etat-d-urgence-un-bilan-et-des-chiffres-cles>.

10 Disponible au lien suivant <http://www2.assemblee-nationale.fr/static/15/lois/bilan_statistique_2017_06_30.pdf>.

11 Avis sur la protection des droits de l'homme dans les situations d'urgence, adopté par la Commission de Venise à sa 66e session plénière, Venise, 17–18 mars 2006, CDL-AD (2006)015, n° 10.

diciaires et autres recours, ils doivent se conformer à l'obligation fondamentale de garantir un recours utile qui est prévu au paragraphe 3 de l'article 2'.[12]

Ce droit au recours, reconnu sur le plan constitutionnel[13], est-il respecté, concrètement, au regard du contrôle exercé par le juge ordinaire ? En pratique, la plupart des demandes sont formées selon la procédure dite du 'référé-liberté', codifiée à l'article L. 521–2 du code de justice administrative[14]. Cette procédure permet une intervention très rapide du juge, dans les jours qui suivent sa saisine voire le jour même. Le juge des référés peut suspendre la décision attaquée ou adresser une injonction à l'autorité administrative en cas d'atteinte grave et manifestement illégale portée à une liberté fondamentale (liberté d'aller et venir, liberté de réunion, liberté du culte, etc.)[15].

Depuis la déclaration de l'état d'urgence le 14 novembre 2015, quelques recours ont été formés contre des interdictions de manifester, la fermeture d'un restaurant et d'une mosquée, ainsi qu'une interdiction de fréquenter un lieu de culte. Toutefois, l'écrasante majorité des demandes a concerné des mesures d'assignation à résidence[16]. C'est par rapport à ces mesures que le Conseil d'État a posé les principes applicables au contrôle juridictionnel des mesures prises au titre de la législation sur l'état d'urgence.[17]

12 Observation générale n° 29/2001 du Comité des droits de l'homme des Nations unies sur les situations d'urgence (article 4 du Pacte international relatif aux droits civils et politiques), CCPR/C/21/Rev.1/Add.11, § 14.

13 Sur le plan constitutionnel, ce droit a été reconnu par le Conseil constitutionnel en 1996; CC, décision n° 96–373 DC du 9 avril 1996, Loi organique portant statut d'autonomie de la Polynésie française, en se basant sur l'exigence de garantie des droits énoncé par l'article 16 de la Déclaration des droits de l'homme et du citoyen (texte qui, en tant qu'élément du 'bloc de constitutionnalité', bénéficie d'une valeur constitutionnelle). Le droit au juge est également reconnu sur le plan conventionnel tant au titre de l'article 13 de la convention européenne des droits de l'homme qu'à celui de l'article 2 § 3 du PIDCP.

14 Saisi d'une demande en ce sens justifiée par l'urgence, le juge des référés peut ordonner toutes mesures nécessaires à la sauvegarde d'une liberté fondamentale à laquelle une personne morale de droit public ou un organisme de droit privé chargé de la gestion d'un service public aurait porté, dans l'exercice d'un de ses pouvoirs, une atteinte grave et manifestement illégale. Le juge des référés se prononce dans un délai de quarante-huit heures.

15 Sur cette procédure, v. O. *Le Bot*, La protection des libertés fondamentales par la procédure du référé-liberté, LGDJ, 2017, 672 p. ; disponible au lien suivant <https://hal.archives-ouvertes.fr/tel-01704108/document>.

16 Par exemple, sur les deux premiers mois d'application du régime : 61 recours, sur les 72 formés devant les tribunaux administratifs; disponible au lien suivant <http://www.conseil-État.fr/Actualites/Communiques/Mesures-prises-au-titre-de-l-État-d-urgence>.

17 CE, Sect., 11 décembre 2015, Gauthier, n° 394990, Lebon; CE, Sect., 11 décembre 2015, Domenjoud, n° 395009, Lebon (2 espèces).

Premièrement, un contrôle de proportionnalité est exercé sur les mesures prises. Le juge prend en compte les circonstances de temps et de lieu, les contraintes et les moyens de l'administration et le cas échéant, s'il était possible d'atteindre l'objectif poursuivi par d'autres mesures moins attentatoires à la liberté considérée. Dans ce contrôle, il s'assure que la personne visée par la mesure représente une réelle menace pour l'ordre public et vérifie que les modalités de la mesure prise sont adaptées et conformes à une exigence de modération dans la restriction apportée.

Deuxièmement, le juge administratif estime que la condition d'urgence, qui justifie son intervention selon une procédure rapide, est présumée satisfaite lorsque se trouve contestée une assignation à résidence. Il entend, par cette présomption, faciliter l'exercice des recours.[18]

Ces principes ont été appliqués par les juridictions administratives. Le juge des référés a ainsi suspendu des arrêtés d'assignation à résidence ne répondant pas aux exigences de nécessité ou de proportionnalité.[19] Il a pu également assouplir certaines modalités, par exemple prévoir un pointage au commissariat deux fois par jour au lieu de trois.[20] De manière générale, les statistiques disponibles sur les trois premiers mois révèlent un taux de réussite des recours se situant à 16 % (auxquels il faut ajouter les cas où l'administration abroge la mesure en cours d'instance, c'est-à-dire 19 % des affaires).[21] Ce taux est globalement comparable à celui observé dans les autres con-

18 Le Conseil d'État a également posé que les mesures prises par l'autorité publique peuvent être fondées sur des menaces différentes de celles ayant justifié la déclaration de l'état d'urgence. Dans le cas présent, l'état d'urgence a été déclaré suite à des attaques terroristes et en vue de contrer la menace d'attentats. Il peut néanmoins être utilisé pour assigner à résidence un individu représentant une menace d'une autre nature. En l'espèce, le Conseil a jugé que l'assignation à résidence de militants engagés dans l'action violente, durant la tenue de la COP21, n'était pas illégale : compte tenu de la mobilisation exceptionnelle des forces de police pour contenir la menace d'attentats et assurer la sécurité d'un sommet international de grande ampleur, ces assignations permettent d'éviter de détourner sur des menaces secondaires des forces mobilisées sur des menaces prioritaires.

19 CE, ord., 22 janv. 2016, *Abdelmalek*, n° 396116, Lebon T et CE, ord. 9 févr. 2016, *Zammouri*, n° 396570, inédit.

20 CE, ord. 6 janv. 2016, *Tarzaeva*, n° 395622, inédit.

21 Commission européenne pour la démocratie par le droit, Avis sur le projet de loi constitutionnelle "de protection de la nation", Avis n° 838/2016 du 14 mars 2016, CDL-AD(2016)006, n° 73: 'Selon les statistiques qui ont été fournies par le Conseil d'État à la délégation de la Commission de Venise, sur les 106 mesures de police administrative examinées à la date du 25 février 2016, les juges des référés (tribunaux administratifs et Conseil d'État) ont donné acte de 20 abrogations par le ministère de l'Intérieur avant que le Conseil d'État ne statue (19 pour cent), ont suspendu totalement ou partiellement 17 mesures (16 pour cent) et ont rejeté le référé dirigé contre 69 mesures (65 pour cent des mesures attaquées)'; disponible sur <http://www.venice.coe.int/webforms/ documents/?pdf=CDL-AD%282016 %29006-f>.

tentieux. C'est là l'indicateur d'un contrôle maintenu du juge administratif ; celui-ci ne fait pas preuve de *self-restraint* du fait du contexte sécuritaire ni de complaisance à l'égard des autorités publiques.

On peut estimer que, sur les mesures d'assignation à résidence (comme, du reste, l'interdiction des réunions ou la fermeture de lieux de réunion), le contrôle juridictionnel assuré présente une efficacité certaine. Le juge est en mesure d'intervenir rapidement et de faire cesser, par une injonction ou une suspension, l'utilisation d'un pouvoir spécial en dehors des hypothèses justifiant sa mise en œuvre. Tel est d'ailleurs le constat auquel parvient la Commission de Venise dans son rapport du 14 mars 2016: 'La Commission de Venise ne voit pas de raison de douter que le contrôle des mesures d'urgence par le juge administratif français, notamment par voie de référé, représente un recours efficace.'[22]

On peut ne pas partager ce constat sur quatre séries de mesures : les perquisitions, les interdictions de séjour, l'instauration de couvre-feux et les autorisations de procéder à des contrôles d'identité et fouilles de bagages et de véhicules.

Ces mesures ont une durée limitée et auront épuisé leurs effets avant que le juge ait pu statuer, voire ait pu être saisi: la décision ordonnant une perquisition est exécutée en quelques heures, l'interdiction de séjour est prise pour le lendemain ou le surlendemain, même chose pour les couvre-feux ; quant aux autorisations de procéder à des contrôles d'identité et fouilles de bagages et de véhicules, ils sont pris pour 24 heures, et renouvelé quotidiennement. Dans tous ces cas, le juge administratif n'a pas le temps d'intervenir avant que la décision ait produit tous ses effets.

Son contrôle s'exerce nécessairement après coup, donc trop tard. Le juge ne peut s'opposer à une mesure illégale mais seulement annuler a posteriori la décision l'ayant ordonné et ordonner la réparation du préjudice subi par la personne indûment perquisitionnée. Le contrôle juridictionnel présente un caractère ineffectif. Il s'exerce après coup et ne présente de ce fait aucun intérêt. Si la mesure a été ordonnée à tort, le mal est fait et il est impossible de revenir en arrière. Quelle a été la position du juge constitutionnel face à ces choix législatifs?

22 Avis précité, n ° 74.

IV. Le Conseil Constitutionnel et le Droit au Juge sous l'État d'Urgence

Sa jurisprudence, sur la question spécifique du droit au juge, s'articule en quatre points.

1. Premier Point: le Conseil Constitutionnel a Posé des Limites à l'Éviction du Juge Judiciaire.

En droit français, l'article 66 de la Constitution prescrit l'intervention du juge judiciaire en cas de privation de la liberté individuelle. Il est important de rappeler la rédaction de cet article afin de comprendre l'interprétation qui lui en est donnée: 'Nul ne peut être arbitrairement détenu. / L'autorité judiciaire, gardienne de la liberté individuelle, assure le respect de ce principe dans les conditions prévues par la loi'.

Il ressort du rapprochement de ces deux phrases que le principe selon lequel l'autorité judiciaire est gardienne de la liberté individuelle se limite à la protection de l'individu contre une détention arbitraire. Il s'agit, pour reprendre une formule souvent citée, de l'*habeas corpus* à la Française. Le principe se limite en conséquence aux seules privations de liberté (garde à vue, détention, rétention, hospitalisation sans consentement).[23]

Il en résulte que les mesures prises au titre de l'état d'urgence ne doivent relever du contrôle de l'autorité judiciaire, en vertu de la Constitution, que si elles emportent privation de liberté.

Une difficulté pouvait en revanche se poser pour les assignations à résidence. Certes, être assigné à résidence n'est pas assimilable à un emprisonnement, mais qu'en serait-il pour une assignation permanente (24 heures sur 24[24]) ou s'appliquant la plus longue partie de la journée? L'atteinte à la liberté d'aller et venir serait à ce point importante qu'elle confinerait à une privation de liberté. Afin d'opérer le départ entre une atteinte 'normale' ou 'ordinaire' à la liberté d'aller et venir et une atteinte à ce point importante qu'elle s'assimile à une privation de liberté, le Conseil a posé qu'une assig-

23 La jurisprudence s'est clairement stabilisée sur ce point depuis une décision de 1999 (n° 99–411 DC du 16 juin 1999), mettant un terme à l'acceptation plus large qui prévalait auparavant. La lecture orthodoxe de l'article 66 (lisant de façon combinée les deux phrases qu'elle comporte) s'est justifiée par l'accroissement des outils mis à la disposition du juge administratif pour assurer une protection efficace des libertés sur les actes relevant de son domaine.

24 Comme cela avait pu être envisagé par un amendement de l'opposition (n° 40), auquel le président de la Commission des lois de l'Assemblée nationale s'était opposé (v. AN, séance du 19 novembre 2015, compte rendu intégral des débats).

nation qui dépasserait les 12 heures devrait être 'regardée comme une mesure privative de liberté, dès lors soumise aux exigences de l'article 66 de la Constitution'.[25] Cette plage de 12 heures n'est pas arbitraire : elle correspond à la distinction jour/nuit. Assigné à résidence la nuit, l'individu visé par la mesure peut circuler librement entre le matin et le soir (sous réserve, selon la modalité les plus fréquemment retenue, d'une obligation de pointage à midi), notamment pour l'exercice d'une activité professionnelle.

En l'état actuel de la législation sur l'état d'urgence, la plage horaire maximum d'astreinte à domicile est précisément de 12 heures. Il en résulte, en l'absence d'atteinte à la liberté individuelle, que le contrôle de ces mesures revient au juge administratif. Si l'amplitude de cette plage horaire devait être étendue, le contrôle de l'autorité judiciaire s'imposerait.

2. Deuxième Point dans la Jurisprudence Constitutionnelle relative au droit au Juge sous l'État d'Urgence: le Conseil Constitutionnel a Défini l'Étendu du Contrôle qu'il Revient au Juge Administratif d'Exercer, notamment sur les Assignations à Résidence.

Il a posé qu'il appartient au juge administratif d'exercer un contrôle de proportionnalité au sens large sur ces mesures, posant 'que le juge administratif est chargé de s'assurer que cette mesure est adaptée, nécessaire et proportionnée à la finalité qu'elle poursuit'.[26]

3. Troisième Point: le Conseil a Accepté, au Regard de l'Intensité de la Menace que l'État d'Urgence vise à Prévenir, une Absence de Contrôle Effectif sur les Mesures dont les Effets s'Épuisent en un Instant.

La question se posait avec une particulière acuité pour les perquisitions administratives, en raison de leurs effets (elles portent atteinte à l'inviolabilité du domicile), de leur utilisation massive et de leur utilisation fréquente en dehors des cas et conditions

25 CC, déc. n° 2015-527 QPC du 22 déc. 2015, M. Cédric D. (Assignations à résidence dans le cadre de l'état d'urgence), cons. 6.

26 CC, déc. n° 2015-527 QPC du 22 déc. 2015, M. Cédric D. (Assignations à résidence dans le cadre de l'état d'urgence), cons 12.

posés par la loi (40 % des perquisitions ayant fait l'objet de recours ont été annulées par le juge en raison de leur illégalité).[27]

Comme cela a été souligné précédemment, une intervention après coup du juge sur cette mesure ne présente aucune utilité pratique pour le juge et le prive de toute intervention juridictionnelle effective.

Pourtant, le Conseil constitutionnel n'y a pas vu d'atteinte inconstitutionnelle au droit au recours, 'au regard des circonstances particulières ayant conduit à la déclaration de l'état d'urgence'.[28] La suppression du droit au juge (ou, pour être plus précis, son intervention uniquement a posteriori, avec pour seuls pouvoirs une annulation sans effet utile et une indemnisation du préjudice) n'a pas été regardée comme contraire à la Constitution du fait, en substance, de la gravité de la menace que les mesures de perquisition visent à prévenir.[29]

27 Rapp. n° 591 du 28 juin 2017 (*M. Mercier*), p. 14, faisant état de 31 annulations sur 78 décisions rendues.

28 CC, décis. n° 2016–536 QPC du 19 février 2016, cons. 11.

29 Qu'en est-il de la conformité à la convention européenne des droits de l'homme ? Selon la jurisprudence européenne, il appartient à la Cour de Strasbourg de 'déterminer si les moyens dont le requérant disposait en droit' interne 'étaient' 'effectifs' en ce sens qu'ils auraient pu empêcher la survenance ou la continuation de la violation alléguée ou auraient pu fournir à l'intéressé un redressement approprié pour toute violation s'étant déjà produite' (CEDH, 26 oct. 2000, *Kudla c/ Pologne*, n° 30210/96. Dans le même sens, voir CEDH, Grande chambre, 4 juillet 2005; *Ramirez Sanchez c/ France*, n° 59450/00, § 160; CEDH, 18 octobre 2005, *Schemkamper c/ France*, n° 75833/01, § 42).
La conjonction de coordination 'ou' laisse une option à l'État: soit mettre en place une procédure a priori, soit prévoir un redressement a posteriori (permettant de sanctionner le droit méconnu sous la forme d'une annulation, d'une réparation ou d'une remise en état). En outre, 'les États contractants jouissent d'une certaine marge d'appréciation quant à la manière de se conformer aux obligations que leur fait cette disposition. La portée de l'obligation découlant de l'article 13 varie en fonction de la nature du grief que le requérant fonde sur la Convention', CEDH, 9 mai 2006, *Pereira Henriques c/ Luxembourg*, n° 60255/00, § 86.
Une menace au regard des articles 2 (droit à la vie) ou 3 (interdiction de la torture, et des traitements inhumains ou dégradants) exigera un recours spécifique, le cas échéant suspensif, CEDH, 26 avril 2007, *Gebremedhin c/ France*, no 25389/05.
En revanche, aucune exigence particulière ne s'impose pour les autres droits. Dans le cadre de la marge d'appréciation qui leur est reconnue, les États sont libres de prévoir une sanction juridictionnelle intervenant exclusivement a posteriori. Tel est le cas s'agissant des mesures de perquisition, qui mettent en cause « seulement » le droit au respect des biens (protégé par l'article 1er du premier protocole additionnel) et le droit au respect de la vie privée (garanti par l'article 8).

4. Quatrième Point: le Conseil Constitutionnel a Censuré, non pas au Titre des Garanties Assurées mais du Mélange des Genres qu'il Opérait, un Dispositif Soumettant au Contrôle Préalable du Juge Administratif le Renouvellement des Assignations de Longue Durée.

Lorsque l'état d'urgence a commencé à s'inscrire dans la durée, après quatre prorogations et un an d'application, la situation des personnes assignées à résidence depuis le début de sa mise en œuvre a commencé à susciter un certain malaise. Il tenait au fait qu'un individu, sans intervention préalable d'un juge et sans s'être vu reprocher la commission d'une infraction, pouvait, sur simple décision de l'administration et par le jeu des renouvellements successifs, se retrouver assigné à résidence pour une durée finalement très longue. Le législateur a en conséquence modifié la loi en soumettant à autorisation préalable du juge administratif (plus exactement du juge des référés du Conseil d'État) le renouvellement d'une assignation au-delà d'une année.[30]

Saisi d'une QPC, le Conseil constitutionnel a censuré ce dispositif au titre du manquement au principe d'impartialité et au droit à un recours juridictionnel effectif. Il estime que le juge de l'autorisation préalable va déterminer ou prédéterminer l'issue du recours qui sera le cas échéant exercé *ex post*. Il va le préjuger puisque les juridictions qui statueront *a posteriori* s'aligneront automatiquement sur la solution arrêtée *a priori*. Selon le Conseil constitutionnel, le recours est vain, les choses sont jouées d'avance : le juge du premier degré ne s'aventurera pas à contredire son juge suprême; le juge suprême ne consentira pas à se déjuge.[31]

30 Le texte adopté, la loi n° 2016–1767 du 19 décembre 2016, a introduit à cette fin deux nouveaux alinéas à l'article 6 de la loi de 1955. Le premier plafonne la durée maximale d'assignation pouvant être atteinte du fait des renouvellements successifs: 'À compter de la déclaration de l'état d'urgence et pour toute sa durée, une même personne ne peut être assignée à résidence pour une durée totale équivalant à plus de douze mois'. Le second alinéa prévoit une possibilité de déroger à cette limite: 'Le ministre de l'intérieur peut toutefois demander au juge des référés du Conseil d'Etat l'autorisation de prolonger une assignation à résidence au-delà de la durée mentionnée' à l'alinéa précédent. La demande 'lui est adressée au plus tôt quinze jours avant l'échéance de cette durée. Le juge des référés statue dans les formes prévues au livre V du code de justice administrative et dans un délai de quarante-huit heures à compter de sa saisine, au vu des éléments produits par l'autorité administrative faisant apparaître les raisons sérieuses de penser que le comportement de la personne continue à constituer une menace pour la sécurité et l'ordre publics. La prolongation autorisée par le juge des référés ne peut excéder une durée de trois mois'.

31 CC, décision n° 2017–624 QPC du 16 mars 2017 *M. Sofiyan I.* (Durée maximale de l'assignation à résidence dans le cadre de l'état d'urgence).

Conclusion

En définitive, le Conseil constitutionnel ne s'est pas montré particulièrement protecteur du droit au juge sous l'état d'urgence. Il a en effet accepté de larges atteints au droit au juge en s'appuyant sur la menace particulière qui avait justifié le déclenchement de ce régime d'exception. Durant les deux années d'application de ce régime, et pour s'en tenir à la seule question du droit au juge, le Conseil n'aura censuré des points relativement secondaires de procédure contentieuse.

Extra Lege Legislative Powers for the Executive during Martial Law in Contemporary Polish Constitutional Law

Maciej Pisz

Abstract

The presented article aims at presenting the issue of *extra lege* legislative powers for the executive during martial law (stan wojenny) in contemporary Polish constitutional law. What is important, executive authorities are equipped with *extra lege* legislative powers in contemporary Polish constitutional law only in – above mentioned – extreme situations of martial law, understood as one of the three states of emergency (stany nadzwyczajne) known in the Polish legal system. Moreover, *extra lege* legislative powers granted to the executive during martial law in contemporary Polish constitutional law are vested only in one of the two executive authorities known in the Polish legal system – the President of the Republic of Poland. Pursuant to art. 234 of the Constitution of the Republic of Poland the President – after fulfilment of the conditions specified in the Constitution – is empowered to issue, under the martial law, specific normative acts of a statutory rank: regulations with the effect of a statute. From the perspective of Polish constitutional law regulations with the effect of a statute are one of sources of law of universal application. Such acts are placed at the same level in the hierarchy of the universally binding sources of law as ordinary statutes. The institution of an act of a statutory rank constitutes the only exception from the accepted in the Polish constitutional order principle of exclusivity of parliamentary rulemaking, meaning passing of acts of a statutory rank.

I. Introduction

The main aim of this paper is to demonstrate the issue of *extra lege* legislative powers for the executive during martial law in the contemporary Polish constitutional law. It is worth to stress at the very beginning that considerations in this article concentrate on both the presentation of – from the perspective of the Polish contemporary constitutional law – the specifics of the general concept of *extra lege* legislative powers for the executive during martial law, as well as introduction to specific cases of realisation of such *extra lege* powers by the executive legal system during martial law, meaning the issuance of regulations with the effect of a statute, regulated in the Constitution of the Republic of Poland dated April 2, 1997.[1]

1 The Constitution of the Republic of Poland of 2 April 2 1997, Journal of Laws 1997, no. 78, item 483, with subsequent amendments.

Firstly, in the paper the doctrinal basis of the issue of *extra lege* legislative powers for the executive during martial law in contemporary Polish constitutional law will be discussed. In this context I present the concept of *extra lege* legislative powers for the executive and the concept of acts of the executive of a statutory rank. Moreover, in this part of the deliberations main assumptions of the institution of states of emergency and the institution of martial law in contemporary Polish constitutional law will be presented.

In further parts, the article is oriented at presentation of the constitutional foundations of the institution of a regulation with the effect of a statute – as well as its assessment – which could be issued in extreme situations of martial law and which is specified in the art. 234 of the Constitution of the Republic of Poland. This institution is analysed, among other, as one of the sources of universally binding law as well as an exception from the principle of exclusivity of parliamentary rulemaking, meaning passing of acts of a statutory rank. Moreover, the institution of a regulation with the effect of a statute is analysed in the context of the security of Poland in international relations. As a consequence, regulation with the effect of a statute is presented in the wider, international context. In the paper research hypotheses, which assumes that in contemporary Polish constitutional law exist close connections between the regulation with the effect of a statue and the Polish situation and its international relations, will be laid down and then analysed.

II. The Doctrinal Basis of the Issuance of *extra Lege* Legislative Powers of the Executive during Martial Law in Contemporary Polish Constitutional Law

1. The Concept of *extra Lege* Legislative Powers of the Executive and the Concept of Acts of a Statutory in Contemporary Polish Constitutional law

At the outset, it should be noted that the concept of *extra lege* legislative powers of the executive is connected to granting the executive (non-parliamentary organs) the powers to issue normative acts of a statutory rank.[2] A view might be expressed, that

2 Cf. for example: *Kazimierz Działocha*, Dekret z mocą ustawy w państwie burżuazyjnym (Decree with the force of law in a bourgeois state), Wrocław 1964, 6, wing; Sławomir *Patyra*, Akty o mocy ustawy w polskim porządku konstytucyjnym. Tradycja a współczesność (Acts with the power of the act in the Polish constitutional order. Tradition and the present), Przegląd Prawa Konstytucyjnego (Review of Constitutional Law) 2014 No. 2, 251, at 253; *Maciej Nowakowski*, Ustawo-

the realisation of statutory powers by the executive is not a commonly applied systemic solution in the Polish constitutional law, as it may only happen in specific systemic circumstances connected to the martial law. It has to be stressed, that in the Polish legal order the acts of a statutory rank are normally issued by the legislative (the parliament). Such solution is connected to the realisation of one of the basic functions of the parliament (the legislative function)[3] and the realisation of the competence – granted to the parliament – consisting on passing statutes.[4]

In this context, it might be indicated that the executive's acts of a statutory rank are viewed in the constitutional law doctrine as an exception from the so called principle of exclusivity of parliamentary realisation of the legislative process (rulemaking). Simplifying, the above mentioned rule is expressed in the fact that the parliament (and not for example the executive) is a body, which shall pass acts of a statutory rank. This rule – in relation to the domestic law – has been approved, among other, in the Polish constitutional law.[5]

Notwithstanding from the above considerations, it is also worth to note that the acts of the executive of a statutory rank are distinguished – in comparison to other sources of the Polish law – by the binding force attributed to them. In the legal sources' hierarchy such acts are issued – despite of their origin – as equally binding as statutes. In consequence, such acts are of the same binding power as statutes.

dawstwo delegowane w polskim prawie konstytucyjnym (Legislation delegated in Polish constitutional law), Przegląd Sejmowy (Sejm Review) 2005 No. 3, 47, at 47; and *Wiesław Skrzydło*, Ustawodawstwo delegowane w polskim prawie konstytucyjnym (Legislation delegated in Polish constitutional law), in: Lech Garlicki/Andrzej Szmyt (ed.), Sześć lat Konstytucji Rzeczypospolitej Polskiej. Doświadczenia i inspiracje (Six years of the Constitution of the Republic of Poland. Experiences and inspirations), Warszawa 2003, 270–278, at 270.

3 In the light of the Polish doctrine, three basic functions of the parliament may be specified: legislative, control and creation; cf. *Maciej Pisz*, Władza ustawodawcza (Legislative power), in: Maciej Pisz/Paweł Ochmann/Ryszard Piotrowski (ed.), Prawo konstytucyjne. Kompendium (Constitutional law. Compendium), Warszawa 2014, 34–98, at 45.

4 Cf. e.g. *Maciej Pisz*, Szczególne tryby ustawodawcze w Konstytucji RP (Special legislative modes in the Constitution of the Republic of Poland), in: Marek Zubik (ed.), Minikomentarz dla Maksiprofesora, Księga Jubileuszowa Profesora Leszka Garlickiego (Minicomessary for Maksiprofesor, Jubilee Book of Professor Leszek Garlicki), Warszawa 2017, 570–586, at 570 ff.

5 Cf. *Lech Garlicki/Marek Zubik*, Ustawa w systemie źródeł prawa (The Act in the system of sources of law), in: Andrzej Szmyt (ed.), Konstytucyjny system źródeł prawa w praktyce (The constitutional system of sources of law in practice), Warszawa 2005, 39–61, at 47; *Kazimierz Działocha*, Instytucja dekretu z mocą ustawy i jej stosunek do zasady wyłączności ustawodawczej parlamentu w prawie europejskich państw socjalistycznych (Institution of a decree with the force of law and its relation to the principle of parliamentary exclusivity in the law of European socialist countries), Wrocław 1969, 62 ff.

Noteworthy is the fact that the statutory (of an equal binding strength) power of the executive's acts of a statutory rank consists of the fact, that regulations contained in them may, in the material scope of statutes (so also regarding matters for which such acts may be issued by the executive), alter and repeal any regulation expressed in a statute or regulate for the first time – with the effect of a statutory regulation – matters regarding the subject matter and not regulated in any statute so far. At the same time, norms of the discussed acts may be altered and repealed only by other norms of such acts or by statutory norms.[6] Moreover, the described possibility of altering or repealing of valid statutes constitutes – in my opinion – the core meaning of issuance of the acts of the executive of a statutory rank.

It is also worth to draw attention to the fact that the acts of the executive of a statutory rank are in the Polish constitutional law a source of law and simultaneously a part of the greater system of the legal system. From the perspective of contemporary Polish law it is of importance, that the acts of the executive of a statutory rank shall be viewed – in regard to the above statements – as one of universally applicable sources of law. Such conclusion is connected to the catalogue of the approved universally binding sources of law and sources of internal law expressed in the Constitution of the Republic of Poland.

2. Main Assumptions of the Institution of the States of Emergency in Contemporary Polish Constitutional Law

In the context of the aforementioned statements, it should be emphasized that – in contemporary Polish constitutional law – the executive authorities are equipped with *extra lege* legislative powers (and have the authority to issue acts of a statutory rank) in extreme situations of martial law (stan wojenny), understood as one of the three states of emergency (stany nadzwyczajne) known in the Polish legal system. Therefore it shall be indicated that during martial states the acts of the executive of a statutory rank may be issued. What is important: the acts of the executive of a statutory rank may neither be issued in Poland during any other emergency state, nor in any other circumstances (when no emergency state is declared).

6 Cf. among others *Kazimierz Działocha*, Ustawodawstwo delegowane (Delegated legislation), in: Janusz Trzciński (ed.), Postępowanie ustawodawcze w polskim prawie konstytucyjnym (Legislative proceedings in Polish constitutional law), Warszawa 1994, 39–60, at 41.

In the Polish legal system three states of emergency (stany nadzwyczajne) are known. Such states are: martial law (stan wojenny), the emergency state during civil unrest (stan wyjątkowy) and the state of natural disaster (stan klęski żywiołowej).[7]

States of emergency may be declared in the Polish legal order only in extraordinary situations, when the use of ordinary constitutional measures would be inadequate. Such situation is currently regulated in art. 228 (1) of the Constitution of the Republic of Poland, in which a statement is expressed that

> 'In situations of particular danger, if ordinary constitutional measures are inadequate, any of the following appropriate extraordinary measures may be introduced: a martial law, an emergency state during civil unrest or a state of natural disaster'.

As it stems from art. 229 of the Constitution of the Republic of Poland, martial law (on a part of or on the whole territory of the state) may be declared on request of the Council of Ministers by the President of the Republic of Poland 'in the case of external threats to the State, acts of armed aggression against the territory of the Republic of Poland or when an obligation of common defence against aggression arises by virtue of international agreements'. The emergency state during civil unrest may be, on the other hand, as specified in art. 230 (1) of the Polish Constitution declared on request of the Council of Ministers by the President of the Republic of Poland 'in the case of threats to the constitutional order of the State, to security of the citizenry or public order'. It might be declared for a definite period, but no longer than 90 days. The third type of the states of emergency – the state of a natural disaster – may be declared by the second executive authority known in the Polish legal system: the Council of Ministers (for a definite period of time, no longer than 30 days in a part of or upon the whole territory of the state) 'in order to prevent or remove the consequences of a natural catastrophe or a technological accident exhibiting characteristics of a natural disaster' (first sentence of art. 232 of the Constitution of the Republic of Poland).

At this moment it is noteworthy that the declaration of martial law (during which issuance of executive's acts of a statutory rank is exclusively possible) is possible in the context of art. 229 of the Polish Constitution in case of existence of at least one of three premises: 1) external threat to the state, 2) act of armed aggression against the territory of Poland, 3) when an obligation of common defence against aggression arises by virtue of international agreement. Above-mentioned premises constitute – in my opinion – not only premises for the declaration of a martial law, but also – deducing logically form the meaning of art. 229 in relation to art 234 of the Constitution

7 Cf. e.g. *Krzysztof Prokop*, Stany nadzwyczajne w Konstytucji Rzeczypospolitej Polskiej (Extraordinary States in the Constitution of the Republic of Poland), Białystok 2005.

of the Republic of Poland – describe a wider context of the institution of an act of a statutory rank in relation to international law and relations indicating Polish systemic circumstances when such an institution may be used. More precisely, the institution of an act of a statutory rank can be applied only when international circumstances (e.g. external threat to the state) justify the introduction of a martial law in Poland.

III. Constitutional Foundations of the Institution of a Regulation with the Effect of a Statute

The institution of a act of a statutory rank has been implemented to the Polish law by art. 234 of the Constitution of the Republic of Poland. Pursuant to this article, the President – after fulfilment of the conditions specified in this regulation – can issue, under the martial law, specific normative acts of a statutory rank: 'regulations with the effect of a statute'.

As it is indicated expressis verbis in art. 234 (1) of the Constitution of the Republic of Poland:

> 'Whenever, during a period of martial law, the Sejm is unable to assemble for a sitting, the President of the Republic shall, on application of the Council of Ministers, and within the scope and limits specified in Article 228, paras. 3–5, issue regulations having the force of statute. Such regulations must be approved by the Sejm at its next sitting'.

According to art. 234 (2) of the Constitution of the Republic of Poland such regulations 'shall have the character of universally binding law'.

It shall be stressed that *extra lege* legislative powers granted to the executive during states of emergency in contemporary Polish constitutional law, meaning the possibility to issue acts of a statutory rank, are vested only in one of two executive authorities known in the Polish legal system – the President of the Republic of Poland. *A contrario*, analogical competences have not been conferred on the second executive authority – the Council of Ministers.[8]

From the perspective of the Constitution of the Republic of Poland regulations with the effect of a statute are one of universally binding sources of law (differentiated in the polish legal order from legal sources of an internal character). The indi-

8 Cf. *Ryszard Mariusz Małajny*, Ustawa a akty ustawowe (Act and statutory acts), in: Jacek Czajnowski/Janusz Karp/Grzegorz Kuca/ Andrzej Kulig/ Piotr Mikuli/Anna Opałek (ed.), Ustroje, doktryny, instytucje polityczne. Księga jubileuszowa Profesora zw. dra hab. Mariana Grzybowskiego (Systems, doctrines, political institutions. Jubilee Book of the Professor Dr. hab. Marian Grzybowski), Kraków 2007, 199–208, at 201.

cated distinction of the commonly binding sources of law of an internal character – as it is often stressed in the polish constitutional law doctrine – originated long time ago and has never been a simple issue.[9] Above-mentioned differentiation constitutes a matter of interest of the polish constitutional law doctrine.[10] It is also the most innovative solution implemented in the 3rd Chapter of the Constitution of the Republic of Poland, which regulates the issue of sources of law.[11]

What is important, regulations with the effect of a statute – similarly to other acts of a statutory rank known in the constitutional regulations of other countries (such as decrees in the Italian Republic or ordinances (ordonanse) in the Fifth Republic of France) – should be placed at the same level in the hierarchy of the sources of universally binding law as ordinary statutes. There exists a view in the Polish law doctrine, that the fact that a regulation with the effect of a statute is of an equal binding power as an ordinary statute may be regarded as the most characteristic and distinct, as it is included in the name of such act, trait of this institution.[12]

It is also worth to add, that regulations with the effect of a statute are in Poland one of the commonly binding sources of law, which has not been listed in art. 87 of the Constitution of Poland, Chapter III, even though it concerns strictly the issue sources of the commonly binding law[13]. In my opinion, such a solution is not contradictory to the Polish Constitution, but – certainly – the regulation in the future of all commonly binding sources of law in one regulation would have an important value in ordering the entire system of sources of law in Poland. In art. 87 only the Constitution, ratified international agreements, statutes, regulations and acts of the local authorities binding in the area of their jurisdiction are listed. Regulations with the effect of a statute were regulated in a completely different article (art. 234 of the Constitu-

9 Cf. *Andrzej Bałaban*, Źródła prawa w polskiej konstytucji z 2 kwietnia 1997 r. (Sources of law in the Polish constitution of April 2, 1997), Przegląd Sejmowy (Sejm Review) 1997 No. 5, 33, at 34–35.

10 Cf. *Henryk Rot*, Koncepcja aktów normatywnych powszechnie i wewnętrznie obowiązujących a nowa Konstytucja (The concept of normative acts universally and internally applicable and the new Constitution), in: Aleksander Patrzałek (ed.), Problemy prawotwórstwa w nowej Konstytucji PRL (Problems of law-making in the new Constitution of the Polish People's Republic), Wrocław 1988, 176–199, at 176 and the following.

11 Cf. *Bałaban*, l. c., 34–35.

12 Cf. *Kazimierz Działocha*, remark no. 2 to art. 234, in: Lech Garlicki (ed.), Konstytucja Rzeczypospolitej Polskiej. Komentarz (Constitution of the Republic of Poland. Comment), vol. IV, Warszawa 2005, 1–4, at 2.

13 Cf. *Bartosz Skwara*, Rozporządzenie jako akt wykonawczy do ustawy w polskim prawie konstytucyjnym (Regulation as an executive act to the statutory law in Polish constitutional law), Warszawa 2010, 60.

tion) and a different chapter, taking into consideration the systematics of the Constitution, namely Chapter XI titled 'States of emergency'.

Noteworthy is that the Constitution of the Republic of Poland contains two types of limitations for issuance of regulations with the effect of a statute – both material (as some matters are excluded from their material scope) and temporary (they might be issued only during certain periods). In that context it shall be stated, that regulations with the effect of a statute – as it stems from above deliberations – may only be issued during martial law and only by the President of the Republic of Poland, and moreover it is necessary to fulfil additional premises constituted by the legislator which condition the application of this institution.

It shall be indicated that regulations with the effect of a statute – mentioning by the way that the competence for their issuance is limited in time to the period for which martial law is declared and personally to the President of the Republic of Poland – may be issued after simultaneous fulfilment of other similar premises indicated below, stemming from art. 234 (1) of the Constitution of the Republic of Poland and indicating that the possibility of issuance of Constitution of regulations with the effect of a statute exists only when the Sejm is not able to assemble for a sitting and upon application of the Council of Ministers to the President of the Republic of Poland. The application of the Council of Ministers is a premise necessary for the issuance of such regulation.[14]

What is more, the regulations with the effect of a statute issued by the President pursuant to art. 234 (1) of the Constitution of 1997 are subject to the Sejm's confirmation on the forthcoming sitting.[15] Refusal of such authorisation of a regulations with the effect of a statute means the loss of its legally binding power. Due to the lack of regulation in this scope, it is the Sejm, which shall specify the moment when this loss takes place.[16]

In the light of the above deliberations, it shall be indicated that there exist also some limitations concerning specification of the matters subject to regulation by means of an act of a statutory rank. As it is expressed in art. 234 (1) of the Constitution of the Republic of Poland, regulations of a statutory rank are issued 'within

14 K. *Działocha*, op. cit. (note 7), 2.

15 In this case, it means the first sitting of the Sejm taking place after issuance of a specific regulation with the effect of a statute.

16 Cf. *Bogusław Banaszak*, remarks to art. 234, in: Bogusław Banaszak, Konstytucja Rzeczypospolitej Polskiej. Komentarz (Constitution of the Republic of Poland. Comment), Warszawa 2012, 1110–1113, at 1113.

the scope and limits specified in Article 228, paras. 3–5'.[17] It means that the material scope of a regulation with the effect of a status – in relation to its personal scope – is limited in two respects. From the strictly material perspective – to regulation of matters included in art. 224 paras. 3 and 4 of the Constitution of the Republic of Poland. The third reference to art. 228 par. 5 of the Polish Constitution has no connection to specifying the scope within which issuance of regulations of a statutory rank is allowed – it is an order of having in regard the rule of proportionality as a fundamental rule applicable during the states of emergency in the course of regulating specified matters by an act of a statutory rank.[18]

IV. Assessment of the Institution of a Regulation with the Effect of a Statute in Extreme Situations of Martial Law

The institution of a regulation with the effect of a statute specified in the Constitution of 1997 – being a manifestation of an act of the executive of a statutory rank – is viewed as a unique institution. It is possible to execute it only when the state and its authorities are acting in the exceptional situation of a martial state.[19] Taking into account the above it shall be said, that the institution of a regulation with the effect of a statute constitutes only an exception form the rule of the exclusivity of parliamentary rulemaking competences approved in the Polish constitutional order. Therefore, the institution of the regulation with the effect of a statute embodies the only exception from the constitutional rule of exclusivity of parliamentary issuance of any acts with the effect of a statute.[20]

What is important, the institution of a regulation with the effect of a statute may *a priori* raise doubts about its compliance with the constitutional principle of the sepa-

17 Art. 228 (3–5) of the Polish Constitution indicates that: "3. The principles for activity by organs of public authority as well as the degree to which the freedoms and rights of persons and citizens may be subject to limitation for the duration of a period requiring any extraordinary measures shall be established by statute. 4. A statute may specify the principles, scope and manner of compensating for loss of property resulting from limitation of the freedoms and rights of persons and citizens during a period requiring introduction of extraordinary measures. 5. Actions undertaken as a result of the introduction of any extraordinary measure shall be proportionate to the degree of threat and shall be intended to achieve the swiftest restoration of conditions allowing for the normal functioning of the State."

18 Cf. K. *Działocha*, op. cit. (note 6), 3.

19 *Patyra*, op. cit. (note 2), 264.

20 Cf. *Garlicki/Zubik*, op. cit. (note 4), 47.

ration of powers. However, given the narrow scope of this regulation and – approved in Poland – a modern way of understanding the constitutional principle of the separation of powers (confirmed in Poland by the Constitutional Tribunal) should be considered that the regulations with the effect of a statute are not contradictory in this respect with the Polish Constitution. Moreover, such regulations should be considered in this context as compatible with other standards resulting from the Polish Constitution, such as principle of the checks and balances.

The possibility of issuance of regulations with the effect of a statute is the effect of granting the President of The Republic of Poland with a special competence during the times of martial law. Such competence – for the purpose of this article – may be described as the right to issue regulations with the effect of a statute.[21]

As I have already signalled it in this article, considering the specific way of arrangement of the three premises necessary for the declaration of martial law in the Constitution of the Republic of Poland – during which regulations with the effect of a statute may be issued – one might also point at the correctness of the research hypotheses, which assumes that in contemporary Polish constitutional law close connections between the regulation with the effect of a statue and the Polish situation and its international relations exists[22]. Limitation of the possibility of issuance of the described regulations only during the state of martial law – which may be declared due to circumstances connected to the international relations of Poland – on the grounds of the Polish Constitution leads to the conclusion, that a close and imminent bond between a regulation with the effect of a statute and the external situation of the state exists.

The indicated research hypothesis seems to be even more likely taking into consideration that on the grounds of the Constitution of the Republic of Poland there do not exist any connections of the regulation with the effect of a statute to the state's internal situation or any other circumstances which may constitute a basis for declaration of any other state of emergency (e.g. in the case of threats to the constitutional order of the state).[23] There also exist no basis for the issuance of regulations with the effect of the statute during times of normal functioning of the state.

21 Cf. *Kazimierz Działocha*, remark no. 1 to art. 234, in: Lech Garlicki (ed.), Konstytucja Rzeczypospolitej Polskiej. Komentarz (Constitution of the Republic of Poland. Comment), vol. IV, Warszawa 2005, 1, at 1.

22 Because the institution of an act of a statutory rank can be applied only when international circumstances (e.g. external threat to the state) justify the introduction of a martial law in Poland.

23 Cf. *Lech Garlicki*, Polskie prawo konstytucyjne. Zarys wykładu (Polish constitutional law. Outline of the lecture), Warszawa 2017, 158.

The close link between the institution of a regulation with the effect of a statute and the Poland's situation in external relations (therefore connecting this institution to circumstances being a basis of declaration of martial law and not any other state of emergency) was a completely intended and rationally justified intention of the Polish rule maker. In the legal doctrine a view may be found in this context that the Polish rule maker assumed that circumstances justifying the declaration of an emergency state during civil unrest or a state of natural disaster, contrary to circumstances being the basis for the declaration of martial law, do not cause that the Sejm is unable to assemble for a sitting, which could justify the application of the institution of regulation with the effect of a statute.[24]

Considering the above it may be said that the institution of a regulation with the effect of a statute is of a particularly narrow scope of application in the contemporary Polish constitutional law. It is also confirmed by the views expressed in the doctrine of the Polish constitutional law. *Andrzej Bałaban's* viev in that context is that the formula of a regulation with the effect of a statute expressed in art. 234 of the Constitution is 'exceptionally narrow'. What is more, in his opinion, such exceptionally narrow formula of a regulation with the effect of a statute actually emphasises the traditional precedence of a statute, and such primacy shall be viewed in the light of the system of sources of commonly binding law.[25]

It is also worth to indicate, that the institution of a regulation with the effect of a statute regulated in art. 234 of the Constitution has not yet ever been applied in the Polish practice. Therefore, so far it is a completely non-functioning institution.

Concerning considerations presented so far it shall now be pointed out, that in the Polish constitutional law doctrine some *de lege ferenda* postulates are formulated, which assume the implementation of systemic alterations in the scope of the institution of the executive's acts of a statutory rank. They concern, among others, the issue of implementation of new types of the executive's acts of a statutory rank into the Polish legal system (completely different from regulations of a statutory rank regulated in art. 234 of the Constitution), which would supposedly be issued not only in extraordinary systemic conditions (as martial law), but also in the course of state's ordinary

24 Cf. *Jerzy Jaskiernia*, Akty normatywne w stanach nadzwyczajnych (Normative acts in extraordinary states), in: Andrzej Szmyt (ed.), Konstytucyjny system źródeł prawa w praktyce (The constitutional system of sources of law in practice), Warszawa 2005, 136–156, at 141.

25 Cf. *Andrzej Bałaban*, Konstytucyjny system źródeł prawa po 15 latach obowiązywania (tezy) (Constitutional system of sources of law after 15 years of validity (thesis)), in: Andrzej Bałaban/Jerzy Ciapała/Przemysław Mijal (ed.), Źródła prawa w Rzeczypospolitej Polskiej w 15 lat po wejściu w życie Konstytucji z 1997 roku (Sources of law in the Republic of Poland in 15 years after the entry into force of the Constitution of 1997), Szczecin 2013, 9–15, at 11.

functioning. In the line with these concepts, such regulations could be used e.g. for the purpose of implementation of the EU law into the Polish legal order[26] (because currently in Poland the implementation of EU law into the state legal order is made only through classical statutory law).

Conclusion

Concluding all of the above deliberations it shall be expressed that *extra lege* legislative powers for the executive during states of emergency constitute an issue which is important and worth taking a closer look at form the perspective of the contemporary Polish constitutional law. The subject matter relates to the – known for many years now in the Polish legal order – institution of the acts of the executive of a statutory rank. What is symptomatic, issuance of such acts in the contemporary Polish constitutional law has been limited only to one of the exceptional situations, the martial law – which is connected to the situation of the state in its external relations – and no other ordinary or exceptional situations of the state empowers the executive to issue such acts.

26 Cf. e.g. *Janusz Trzciński/Marcin Wiącek*, W sprawie wprowadzenia do Konstytucji RP instytucji rozporządzenia z mocą ustawy w celu implementacji prawa Unii Europejskiej (On the introduction of the institution of a regulation with the force of law into the Constitution of the Republic of Poland in order to implement the law of the European Union), in: Piotr Radziewicz/Jan Wawrzyniak (ed.), Konstytucja Rząd Parlament. Księga Jubileuszowa Profesora Jerzego Ciemniewskiego (Constitution Government Parliament. Jubilee Book of Professor Jerzy Ciemniewski), Warszawa 2014, 340–347, at 340 and the following; cf. also *Ryszard Piotrowski*, O potrzebie rozporządzeń z mocą ustawy w polskim systemie stanowienia prawa (On the need for regulations with the force of law in the Polish law-making system), in: Andrzej Bałaban/Przemysław Mijal (ed.), Zasady naczelne w Konstytucji RP z 2 kwietnia 1997 roku (Supreme principles in the Constitution of the Republic of Poland of April 2, 1997), Szczecin 2011, 259–287, at 259 ff.

Resilience of Law in Times of Crisis. The Austrian Perspective with a View to other European Countries

Eva Schulev-Steindl

Abstract

Facing various terrorist attacks in Europe during the last years, Austria has to put the question, whether its legal order is sufficiently 'resilient' in a way that it is prepared to face various situations of crisis: A closer look at its present legal instruments (mainly emergency decrees by the Federal President, which up to now have never been issued) shows, that from an overall perspective the instruments seem to be basically suitable, but fragmented, not well coordinated and, to some extent, not efficient enough. Therefore, with a view to other European countries (Britain, France, Germany, Hungary, and Switzerland) the paper develops a regulatory model for times of emergency, trying to overcome these deficiencies while fully complying with rule of law and constitutional standards.

I. 'Resilience' of Law

Asking for the responsiveness of a legal order in events of crisis can be understood as raising the question of its 'resilience'. This concept generally means the ability of complex systems to return to their original state despite massive external or internal disturbances.[1] It is well known in engineering, ecology, psychology and other fields of science – but not yet widely used in jurisprudence. However, lawyers increasingly refer to 'resilience' when discussing, whether legal systems are sufficiently prepared to cope with unusual situations, such as disasters and crises in an adequate manner.[2]

Speaking of 'resilience' in the context of law though may be somewhat euphemistic. After all, when it comes to legal issues in the event of a crisis it is ultimately about 'hard facts', meaning powers – namely extended powers – of the state as well as associated coercive measures, with which the law tries to react to extraordinary situa-

1 Available at <https://de.wikipedia.org/wiki/Resilienz_(Ingenieurwissenschaften)#cite_note-AvG-3>, 29 August 2018; *Benjamin Scharte/Klaus Thoma*, Resilienz – Ingenieurwissenschaftliche Perspektive (Resilience – Engineering Perspective), Wiesbaden 2016; *Klaus Fröhlich-Gildhoff/Maike Rönnau-Böse*, Resilienz (Resilience), Munich 2015.

2 Cf. *Kai von Lewinski* (ed.), Resilienz des Rechts (Resilience of Law), Baden-Baden 2016.

tions, such as state dangers, crises or disasters.[3] So nothing must be glossed over: in question are instruments that clearly show the 'Gorgon's head' of power[4] behind law, and which are – what weighs heavily historically, but unfortunately today as well – very prone to abuse!

Nevertheless, the issue cannot be negated – the thing about crises is that they usually come unexpectedly. The state must be prepared. It is important and indispensable however, that reaction to such crises, law is entitled to, does not exceed the absolute necessary. Thus, even in a crisis, law and state must be bound by essential guarantees, namely fundamental rights and the rule of law in the material sense with all its fundamental principles, such as proportionality, the prohibition of arbitrariness and the principles of a fair trial.[5]

The ability to react to crises, the question of powers state should have in crisis situations, is a topical issue. Especially since the terrorist attacks of recent years, as we know them from France, Germany and Britain. However, other threat scenarios affecting the security situation of states nowadays are natural disasters, being likely to become more frequent due to climate change, as well as pandemics or attacks on critical infrastructures.

In the following therefore, based on a study[6] of a project team of the Universities of Vienna – *Susanne Reindl-Krauskopf, Farsam Salimi, Barbara Kraml* – and Graz – *Eva Schulev-Steindl, Markus Scharler, Julian Pekler* – Austrian law's ability of responding to situations of crises, i.e, its 'resilience', shall be examined closer. Thereby in comparison with Britain, France, Germany, Hungary and Switzerland – de lege lata as well as de lege ferenda – it will be discussed what kind of scenarios are to be seen as forms of crisis, what kind of competences and legal instruments exist in Austria and the other countries, what mechanisms are there to maintain the rule of law and protect human

3 So insistently *Ewald Wiederin*, Das Recht des Staatsnotstands in Österreich (The Law of State Emergency in Austria), in: Christian Grafl/ Bernhard Klob/Susanne Reindl-Krauskopf, 5. ALES-Tagung 2016 Freiheit versus Sicherheit (5th ALES Conference 2016 Freedom versus Security), Vienna 2017, 115–146, at 115 et seq.

4 *Hans Kelsen* in: Veröffentlichungen der Vereinigung der Deutschen Staatsrechtslehrer [VVDStRl] (Publications of the Association of German Constitutional Law Teachers) 3, Berlin 1927, 55.

5 In detail *ICJ*, Legal Commentary on the ICJ Geneva Declaration 2011.

6 For the following cf. *Susanne Reindl-Krauskopf/Eva Schulev-Steindl*, Reaktionsfähigkeit des österreichischen Rechts im Krisenfall (Responsiveness of Austrian law in events of crisis), in: ÖJK [Österreichische Juristenkommission – Austrian Section of the International Commission of Jurists – ICJ], (ed.), Krise der liberalen Demokratie? (Crisis of liberal democracy?), 2019, 229 et seq; *Susanne Reindl-Krauskopf/Eva Schulev-Steindl/Farsam Salimi/Barbara Kraml/Markus Scharler/Julian Pekler*, Resilienz des Rechts in Krisenzeiten (Resilience of law in times of crises), 2016; available at <http://bmi.gv.at/bmi_documents/2025.pdf>.

rights and finally, with regard to the Austrian legal background, what kind of regulatory model in compliance with the rule of law and constitutional standards seems to be suitable for times of crisis.

II. States of Emergency and Definition of Crisis

While political science understands the term 'crisis'[7] generally as an 'unplanned, unexpected, incalculable and untried situation' that 'places special demands on the actors' and cannot be controlled by 'daily routines' of organizations, authorities and companies[8] and is further characterized by a 'grave threat, a high degree of insecurity and immediate need for action',[9] jurisprudence often focuses on the notion of 'state calamity' as a state of emergency.[10] According to *Koja*[11], such a state of emergency constitutes a highly dangerous situation that urgently requires the rapid establishment and implementation of certain measures, without being able to accomplish this in the required hurry with the 'normal' legislative procedure, i. e. with the 'normally provided' organizational competences, procedures and substantive determinants of legal production.

In this sense, and against the background that an adequate legal regime should be able to cover a wide range of different, perhaps even unknown, crisis scenarios, it makes sense to understand the concept of a crisis as a risk or danger to the state, which makes certain measures urgently necessary (imminent danger) and for the accomplishment of which regular state (legal) procedures are inadequate (impending excessive demand on state structures).[12]

7 Cf. *Boris Porfiriev*, Disaster and Disaster Areas: Methodological Issues of Definition and Delination, International Journal of Mass Emergencies and Disasters 1995, Vol 13, No. 3, at 286 et seq.

8 *Thomas Jäger*, Strategische Führung in Krisen (Strategic Leadership in Crises), in: Thomas Jäger/Anna Daun/Dirk Freudenberg (ed.), Politisches Krisenmanagement (Political crisis management), Wiesbaden 2016, 3–16, at 3 and 8.

9 *Michael Herzog/ Tim Prior*, Krisenmanagement im internationalen Vergleich (Crisis management in international comparison), Center for Security Studies, Zürich 2013, 8.

10 Cf. *Oren Gross/Fionnualla N. Aoláin*, Law in Times of Crisis: Emergency Powers in Theory and Practice, Cambridge 2006, 249 et seq.; *Thomas Jäger* in: Thomas Jäger/Anna Daun/Dirk Freudenberg (ed.), Krisenmanagement (Crisis Management), 8.

11 *Friedrich Koja*, Der Staatsnotstand als Rechtsbegriff (State necessity as a legal definition), Pustet 1979, 18 with further notes; cf. also *Felix Ermacora*, Allgemeine Staatslehre (General State Theory), Berlin 1970, 860.

12 *Susanne Reindl-Krauskopf/Eva Schulev-Steindl/Farsam Salimi/Barbara Kraml/Markus Scharler/Julian Pekler*, Resilienz, 20 et seq.

1. State Risk

Therefore, in order to speak of a crisis in the above sense, an unexpected danger must arise for the state or the fulfillment of its essential functions. This may result from internal or exogenous factors, which is why the concept of state risk has traditionally been divided into three categories: an 'external danger' (esp. military threats from outside – which are not treated further here), an 'internal danger' (e. g. riots, terrorist attacks, paralysis of public life) and a 'state of disasters' (natural disasters, pandemics or economic crises)[13]. This differentiation however is increasingly losing its importance today and appears to be of little use in the given context: On the one hand the danger manifests itself always in the national territory, even if it is 'external' from its origin, and on the other hand a danger may arise in the interior by a threat from outside, whose avoidance is not a case of military defense, but lies in the competence of civil security authorities. Just consider a widespread threat from abroad for a large-scale terrorist attack inside the country.[14] It is therefore better to focus on specific phenomena causing dangers, such as natural disasters, anthropogenic disasters (e. g. traffic disasters, power plant accidents or industrial disasters), terrorist acts, or pandemics, i. e. cross-border epidemics with a large number of affected people.[15] So-called 'constitutional disturbances' (or constitutional crises), meaning 'abnormal state law situations' not triggered by factors outside the state structure, but by internal parameters, remain excluded.[16] In historical retrospective, a so-called 'self-disengagement' of the parliament by special political constellations is to be considered in this context.[17]

13 *Friedrich Koja*, l. c., at 29; *Schweigmann*, in: Dieter Nohlen/Rainer-Olaf Schultze, Lexikon der Politikwissenschaft (Lexicon of Political Science), Munich 2010, 666; cf. also. the German Constitution (dGG), which knows in its Art 87a (3) the 'external emergency' and in Art 87a (4) the 'internal emergency', more details cf. *Veit Petzoldt*, Schnittstellen polizeilicher und militärischer Sicherheit. Hilfeleistungen der Bundeswehr im Inneren angesichts zunehmend multipler Katastrophen- und Bedrohungslagen (Interfaces of police and military security. Assistance provided by the military internally in view of increasingly multiple catastrophes and threats), SIAK-Journal 2015 No. 3, 68, at 69.

14 Cf. *Friedrich Koja*, l. c.

15 More details cf. *Susanne Reindl-Krauskopf/Eva Schulev-Steindl/Farsam Salimi/Barbara Kraml/Markus Scharler/Julian Pekler* (note 6), 23 et seq.

16 Cf. *Johannes Heckel*, Diktatur, Notverordnungsrecht, Verfassungsnotstand: Archiv des öffentlichen Rechts (Dictatorship, Emergency Ordinance Law, Constitutional Emergency: Public Law Archive), 1932, 257 et seq.; *Heinz Kreutzer*, Der Ausnahmezustand im deutschen Verfassungsrecht (The state of emergency in German constitutional law), in: Ernst Fraenkel (ed.) Der Staatsnotstand (State emergency), Berlin 1965, 9 et seq.; *Friedrich Koja*, l. c., 29 et seq.

17 For the so-called 'self-disengagement' of the Austrian Federal Parliament in 1933 cf. *Ludwig Adamovich*, Das autoritäre System 1933–1938 zwischen Rechtsbruch und Gewissensentscheidung

Danger for the state will be given if at least one of the state functions of legislation, jurisdiction and administration is at risk. The state as a whole does not necessarily have to be affected, it can already be spoken of state risk when an important part of the state is affected. In this way, the term 'police emergency' may be used in the sense of 'a threat to the maintenance of public order and security', thus expressing that even a partial threat for the functioning of the state can represent a situation of crisis.[18] Furthermore such a sub-area risk exists if not the entire state is affected by a crisis, but only parts of its territory, such as a federal state. In this case, the sub-area is not to be understood functionally, but territorially.

2. Imminent Danger

A risk can only trigger a crisis if it requires rapid counteraction by public authorities,[19] in particular if state inaction increases the damage that has occurred or threatens. Whether there is such a risk of delay or even a present danger can be determined concretely only at the time of evaluation. The decisive factor is whether an acute obligation to act quickly must be assumed. Also, it is essential whether swift state action is possible through regular state acts and usual mechanisms of state decision-making are sufficient, or, due to the acute situation, a different set of instruments is needed.

Usually a danger in the above sense will occur suddenly and unpredictably (as in terrorist attacks or natural disasters). Threats that are known to the state for a longer period of time and are unlikely to realize in the near future – to what extent ever – leave (theoretically) enough time for legal and executive measures. The state can counter such risks with regular administrative processes and legal procedures. If, of course, it fails to take the necessary steps with regard to foreseeable events (e. g. an economic crisis or a crisis in the context of migration), due to misjudgment or neglect, nevertheless it is possible to speak of a crisis case, if the realizing danger cannot be combated with regular instruments.

(The authoritarian system 1933–1938 between breach of law and decision of conscience), Journal für Rechtspolitik 2015 No 2, 126, at 126.

18 Cf. *Ludwig Adamovich*, Handbuch des österreichischen Verfassungsrechts (Handbook of Austrian Constitutional Law), Vienna 6th ed. 1971, 106; *Felix Ermacora*, Österreichische Verfassungslehre (Austrian constitutional theory), Vienna 1980, 413; *Friedrich Koja*, l. c., 23 et seq.

19 *Friedrich Koja*, l. c., at 19.

3. Impending Excessive Demand on State Structures

Thus, essential for assuming a situation of crisis is furthermore, that a state's regular (decision) structures are in danger of being overburdened and ultimately a (partial) state failure is impending.[20] This is the case when the relevant risk and the consequent urgency of state action are particularly high. By this criterion emergency situations manageable with regular means (e. g. small-scale floods, a limited terrorist attack) can be distinguished from real crisis situations. At the same time, this point is very difficult to define in concrete terms. Depending on the state's function involved or its particular area concerned, excessive demand on state decision-making structures can be shown in various ways. So for example, a pandemic can bring excessive demands on public health, while a widespread natural disaster can lead to a collapse in the supply of essential services and goods.

III. The Crisis Case in Selected Legal Systems

When examining the legal framework for situations of crisis in various states[21] and (in a next step) comparing it to the Austrian legal system, it seems appropriate to distinguish between 'situations", 'responsibilities" and 'measures" covered by the relevant laws. As for the countries to be included in the comparison, Germany and Switzerland seem to be a good choice because their legal systems are similar to the Austrian. Furthermore, a comparison with Britain (UK), France and Hungary, despite their legal systems being less close, seems rewarding and appropriate: Britain is looking back on many decades of experience in dealing with acts of terrorism; France has had to

20 *Andrej Zwitter*, Rechtstheoretische Erläuterungen zur Begrifflichkeit und Theorie des Staatsnotstandsrechts (Legal Theoretical Explanations on the Concept and Theory of State Emergency Law), in: Andrej Zwitter (ed.), Notstand und Recht (Emergency and Law), Baden-Baden 2012, 20–46, at 24 et seq. deals with this aspect under the term 'enforcement emergency'.

21 The comparison is based on the following legal acts: Germany: Grundgesetz für die Bundesrepublik Deutschland (Basic Law for the Federal Republic of Germany, GG), in the version dated 13 July 2017; Switzerland: Bundesverfassung der Schweizerischen Eidgenossenschaft (Federal Constitution of the Swiss Confederation, Swiss Constitution), in the version dated 1 January 2016; Government and administrative organization law of 21 March 1997 (SchwRVOG), in the version of 1 January 2016; France : Loi n°55 385 du 3 avril 1955 relative à l'état d'urgence (French Emergency Provision Act), Version consolidée au 05 octobre 2016; Britain: Civil Contingencies Act 2004 (CCA 2004), in the version dated 18 November 2004; Hungary: The Fundamental Law of Hungary (Constitution of Hungary), in the version dated 25 April 2011.

react to several terroristic attacks during the last years and Hungary has moved into the center of debate in connection with enormous refugee flows recently.

Comparing these countries' laws reveals considerable similarities as well as various differences, the results being summarized as follows:

There is general consensus on whether and how a crisis should be defined. None of the examined states fully dispenses with a legal definition. In most countries, the case of crisis is determined broadly (Germany, Switzerland, France, and Hungary).[22] Britain[23] has chosen a combination of a general definition of three variations of emergency[24] with detailed specifications[25] and a 'catch-all clause' for further cases.[26]

Stronger differences can be identified when it comes to the question whether a crisis should be declared formally and who should be in charge of this act:

- Partly there is no formal declaration; thus, the presence of a crisis situation implicitly follows from the fact that emergency powers are exercised by the competent authorities (Germany, Switzerland).[27]
- Most states on the other hand have provided for a formal declaration of crisis, the relevant competence lying mainly with the executive (France: Council of Ministers, Britain: Chief Minister of the Crown, Hungary: Government),[28] while in Hungary[29] Parliament and in Britain[30] the Head of State also can declare a situation of crisis under specific circumstances.

22 Art 35 and Art 91 dGG, Art 173 (1) lit c and Art 185 (3) Swiss Constitution, Art 1 French Emergency Provision Act and Art 49 (1) lit b and Art 50 (1) Constitution of Hungary.

23 Art 19 paragraphs 1–4 CCA 2004.

24 This is the 'event or situation which threatens serious damage to human welfare' and the 'event or situation which threatens serious damage to the environment' in relation to the whole country or one of its parts or a region, furthermore 'war, or terrorism, which threatens serious damage to the security' of the country.

25 So in relation to an event or situation which threatens serious damage to human welfare, the loss of human life, disruption of a supply in money, food, water, energy and fuel, disruption of a system of communication or of services relating to health etc.

26 Thereafter, events or situations involving or causing disruption of a specified supplies, systems, facilities or services may be declared public policy threats by order of the Administration and by reconnection to Parliament.

27 Art 35 and Art 91 dGG, Art 173 (1) lit c and Art 185 (3) Swiss Constitution.

28 Art 2 French Emergency Provision Act, Art 20 (2 in connection with 5) CCA 2004, Art 53 (1) Constitution of Hungary.

29 Art 48 (1) lit b Constitution of Hungary.

30 Art 20 (1 in connection with 5) CCA 2004.

Differentiations too are to be seen with regard to a possible separation between the organ declaring a crisis and the one enabled to take concrete measures.

- On one hand, there exist strict rules for such a separation (e.g. in Hungary Parliament declares an emergency and the President then has the right to rule with emergency decrees).[31]
- On the other hand, one can find a complete concurrence of the declaring and the acting organ (Britain, Hungary: concerning 'dangerous condition)[32] or several hybrid forms (e.g. in France the Minister of Interior is part of the declaring cabinet and is subsequently empowered to take far reaching measures by himself).[33]

A key issue is who should be given the *competences* to take extraordinary action to handle the crisis. In this regard, agreement among the compared countries is not quite evident in the legal answers to this question.

- In some cases only this competence lies with organs of the legislature (Switzerland)[34] or the Head of State (Britain, Hungary).[35]
- For most constellations of crisis, the capacity to act is delegated to the executive; either to Government as a collective (Germany, Switzerland, Hungary),[36] or individual ministers (France, Britain),[37] furthermore to administrative heads of affected federal states (Germany)[38] or departments (France).[39]

While there are differences with regard to exceptional (administrative) *measures* in reaction to a crisis between the compared states, nearly all of them know exceptional regulatory competences in times of crisis.

31 Art 48 (1) lit b and Art 50 (3) Constitution of Hungary.

32 Art 20 (5) CCA 2004, Art 53 (1 and 2) Constitution of Hungary.

33 E.g. Art 2 in connection with Art 6 French Emergency Provision Act.

34 Art 173 (1) lit c Swiss Constitution.

35 Art 20 (1) CCA 2004, Art 50 (3) Constitution of Hungary.

36 Art 35 (3) and Art 91 (2) dGG, Art 185 (3) Swiss Constitution, Art 53 (2) Constitution of Hungary.

37 E.g. Art 6, 8 and 11 French Emergency Provision Act (Minister of Interior), Art 20 (2) CCA 2004 (Chief Minister of the Crown).

38 Art 35 (2) and Art 91 (1) dGG.

39 E.g. Art 8 and 9 French Emergency Provision Act.

- In Germany, exceptional measures are limited to the right of the federal states to request assistance and to the Federal Government's subsidiary competence of intervention.[40]
- Most of the compared states have provided for emergency decrees as a means of reacting to critical situations (Switzerland, France, Britain, Hungary)[41].
- In addition, there exist a few other forms of intervention like ordinary federal decrees.[42]
- Britain and France have, contained in a specific act, the most detailed rules concerning substantive and formal requirements for emergency measures.[43]

Legal comparison in all countries shows *constitutional limitations and restrictions* based on fundamental rights and the rule of law that have to be observed while taking extraordinary measures, esp. emergency decrees.

- Therefore, it is requested regularly, that in general an intervention must be necessary and proportionate (explicitly: Switzerland, Britain)[44]. Specific restrictions result from fundamental rights regularly allowing no or only limited interference.[45]
- When it comes to emergency law in form of decrees content-related restrictions can be found in constitutional and ordinary laws (Switzerland).[46].
- Partly, there is an obligation to limit emergency law to a certain period of time (Switzerland).[47] With regard to emergency decrees, there is often a maximum period of validity after which the decree ceases to be in force (Switzerland,

40 Art 35 (2 and 3) and Art 91 dGG.

41 Art 173 (1) lit c and Art 185 (3) Swiss Constitution, Art 5 (2) French Emergency Provision Act, Art 20 et seq. CCA 2004, Art 50 (3) and Art 53 (2) Constitution of Hungary.

42 Art 173 (1) lit c and Art 185 (3) Swiss Constitution, Art 6-1 (1) French Emergency Provision Act.

43 Art 5 et seq. French Emergency Provision Act, Art 22 CCA 2004.

44 Art 5 (2) Swiss Constitution and Art 23 (1) CCA 2004.

45 Cf. for example Art 36 Swiss Constitution, Art 23 (5) lit b CCA 2004, Art 54 (1) Constitution of Hungary.

46 Art 185 (3) Swiss Constitution.

47 Art 185 (3) Swiss Constitution.

Britain, Hungary)[48] and the relevant measures can only be prolonged by legislature or with its consent.

Finally, the compared legal systems provide for different *types of legal protection and subsequent control through legislative and executive.*

- Some of the states have established subsequent parliamentary control relating to emergency decrees (Britain)[49].
- When it comes to intensive interventions, participation of public prosecution or jurisdiction can be necessary (France).[50]
- Emergency measures taken can be subject to specific judicial control as in France by administrative courts.[51] Partly, an appeal to the constitutional court is available, especially in disputes concerning conflicts of competences (Germany).[52]

IV. Crisis Regulation in Austrian Law

In order to determine the reactivity or 'resilience' of Austrian law in more detail, it is first necessary to identify the relevant competences and legal instruments related to the crisis at federal and state level and to define their basic rights framework. Taking into account the findings of the legal comparison, their usefulness and effectiveness can then be assessed, and approaches can be taken to improve the legal situation.

1. Emergency Decrees of the Federal President

The Austrian Federal Constitution (Bundes-Verfassungsgesetz – B-VG[53]) only deals explicitly with a crisis in a few articles, the most important being Art 18 (3–5) B-VG. It contains the emergency prescription right of the Federal President and authorizes him to take measures by means of provisional ordinances amending the law, but only

48 Art 7d (2) and (3) SchwRVOG, Art 26 (1) CCA 2004, Art 50 (5) and Art 53 (3) Constitution of Hungary.

49 Art 27 and the following CCA 2004.

50 Art 11 French Emergency Provision Act.

51 Art 14–1 French Emergency Provision Act.

52 Art 93 (1) dGG.

53 BGBl (Federal Law Gazette) 1930/1 (repeated issue) in the version of BGBl I 2017/138.

under three conditions.[54] Thus, firstly, the immediate adoption of such measures must be necessary to avert obvious, irreparable damage to the general public; secondly, this must occur at a time when Parliament ('National Council') is not convened, cannot meet in time or is hindered in its activities by force majeure; and thirdly, the president also requires the cooperation (proposal) of the Federal Government and the standing subcommittee of the parliament. Subsequently, the ordinances must also be countersigned by Government. Other provisos are the reconnection of emergency ordinances amending the law to Parliament, namely, on the one hand, the obligation to submit the ordinance to the National Council, and on the other hand, the possibility for the latter to confirm the ordinance by law within four weeks or to demand its repeal by Government. Areas of law considered particularly sensitive (federal constitutional law, right of association, tenant protection law, labour and social security law) may not be amended by the emergency ordinance law. In addition, measures are prohibited which imply a sale of federal assets or a permanent financial burden on the federation or a financial burden at all on the Länder (states), municipalities or citizens.

In an overall view, it becomes apparent that the emergency prescription law of the Federal President only appears at first glance to be an instrument for rapid action in a crisis; the large number of conditions and restrictions make it seem impractical for emergencies. Without a doubt, the historical legislator was very keen to prevent abuse or unilateral political exploitation of the emergency ordinance right by the numerous hurdles.[55] The fact that emergency ordinance has never been used in the second republic (since 1945) confirms the assessment of only limited applicability; however, it should not be considered as a completely ineffective instrument. Especially in combination with the other means of the Federal President, especially the right to dissolve the National Council, the emergency ordinance right should not be underestimated.[56]

54 More details *Heinz Mayer/Gabriele Kucsko-Stadlmayer/Karl Stöger*, Grundriss des österreichischen Bundesverfassungsrechts (Basic Plan of the Austrian Federal Constitutional Law), Vienna 11th ed. 2015, notes 639 et seq.; *Heinz Mayer/Gerhard Muzak*, Das österreichische Bundes-Verfassungsrecht (Austrian Federal Constitutional Law), Vienna 5th ed. 2015, 150; *Bernhard Raschauer*, Art 18 Abs 3 bis 5 B-VG, in: Karl Korinek/Michael Holoubek et al (ed.), Österreichisches Bundesverfassungsrecht (Austrian Federal Constitutional Law), Vienna 6th ed. 2003.

55 Also *Mathis Fister*, Staatsnotstandsrecht in Österreich (State emergency law in Austria), in Andrej Zwitter (ed.), Notstand und Recht (Emergency and Law), Baden-Baden 2012, 160–200, 165.

56 In this sense also *Mathis Fister*, Staatsnotstandsrecht 166; *Ewald Wiederin*, in: Christian Grafl/Bernhard Klob/Susanne Reindl-Krauskopf (note 3), at 145.

2. Transfer of Residence, Dismissal of the Highest Authorities and Dissolution of the National Council

Not expressly for a crisis, but for 'the duration of extraordinary circumstances', the Federal President may under Art 25 (2) B-VG transfer the seat of the National Council and under Art 5 (2) B-VG the seat of the highest authorities to another location in Austrian territory at the request of the Federal Government.

The Federal President, the Federal Government and the majority in the National Council cannot only be the main persons responsible for dealing with a crisis, but potentially may also belong to its perpetrators. Theoretically, there is a danger that the representatives elected by the people will not fulfil their constitutional duties but will act against the interests of the people or the Republic of Austria for personal, ideological or other reasons. This addresses serious violations that reach the threat level of a crisis in the above sense. For this case, the legislature provides for the possibility of dismissing the Federal President (Art 60 (6) B-VG), the Federal Government, the Federal Chancellor or one or more Federal Ministers (Art 70 (1) B-VG), and to dissolve the National Council in its entirety (Art 29 (1) B-VG).

3. Assistance by the Austrian Armed Forces

The Austrian Armed Forces also play an important role in three specific areas of crisis management. For the 'protection of constitutional institutions and their capacity to act and the democratic freedoms of their inhabitants', the 'maintenance of order and internal security' and – of particular importance in practice – 'the provision of assistance in the event of natural disasters and accidents of exceptional scope', the Federal Constitution contains so-called special powers of the 'lawful civil authority' (Art 79 (2) B-VG).[57] In principle, the Federal Armed Forces are called upon by instructions establishing an ad hoc subordination relationship with the requesting authority. In addition, the Federal Armed Forces are also to intervene independently for the three purposes mentioned in the B-VG, namely when the competent authorities are unable to bring about military intervention due to force majeure, while immediate action is required. It should be mentioned, however, that this competence of the armed forces ends when the competent authority regains its ability to function.

57 *Michael Truppe*, Art 79 B-VG, in: Benjamin Kneihs/Georg Lienbacher, Rill-Schäffer-Kommentar Bundesverfassungsrecht (Rill-Schäffer commentary Federal constitutional law), Vienna 9th ed. 2012, notes 23 et seq.

4. Declaration of Crisis and Competences

The Austrian B-VG does not contain any explicit competence for the Federal Government, the Federal President or any other body to officially declare – at federal level – the existence of a crisis. This is an important difference to other legal systems, such as the dGG, which stipulates in Art 80a that the Bundestag may determine by a two-thirds majority that such a 'tension case' exists. This statement is then followed by specific legal consequences and mechanisms in the event of a crisis. The B-VG does not grant comparable competence to any organ, which is not beneficial for legal certainty. Thus, for example with regard to powers such as the competence for emergency regulation, it may only be decided ex post (by the Constitutional Court) whether the conditions for its use have been met. However, the B-VG itself does not contain any specific instruments relating to crises, apart from the broad and scarcely determined authorization of Art 18 (3–5) B-VG.

But certain instruments that can be used in crisis situations are to be found at an ordinary law level. In particular, the powers of security police law, such as the imposition of street bans, the dissolution of occupations and eviction orders, are to be considered.[58] These instruments are limited in time and territory.

In asylum law, the Federal Government was authorized to declare, in agreement with the main committee of the National Council (with written justification to it), by ordinance that there is a threat to the maintenance of public order or the protection of internal security.[59] If the government issues such a regulation, which according to the legislative materials is not only permissible in acute but already in foreseeable danger situations, specific (stricter) criteria for the submission of applications for international protection by foreigners before Austrian authorities apply as long as the regulation is valid and – in derogation from Art 67 (2) Treaty on the Functioning of the European Union (TFEU) – border controls at the EU internal borders are carried out. This regulation was adopted in 2016 explicitly 'against the background of the… [then] migration process and the resulting challenges in the area of asylum and migration' in order to prevent an internal crisis due to an overload of the Austrian asylum system by too large a number of asylum seekers to be cared for. This provision can certainly help to counteract such an overstraining of the asylum sys-

58 Closer *Ludwig Adamovich/Bernd-Christian Funk/Gerhart Holzinger/Stefan L. Frank,* Österreichisches Staatsrecht (Austrian constitutional law), Vienna Volume 4 2nd ed. 2017, notes 53.028 et seq.; *Karim J. Giese,* Sicherheitspolizeirecht (Security police law), in: Susanne Bachmann et al (eds.), Besonderes Verwaltungsrecht (Special administrative law), Vienna 11th ed. 2016, 41–84, 41 et seq.

59 § 36 Asylgesetz (Asylum Law), BGBl I 2005/100 in the version of BGBl I 2016/24.

tem, but, since it does not refer, at least in the light of the circumstances, to a danger to the state in the proper sense, it should not be qualified as typical emergency law.

5. Securing the Functionality of Authorities

Cases are conceivable in which necessary administrative procedures or workflows become (technically) unfeasible (a large number of employees cannot reach the authority due to extraordinary elementary events or circumstances; the publication of legal provisions on the internet is impossible because of a blackout). In this context, the instruments of administrative assistance (Art 22 B-VG) and the first general duty of the security authorities to provide assistance can be made fruitful. In the event of a blackout (when internet is not available), there is the obligation to publish laws in other forms (in the sense of Art 49 (3) B-VG), which means that they must be generally accessible and completely and permanently identifiable. On the whole, the impression is that there are merely isolated regulations instead of a clear concept.

6. Modification of Law in Times of Crisis

A central problem in a crisis situation is often that a solution to existing problems is practically possible, but not permissible within the framework of existing law, which primarily was created for regulatory rather than crisis situations. Austria was confronted with a comparable problem in 2015, when the supply and accommodation of a number of asylum seekers far above the long-term average[60] was in fact possible in federal real estate, but this was prevented by the need to comply with various legal provisions (e. g. building law) falling within the competence of the Länder or the municipalities. This 'stalemate' was finally resolved by amending the division of competences and introducing a so-called 'right of the Federation to intervene' by means of a constitutional law.[61] On the basis of this, the Federal Minister of the Interior can order the corresponding uses or conversions of buildings owned by or available to the Federal Government and approve them in a shortened procedure; all other necessary permits will be replaced.

60 In 2015, 88,340 asylum applications were filed in Austria, approximately the same number as in the five previous years (2010–2014); in the period 2006–2015, a total of 230,680 asylum applications were filed; cf. *Migrationsrat für Österreich* (ed.), Bericht des Migrationsrats (Report of the Migration Council), Vienna 2016, 17 f.

61 Cf. Art 3 Abs 1 and 6 BVG über die Unterbringung und Aufteilung von hilfs- und schutzbedürftigen Fremden (Federal Constitutional Law on the Accommodation and Distribution of Foreigners in Need of Help and Protection), BGBl I 2015/120.

This example shows that, in a European legal comparison, Austrian constitutional law belongs to the group of constitutions that are more flexible and easier to amend. Commandments of inviolability or guarantees of eternity as in France or Germany do not exist. Yet, unlike 'normal' constitutional law, the basic principles of the Federal Constitution can only be amended by an additional referendum and not merely by a majority in Parliament that changes the constitution.[62] This 'rigidity' of the basic principles gives them a higher rank than the rest of constitutional law.

With regard to this hierarchy of the legal system, it can be generally said that, according to prevailing opinion, any Austrian legal norm can be amended in the formal procedure provided for this in legal continuity; but the higher the norm stands in hierarchy the more difficult this is. However, this structure is broken – among the provisos outlined above – by the law-changing emergency ordinances of the Federal President or the State Governments (see below).

In contrast to the German Constitution, which provides for a simplified procedure for legislation in the case of defence (Art 115a ff dGG), the Austrian Federal Constitution does not have a modified legislative procedure in the case of crisis; such a procedure results only indirectly from the aforementioned emergency ordinance law. Constitutional law (Art 10 (1) no 15 B-VG) on the other hand, provides for a temporary change in the distribution of powers (towards the federation), 'on the occasion of or in the wake of a war to ensure uniform economic management, in particular also with regard to the supply of the population with consumer goods'.[63]

Apart from the question of formal enactment or amendability of Austrian legislation, it should be noted that a large part of the law applicable in Austria is of a European Union nature, which is why Austria no longer or only under special conditions can legislate in these areas. It should also be emphasized that, in addition to the formal procedure, the substantive provisos, in particular fundamental rights and freedoms, must always be observed in lawmaking – also and especially in the event of a crisis.

7. Provisions for Crisis Management on a State Level

The most prominent constitutional mechanism for times of crisis on the level of federal states (Länder) is on the one hand the right of the State Government to issue emergency decrees under Art 97 (3 and 4) B-VG. This competence is bound to sim-

62 'Overall modification of the constitution', Art 44 (3) B-VG.

63 Cf. *Michael Truppe*, Art 10 Abs 1 Z 15 B-VG, in: Benjamin Kneihs/Georg Lienbacher (note 20).

ilar conditions and restrictions as the corresponding right of the Federal President,[64] yet limited in its scope to the territory and law of the land.[65] On the other hand there is the State Governor's competence to take emergency executive measures (e. g. asking for assistance by the army in case of a disaster) within the area of direct federal administration under Art 102 (5) B-VG,[66] which again is limited to the borders of the state.[67]

Those rules are accompanied by many state laws, among which disaster protection laws play the key part: While the federation is responsible for legal measures aiming at the prevention of disasters, states have the competence to combat concrete disasters.[68] The states' disaster protection laws[69] usually characterize a disaster as an unexpected, occurred or imminent damage to humans and material assets of an exceptional scale based on natural phenomena or other causes. Competences to take measures often are distributed according to the dimension of the disaster to authorities on a municipal or district level. The competent authority functions as head of operations and can use assistance services (like ambulance and fire brigades). Some states require a declaration of a state of emergency to apply disaster protection law while others leave it to the discretion of the authority to decide when and which measures should be taken. Concrete measures for situations of crisis are: requiring everybody's assistance within reasonable bounds, entering and using properties, evicting bystanders from the disaster area, imposing area-based closures and so on. To enforce

64 *Willibald Liehr*, Art 97 Abs 3 bis 4 VG in: Karl Korinek/Michael Holoubek et al (ed.), Österreichisches Bundesverfassungsrecht (Austrian Federal Constitutional Law), Vienna 4th ed. 2001.

65 *Wolfgang Pesendorfer*, Art 97 B-VG in: Benjamin Kneihs/Georg Lienbacher, Rill-Schäffer-Kommentar Bundesverfassungsrecht (Austrian Federal Constitutional Law), Vienna 2nd ed. 2002 (note 25).

66 This regulation should not replace legislative procedures (in contrast to Art 97 B-VG), but it should rather compensate failures of the highest federal organs by acting with emergency decrees in the field of direct federal administration under Art 97 B-VG, *Mathis Fister* (note 55), at 170.

67 Cf. *Gerhart Holzinger*, Die Notstandskompetenz des Landeshauptmannes im Sinne der B-VG-Novelle 1984 (The emergency competence of the state governor in the sense of the B-VG amendment 1984), Vienna 1988, 8.

68 *Peter Bußjäger*, Katastrophenprävention und Katastrophenbekämpfung im Bundesstaat (Disaster prevention and disaster control in the federal state), Vienna 2003, 46. Agreeing *Helmut Hörtenhuber*, Katastrophenschutz als Problem der bundesstaatlichen Kompetenzverteilung (Disaster control as a problem of the federal distribution of competences), Zeitschrift für Verwaltung (Journal for Administration) 2007 No. 2, 154, at 161.

69 For details of federal states legislation, addressed in the following, cf. *Susanne Reindl-Krauskopf/Eva Schulev-Steindl/Farsam Salimi/Barbara Kraml/Markus Scharler/Julian Pekler* (note 6), 162 et seq.; in general *Josef Müllner*, Rechtliche Rahmenbedingungen der Katastrophenbekämpfung (Legal framework for disaster control), Vienna 2014, 228.

such measures authorities and emergency forces are entitled to use direct administrative command and coercive power.

Existing disaster protection law appears to be doing fairly well in its task of combating disasters. A problem yet seems to lie in the complicated division of competences which can result in a delay of necessary actions and in the fact that competences are restricted to the territory of the states. As a result, cross-border alert and disaster response facilities have been established in practice on a more or less informal way, such as the so-called 'State Crisis and Disaster Management' coordinated by the Federal Ministry of the Interior.

8. Fundamental Rights in Times of Crisis

Executive and legislative measures in times of crisis often are very invasive. In the event of crisis aspects of effectiveness, flexibility and speed of government action are in conflict with indispensable guarantees of the rule of law, as enshrined in the fundamental rights and freedoms of Austrian and European law, esp. in the relevant Austrian 'Staatsgrundgesetz' (StGG),[70] the European Convention on Human Rights (ECHR) and the Charter of Fundamental Rights of the European Union (CFR). The question arises whether these tensions can be resolved by mechanisms inherent in fundamental rights, such as the requirement of proportionality, or whether further steps, such as a temporary suspension of certain fundamental rights, might be necessary.

Leaving apart the principle of equality,[71] with its prohibition of discrimination and general requirement of objectivity, fundamental rights of community and economic life (e. g. freedom of expression and property[72]) as well as organizational and procedural guarantees,[73] in times of crisis fundamental rights of the person are of great relevance. The numerous aspects in this context can only be highlighted:

70 Staatsgrundgesetz vom 21. December 1867, über die allgemeinen Rechte der Staatsbürger für die im Reichsrathe vertretenen Königreiche und Länder (StGG – Basic Law of 21 December 1867 on the General Rights of Nationals in the Kingdoms and Länder represented in the Council of the Realm), RGBl (Reichsgesetzblatt – Imperial Law Gazette) 1867/142 in the version of BGBl 1988/684.

71 Art 7 B-VG and 2 StGG.

72 Freedom of expression: Art 10 ECHR, Art 13 StGG, Art 11 CFR; Freedom of association and assembly: Art 12 StGG, Art 11 ECHR, Art 12 CFR; Guarantee of property: Art 5 StGG, Art 1 1st additional protocol of ECHR, Art 17 CFR.

73 In particular, the right to the statutory judge (Art 83 (2) B-VG), the right to a fair trial (Art 6 ECHR, Art 47 and 48 CFR), the prohibition of retroactive penal law (Art 7 ECHR), the double punishment ban (Art 4 7th additional protocol of ECHR) and the right to an effective complaint (Art 13 ECHR).

The fundamental right to life (Art 85 B-VG, Art 2 ECHR with its 6th and 13th additional protocol, Art 2 CFR) includes the absolute right not to be sentenced to death and the states' obligation to protect human life, which for example could be violated if a state fails to take sufficient precautionary measures against life-threatening disasters.[74] On the other hand under Art 2 (2) ECHR it is, when absolutely necessary, allowed to interfere with the right to life in cases of defense of any person from unlawful violence (lit a), of ensuring a proper arrest or preventing the escape of a prisoner (lit b) or of suppression of revolts (lit c) within the rules of law.

Art 3 ECHR (Art 4 CFR) – absolutely and reflecting the respect for human dignity (Art 1 CFR) – prohibits torture and inhuman or humiliating punishment and treatment.[75] The prohibition of slavery and forced labour (Art 4 ECHR, Art 5 CFR) on the other hand knows exemptions for emergency situations and disasters (thus allowing disaster protection law to require everybody's assistance).[76]

There are undoubtedly many points of contact between crisis management measures and the right to personal freedom, as enshrined in the Constitutional Act on the Protection of Personal Freedom (BVGPersFr[77]) in conjunction with Art 5 ECHR (Art 6 CFR)[78] – arrest, house detention or curfew being interferences with this right. Personal freedom may only be interfered with if this is provided for by law and proportionate and if one of the cases listed in Art 2 (1) BVGPersFr is present: for example, what is relevant for combating pandemics, if the person concerned constitutes a source of danger for the spread of infectious diseases, and also, for example in connection with terrorist acts, if a criminal offence is suspected. In certain constellations, e. g. where there is a risk of escape or collusion, arrest is only permissible with a court order. In case of imminent danger (or termination of an attack etc.), a judicial order can be waived, but only under the strict condition that a judge cannot actually be reached – using today's technical means – and that the existence of grounds for detention must result from a concrete fact. Arrest or detention must therefore only be used as a last resort.

74 Cf. European Court of Human Rights (ECtHR) 20.03.2008, 15339/02, *Budayeva*.

75 More details *Francis G. Jacobs/Robin C. A. White/Claire Ovey*, The European Convention on Human Rights, Oxford 7th ed. 2017, 183 et seq.

76 In detail *Pieter van Dijk/Fried van Hoof/Arjen B. van Rijn/Leo Zwaak*, Theory and Practice of the European Convention on Human Rights, Cambridge 5th ed. 2018, 434 et seq.

77 Bundesverfassungsgesetz über den Schutz der persönlichen Freiheit (Federal Constitutional Law on the Protection of Personal Freedom), BGBl 1988/684 in the version of BGBl I 2008/2.

78 More details *Andreas Hauer*, Freiheit der Person und Freizügigkeit (Freedom of the person and freedom of movement), in: Detlef Merten/Hans-Jürgen Papier/Gabriele Kucsko-Stadlmayer, Grundrechte (Fundamental Rights), Heidelberg 2nd ed. 2014, § 11.

Art 8 ECHR (Art 7 CFR) guarantees the right to protection and respect of privacy,[79] including data from private communications (location data, call data, etc.). In the event of a crisis, measures such as mobile phone location, search, surveillance or data retention therefore interfere with the fundamental right to privacy and must also be measured against the fundamental right to data protection.[80] According to this, state restrictions on the right to confidentiality of personal data – apart from the vital self-interest of this person or with his or her consent – are only permissible if this is done legally and is necessary to safeguard a public interest within the meaning of the legal reservation in Art 8 ECHR.[81] Forms of covert data collection, such as those used in observation and covert investigations, therefore require a particularly conscientious consideration of the necessity and appropriateness of these investigations by the legislator.

The right to privacy also comprises the right to respect one's home, which specifically is guaranteed in Art 9 StGG in conjunction with the Rights of the Home Act[82]. According to the latter house searches are only permitted with a court order, which can only be waived in certain cases (imminent danger, or entry in the act etc.).

All in all, this brief overview shows that fundamental rights – with the exception of those that are absolutely guaranteed, such as the prohibition of torture – may regularly be subject to certain legal and administrative restrictions. The precondition for their constitutional conformity is in general that they comply with the principle of proportionality,[83] i. e. pursue a legitimate objective in the public interest (e. g. the protection of public order and security) and represent an appropriate, necessary and adequate means of achieving this objective. With regard to crisis situations, it should be borne in mind that more important public interests (such as combating terrorism[84] or the security of life and health in connection with natural disasters) – pro-

79 *Francis G. Jacobs/Robin C. A. White/Claire Ovey* (note 75), 369 et seq.

80 As enshrined in § 1 Datenschutzgesetz (Data Protection Act), BGBl I 1999/165 in the version of BGBl I 2017/120.

81 In detail *Pieter van Dijk/Fried van Hoof/Arjen B. van Rijn/Leo Zwaak*, l. c., 674 et seq.

82 Gesetz vom 27. October 1862 zum Schutze des Hausrechtes (Law of 27 October 1862 on the protection of domestic rights), RGBl 1862/88 in the version of BGBl 1974/422.

83 In recent years, in particular, in the wake of the Austrian Constitutional Court's case-law the requirement of proportionality has developed into a general standard for the admissibility of restrictions on fundamental rights, *Gabriele Kucsko-Stadlmayer*, The general structures of fundamental rights, in: Merten/Papier/Kucsko-Stadlmayer (note 78), § 3 notes 98 et seq.

84 Cf. *Andrew Byrnes*, More Law or Less Law? The Resilience of Human Rights Law and Institutions in the 'War on Terror', in: Miriam Gani/ Penelope Mathew, Fresh Perspectives on the 'War on Terror', Canberra 2008, 127–158, at 127 et seq.

vided that the relevant measures are appropriate and necessary – tend to justify more intensive interventions.[85] As to some fundamental rights (personal freedom, protection of home rights) the admissibility of restrictions depends not only, or primarily, on proportionality, but also on the fulfilment of specific conditions – such as a judicial order. These can also be dispensed with in various constellations relevant in times of crisis (imminent danger, termination of an attack etc.).

Fundamental rights thus form a relatively dense network of constitutional provisos to protect the individual from state power, which by some might be perceived as too tight a corset in the event of a crisis, where rapid and flexible action is required. The question therefore arises as to what extent there is, or should be, the possibility of suspending fundamental rights in the sense of temporarily withdrawing fundamental rights obligations in the event of a crisis.[86]

While Art 20 StGG originally allowed for a suspension of certain fundamental rights (freedom of the person, rights of home, secrecy of correspondence, freedom of assembly and association, freedom of expression), after its abrogation by the B-VG[87] in 1920, genuine Austrian constitutional law no longer contains such a possibility, nor does the CFR.

However, Art 15 ECHR enables the state to suspend some of the obligations from fundamental rights 'in time of war or other public emergency threatening the life of the nation',[88] but excludes certain fundamental rights (e.g. Art 3 ECHR – prohibition of torture) as 'emergency- or derogation-proof'.[89] Moreover, suspension is only permitted on condition that there is no conflict with other obligations under international law and only to the extent strictly required by the situation. This means that

85 More details *Tiberiu Dragu/Mattias Polborn*, The Rule of Law in the Fight against Terrorism, American Journal of Political Science, Vol 58, No 2 (April 2014), 511 et seq.; *Katharina Pabel*, Bewährungsproben des Rechtsstaates und Reaktionsmöglichkeiten im Rechtsschutzsystem der EMRK (The rule of law put to the test and the possibilities for response in the ECHR's legal protection system), in: Grafl/Klob/Reindl-Krauskopf (note 3), 61–88, 78 et seq.

86 Cf. also *Ross J. Corbett*, Suspension of Law during Crisis, Political Science Quarterly, Winter 2012–13 Vol 127 No. 4, at 627 et seq.; *Guillaume Tusseau*, The Concept of Constitutional Emergency Power: A theoretical and comparative Approach, Archives for Philosophy of Law and Social Philosophy 2011 Vol 97 No. 4 , 498, at 511 et seq.

87 Art 149 (2) B-VG.

88 *William Schabas*, The European Convention on Human Rights, Oxford 2015, 596 et seq. public emergency exists when regular measures or restrictions on fundamental rights are clearly not sufficient to deal with the crisis, *Jacobs/White/ Ovey* (note 75), 118 et seq.; *Katharina Pabel*, l. c., 64 et seq. with further notes.

89 More details *David Harris/Michael O´Boyle and Warbick*, Law of the European Convention on Human Rights, Oxford 3rd ed. 2014, 844 and the following; Katharina *Pabel*, l. c., 61 et seq.

when Article 15 of the ECHR is invoked, it is not convention guarantees as a whole that are temporarily invalidated, but specific aspects of these guarantees in connection with concrete state measures.[90] And further that these measures must comply with the principle of proportionality,[91] which can be verified by the European Court of Human Rights (ECtHR). Even in an emergency, according to the jurisprudence of the ECtHR, e. g. a deprivation of liberty of two weeks or more without being brought before a judge is disproportionate.[92]

The suspension of fundamental rights permitted under the ECHR therefore amounts to a certain flexibility of its guarantees, which in many cases already results from the general requirement of proportionality outlined above. In any case, a more far-reaching possibility of suspending fundamental rights, e. g. enshrined in national law, does not seem necessary.

On the whole, the Austrian legal situation must be regarded as sufficiently 'resilient' against the background of national and European fundamental rights: Appropriate and necessary interference in fundamental rights caused by crisis situations can be justified by the principle of proportionality; specific admissibility conditions required by some fundamental rights can be waived under certain circumstances, for example in the event of imminent danger.

V. State of Emergency – Assessment in the Legal Comparison

If one tries now, with reference to the comparison outlined above with other selected legal systems, to specify or assess the responsiveness of Austrian law in the event of a crisis, the following can be stated:

1. Elementary Criteria

All legal systems examined (Britain, France, Germany, Hungary, Switzerland and Austria) know legally defined situations that trigger an emergency competence of a constitutional institution. Such situations are essentially threats to public security and

90 ECtHR 26.05.1993, 14553/98 ua, *Brannigan u McBride*; *Christoph Grabenwarter/Katharina Pabel*, Europäische Menschenrechtskonvention (European Convention on Human Rights), Munich, 6th ed. 2016, § 2 note 8.

91 *Pieter van Dijk/Fried van Hoof/Arjen B. van Rijn/Leo Zwaak* (note 76), 1070.

92 *Christoph Grabenwarter/Katharina Pabel*, l. c., § 2 note 11 with further references.

order, whereby the states examined formulate this threat differently and in part distinguish between threats to internal and external security.

All the legal systems examined define crisis in law, whereby a general definition is predominantly chosen, partly combined with specifications (Britain). The Austrian Federal Constitution in Art 18 (3) to (5) B-VG with the emergency ordinance right of the Federal President (and the similar rights of the State Governments) has a comparable competence for setting extraordinary legal acts in times of crisis – and thus a (rather general) definition of the crisis situation.

While some legal systems provide for the explicit declaration of crisis, such as Hungary (by Parliament or Government), Britain (by the Head of State or Senior Minister) and France (by decree of the Council of Ministers), this is not the case in Germany and Switzerland. A formal declaration of crisis is currently also unknown to the Austrian legal system (apart from the determination of the catastrophe according to some disaster control laws). The Federal President's emergency prescription right can be exercised if the relevant legal requirements are met. However, a constitutive determination of the circumstances of Art 18 (3) B-VG is not required.

As to the *competence* to declare a crisis case, legal comparison has shown that it is either separated from or coincides with the competence to take extraordinary measures for crisis management (there exist mixed forms too). In order to prevent abuse, the body proclaiming the crisis should be strictly *separated* from the organ enabled to take concrete measures.

2. Special Legal Emergency Powers

Competences and permissible measures in crisis situations are regulated very differently in the countries examined. Under German law, for example, the federal states (Länder) concerned (only) have rights to request aid, while the Federal Government in turn has subsidiary intervention powers. In all other legal systems examined, an *extraordinary emergency ordinance right* is provided for – in varying forms and detail. In Switzerland, the Federal Assembly as well as the Federal Council has such a right, thus existing special crisis competences of both the legislative and executive branches. In France, the Minister of the Interior and the Prefects have extensive emergency powers. In Britain, the Head of State or the Senior Minister who has declared a state of emergency can issue emergency ordinances, with Parliament having full powers of control. Both countries have adopted *special laws* to combat crises containing substantive and formal requirements for emergency measures. In Hungary, the emergency powers are vested in the Government (in case of 'danger') or the President of the Republic (in case of 'emergency'), the measures permitted in each case being regulated by specific laws.

The Austrian legal system, apart from the federal states' disaster protection laws, essentially only provides for an emergency decree competence of the Federal President under the provisos described above and a similar right of the State Governments. These competences are rather specific in terms of their scope and bound to the condition that the legislator is prevented from taking regular decisions. The other legal systems examined do not require legislature being prevented this way in crisis situations triggered by external factors; rather they call for interaction between Parliament and the executive branch.

Thus, the Austrian legal system, unlike others, neither has a general executive competence for the adoption of legal acts (general abstract provisions and individual measures) in crisis situations nor does it provide for a closer specification of possible measures and their boundaries in a special law constituting a comprehensive system of national crisis management.

3. Limits in Time and Scope

The legal systems examined have different restrictions on the content of special measures permitted in the event of a crisis. These must normally be *necessary* and *proportionate*. Further barriers result from the fundamental rights, into which, as a rule, only limited intervention is allowed. Furthermore, measures taken must not contradict to other constitutional provisos or even ordinary laws in general.

As to Austria, the emergency prescription competence of the Federal President is subject to a large number of such and other restrictions (e.g. prohibition on the sale of federal assets). Similar restraints exist for the analogous emergency ordinance right at state level. There are numerous restrictions due to the requirements of national and European fundamental rights, which on the other hand leave enough flexibility for effective measures to combat crises.

In addition, the legal systems analysed provide for mandatory time limits for the extraordinary measures taken in the event of a crisis (e.g. Switzerland) as well as absolute maximum periods after which crisis law expires (Switzerland, Britain, Hungary) and may only be extended by the legislature or with its consent.

With respect to the Austrian Federal President's right to issue emergency decrees a time limit results insofar as a decree issued by the President must, without delay, be submitted by the Federal Government to Parliament, which within four weeks must either pass a corresponding federal law replacing the ordinance or demand that the ordinance be immediately repealed by the Federal Government (the analogous applies for the emergency ordinance law of the State Government).

4. Maintaining the Rule of Law

The regulatory systems studied also include various forms of legal protection and scrutinizing parliamentary control. Partially a formal parliamentary control of the emergency measures previously taken by executive bodies is provided for (Britain). In addition, there is reviewing judicial control of the measures taken, e.g. in France, where emergency measures are examined by administrative courts. In Germany, appeal to the Federal Constitutional court on the applicability of crisis competences is also permissible.

In Austria, like all general legal acts, the emergency ordinances of the Federal President and the State Governments are subject to reviewing control by the Constitutional Court. Individual acts of authorities are reviewed by the administrative courts. Yet there are no specific legal protection and control mechanisms for extraordinary measures in the event of a crisis. The Austrian remedies system provides for the same substantive and temporal conditions in times of crises as under regular circumstances, which may lead to unsatisfactory results in serious crisis situations.

5. Result

Overall, it can be stated that although there are isolated regulations for crises in the Austrian Federal Constitution, their scope and detail cannot be compared with those of the other legal systems examined, even in combination with the further, rather fragmented, provisions found in ordinary law. After all, the legal comparison shows that, other than Austrian law, fully 'resilient legal systems not only provide a separate framework for nationwide coordination tasks in crisis situations, but also allocate competences for a nationwide crisis situation as a whole, provide special crisis management measures and have specific control mechanisms in place that, in the sense of checks and balances, are intended to prevent the abuse of crisis powers and the overstretching (in terms of content and time) of the case of crisis as far as possible.

In contrast, with the exception of the emergency prescription rights of the Federal President and the State Governments – which are tied to particularly strict provisos -, there is no regulation for Austria concerning the adoption of individual or general legal acts in crisis situations which would be suitable for the effective management of crisis situations as described above. In this respect, the reaction mechanisms of the Austrian legal system cannot be classified as fully adequate to deal efficiently and quickly with serious crisis scenarios.

VI. Regulatory Model de lege ferenda

If one therefore wants to improve the ability of the Austrian legal system to react to crises, approaches to an adequate regulatory regime can be worked out on the basis of the above analysis and the results of the legal comparison.[93] Such a legal regime should comprise the necessary constitutional foundations on the one hand and a specific legal basis ('Crisis Act") on the other hand. On a constitutional level the following key points should be regulated:

- For reasons of legal certainty and subsequent verifiability of concrete measures as well as to reduce the potential for abuse, a definition of the crisis case should be made. A general definition with an exemplary list of typical (overall) state crisis situations (such as in Britain) is recommended.

In order to increase publicity and avoid abuse, the applicability of the crisis regime should require a formal-constitutive act of declaring a crisis. The proclaiming body should be subject to a duty to state reasons for the specific occurrence of the crisis and should not be authorized to take the (first) crisis measures itself. There should be a link to the democratically legitimized legislature, for example by giving a 'Crisis Committee' of the National Council the power to declare a state of crisis. The proclamation should be specified according to the nature and extent of the crisis, should be limited to a maximum duration of six months and should be published in an appropriate form. If the conditions are met no longer, the crisis situation should also have to be declared over by the competent body before the end of six months.

- In the event of a crisis, a collegial body ('Crisis Cabinet') should ensure rapid action and be authorized to take crisis measures. This should in any case consist of the Federal Chancellor, the Minister of the Interior, the Minister of Defense and the Minister of Health. The involvement of the federal states should also be provided for in an appropriate form; furthermore, other decision-makers could also be co-opted and experts in an advisory capacity consulted.

In addition, constitution should authorize the ordinary federal legislature to adopt a 'Crisis Act', which, without having constitutional status itself, should have to be

93 In detail *Reindl-Krauskopf/Schulev-Steindl/Salimi/Kraml/Scharler/Pekler* (note 6), 216 et seq.

passed with increased quorums (presence of at least half of the members of Parliament and majority of two-thirds of the votes cast). Basic substantive determinants of the 'Crisis Act' should be:

- In the event of a crisis, the Crisis Cabinet should be authorized to adopt justified and proportionate measures (general and individual acts) to deal with the crisis, which will expire at the latest six weeks after their adoption, unless they are extended by Parliament.
- A demonstrative list of possible measures in the crisis act should be considered.
- Ordinances of the Crisis Cabinet should have possibly law-altering as well as law-complementing character. In any case, neither the amendment of federal constitutional law nor the crisis act itself should be permissible. A preliminary check of the legality of crisis cabinet regulations should be considered. This could be done by summary proceedings before the Constitutional Court or a special body, e. g. consisting of the presidents of the three high courts.
- The Crisis Cabinet should be empowered to enforce existing substantial law in the event that the competent authority is unable to act (subsidiary enforcement competence).
- The Crisis Cabinet should be obliged to report continuously on all crisis measures and to submit a final report to Parliament.

This should be accompanied by appropriate legal protection. Thus, existing provisions of the constitution would have to be adapted, e. g. with regard to the jurisdiction of the Federal Administrative Court concerning complaints against individual administrative acts of the Crisis Cabinet or the conditions and legal consequences of the review of ordinances by the Constitutional Court. An accelerated procedure and a supplementary compensation model (e. g. appropriate compensation regardless of fault for those affected by emergency measures) could also be considered.

VII. Concluding Remarks

The legal comparison has shown that the various legal systems deal with crises in rather different ways. What the regulatory systems nevertheless have in common is that they regard crisis law as a special regime and accordingly not only keep an eye on the efficiency and effectiveness of measures to overcome the crisis, but also on checks and balances to ensure the proportionality of the measures employed. Not least in this way, the potential for abuse, which is inherent in special regimes, is to be largely reduced. In particular, the aim is to prevent restrictions on civil rights being introduced into the regular body of law as permanent measures by way of a crisis law, and ultimately to undermine the guarantees of the rule of law and to permanently lower standards of fundamental and human rights.

Against this background, and despite the need to provide instruments enabling rapid and efficient action in a crisis, particular attention must be paid to a system of checks and balances for emergency regulations, which was also given specific importance with respect to the regulatory proposals outlined above. Furthermore, interdependencies between the individual building blocks of a possible legal framework for crises, as well as between these and the rest of the constitutional structure, must always be explored. Since a special law for crisis cases means a significant deviation from regular legislative and executive powers, the ultimate (socio-) political decision on such a special regime should not only fit as harmoniously as possible into the overall constitutional structure but also be based on a broad and thoroughly conducted social, political and scientific discussion.

Peace through Democracy? The Use of Constitutions in Post-conflict Situations

Manon Bonnet

Abstract

The end of the decolonization process and the change in the nature of armed conflicts slowly changed the understanding of peace among international actors. Going beyond the bare absence of armed conflicts, they came to focus on elements that are more likely to ensure sustainable peace. In other words, there has been a shift in the understanding of what peace is, moving from negative peace to positive peace. Among the tools identified as peace building elements, democracy has emerged as the political regime most capable of ensuring lasting peace. In this paper, I will question the grounds to use democracy as a peace making tool, but also its limits in an international society that has changed a lot since *Kant* published his 'Perpetual peace'.

I. Introduction

The international peace and security system was renewed after the end of WW2. New tools were created in order to guarantee that traumatic past events will not occur again. This commitment to avoid violent conflicts led to the identification of tools thought to be able to create sustainable peace. Democracy is nowadays one of these tools. The end of the decolonization process and the change in the nature of armed conflicts slowly changed the understanding of peace among international actors. Going beyond the bare absence of armed conflicts, they came to focus on elements that are more likely to ensure sustainable peace. In other words, there has been a shift in the understanding of what peace is, moving from negative peace to positive peace. Among the tools identified as peace building elements, democracy has emerged as the political regime most capable of ensuring lasting peace.

Democracy is generally understood under *A. Lincoln's* vision as the 'government of the people, by the people and for the people'. As such, democracy is a link between the people and its government. A democratic regime is 'an organization of a society, where those who govern do so for, with the consent of, and with regular consultation of the governed'.[1] Beyond this basic idea of what democracy is, its implementation takes different forms. From *Rousseau's* direct democracy, to *Montesquieu's* represent-

1 *Rein A. Müllerson*, Democracy promotion: Institutions, international law and politics, vol. 2008, Recueil des cours de l'Académie de droit international de La Haye, 2009, 9, 33.

ative democracy, including *Habermas'* deliberative democracy, there are many ways to realise the democratic ideal. Elections have emerged as a crucial factor of identification of democratic regimes. Furthermore, 'materially, democracy became non-detachable from the protection of human rights which content has extended among the different generation. From a procedural approach, the rule of law became an essential requirement of democratic regime'.[2]

The recognition of democracy as a peace building tool is due to the idea that democracy leads to peace. Rooted in *Immanuel Kant's* theory, this idea – commonly called democratic peace – is a cornerstone of contemporary international relations.[3] By including the domestic organisation of the state as a mean to ensure international peace, democratic peace has changed the international political and legal order. Even though this idea is widely accepted and used, democracy is not a self-evident peace building tool.

In this paper, I will question the grounds to use democracy as a peace making tool, but also its limits in an international society which has substantially changed since *Kant* published his 'Perpetual peace'.

II. Peaceful Perception of Democracy

The use of democracy as a tool to build peace results from the belief that such a regime is the most likely to bring out peace, if not that it is able to create peace. The use of the democratic peace paradigm by international decision-makers has participated in making democracy a tool of post-conflict state reconstruction.

1. Birth of the democratic paradism

One of the arguments in favour of the promotion of liberal democracy all over the world is the belief in so-called 'democratic peace theory', which finds its philosophical groundings in *Immanuel Kant's* 1795 essay 'Perpetual Peace: A philosophical study'.[4]

2 *Magalie Besse,* Les transitions constitutionnelles démocratisantes – Analyse comparative à partir de l'expérience du Bénin, Thèse en vue de l'obtention du grade de docteur en droit, Université Clermont Auvergne, Clermont-Ferrand, 2017, 21: 'matériellement, la Démocratie est notamment devenue inséparable de la protection des droits et libertés dont le contenu a prospéré au travers de leurs différentes générations. D'un point de vue procédural, le respect de l'Etat de droit est enfin devenu un critère incontournable des régimes démocratiques'.

3 *Immanuel Kant,* Perpetual peace, New York, 2005.

4 *Rein A. Müllerson,* Regime change: from democratic peace theories to forcible regime change, Leiden, Boston, Brill, 2013, 161.

Kant's essay attempts to imagine a system in which peace would be self-sustained.[5] It establishes a specific form of domestic organisation of the State, called republican – but refers materially to what is now called democracy –,[6] and a system gathering the states, called Republican states federation.

Regarding the peaceful dimension of republican constitutions, *Kant's* argument is twofold: the involvement of the people in the decision-making process lowers the likelihood for a state to go to war; and the republican system has an internal stabilising effect. [7] In order to create an inter-states peace, peace must pre-exist internally. According to Kant, Republican states are less likely to go to war as the people participates in the choice to go to war. Moreover, the people directly suffers the consequences of war, and therefore, it is less likely to lightly take the decision to fight a war. On the contrary, a state whose government is not democratic will take less seriously the decision to go to war and thus be more likely to enter violent conflicts.[8] Thus, *Kant's* democratic peace relies on the republican organisation of states that, according to him, will lead to the end of interstates conflicts. It should be highlighted here that the Kantian democratic peace only establishes that a world in which all states have gradually come to a democratic regime will be peaceful. It is based on the internal and autonomous transformation of internal regimes of states. International peace would thus result from the natural transformation of every state into a democracy. *Kant's* project does not include the use of democracy as a tool to forcibly change national political regimes in order to create international peace.

His theory was rather an utopic ideal until the 70's. Democratic peace has then known a renewal due to empirical researches conducted in order to question the causal link between peace and democracy. First, researchers started to show that there is an empirical correlation between democracy and peace.[9] Second, they attempted to explain the causal link behind this finding through normative and structural approaches. Thirdly, they focused their researches on democratic peace taking

5 *Immanuel Kant*, op. cit. (note 3).

6 *Vesna Danilovic/Joe. Clare*, The Kantian Liberal Peace (Revisited), vol. 51(2), American Journal of Political Science (2007), 397, 398-399.

7 *Immanuel Kant*, op. cit. (note 3),122-123.

8 *Immanuel Kant*, op. cit. (note 3), 123. Kant explique: 'or the ruler is not a citizen, but the owner of the state, and does not lose a whit by the war, while he goes on enjoying the delights of his table or sport, or of his pleasure palaces and gala days. He can therefore decide on war for the most trifling reasons, as if it were a kind of pleasure party.'

9 *Dean V. Babst*, A force for peace, vol. 14, Industrial Research (1972), 55.

constructivist, psychological and evolutionist approaches.[10] Gradually the democratic peace migrated from the academic world to the international decision-making sphere, slowly turning into a paradigm of international relations. It became the ground for a plurality of policies used by international decision-makers to promote peace. Numerous international decision-makers integrated democratic peace in both their speeches and actions, slowly turning it into a truism of international relations. This movement from the academic world to the political sphere is called public convention[11]: 'In other words, it was transformed from a theoretical discourse to a public discourse, and converted from a mere theoretical construction into a public convention. Put differently, it eventually came to be taken for granted and to shape common sensical codes of thinking and behaviour'.[12]

Several factors participated in the movement of democratic peace into the political sphere. The idea that democracy creates peace had entered the political sphere before *Babst's* work[13], but the use of the democratic peace paradigm mostly happened at the end of the Cold War. This transformation of democratic peace into a public convention led to a new understanding of this theory. Its vulgarisation also led to its simplification. The decision-makers who based their actions on democratic peace sometimes misunderstood some of its dimensions. This phenomenon is inherent to the difference of nature between the academics and the political world: 'Because of its structural duality, the subtle minutia of theorizing are lost when theory migrates to the public and political spheres, causing distorted understandings of theory that are both politicized and simplifies'.[14] Indeed, where academics make 'meticulous claims of the relations between different phenomena, articulated to deliver the subtlest minutia of a theory's contentions as were established through strict and careful theorization', decision-makers use a simpler vocabulary, that does not take into account the subtleties of scientific work. Thus, whereas theorists struggle to establish the causal link between democracy and peace, the use of the democratic peace paradigm lead to a will to spread democracy among the world: 'The gist of this theory is the assertion that as democracies do not wage wars against one another, the more democracies there are in the world, the less there is the chance of a military breaking out'.[15]

10 See. infra. 2.

11 *Piki Ish-Shalom,* Democratic peace: a political biography, Ann Arbor, 2013, 69.

12 *Piki Ish-Shalom,* op. cit. (note 11), 69.

13 *Babst,* A Force for Peace, op. cit. (note 9).

14 *Piki Ish-Shalom,* Theorization, Harm, and the Democratic Imperative: Lessons from the Politicization of the Democratic-Peace Thesis, vol. 10 (4), International Studies Review 2008, 680, 682.

15 *Rein A. Müllerson,* op. cit. (note 4), 162.

2. Democracy Promotion by the UN

This mutation of the democratic peace idea had important repercussion on the United Nations, especially through a renewed reading of the Charter which caused the development of intervention policies to promote democracy. The Charter itself relies on the idea that the Organisation should directly participate in the promotion of international peace, including through the realisation of democratic peace. The object of the Charter is dual: 'on the one hand, it offers a ground for a renewed vision of the international order, on the other hand, it reaffirms strongly the principles of the 'Westphalian system'' .[16] Moreover, its role in international peace reveals this duality. The institutional deadlocks caused by the Cold War prevented the implementation of the mechanisms created by the Charter; nevertheless, the dislocation of the soviet bloc allowed a re-interpretation bringing the organisation closer to the idea of Kant's democratic peace of which it was inspired. The UN is indeed 'at the heart of a reality of which it endorses the structures in a legal form. It is in this deep duality of the world organisation that lies its nature'.[17]

Peace is the quintessential goal of the Charter, which seems to be a logical consequence of the context of its birth.[18] The Charter's preamble is quite eloquent on this matter: 'Determined to save succeeding generations from the scourge of war, which twice in our lifetime has brought untold sorrow to mankind, and [...] to practice tolerance and live together in peace with one another as good neighbours, and to unite our strength to maintain international peace and security, [...] have resolved to combine our efforts to accomplish these aims'.[19] Moreover, Article 1 of the Charter that sets the goals of the United Nations, puts maintaining international peace and security at the top of the aims of the organisation. [20] The term peace is however equivocal. Following *J. Galtung's* distinction[21], there is a difference between negative and posi-

16 *Olivier de Frouville*, Une conception démocratique du droit international, vol. XXXIX-120, Revue européenne des sciences sociales, juillet 2001, 101, 139.

17 *Olivier de Frouville*, op. cit. (note 16), 134: 'au cœur d'une réalité dont elle entérine les structures sous forme de normes juridiques. C'est dans cette profonde dualité de l'Organisation mondiale que réside sa nature'.

18 *Mohammed Bedjaoui*, Chapitre I : Buts et Principes – Article 1 : Commentaire général', in: Alain Pellet et Jean-Pierre Cot (ed.), La Charte des Nations Unies : Commentaire article par article, 2ème Ed., s. l., 1991, 24.

19 *Charte des Nations Unies*, signed 26 june 1945 in San Francisco, Preamble. Hereinafter UN Charter.

20 UN Charter, Art. 1.

21 *Johan Galtung*, Theories of peace : A synthetic approach to peace thinking, Oslo, 1967.

tive peace. In its negative meaning, peace means the absence of armed confrontations, whereas the positive reading of peace means that 'peace in its Kantian understanding, as a future state of society, a project, a piece to realize'.[22] The negative understanding of peace in the Charter keeps the Organisation's role down to avoid armed conflicts. On the opposite, a positive understanding of peace in the Charter involves that the Organisation should act in such a way as to create the conditions to accomplish Justice. As *A. Cassese* highlights, the new reading of the Charter following the Cold War: 'One might say that the Organisation moved from a negative understanding of peace (the absence of armed conflict) to a positive understanding of peace (the realisation of the principle of justice) [...]'.[23] Therefore, peace involves more than a security system to avoid armed conflicts. The idea of positive peace implies on the one hand to identify the roots of conflict, and, on the other hand, to suppress them.[24] Combined to the democratic peace theory, this reading of the Charter leads to the use of some of the Charter's mechanisms in order to implement democracy.

Partly due to previous failures of the international society to prevent war and protect negative peace, the Charter has gradually been read in order to promote positive peace.[25] The UN's involvement in the promotion of positive peace, especially in favour of democratic regimes, took a turn when *B. Boutros-Ghali,* who was openly in favour of the involvement of the Organisation in the promotion of democratic peace,[26] was elected as Secretary General of the United Nations. This new policy of the UN lead to an important conflict between two main characteristics of the UN: 'on the one hand, the Organisation's neutrality regarding the member states' choice of their political regime, and on the other hand, concerning international human rights protection, the criticism of arbitrary decisions in authoritarian regimes and their consequences on human rights'.[27]

The inclusion of democratic principles in the UN's policies arises from the combined perception of democracy as a peace building tool and of the UN's role in the promotion of human rights. Democracy was gradually linked to human rights pro-

22 *Olivier de Frouville,* op. cit. (note 16), 136: 'la paix entendue dans le sens kantien, comme un état futur de la société, un projet, une œuvre à réaliser'.

23 *Antonio Cassese,* Article 1 : Paragraphe 2, in: Allain Pellet et Jean-Pierre Cot (ed.), op. cit. (note 18), 49.

24 *Olivier de Frouville,* op. cit. (note 16), 136.

25 *Russell Buchan,* International law and the construction of the liberal peace, Oxford, 2013, 74.

26 This is illustrated by his *Agenda for peace. Boutros Boutros-Ghali,* An agenda for peace, New York, Secretary General of the United Nations, 1992.

27 *Kathia Martin-Chenut,* Droit international et démocratie, vol. 220 (4), Diogène (2007), 37.

motion and to economic development, resulting in the enlargement of the UN's actions regarding political regimes. Virtues of democracy seem to be many: 'Viewed as essential to sustaining social and economic assistance, democratic legal authority – once firmly embedded in a society – is also believed to perform better than other forms of authority in maintaining stability and fostering a durable peace'.[28] This new conception of the international order leads to a gradual rooting of democratic standards in international law, resulting in the use of new tools to promote peace such as state building or peace building. Such tools are rooted in an ideological willingness to create favourable conditions to sustainable peace. This will to increasingly use democracy in peace keeping or peace building policies, made constitutions a first-choice tool in post-conflict settings. However, the relevance of those tools should be questioned.

II. Neo-constitutionalism: a Modern Post-conflict Peacebuilding Tool?

From a constitutional perspective, the will to promote peace trough democracy materialises in the implementation of various legal instruments. Even though it is not their only purpose, post-conflict constitutions reflect the will to promote democracy. Among various constitutional mechanisms used by decision-makers, a set of tools is largely used: constitutionalism.[29] However, it is necessary to question the relevance of this tool regarding its peace building purpose. I will first discuss the causality link between democracy and peace (1), and second its link with the mechanisms used to promote democracy (2).

1. Causal Link between Democracy and Peace

The empirical correlation between democracy and peace leads to question the causal link between the two. This issue has a practical interest: if one admits that democracy creates peace, it is necessary to establish what it is within democracy that creates peace in order to implement such elements with a view to create peace. Literature on the subject attempts to explain the link between the two. Researches on this matter may be divided in different groups: those that focus on the structural aspect

28 *Richard Ponzio*, Democratic peacebuilding: aiding Afghanistan and other fragile states, Oxford, New York, 2011, 35.

29 DRI, Le Nouveau Constitutionnalisme : Une Forme de Processus Constitutionnel' (DRI, November 2012).

of democracy; those that rather focus on a normative explanation; those that use a holistic approach; and those that use constructivist, evolutionist and psychological approaches. Yet, those researches have struggled to give a satisfying and comprehensive explanation of the link between democracy and peace.

The first type of studies started in early 1990's. They meant to question the link between democratic structures and peace. Thus, they focus on the consequences of democratic structures on international relations in order to explain democratic peace. The pacifying effect of democracy would then rely on modalities of the domestic decision-making process. The link between democracy and peace is due to democratic settings such as 'separation of power, check and balances, leader's accountability regarding public opinion' which tend to slow down the decision-making process, thus allowing peaceful conflict resolution. [30] Those explanations understand democracy as a specific decisional structure that inherently creates peaceful settings: democratic decision-making is the essential characteristic that ensures that democracies do not fight each other.

The second type of explicative theories relies on the normative dimension of democracy. They tend to demonstrate that the absorption of democratic norms in domestic practice reflects on state's international relations. According to such theory, democracies project their own democratic norms in the international system.[31] Consequently, democratic peace 'arises when two democratic states, projecting their norms onto the international system, create a zone of shared norms that enables peaceful transactions.'[32] Most normative explanations rely on the idea of projection of norms on the international system, [33] yet the definition of those norms brings struggle. Some authors consider that the projection of the norm of peaceful conflict resolution, creating a culture of compromise, including the use of third party resolution or conflict

30 *Piki Ish-Shalom,* op. cit. (note 11), 39.

31 *Piki Ish-Shalom,* op. cit. (note 11), 40, arguing that the norms of tolerance and openness within these states extend into the relations between them, producing greater willingness to use conflict-resolution techniques and to reach compromises, so that conflicts are settled peacefull".

32 *Jarrod Hayes,* The democratic peace and the new evolution of an old idea, vol. 18 (4), European Journal of International Relations, December 2012) 767, 774.

33 *Kurt T. Gaubatz,* Democratic States and Commitment in International Relations, vol. 50 (1), International Organization 1996, 109-139; *Zeev Maoz/Bruce Russett,* Normative and Structural Causes of Democratic Peace, 1946–1986, vol. 87 (3), American Political Science Review (September 1993), 624-638; *Gregory A. Raymond,* Democracies, Disputes, and Third-Party Intermediaries, vol. 38 (1), The Journal of Conflict Resolution (1994), 24-42.

resolution organ,[34] protected by the rule of law, creates democratic peace.[35] Other researchers[36] highlighted the transfer of 'behavioural norms of exchange and cooperation rather than coercion.'[37] Separation of powers and democratic organisation of the states lead to the use of negotiated solutions to political disputes rather than imposed ones, hence creating a culture of cooperation.[38] Moreover, projection of norms by a state depends on its interlocutor: democracies will refer to democratic norms only when dealing with other democratic states.[39] Democracies then form a trust circle in which they act along cooperation and negotiation norms, excluding non-democratic states. This increases the risks that democracy will react with violence in their interaction with those later states.[40]

In late 90's early 2000's, some authors tried to combine both approaches through holistic researches on the subject.[41] For instance, *Michael W. Doyle* argues that representation of the people (the structural element of democracy) implies that wars are fought only if they are in adequacy with liberal goals (normative element).[42] Moreover, a third category of researches on the topic has emerged at the same time.[43] Those theses include a wide range of approaches, including constructivism, psychological and evolutionism. For instance, studies such as those of *Sara M. Mitchell*[44] and of

34 *Zeev Maoz/Bruce Russett*, l. c.; *Kurt T. Gaubatz*, op. cit. (note 33); Gregory A. Raymond, op. cit. (note 33).

35 *Zeev Maoz/Bruce Russett*, l. c., *T. Gaubatz*, l. c.; *Gregory A. Raymond*, l. c.

36 *William J. Dixon/Paul D. Senese*, Democracy, Disputes, and Negotiated Settlements, vol. 46 (4), The Journal of Conflict Resolution 2002, 547-571; *Bear F. Braumoeller*, Deadly Doves: Liberal Nationalism and the Democratic Peace in the Soviet Successor States, vol. 41 (3), International Studies Quarterly 1997, 375-402; *Paul K. Huth / Todd L. Allee*, The democratic peace and territorial conflict in the twentieth century, Cambridge, New York, 2002.

37 *Bear F. Braumoeller*, l. c., at 380.

38 *Bear F. Braumoeller*, l. c.

39 *William J. Dixon/Paul D. Senese*, l. c., at 565.

40 *Jarrod Hayes*, op. cit. (note 32), 774.

41 *Charles Lipson*, Reliable Partners: How Democracies Have Made a Separate Peace, s. l., Princeton University Press, 2003; *John R. Oneal et al.*, The Liberal Peace: Interdependence, Democracy, and International Conflict, 1950–85, vol. 33 (1), Journal of Peace Research 1996, 11-28; *Michael W. Doyle*, Kant, Liberal Legacies, and Foreign Affairs vol. 12 (3), Philosophy & Public Affairs 1983, 205-235; *Michael W. Doyle*, Three Pillars of the Liberal Peace, vol. 99 (3), American Political Science Review, August 2005, 463-466.

42 *Jarrod Hayes*, op. cit. (note 32), 776.

43 *Jarrod Hayes*, l. c., at 769.

44 *Sara McLaughlin Mitchell/Scott Gates/Håvard Hegre*, Evolution in Democracy-War Dynamics, vol. 43 (6), The Journal of Conflict Resolution 1999, 771-792; *Sara McLaughlin Mitchell*, A Kan-

Lars-Erik Cederman[45] offer historical systemic approaches. They argue that the expansion of democratic states together with the emergence of an international forum pushed non-democratic states to absorb democratic norms and peaceful conflict resolution.[46] Social constructivism has also been used as an analysis prism of democratic peace. In this respect, *Thomas Risse-Kappen* argues that democratic states create a 'we' in opposition to the 'others' based on common democratic norms.[47]

Explanative theories of democratic peace are very various. They rely on different elements and methodologies beyond structural and normative characteristics of democracies. Besides the remaining uncertainties regarding the existence of a causal link between democracy and peace – and not the other way around –, the tools used in order to promote peace through democracy must be analysed with regard to the said link.

2. Creating Democratic Constitutions: a Mean to Create Peace?

In this part, I will address two main critics to the use of democratic constitutions in order to promote peace. First, democratic standards promoted by international decision-makers seem not to match the elements identified as pacifying factors of democracy. Second, the change in the nature of armed conflict since the end of the Cold war led to a change in the nature of threats to peace, that now rather come from within than outside the state.

Constitutionalism tools mainly focus on the implementation and protection of a hierarchy of norms on the top of which there is a democratic constitution. Explicative theories of democratic peace explain the causal link between democracy and peace through elements such as: the decision-making process, the set of democratic

tian System? Democracy and Third-Party Conflict Resolution, vol. 46 (4), American Journal of Political Science 2002, 749-759.

45 *Lars-Erik Cederman*, Back to Kant: Reinterpreting the Democratic Peace as a Macrohistorical Learning Process, vol. 95 (1), The American Political Science Review 2001, 15-31; *Lars-Erik Cederman*, Modeling the Democratic Peace as a Kantian Selection Process, vol. 45 (4), The Journal of Conflict Resolution 2001, 470-502; *Lars-Erik Cederman/Kristian S. Gleditsch*, Conquest and Regime Change: An Evolutionary Model of the Spread of Democracy and Peace, vol. 48 (3), International Studies Quarterly 2004, 603-629; *Lars-Erik Cederma/Mohan P. Rao*, Exploring the Dynamics of the Democratic Peace, vol. 45 (6), The Journal of Conflict Resolution 2001, 818-833.

46 Cf. also *Errol A. Henderson*, Neoidealism and the Democratic Peace, vol. 36 (2), Journal of Peace Research 1999, 203-231.

47 *Thomas Risse-Kappen*, Democratic Peace — Warlike Democracies?: A Social Constructivist Interpretation of the Liberal Argument, vol. 1 (4), European Journal of International Relations, December 1995, 491-517; repeated by *Harald Mülle /Jonas Wolff*, Dyadic democratic peace strikes back: Reconstructing the social constructivist approach after the monadic renaissance, La Haye, 2004.

values, accountability of decision-makers and leaders, and democracy's self-perception.[48] The implementation of democratic constitutions through neo-constitutionalism includes various mechanisms which intent to ensure that the constitution reflects all the guaranties 'inherent to rule of law requirement'.[49] Among this arsenal of legal tools, there are instruments such as: separation and balance of powers, mechanisms to ensure coherence among different norms, control and accountability mechanisms, constitutional review and human rights protection.[50] Those tools mainly focus on the will to implement (and guaranty) formal democratic mechanisms. The extensive use of electoral mechanisms, highly used in post-colonial African transition to legitimise new regimes,[51] is one example of this phenomenon. Set aside the issues related to the efficiency of such mechanisms when it comes to avoid that the regime deviates into an authoritarian regime, the pacifying capacity of normative techniques might be questioned. The use of such tools by actors of constitutional transitions tend to lead to a standardisation of political regimes and to the use of turnkey solutions hardly able to create favourable conditions for democratic peace. Thus constitutionalism, yet often able to protect democratic mechanisms against power, does not necessarily appear as appropriate to promote democratic peace.

The second limit to the use of democratic peace as a paradigm of international relations is due to the increased proportion of internal conflict, where democratic peace was mainly thought to fight international threat to peace. Moreover, the idea of peace at the heart of the international peace and security system design is an idea of international peace, 'which is important here, as it is not the general idea of peace that is aimed to, meaning that internal tensions or conflicts might continue'.[52] This must be connected to the principle of states' sovereignty that excludes interference with internal affairs.[53] The collapse of the soviet bloc marked the beginning of a growth in the number of internal armed conflicts and a decrease of international conflicts. The UN was thus called to intervene more and more in internal conflicts and to coordinate

48 See supra, II-1.

49 DRI, Le Nouveau Constitutionnalisme : Une Forme de Processus Constitutionnel, 5.

50 DRI, l. c.

51 Cf. *Babacar Gueye/M. P. Tine*, La légitimité et la légitimation de la transition constitutionnelle par les élections en Afrique, in: Xavier Philippe (ed.), Transitions constitutionnelles et Constitutions transitionnelles, Quelles solutions pour une meilleure gestion des fins de conflit, Paris, 2014, 197.

52 *Manfred Lachs*, Article 1: Paragraphe 1, in: Allain Pellet et Jean-Pierre Cot, op. cit. (note 18), 38: ce qui est important dans notre contexte, car on ne vise pas ici la paix au sens général, s'appliquant aussi à l'intérieur des États, où les troubles, conflits et affrontements peuvent persister.

53 *Hurst Hannum*, Rethinking Self Determination, vol. 34, Virginia Journal of International Law 1993, 1–69.

the internal war-peace transition of states.[54] Moreover, phenomena linked to state's deliquescence, usually known as failed states, became an important stake for international peace and security[55]. Those phenomena of internal collapse of government are not new, however, 'in a modern era when national states constitute the building blocks of legitimate world order the violent disintegration and palpable weakness of selected African, Asian, Oceanic, and Latin American states threaten the very foundation of that system'.[56] The rise of internal instabilities as a matter of international peace creates new struggles. Internal stabilisation is linked to the interaction between the State as a power and the society, both physically and symbolically, making it difficult for international actors to interfere with the process. [57] This fundamental change in the nature of threats to peace induces a need to question peacebuilding tools, such as formal democratic mechanisms, that were designed to bring international peace. Such tools seem only to be able to label regimes as democratic without creating peaceful democracies.

Conclusion

Democratic peace, understood as the idea that democratisation will naturally create peace has led to the promotion of democracy, sometimes even in a forcible way. However, this idea has significant limits. First, Constitutions, as the legal medium of democracy, have a limited role in post-conflict settings, especially following internal conflicts. They are just one of the numerous factors of stabilisation, such as demilitarisation, transitional justice, demobilisation, effective control on the territory. Second, the ability of constitutions to change individual social behaviours may be ques-

54 The end of the competitive logic which led both blocs to offer 'strategic annuity' to governments in difficulty, coupled to a geopolitical marginalisation (especially in Africa) created a 'deliquescence' of numerous sates, *François Polet*, State building au Sud : de la doctrine à la réalité, in: François Polet (ed.), (Re)-construire les États, nouvelles frontières de l'ingérence, Paris, 2012, 9.

55 *Daniel Thürer*, The 'failed State' and international law, (836), International Review of the Red Cross 1999.

56 *Robert I. Rotberg*, Failed States, Collapsed States, Weak States: Causes and Indicators, in: Robert I. Rotberg (ed.), When states fail: causes and consequences, Princeton, 2004, 1.N.J","source":"Library of Congress ISBN","event-place":"Princeton, N.J","ISBN":"0-691-11671-7","call-number":"JF60 .W46 2004","editor":[{"family":"Rotberg","given":"R.I."}],"author":[{"family":"Rotberg","given ":"R.I."}],"issued":{"date-parts":[["2004"]]},"locator":"1"}],"schema":"https://github.com/citation-style-language/schema/raw/master/csl-citation.json"}.

57 *Béatrice Pouligny*, La construction de la paix, vol. 4, Annuaire Français de Relations internationales 2003, 292.

tioned.[58] The standards brought by constitutional *instrumentum* tend to be quite far from the actual practice. Finally, the idea of democracy as thought through democratic peace goes beyond formal democracy promoted by international decision-makers.

58 *Nehal Bhuta*, New Modes and Orders: The Difficulties of a Jus Post Bellum of Constitutional Transformation, vol. 60, University of Toronto Law Journal 2010, 799-854.

Index of Authors

Oesten Baller has been full Professor of Public Law at the Berlin School of Economics and Law since 1997. He also is Director of the Institute for Cooperation with Central and Eastern European Countries in Public Reform and President of the German-Ukrainian School of Governance e. V. Professor Baller has more than twenty years of experience in managing projects (project director and key expert), in public consultation, policy advice, capacity and training, in implementing and enforcing of administrative and economic reforms and institution building in Eastern Europe. E-mail: oesten.baller@hwr-berlin.de

Rubens Beçak is a full Professor at the University of Sao Paulo (USP). He is a visiting Professor at the University of Salamanca linked to the Brazilian Studies Center and co-Editor of the Journal of Brazilian Studies. In the University of Sao Paulo he headed the Center of Rights (Núcleo de Direitos) and worked as the General-Secretary of the University (2010–2014). Currently, he is the President of the Postgraduate Commission in Law at the Ribeirão Preto Law School (USP). His main focus in teaching and researching is Theory of State. E-mail: rubens.becak@gmail.com

Olivier Le Bot is Professor of public law in Aix-Marseille University. He is the director of the master 'Public litigation'. His researches are focused on public litigations, constitutional law and administrative law. E-mail: olivier.le-bot@univ-amu.fr

Manon Bonnet is a PhD student at Aix Marseille University, France with the Louis Favoreu Institute. As a visiting researcher, she spent time at the European University institute in Florence (Italy) and the Grotius center for International Law in Leiden (Netherlands). Her dissertation focuses on international constitution-making as a peace-building tool. She teaches international criminal law moot court, constitutional law, constitutional litigation, fundamental rights, international humanitarian law, and introduction to legal studies. She also worked with the human rights clinic at Aix Marseille University. E-mail: mbonnet.gerjc@gmail.com.

David KC Huang has been a visiting fellow in constitutional law at the O. P. Jindal Global Law School in Delhi, India since 2018. He is a Taiwanese scholar specialising in constitutional law, administrative law, judicial politics and behaviourism, philosophy, sinology and mathematics. He received fundamental legal education in both civil law (Taiwan) and common law (England and Wales) jurisdictions, by which he can compare civil law jurisprudence with that of common law in detail. He also majored in philosophy and can read any classical Chinese literature within the past four millennia without a dictionary. He obtained his Ph.D. degree in constitutional law at SOAS Law School, University of London, with a thesis about Taiwan's judicial supremacy through strategic decision-making in the 1990s. E-mail: dr.david.kc.huang@gmail.com

Priscilla Jensel-Monge is Associate Professor at the University of Aix-Marseille. She is member of the Institute Louis Favoreu (Study and Research Group on Constitutional Justice). She teaches constitutional law, constitutional litigation and fundamental rights and freedoms. Hers research focuses on institutional constitutional law and particularly on Parliament. E-mail: priscilla.monge@univ-amu.fr

Jairo Lima is Professor at Universidade Estadual do Norte do Paraná (Brazil). He obtained his Ph.D. degree in Constitutional Law at Universidade de São Paulo (Brazil) with a thesis on unconstitutional constitutional amendments. This paper is part of his general argument in the thesis. In 2016, he was visiting Researcher at University of Glasgow. His current research focuses on the tension between constitutionalism and democracy. E-mail: jaironlima@yahoo.com.br

Xavier Miny obtained his master's degree, with a specialisation in public and administrative law, in 2013 and an executive master's degree in tax law in 2015. From 2013 to 2017, he was a teaching & research assistant in public, constitutional and public international law at the Law School of University of Liège, in Belgium. Since 2018, he is lecturer at the University of Liège and FRESH grantee (National Fund for Scientific Research). He is preparing a doctoral research under the supervision of Prof. Dr. Christian Behrendt (promoter). His current research as a Ph.D. candidate focuses on the economic policy of the federal states. E-mail: xavier.miny@uliege.be

Audrey de Montis is Associate Professor at the University of Rennes 1. She is member of the Institute of Public Law and Political Science. She teaches in particular general constitutional law, the history of constitutional law and international relations. Her research focuses on French institutional constitutional law. E-mail: audrey.demontis@univ-rennes1.fr

Abiodun Odusote, PhD in Law, is a Senior Lecturer with the Department of Public Law, Faculty of Law, University of Lagos, Akoka-Nigeria. His research interests focus on enjoyment and enforcement of socio-economic rights, enthronement of good governance, accountability in leadership, access to qualitative education, access to justice, promotion of democracy and peace studies. E-mail: aodusote@unilag.edu.ng

Oyelowo Oyewo, Professor of Public Law, Faculty of Law, University of Lagos, Nigeria. Presently, the Head of Department of Public Law of the Faculty. The Convener/ Leader of the Nigerian Association of Constitutional Law (NACL). Past President of the African Network of Constitutional Lawyers (ANCL) and the Nigerian Association of Law Teachers (NALT), respectively. A Fulbright Scholar at University of California Los Angeles (UCLA), and was admitted into the State Bar of California, USA, in 1991. His areas of interest in research and writing are: constitutional law and constitutionalism; democracy and nation-building; federalism and development; human rights; administrative law and governance; and environmental law and justice. E-mail: eoyewo@unilag.edu.ng

Quentin Pironnet obtained his master's degree, with a specialisation in public and administrative law, in 2015 after an internship at the Belgian Constitutional Court. He worked for two years as a lawyer in a firm specialized in labour law. Since 2015 he has been an assistant in constitutional law. His research areas cover Belgian public and constitutional law and comparative law. He also teaches at the University of Liège as a lecturer where he gives the course of "Introduction to Public Law" to Erasmus students, in French and then in English since 2018. E-mail: quentin.pironnet@uliege.be

Maciej Pisz has been PhD student at the Faculty of Law and Administration (University of Warsaw, Poland) since 2014. Lecturer at the Faculty of Law and Administration, University of Warsaw. He teaches human and civil rights and constitutional law. Author of five books and various scientific articles in the field of law. He was granted a scholarship by the Minister of Science and Higher Education for PhD students for outstanding scientific achievements in the field of legal sciences. E-mail: m.pisz@kancelaria.eu

Anne-Laure Youhnovski Sagon is a PhD candidate since 2015 in Jean Moulin Lyon 3 University, France. Her dissertation is about the right to life as a fundamental right. She teaches constitutional law, legal methodology, administrative law and fundamental rights. Her main research focuses on fundamental rights, European law and bioethics. E-mail: annelaure.ysagon@gmail.com

Eva Schulev-Steindl is full professor of Public Law and Economic Law at the University of Graz. After studies at the Vienna University of Economics and Business (WU), the University of Vienna and the London School of Economics and Political Science (LSE) she habilitated 2003 at the University of Vienna and held after visiting professorships at WU and the University of Klagenfurt from 2008–14 a professorship for Law at the University of Natural Resources and Life Sciences, Vienna

(BOKU). She publishes in the fields of Austrian and European Public Law, Economic Law, Environmental Law, University Law as well as Legal Theory. E-mail: eva.schulev-steindl@uni-graz.at

Sacha Sydoryk is a PhD candidate since 2014 in Toulouse Capitole University, France. His dissertation is about French constitutional legal doctrine: study of the production of knowledge about contemporary French constitutional law. He teaches constitutional law, legal methodology, international law and fundamental rights. His main research focus on legal theory, constitutional law and European law. E-mail: sacha.sydoryk@gmail.com

Paul Zibi has been a Lecturer at the Faculty of Law and Political Science of the University of Bamenda, Cameroon. He served as an Assistant Lecturer at the Department of Law of the Higher Technical Teacher Training College in the same university. He teaches Constitutional Law, Comparative Political Regimes, Public Finance Law, Taxation Law and Research Methodology and Legal Writing at the Department of Public Law in the said faculty. He obtained his PhD in Public Law in June 2015 at the University of Yaoundé II with a thesis written on a genuine multidisciplinary law topic that is: The law of governance in Cameroon (in French). In June 2018 he has been part of the Global Youth Programme for Young Scholars of Constitutional Law (GYIP) organized alongside the World Congress of Constitutional Law (WCCL) in Seoul, Republic of Korea. E-mail: paulzibi17@gmail.com

Oesten Baller, Burkhard Breig (Hrsg.)

Justiz in Mittel- und Osteuropa

Eine unabhängige und funktionsfähige Justiz ist eine unverzichtbare Voraussetzung für einen demokratischen Rechtsstaat und eine stabile wirtschaftliche Entwicklung. In den beiden größten Ländern im postsowjetischen Raum, in Russland und der Ukraine, ist es ein weiter Weg hin zu einer unabhängigen Justiz, gerade wenn man die gerichtliche Kontrolle des Präsidenten und der Regierung in den Blick nimmt. Aber auch in Ungarn und Polen, Mitglieder der Europäischen Union seit 2004, ist die Verfassungsjustiz auf Grund zunehmenden politischen Drucks in ihrer Unabhängigkeit bedroht. Juristen aus diesen Ländern sowie aus Deutschland und aus Israel untersuchen unterschiedliche Fragen des Zustands und der Entwicklung der Justiz, primär in den Ländern Russland, Ukraine, Polen und Ungarn. Ein Schwerpunkt ist die Rechtsentwicklung in Russland, vor allem die sehr umstrittene Abschaffung des russischen Obersten Arbitragegerichts und die Übertragung seiner Funktionen auf das Oberste Gericht.

2017, 180 S., 2 s/w Abb., kart., dt./engl.,
39,– €, 978-3-8305-3777-9
eBook PDF 978-3-8305-2214-0
(Recht, Sicherheit und Verwaltung in internationaler Perspektive, Bd. 5)
ISSN Print 2367-086X
ISSN Online 2367-0878

DIE HERAUSGEBER

Oesten Baller ist Professor und Doktor der Rechtswissenschaften am Fachbereich Polizei und Sicherheitsmanagement der Hochschule für Wirtschaft und Recht Berlin, Direktor des Instituts für Verwaltungsmodernisierung und Polizeireform in Mittel- und Osteuropa (IMO) an der HWR Berlin und Direktor der German-Ukrainian School of Governance e. V. Zahlreiche Veröffentlichungen zum Polizei- und Sicherheitsrecht sowie zum Verwaltungs- und Verfassungsrecht in Russland und der Ukraine.

Burkhard Breig studierte Rechtswissenschaften an den Universitäten Bayreuth und Bonn. Er promovierte mit einer Arbeit zum russischen Privatrecht an der Christian-Albrechts-Universität zu Kiel. Derzeit ist er Inhaber der Professur für Bürgerliches Recht, Handels- und Gesellschaftsrecht und osteuropäisches Recht mit besonderer Berücksichtigung Russlands an der Freien Universität Berlin.

Berliner Wissenschafts-Verlag | Markgrafenstr. 12–14 | 10969 Berlin
Tel. 030 84 17 70-0 | Fax 030 84 17 70-21
www.bwv-verlag.de | bwv@bwv-verlag.de

Berliner
Wissenschafts-Verlag

DER HERAUSGEBER

Oesten Baller ist Professor und Doktor der Rechtswissenschaften am Fachbereich Polizei und Sicherheitsmanagement der Hochschule für Wirtschaft und Recht Berlin, Direktor des Instituts für Verwaltungsmodernisierung und Polizeireform in Mittel- und Osteuropa (IMO) an der HWR Berlin und Direktor der German-Ukrainian School of Governance e. V. Zahlreiche Veröffentlichungen zum Polizei- und Sicherheitsrecht sowie zum Verwaltungs- und Verfassungsrecht in Russland und der Ukraine.

MIT BEITRÄGEN VON

Joachim R. Daduna | Lotfi Mechichi | Zohra Smaali | Zouheir Buchaddakh | Hartmut Aden | Dörte Busch | Wolfgang Strehl | Abdelfattah Triki | Samiha Mjahed Hammami | Chérifa Turki Sassi | Ursula Walter | M. Naceur Azaiez | Asma Ben Yaghlane | Karim Chaabouni | Fatma Siala Guermazi | Asma Zantour | Sabrina Schönrock | Arafet Farroukh | Messaoud Boudhiaf

Oesten Baller (ed.)

Public-Private Partnership in Germany and Tunisia

Public-Private Partnership models are often controversially discussed with regard to not only their benefits and advantages, but also the chances and risks inherent in their realisation. However, there is no doubt that in developing countries the involvement of private investment and private partners can contribute to economic growth and the expansion of infrastructure. In Tunisia, the government is actively supporting PPP projects, believing that they are crucial for the further development of the country's economy and the welfare of the people.

The contributions in this book are the result of the cooperation between Tunisian and German scholars and reflect general as well as country-specific current and future frameworks of PPP and best practices of both countries. A comparison of Tunisia's concession-based concept with the infrastructure- and construction-focused approach in Germany leads to the conclusion that an open framework for PPP is desirable. The volume provides not only scholars, but also policymakers in Maghreb countries and development and investment protagonists with an overview of the PPP sector's current development in Tunisia and Germany.

2016, 182 S., kart., engl., 39,– €,
978-3-8305-3518-8
eBook PDF 978-3-8305-2164-8
(Recht, Sicherheit und Verwaltung
in internationaler Perspektive, Bd. 4)
ISSN Print 2367-086X
ISSN Online 2367-0878

Berliner Wissenschafts-Verlag | Markgrafenstr. 12–14 | 10969 Berlin
Tel. 030 84 17 70-0 | Fax 030 84 17 70-21
www.bwv-verlag.de | bwv@bwv-verlag.de

Berliner Wissenschafts-Verlag